Caregiving

Research • Practice • Policy

Ronda C. Talley, Series Editor

An official publication of
The Rosalynn Carter Institute for Caregiving

For further volumes:
http://www.springer.com/series/8274

Ronda C. Talley • Gregory L. Fricchione
Benjamin G. Druss
Editors

The Challenges of Mental Health Caregiving

Research • Practice • Policy

Editors
Ronda C. Talley
Western Kentucky University
Bowling Green
Kentucky
USA

Gregory L. Fricchione
Massachusetts General Hospital
Department Health Policy and Management
Boston
Massachusetts
USA

Benjamin G. Druss
Rollins School of Public Health
Department of Health Policy and Management
Emory University
Atlanta
Georgia
USA

ISSN 2192-340X ISSN 2192-3418 (electronic)
ISBN 978-1-4614-8790-6 ISBN 978-1-4614-8791-3 (eBook)
DOI 10.1007/978-1-4614-8791-3
Springer New York Heidelberg Dordrecht London

Library of Congress Control Number: 2013951784

Printed on acid-free paper

Springer is part of Springer Science+Business Media (www.springer.com)

To Rosalynn Carter
Champion for those with mental illnesses and their caregivers

Ronda C. Talley
Gregory L. Fricchione
Benjamin G. Druss

Editorial Board

Series Foreword

From its inception in 1987, the Rosalynn Carter Institute for Caregiving (RCI) has sought to bring attention to the extraordinary contributions made by caregivers to their loved ones. I grew up in a home that was regularly transformed into a caregiving household when members of my family became seriously ill, disabled, or frail with age, so my interest in the issue is personal. In my hometown of Plains, Georgia, as in most communities across our country, it was expected that family members and neighbors would take on the responsibility of providing care whenever illness struck close to home. Delivering such care with the love, respect, and attention it deserves is both labor-intensive and personally demanding. Those who do so represent one of this nation's most significant yet underappreciated assets in our health delivery system.

When the RCI began, "caregiving" was found nowhere in the nation's health lexicon. Its existence was not a secret but rather simply accepted as a fact of life. In deciding on the direction and priorities of the new institute, we convened groups of family and professional caregivers from around the region to tell their personal stories. As I listened to neighbors describe caring for aged and/or chronically ill or disabled family members, I recognized that their experiences reflected mine. They testified that, while caregiving for them was full of personal meaning and significance and could be extremely rewarding, it could also be fraught with anxiety, stress, and feelings of isolation. Many felt unprepared and most were overwhelmed at times. A critical issue in the "field" of caregiving, I realized, was the need to better understand the kinds of policies and programs necessary to support those who quietly and consistently care for loved ones.

With the aging of America's Baby Boomers expecting to double the elderly population in the next 20 years, deinstitutionalization of individuals with chronic mental illnesses and developmental disabilities, a rising percentage of women in the workforce, smaller and more dispersed families, changes in the role of hospitals, and a range of other factors, caregiving has become one of the most significant issues of our time. Caregiving as an area of research, as a focus and concern of policy making, and as an area of professional training and practice has reached a new and unparalleled level of importance in our society and indeed globally.

As we survey the field of caregiving today, we now recognize that it is an essential component of long-term care in the community, yet also a potential health risk for those who provide care. The basic features of a public health approach have emerged: a focus on populations of caregivers and recipients, tracking and surveillance of health risks, understanding the factors associated with risk status, and the development and testing of the effectiveness of various interventions to maximize benefits for both the recipients of care and their providers.

The accumulated wisdom from this work is represented in the volumes that make up the Springer Caregiving Series. This series presents a broad portrait of the nature of caregiving in the USA in the twenty-first century. Most Americans have been, are now, or will be caregivers. With our society's increasing demands for care, we cannot expect a high quality of life for our seniors and others living with limitations due to illness or disability unless we understand and support the work of caregivers. Without thoughtful planning, intelligent policies, and sensitive interventions, there is the risk that the work of family, paraprofessional, and professional caregivers will become intolerably difficult and burdensome. We cannot let this happen.

This volume focuses on a topic of longstanding and deep concern for me. During our time in the White House, President Carter and I were committed to bringing the nation's attention to the needs of those who suffered from emotional and behavioral disorders and of those who lived with them, cared for them, and sought appropriate and affordable services for their care. Shortly after the inauguration, President Carter created the President's Commission on Mental Health to examine problems with the nation's mental health system and its capacity to serve the needs of those with chronic mental illnesses. I served as Honorary Chair of that Commission; our work led to passage of the Mental Health Systems Act, which unfortunately was never implemented by the next administration. Our work before entering the White House and since that time has consistently focused on the need for new and ever more effective treatments but especially on the need to remove the stigma from those who suffer from mental illnesses. This stigma remains a significant obstacle to seeking treatment and an impediment to family members to obtain help for their loved ones and for themselves. The chapters within this volume provide a timely reminder of how much remains to be done if we are to serve effectively those with mental illnesses and those who care for them. As with many conditions that result in the need for short- and long-term caregiving, mental disorders occur across the life span and thus, like other conditions addressed in this book series, affect the lives of caregivers across much of their life span. These disorders know neither cultural nor economic boundaries. The stigma attached to them influences the reactions of far too many of the nation's population! Caring for a loved one with a mental illness taxes the financial and emotional resources of all involved. Readers of this volume will see some evidence of progress in this arena but they will also recognize how much more needs to be done in public policy, service delivery, and basic and applied research. The volume closes with a call to arms that I hope readers and those they touch will heed!

Readers of this series will find hope and evidence that improved support for family and professional caregivers lies within our reach. The field of caregiving has matured and, as evidenced in these volumes, has generated rigorous and practical research findings to guide effective and enlightened policy and program options. My hope is that these volumes will play an important role in documenting the research base, guiding practice, and moving our nation toward effective polices to support all of America's caregivers.

Rosalynn Carter

Contents

1 **Introduction: Caregiving to Promote Mental Health and Prevent Mental Illness** 1
Ronda C. Talley, Gregory L. Fricchione and Benjamin G. Druss

Part I Developmental Issues in Mental Health Caregiving

2 **The Impact of Caregiving on Physical and Mental Health: Implications for Research, Practice, Education, and Policy** 15
Diane L. Elmore

3 **Cultural Considerations in Caring for Persons with Mental Illness** ... 33
Brent E. Gibson

4 **Chronic Illness and Primary Care: Integrating Mental Health and Primary Care** 55
Susan Taylor-Brown, Tziporah Rosenberg and Susan H. McDaniel

Part II The Mental Health Caregiving Context

5 **Mental Illness Prevention and Promotion** 83
William R. Beardslee and Tracy R. G. Gladstone

6 **Systems of Caregiving: The Promotion of Positive Mental Health Outcomes in Children and Adolescents** 103
Patricia Stone Motes and Chaundrissa Oyeshiku Smith

7 **Midlife Concerns and Caregiving Experiences: Intersecting Life Issues Affecting Mental Health** 123
Jane E. Myers and Melanie C. Harper

Part III Local, State, and National Issues Effecting Caregivers and Mental Health Caregiving

8 Loss, Grief, and Bereavement: Implications for Family Caregivers and Health Care Professionals of the Mentally Ill 145
Sherry R. Schachter and Jimmie C. Holland

9 Caring for a Family Member with Mental Illness: Exploring Spirituality 161
Thomas R. Smith and Mary G. Milano

Part IV Issues in Policy and Research

10 Caregiving and Mental Health: Policy Implications 181
Michael J. English, David de Voursney and Kana Enomoto

11 Research in Caregiving 205
Elizabeth A. Crocco and Carl Eisdorfer

Part V Conclusions

12 Mental Health Caregiving: A Call to Professional Providers, Family Caregivers, and Individuals with Mental Health Challenges 225
Donald Lollar and Ronda C. Talley

Index 231

Contributors

William R. Beardslee MD Judge Baker Children's Center, Principal Investigator, TEAMS, Children's Hospital, Boston, MA, USA

Children's Hospital Boston, 21 Autumn Street, Boston, MA, USA

Dr. Elizabeth Crocco MD Division of Geriatric Psychiatry, Department of Psychiatry and Behavioral Sciences, Jackson Memorial Hospital, Miller School of Medicine/University of Miami, Miami, FL, USA

Dr. Benjamin G. Druss MD, MPH Health Policy and Management, Behavioral Sciences and Health Education, Rollins School of Public Health, Atlanta, GA, USA

Dr. Carl Eisdorfer Division of Geriatric Psychiatry, Department of Psychiatry and Behavioral Sciences, Jackson Memorial Hospital, Miller School of Medicine/University of Miami, Miami, FL, USA

Diane Elmore, PhD, MPH National Center For Child Traumatic Stress, UCLA/Duke University, NCCTS—Duke University, 27701 Durham, NC, USA

Michael J. English JD (deceased) Substance Abuse and Mental Health Services Administration, U.S. Department of Health and Human Services, Rockville, MD, USA

Kana Enomoto Substance Abuse and Mental Health Services Administration, U.S. Department of Health and Human Services, Rockville, MD, USA

Gregory L. Fricchione, MD Division of Psychiatry and Medicine, Division of International Psychiatry, Harvard Medical School, Massachusetts General Hospital, Boston, MA, USA

Dr. Brent E. Gibson PhD Research Institute on Aging, Jewish Home Lifecare, New York, NY, USA

Arlene R. Gordon Research Institute of Lighthouse International, NewYork, NY, USA

Tracy R. G. Gladstone PhD Director, Robert S. and GraceW. Stone Primary Prevention Initiatives, Wellesley Centers for Women, Wellesley College, Wellesley, MA, USA

Melanie C. Harper Ph.D., LPC, NCC St. Mary's University, San Antonio, TX, USA

Dr. Jimmie C. Holland MD Department of Psychiatry and Behavioral Sciences, Memorial Sloan-Kettering Cancer Center, NewYork, NY, USA

Dr. Donald Lollar EdD Oregon Institute on Disability & Development, Oregon Health & Science University, Portland, OR, USA

Dr. Susan H. McDaniel PhD, ABPP Department of Family Medicine, University of Rochester Medical Center, Rochester, NY, USA

Department of Psychiatry, University of Rochester Medical Center, Rochester, NY, USA

Jane E. Myers PhD, LPC, NCC Department of Counseling & Educational Development, The University of North Carolina at Greensboro, Greensboro, NC, USA

Mary G. Milano BA International Center for the Integration of Health and Spirituality, Ellicott City, MD, USA

Dr. Patricia Stone Motes PhD Division of Policy and Research on Medicaid and Medicare, Institute for Families in Society, University of South Carolina, Columbia, SC, USA

Dr. Sherry R. Schachter PhD, FT Bereavement Services, Calvary Hospital/Hospice, Bronx, NY, USA

Dr. Chaundrissa Oyeshiku Smith Department of Psychiatry and Behavioral Sciences, Emory University School of Medicine, Atlanta, USA

Dr. Thomas R. Smith Cheaha District, The United Methodist Church,Oxford, AL, USA

Ronda C. Talley, PhD, MPH Department of Psychology, Western Kentucky University, 1906 College Heights Boulevard, Bowling Green, KY, USA

Susan Taylor-Brown Department of Pediatrics, Golisano Children's Hospital, University of Rochester, School of Medicine & Dentistry, Rochester, NY, USA

Department of Family Medicine, University of Rochester Medical Center, Rochester, NY, USA

David de Voursney Office of the Assistant Secretary for Planning and Evaluation, U.S. Department of Health and Human Services, Rockville, MD, USA

About the Editors

Dr. Ronda C. Talley, PhD, MPH is Professor of Psychology at Western Kentucky University. Dr. Talley's professional experience includes providing national leadership on caregiving issues and organizational development as Executive Director of the Rosalynn Carter Institute for Caregiving and the National Quality Caregiving Coalition; working with federal government groups to promote caregiving issues as Associate Director of Legislation, Policy, and Planning/Health Scientist for the Centers for Disease Control and Prevention, U.S. Department of Health and Human Services, in Atlanta, GA; and promoting the science and practice of psychology in the schools as Associate Executive Director of Education and Director of School Policy and Practice at the American Psychological Association in Washington, DC. Dr. Talley taught ethics and legal issues in school psychology at the University of Maryland, College Park, and clinical, counseling, and school psychology students at Spalding University in Louisville, KY. Prior to that time, Dr. Talley worked a teacher of students with special needs and school administrator for almost 20 years in the Jefferson County (KY) Public Schools where she supervised a multidisciplinary private practice. Dr. Talley received the Outstanding Alumni Award from Indiana University and the Jack Bardon Distinguished Service Award from the Division of School Psychology of the American Psychological Association. She serves on the national board of the American Association of Caregiving Youth, the Indiana University School of Education Board of Visitors, and the Western Kentucky University National Alumni Advisory Board. Dr. Talley is Editor-in-Chief of the Springer CARE book series on diverse caregiving issues. Dr. Talley may be reached at 1906 College Heights Boulevard, GRH 3023, Bowling Green, KY 42101; by telephone at (270) 745-2780. e-mail: Ronda.Talley@wku.edu.

Dr. Gregory L. Fricchione, MD is Director of the Benson-Henry Institute for Mind Body Medicine at Massachusetts General Hospital. He also serves as Associate Chief of Psychiatry at MGH and is a Professor of Psychiatry at Harvard Medical School. He is a 1978 graduate of the New York University School of Medicine and did his postgraduate training in psychiatry at NYU-Bellevue and in psychosomatic medicine at Massachusetts General Hospital. From 2000 to 2002, he served as Director of the Mental Health Task Force at the Carter Center in Atlanta, Georgia, while on leave of absence from HMS. While there he worked with Mrs. Rosalynn Carter and former President Jimmy Carter on public and international mental health issues and policy. Dr. Fricchione has published more than 100 journal articles and has coauthored five books. He has overall responsibility for the clinical, educational and research missions of BHI.

Dr. Benjamin G. Druss, MD, MPH is Professor of Health Policy and Management and Behavioral Sciences and Health Education at the Rollins School of Health, Emory University. As the first Rosalynn Carter Chair in Mental Health at Emory University, Dr. Druss is working to build linkages between mental health, general medical health, and public health. He works closely with Carter Center Mental Health Program, where he is a member of the Mental Health Task Force and Journalism Task Force. He has been a member of two Institute of Medicine Committees and has served as an expert consultant to the Substance Abuse and Mental Health Services Administration, the Centers for Disease Control, and the Assistant Secretary for Planning and Evaluation. Dr. Druss's research focuses on improving physical health and healthcare among persons with serious mental disorders. He has published more than 100 peer-reviewed articles on this and related topics, including the first randomized trial of an intervention to improve medical care in this population in 2001. His research is funded by grants from the National Institute of Mental Health and the Agency for Healthcare Quality and Research, and he serves as a standing member of an NIMH study section. He has received a number of national awards for his work, including the American Psychiatric Association Early Career Health Services Research Award, the AcademyHealth Article-of-the-Year Award, and the AcademyHealth Alice S. Hersh New Investigator Award.

About the Authors

William R. Beardslee, MD directs the Baer Prevention Initiative, Department of Psychiatry, Boston Children's Hospital. He is Chairman Emeritus of the Department of Psychiatry at Boston Children's Hospital and Gardner/Monks Professor of Child Psychiatry at Harvard Medical School. He is a senior research scientist at Judge Baker Children's Center. His work is focused on developing effective preventive intervention strategies for families facing multiple adversities including parental depression and poverty.

Dr. Elizabeth Crocco, MD received her MD from the University of Medicine and Dentistry, Robert Wood Johnson Medical School in Piscataway, New Jersey. She then completed her residency training in general psychiatry at The Mount Sinai Medical Center in New York. She specializes in geriatric psychiatry, and completed her fellowship at University of Miami/Jackson Memorial Hospital. Dr. Crocco is currently the Chief of Geriatric Psychiatry in the Department of Psychiatry and Behavioral Sciences at the Miller School of Medicine. As the Medical Director of the University of Miami Memory Disorder Clinic, she oversees the coordination of clinical services at the MDC and participates actively in the overall research efforts of the clinic. She also serves as the geriatric psychiatry training director at Jackson Memorial Hospital and facilitates the primary training and supervision of all geriatric psychiatry fellows, psychiatry residents, medical students, and other physicians/health care professionals.

Dr. Carol Eisdorfer received his BA, MA, and PhD from NYU, his MD and Psychiatric training at Duke, and completed the Program for Health Systems Management at Harvard. At Duke, he rose to become Professor of Psychiatry, Head of Med Psych, Director of Medical Studies in Behavioral Sciences, and Director of the Duke University Center for the Study of Aging. He spent a sabbatical year at the University of California Berkeley as Visiting Professor of Architecture and as Professor of Psychiatry. He left Duke to become Professor and Chair of Psychiatry and Behavioral Sciences at the University of Washington in Seattle, where he founded and directed the University of Washington's Institute on Aging. He was invited to Washington, D.C. as a Senior Scholar at the Institute of Medicine of the National Academy of

Science, chairing an international commission on stress and disease. From 1981–1985, he served as President and CEO of Montifiore Medical Center and Professor of Neuroscience and Psychiatry at the Albert Einstein Medical School in the Bronx, New York. In 1986, he joined the University of Miami as Professor and Chair of Psychiatry, Prof of Psychology, & Family and Community Medicine. He founded the Alzheimer's Disease Centers at the University of Miami and the Mount Sinai Medical Center of Miami Beach. He also directed the University of Miami Center for Biopsychosocial Studies of AIDS. In 2005, he was named the Knight Professor and Director of the University of Miami Center on Aging. His work has been principally in aging, stress, learning, memory and dementia, as well as psychoneuroimmunology and depression in later life. He has also worked in health policy and problems associated with Family Caregiving. His most recent interests have been in the transition from work and in cognitive impairment related to anesthesia. He has authored over 330 scientific and professional articles including 21 books. His books include Health Care Policy for the Aged, published by John Hopkins Press and Loss of Self for caregivers of patients with Alzheimer's Disease (which he wrote with Dr. Donna Cohen). He has served as President of the Gerontological Society of America, the American Society on Aging, and the American Federation for Aging Research. He has served on a number of national advisory panels including the Federal Council on Aging and the Commission on the Future of Veterans Health Care. He also worked with the Peace Corps from 1966–1972. He was a delegate at the 2005 White House Conference on Aging and has recently been appointed to the National Advisory Council of the National Institute on Aging. He is the recipient of numerous awards for his research and public service. These include the Allied Signal Award for Distinguished Contribution to Aging, and major awards from the American Psychiatric Association, the American Psychological Association, and the American College of Physicians and the International Psychogeriatrics Association. He is the only recipient of both the Kent Award for public service and the Kleemeir Award for research from the Gerontological Society of America. He is a member of the Institute of Medicine of the National Academy of Science and chairs the Group on Biology of Aging/Geriatrics. A founding member of the national Alzheimer's Association, he has received its Founders Award and Genesis Awards well as a Lifetime Achievement Award from the American Association for Geriatric Psychiatry, the Grey Panthers (Dade Chapter) named him Citizen of the year and he has been included in every edition of Best Doctors in America.

Dr. Diane Elmore, PhD, MPH Associate Executive Director of the American Psychological Association's (APA) Public Interest Government Relations Office, Director of the APA Congressional Fellowship Program, and coordinator of activities related to military service members, veterans, and their families. She is also an Adjunct Professor in the School of Public Affairs at the American University. Previously, Dr. Elmore served as an APA/AAAS Health Policy Fellow in the Office of U.S. Senator Hillary Rodham Clinton and as the SPSSI James Marshall Public Policy Scholar at APA. She received her PhD in Counseling Psychology from the University of Houston, MA and BA in Psychology from Pepperdine University, and

MPH from Johns Hopkins University with a dual concentration in health policy and public health preparedness. She completed her predoctoral internship at the Honolulu Veterans Affairs Medical Center/National Center for PTSD, Pacific Islands Division. Dr. Elmore currently serves as a Member of the Board of Directors and the Executive Committee for the International Society for Traumatic Stress Studies (ISTSS); Chair of the ISTSS Public Policy Committee; Chair of the Board of Directors for the National Alliance for Caregiving; Member of the Advisory Board for Voices of September 11th; and Member of the Advisory Board for the National Child Traumatic Stress Network. Her areas of expertise include trauma and PTSD, intergenerational issues, and emergency preparedness and response.

Michael J. English, JD (deceased) retired from the Center for Mental Health Services, Substance Abuse and Mental Health Services Administration (SAMHSA), where he served as Director of the Division of Knowledge Development and Systems Change. In this capacity, he led the Systems of Care and PATHS programs, among others. Mr. English was a recipient of the Department of Health and Human Services Secretary's Award for Distinguished Service. Before joining SAMHSA in 1992, Mr. English served for many years in the public mental health system in the District of Columbia (DC) as a litigating attorney and administrator, culminating in a position as Chief Administrator of the DC Commission on Mental Health Services. A graduate of Georgetown Law School, Mr. English devoted more than more than 20 years to delivering mental health services effectively to those who need them most.

Kana Enomoto is the Principal Deputy Administrator of the Substance Abuse and Mental Health Services Administration (SAMHSA), at the U.S. Department of Health and Human Services (HHS). In this capacity, Ms. Enomoto is the senior non-political official at SAMHSA and she assists SAMSHA's Administrator in providing executive direction and policy leadership for the agency. Ms. Enomoto began her tenure at SAMHSA in 1998 as a Presidential Management Fellow. Since that time, she has held the positions of Director of the Office of Policy, Planning, and Innovation; Acting Deputy Administrator; and Principal Senior Advisor to the Administrator. Ms. Enomoto has been the immediate policy advisor to four Administrators across two administrations and to the Director of the Center for Mental Health Services. Ms. Enomoto has maintained a focus on the behavioral health issues of women and Asian and Pacific Islanders throughout her career. She received her bachelor's and master's degrees in psychology from the University of California, Los Angeles and is a 2011 graduate of Harvard University's Kennedy School of Senior Managers in Government Program.

Dr. Brent E. Gibson, PhD is a Gerontologist with a multidisciplinary background in Human Development and Family Studies. His research is focused mainly on family caregiving and people's perceptions of illness and disability at individual, family, and cultural levels. He has studied caregivers from ethnically and culturally diverse populations within the United States. Dr. Gibson is also President of HaitiCorps International, a non-profit organization focusing on workforce development in Haiti.

Tracy R.G. Gladstone, PhD is the inaugural director of the Robert S. and Grace W. Stone Primary Prevention Initiatives at the Wellesley Centers for Women, Wellesley College, which focuses on research and evaluation designed to prevent the onset of mental health concerns in children and adolescents. She is an assistant in psychology at Boston Children's Hospital, an instructor at Harvard Medical School, and a research scientist at Judge Baker Children's Center. Her work focuses on the prevention of depression in adolescents.

Melanie C. Harper, Ph.D., LPC, NCC is an Associate Professor of Counselor Education at St. Mary's University in San Antonio, TX. She has written a number of publications and presented at national and international conferences on counseling topics, including counseling retirees and older adults and integrating spirituality and religion in counseling.

Dr. Jimmie C. Holland, MD recognized internationally as the founder of the subspecialty of psycho-oncology, is Attending Psychiatrist and holds the first endowed chair in Psychiatric Oncology, the Wayne E. Chapman Chair at Memorial Sloan-Kettering Cancer Center. She is Professor of Psychiatry at Weill Medical College of Cornell University. She began the first fulltime psychiatric service in a cancer hospital in 1977 at Memorial Sloan-Kettering Cancer Center. From this base, the concept of psycho-oncology evolved to become a nationally recognized subspecialty of oncology. The Department of Psychiatry & Behavioral Sciences has trained over 300 psychologists and psychiatrists. Dr. Holland was PI of the first research grant in psycho-oncology which has continued uninterrupted for 26 years. Several key figures in psycho-oncology trained in the program: David Cella, Paul Jacobsen, Julia Rowland, Jamie Ostroff, Bill Redd, Bill Breitbart, as well as several in Europe. Dr. Holland studied the prevalence and nature of psychological problems in patients with cancer in the 1970s and established the first committee studying psychological issues in a cooperative group, the Cancer Leukemia Group B. In the 1980s she became the Founding President of the International Psycho-oncology Society (1984) and of the American Psychosocial Oncology Society (1986). Dr. Holland has been senior editor of the Oxford University Press textbooks in psycho-oncology, first The Handbook of Psychooncology, (1989); Psycho-Oncology, (1998); and the 2nd Edition (2010). In 1992, she started the first international journal in the field, Psycho-Oncology, and continues as co-editor. Dr. Holland and Sheldon Lewis co-authored a book to help patients and their families cope with cancer, The Human Side of Cancer, (HarperCollins, 2000). Dr. Holland has chaired the National Comprehensive Cancer Network's (NCCN) Panel on Management of Distress since its beginning in 1997. She served on the Institute of Medicine Multidisciplinary Committee which reported in 2007 that there is a new standard of quality cancer care today which demands that psychosocial interventions must be integrated into routine cancer care and clinical practice guidelines. Dr. Holland has received awards from the American Cancer Society, ASCO, AACR and the American Psychiatric Association. She was elected Member of the Institute of Medicine in 1995. In Nov, 2011 she received the Alexander Ming Fisher Lecturer/Award at the Columbia College of Physicians and Surgeons in New York and on December 7th, 2011, Dr. Holland received the Marie

Curie Award kicking off the first Marie Curie Campaign presented during the Marie Curie Charity Gala at the French Embassy in Washington DC. Now in April, attending the AACR annual meeting, Dr. Holland received the first Scientist↔Survivor Program Emeritus Mentor Award. She is married to Dr. James Holland, pioneer medical oncologist and Editor of the Holland-Frei textbook, Cancer Medicine. They have 6 children and 10 grandchildren.

Dr. Donald Lollar, EdD is the Director of the Oregon Health & Science University's (OHSU) University Center for Excellence in Developmental Disabilities (UCEDD) and a Professor in the Department of Public Health and Preventive Medicine. Previous to his position with OHSU, Dr. Lollar was a Senior Research Scientist at the National Center on Birth Defects and Developmental Disabilities (NCBDDD) at the Centers for Disease Control and Prevention (CDC) in Atlanta, Georgia. Dr. Lollar received his graduate degrees (MS and EdD) in Rehabilitation Counseling at Indiana University. He served in a variety of leadership positions at the CDC including directing the Office on Disability and Health and the Office of Extramural Research. He is a nationally recognized expert in the areas of disability and health—particularly in the prevention of secondary conditions and health promotion, and the development and implementation of the International Classification of Functioning, Disability and Health (ICF). He was a practicing psychologist for 25 years in states of Maine, Kentucky, and Georgia before being recruited to the CDC. His accomplishments have been acknowledged by the American Academy of Pediatrics (Distinguished Service Citation), and the American Public Health Association (Outstanding Leadership Award). In addition, Dr. Lollar has published extensively in the areas of child disability, public health and disability, and measurement of disability.

Dr. Susan H. McDaniel, PhD, ABPP a family psychologist, is the Dr. Laurie Sands Distinguished Professor of Psychiatry and Family Medicine, Director of the Institute for the Family in Psychiatry, and Associate Chair of Family Medicine at the University of Rochester School of Medicine & Dentistry. She is known for her publications in the areas of behavioral health and primary care, genetic conditions and family dynamics, and doctor-patient communication. Dr. McDaniel a member of the American Psychological Association Leadership Institute for Women in Psychology, She has published 85 peer-reviewed journal articles and co-authored or co-edited 12 books. In 2012, Dr. McDaniel received a 2011 Elizabeth Hurlock Beckman Award, which recognizes educators in psychology, medicine, and law who have inspired a student or students to create an organization which has demonstrably benefited the community at large.

Mary G. Milano, BA is a former staff writer at the International Center for the Integration of Health and Spirituality.

Dr. Patricia Stone Motes, PhD is a research professor with the University of South Carolina's Institute for Families in Society, Division of Policy and Research on Medicaid and Medicare. In this role, Dr. Motes' research and scholarship will focus on enhancing the health and well-being of families through improved systems of healthcare. With a focus on the promotion of positive youth development through community collaboration, Dr. Motes has led a range of research projects including efforts focusing on the prevention of youth violence and systems of care to promote positive mental health outcomes for children, youth, and their families. Dr. Motes recently concluded research projects that included a statewide policy study on the overrepresentation of minority youth in the juvenile justice system, a volunteer community-based program of support to families in crisis or with acute needs, and a mentoring initiative that supports children and families affected by incarceration. Dr. Motes is a national consultant to the Olweus Bullying Prevention Program, Blueprints for Violence Prevention Program. A clinical-community psychologist, Dr. Motes was formerly research professor at Clemson University in the Institute on Families and Neighborhood Life. She began her post-doctoral career at South Carolina State, where she taught in the Department of Psychology and Sociology. Her publications include a co-edited book, Collaborating with Community-Based Organizations Through Consultation and Technical Assistance (Columbia University Press).

Jane E. Myers, PhD, LPC, NCC is a Professor of Counselor Education at the University of North Carolina at Greensboro. A Fellow of the American Counseling Association and the Chi Sigma Iota Academy of Leaders for Excellence, she is a past-president of the American Counseling Association, the Association for Adult Development and Aging, the Association for Assessment in Counseling, and Chi Sigma Iota, International. She is past Chair of the Council for Accreditation of Counseling and Related Educational Programs (CACREP). She has written and edited numerous publications in the areas of adult development, gerontology and wellness, and was noted twice, most recently in 2010, as being in the top 1 % of contributors to the Journal of Counseling & Development, ACAs flagship journal. Most recently, she is the Executive Director of Chi Sigma Iota, International.

Dr. Sherry R. Schachter, PhD, FT the Director of Bereavement Services for Calvary Hospital/ Hospice where she develops, coordinates, and facilitates educational services for staff and develops and oversees an extensive bereavement program for families and bereaved members of the community. Dr. Schachter also directs Camp Compass®, the hospital's summer camp for bereaved children and adolescents. Dr. Schachter is a recipient of the prestigious Lane Adams Award for Excellence in Cancer Nursing from the American Cancer Society and for over 30 years has worked with dying patients and their family caregivers. She is a past president of the Association for Death Education and Counseling, The Thanatology Association (ADEC). Dr. Schachter is also a member of the International Work Group on Death, Dying and Bereavement (IWG). In addition, Dr. Schachter has a private practice in New York City and Pennsylvania, writes a monthly column for Journeys, a publication from the Hospice Foundation of America and also publishes and lectures on issues related to dying, death and loss.

Dr. Chaundrissa Oyeshiku Smith, PhD, APBB is a psychologist with Kaiser Permanente. Previously an assistant professor in the Department of Psychiatry and Behavioral Sciences at Emory University School of Medicine and Clinical Director of the Child and Adolescent Psychiatry Outpatient Clinic at Grady Health System in Atlanta, Dr. Smith is a licensed clinical psychologist. She received her undergraduate degree in psychology from Morgan State University and her doctorate in clinical-community psychology from the University of South Carolina. Dr. Smith completed a psychology postdoctoral fellowship at Emory University School of Medicine and is Board Certified in Child and Adolescent Psychology by the American Board of Professional Psychology. Dr. Smith has co-authored manuscripts and book chapters related to child and adolescent depression, evidence-based interventions for childhood and adolescent disorders, pediatric health psychology, racial identity development, intimate partner violence and child maltreatment, juvenile delinquency, and competencies in psychology related to family therapy interventions. For more than 10 years, Dr. Smith's professional training and career has been in child and adolescent psychology. She has myriad experience providing mental health care to low-income, African American children and their families through the implementation of evidence-based and culturally sensitive family interventions. She maintains specific expertise in the treatment of childhood externalizing disorders (e.g., Attention Deficit-Hyperactivity Disorder, Oppositional Defiant Disorder) and the implementation of evidence-based parenting interventions. Dr. Smith has also lectured in the areas of cultural competence in family interventions, cognitive-behavioral therapy for children and adolescents, and consultation with educational systems.

Dr. Thomas R. Smith, MDiv, PhD is a graduate of Florida State University's doctoral program in Marriage and Family Living. As an army chaplain, Dr. Smith was the founding director of the army's first academically based program to train chaplains in family therapy. After retirement from the Army, he held the positions of President and Deputy Executive Director of the International Center for the Integration of Health and Spirituality. As retired Chaplain (Colonel), USA, Dr. Smith also serves as Vice-President for Local Chapters for the U.S. Army Chaplain Corps Regimental Association.

Pamela Jumper Thurman, PhD a Western Cherokee, is a Senior Research Scientist and Director of the National Center for Community Readiness and the CA7AE Project at Colorado State University. She has 21 years of experience in mental health, substance abuse/epidemiology research, and HIV/AIDS Capacity Building Assistance, as well as 35 years in the provision of direct treatment and prevention services as well as community work. She is a co-developer and co-author of the Community Readiness Model and has applied the model in over 2,000 communities throughout the US as well as over 23 communities internationally. She has worked with cultural issues utilizing community participatory research, prevention of ATOD, methamphetamine treatment and prevention, prevention of violence and victimization, rural women's concerns, HIV/AIDS, and solvent abuse. She currently serves or has served as principal investigator or co-principal investigator for 17 federally funded grants that examine community/grassroots prevention of intimate partner violence, state wide initiatives to prevent methamphetamine use, epidemiology of American Indian substance use, prevention of HIV/AIDS, and epidemiology and prevention of solvent use among youth. She is the Project Director of a CDC funded effort to provide capacity building assistance aimed at community mobilization for HIV/AIDS prevention in Ethnic communities throughout the United States. She has served as a member of the National CSAT Advisory Council and was also a member of one of Roslyn Carter's Caregiving Panels as well as participating in First Lady Laura Bush's "Helping Americas Youth" initiative. She worked collaboratively with Ohio's First Lady, Hope Taft in the integration of community readiness into Mrs. Taft's Building Bridges Project to reduce underage drinking throughout the state of Ohio. She has published extensively on a variety of topics in various books chapters and journals.

Susan Taylor-Brown, PhD, MPH, ACSW is Clinical Professor of Pediatrics, Strong Center for Developmental Disabilities, Department of Pediatrics, University of Rochester has dedicated her career to training health care practitioners to provide family-centered care and research. She has focused on delivering strengths-oriented services to individuals and families coping with chronic or life-threatening conditions. This manuscript was part of her work with Project on Death in America, Soros Foundation. Currently her research focus is on the use of animal-assisted interventions using dogs and horses for a variety of conditions ranging from Alzheimers, autism, progressive neuromuscular disorders, spinal cord injuries to Iraq/Afghanistan veterans who are disabled. Her career was profoundly enhanced by caring for her parents until their deaths in 2009 and 2010. Susan and her husband, Marc, have two grown children, David and Marian who involved in similar efforts.

David de Voursney, MPP is an analyst in the Office of the Assistant Secretary for Planning and Evaluation (ASPE) in the Department of Health and Human Services. He started his career working with children and youth at a community mental health center in rural Indiana and a group home serving justice-involved youth in central Virginia. Mr. de Voursney joined the Substance Abuse and Mental Health Services Administration (SAMSHA) through the Presidential Management Fellowship in the fall of 2005. At SAMHSA, he served as a project officer on the Safe Schools/Healthy Students program, coordinated the development of Project LAUNCH, and supported agency leadership as an analyst in the Office of Policy, Planning, and Innovation until 2012. He has a bachelor's degree in psychology from Earlham College and a master's degree in public policy from the University of Michigan.

Introduction: Caregiving to Promote Mental Health and Prevent Mental Illness

Ronda C. Talley, Gregory L. Fricchione and Benjamin G. Druss

Former First Lady Rosalynn Carter captures the essence of caregiving's universal nature in the following quote:

There are only four kinds of people in this world:

> Those who have been caregivers;
> Those who currently are caregivers;
> Those who will be caregivers; and
> Those who will need caregivers. (1999)

As Mrs. Carter suggests, caregiving is a universal proposition that almost every human will face at some point in their lifetime (Carter and Golant 1999; Carter et al. 2010). While caregiving—providing care for an individual with special needs or illnesses—is most often a selfless act of love, the process involves deep personal commitment to situations with great variety, and for some, it also demands incredible personal sacrifice.

Consider the individual who requires care or the care recipient. The length of time care is needed or its duration is one factor influencing the caregiving situation. For example, a care recipient may be ill for a relatively short time period. Alternatively, if the individual has a chronic illness or long-term disability, the demands on the caregiver are dramatically increased. Second, severity also dictates care needs. For

R. C. Talley (✉)
Department of Psychology, Western Kentucky University,
1906 College Heights Boulevard, 3023 Gary Ransdell Hall,
Bowling Green, KY 42101, USA
e-mail: Ronda.Talley@wku.edu

G. L. Fricchione
Division of Psychiatry and Medicine, Division of International Psychiatry,
Harvard Medical School, Massachusetts General Hospital,
55 Fruit Street, Boston, MA 02114, USA

B. G. Druss
Health Policy and Management, Behavioral Sciences and Health Education,
Rollins School of Public Health, 1518 Clifton Road NE, Atlanta, GA 30322, USA
e-mail: bdruss@emory.edu

R. C. Talley et al. (eds.), *The Challenges of Mental Health Caregiving*,
Caregiving: Research • Practice • Policy, DOI 10.1007/978-1-4614-8791-3_1,

example, the nature of the illness or condition that triggers care may range from a limited to generalized disability. Obviously, an individual with a limited disability will produce fewer care demands than someone with a substantial disability. Third, what is the family's level of support, both human and fiscal? Does the caregiver have resources in terms of other individuals who will assist in providing care, and are there funds to pay for respite and other resources that may relieve the stress of caregiving ? The duration, severity, and support levels experienced by caregivers interact to provide a unique caregiving experience for each caregiver–care recipient dyad.

For individuals with mental illness or behavioral health challenges, the care dynamics are often even more complex. For example, depression may require ongoing treatment throughout one's lifetime, but, at some periods, the caregiving experience may be like a roller coaster ride. That is, caregiving may be more or less intense at some points compared to others as the care recipient's condition degrades or improves. In other words, for individuals with mental health challenges and their caregivers, the caregiving trajectory is often more unpredictable than it is with other kinds of caregiving, and the end result can be uncertain depending on factors such as medication management, social support, insurance availability, and workplace accommodation. Although great strides have been made in the medical treatment of mental illness, we are a long way from consistently providing a system of supports that allows individuals with mental health challenges to have a smooth trajectory toward freedom from the symptoms of their diseases. For caregivers of individuals with mental health challenges, the burden and stress of caregiving is complicated by this unpredictability.

Mental health issues, while long in the nation's conscience, have often been ignored and neglected due to tremendous public stigma against those who exhibit mental health challenges (Thompson 2003). Within the last decade, fortunately, great strides have been made to acknowledge and provide appropriate services for individuals with mental and behavioral health challenges (Agency for Healthcare Quality 2013; Centers for Disease Control and Prevention 2013; Center for Mental Health Services 2006; New Freedom Commission on Mental Health 2003; U.S. Department of Health and Human Services 2005).

Current public health data suggest that mental health caregiving is a critical national health care issue (U.S. Department of Health and Human Services (2001a, b). Very recently, the Centers for Disease Control and Prevention (CDC) issued several reports addressing the topic (2011, 2013). This work has focused the nation's attention on caregiving and mental health. To produce this picture of mental health in the United States, CDC compiled data from eight of their surveillance systems: Pregnancy Risk Assessment Monitoring System (PRAMS), National Nursing Home Survey (NNHS), National Health Interview Survey (NHIS), National Hospital Discharge Survey (NHDS), National Health and Nutrition Examination Survey (NHANES), National Ambulatory Medical Care Survey (NAMCS), National Hospital Ambulatory Medical Care Survey (NHAMCS), and the Behavioral Risk Factor Surveillance System (BRFSS).

From these data, CDC (2011, 2013) notes that the economic burden of mental illness in the United States is substantial—about US$ 300 billion in 2002. Approximately 25 % of U.S. adults have a mental illness. Increasingly, scientists are documenting the connection between functioning of the mind and body. For instance, often individuals with mental illnesses also have physical illnesses, such as cancer, cardiovascular disease, obesity, and diabetes (SAMHSA 2013).

Definitions

For purposes of consistency throughout this book, several concepts will be defined here.

Mental Health, Mental Disorders, and Mental Illness

First, we embrace the World Health Organization's (2011) definitions of mental health, mental disorders, and mental illness as noted below. WHO states:

> Mental health is a state of successful performance of mental function, resulting in productive activities, fulfilling relationships with other people, and the ability to adapt to change and to cope with adversity. Mental health is indispensable to personal well-being, family and interpersonal relationships, and contribution to community or society.

WHO (2011) goes on to define mental disorders as "health conditions that are characterized by alterations in thinking, mood, or behavior (or some combination thereof), which are associated with distress and/or impaired functioning and spawn a host of human problems that may include disability, pain, or death. " In expanding on this definition, the U.S. Surgeon General specifically addresses mental disorders among children, which was described by that office as "serious deviations from expected cognitive, social, and emotional development" (U.S. Department of Health and Human Services 1999).

Lastly, WHO uses the term "mental illness" to refer collectively to all diagnosable mental disorders.

Note that in our work, we consider the care needs of individuals who may function at suboptimal levels as well as those who exhibit clear signs of mental illness. Since care of an individual with suboptimal mental health status or serious mental health problems affect both the individual with the mental health issues and those who live and work with that person, professional caregivers need to provide services that are ecological in nature and take into account the needs of the mental-health-challenged individual and those who are stressed in their care.

We also emphasize the mind–body connection throughout this book. Due to the rapidly expanding knowledge base supporting strong correlations between physical and mental health, an individual's status in one area is known to directly influence their ability to perform in the other. This has direct bearing on the treatment and care of individuals with mental health challenges as well as individuals who suffer from other diseases or conditions that contribute to suboptimal life functioning.

Disability

Disability, for our purposes, is defined as mobility, sensory, intellectual, or mental impairments that lead to activity limitations. While individuals may be born or become disabled for many reasons, or, in the case of mental illness, symptoms may manifest later in life, we focus on issues related to their care rather than the cause or type of disability. Our rationale stems from the knowledge that caregivers have common needs regardless of the disability name or genesis (Talley and Crews 2013). CDC notes that mental disorders are among the highest causes of disability (2001).

Caregiving, Care Recipient, and Family Caregiver

There are several definitions of *caregiving*. To define caregiving, we turn to several of the well-known caregiving researchers and advocacy groups . The National Alliance for Caregiving (NAC) and the American Association of Retired Persons (AARP) define caregiving as "caring for an adult family member or friend." A second definition of caregiving, promoted by the National Family Caregivers Association (NFCA), is "offering the necessary physical and mental health support to care for a family member." Among the descriptions of informal or family caregiving, one that has been widely accepted over time was offered in 1985 by Horowitz (1985), who indicated that informal care involves four dimensions: *direct care* (helping to dress, managing medications); *emotional care* (providing social support and encouragement); *mediation care* (negotiating with others on behalf of the care receiver); and *financial care* (through managing fiscal resources, including gifts or service purchases). The challenges of actually providing informal or family caregiving have been attributed to the level of intensity and physical intimacy required to provide care (Montgomery et al. 1985); the amount of burden, distress, and role strain that care engenders for the caregiver (Aneshensel et al. 1993; Berg-Weger et al. 2000; Seltzer and Li 2000); and the skill required to master care tasks (Schumacher et al. 2000).

Relatedly, the Administration on Aging defines a *caregive*r as "anyone who provides assistance to another in need." More specifically, *family caregiver* is defined by the Health Plan of New York and NAC as "a person who cares for relatives and loved ones." Metlife and NAC (2006) expanded on this by specifying additional qualifiers in that a family caregiver is "a person who cares for relatives and loved ones who are frail, elderly, or who have a physical or mental disability . " Similarly, the NFCA adds that family caregivers provide a vast array of emotional, financial, nursing, social, homemaking, and other services on a daily or intermittent basis. The NFCA advocates for the term *family caregiver* to be defined broadly and to include friends and neighbors who assist with care by providing respite, running errands, or a whole host of other tasks that support the caregiver and care recipient. In this volume, we will use the terms *informal caregiver* and *family caregiver* interchangeably and employ the comprehensive definition of *family caregiver* to refer to caring relatives, friends, and neighbors.

Professional Caregiver

Throughout the book, we use the term *professional caregivers* to refer to paid care providers such as physicians, nurses, social workers, psychologists, case managers, hospice workers, home health aides, and many others. The designation as professional caregiver excludes those family caregivers who may receive funds to provide care from new and emerging sources, such and the Medicaid Cash and Counseling Demonstration Program.

Genesis of the Rosalynn Carter Institute Caregiving Book Series

Efforts to develop this book began in 2000, when Johnson & Johnson, an international health care business leader, and Dr. Ronda Talley, executive director of the Rosalynn Carter Institute for Caregiving, began discussions that led to the development of the Johnson & Johnson/Rosalynn Carter Institute Caregivers Program. Through this program, the Rosalynn Carter Institute (RCI) convened a series of ten expert panels over a period of several years to address a wide variety of caregiving issues. These included disability, Alzheimer's disease, cancer, life span caregiving, rural caregiving, intergenerational caregiving, education and support for caregivers, interdisciplinary approaches to caregiving, building community caregiving capacity, and, the topic of this volume, mental health. With Springer as our partner, the RCI books were integrated into the Springer caregiving book series, *Caregiving: Research, Policy , and Practice* with Dr. Talley as editor-in-chief. The current book, *The Challenges of Mental Health Caregiving*, is the eighth book to be published in the series.

Organization of the Book

The Challenges of Mental Health Caregiving is divided into three sections. In the first section, *Developmental Issues in Mental Health Caregiving*, authors Elmore, Gibson, Taylor-Brown, and McDaniel explore issues of relevance to specific populations. Section two, *The Mental Health Caregiving Context*, deals with a variety of environmental settings and concerns, such as environmental issues, spirituality, and aging. In section three, *Local, State, and National Issues Effecting Caregivers and Mental Health Caregiving*, the authors address prominent legislative and policy issues in both mental health and caregiving, including reimbursement for services. The book is summarized by Lollar and Talley in the concluding chapter.

Section I: Developmental Issues in Mental Health Caregiving

Elmore. Diane Elmore's chapter provides an overview of the relationship between physical health, mental health, and caregiving. Elmore notes that although caregiving can be a rewarding opportunity for many family caregivers, this labor of love can put individuals at risk for substantial stressors, including financial, physical, and psychological hardship. Elmore provides evidence that suggests that caregiving, if not overly strenuous, can actually be associated with mental health benefits to the caregiver. Lessons learned from relevant research, clinical practice, education and training, and public policy are highlighted. In addition, implications and opportunities for future directions in each of these areas are offered.

Gibson: In his chapter on cultural considerations in caring for persons with mental illness, Brent Gibson highlights the importance of culture in determining illness meaning, family caregivers' experiences of burden and reward, and culturally competent formal service provision for persons with mental illness and their families. He highlights the research, practice, and policy dimensions of each of these key issues.

Taylor-Brown and McDaniel. In their chapter, Susan Taylor-Brown and Susan McDaniel stress that many families are stretched thin with simultaneous care demands. Family-oriented approaches are widely called for, but there are few primary care providers who are capable of delivering this model of care in today's managed care environment. At the same time, collaborative care is not yet valued as a central practice in health care delivery despite the fact that it is integral to the successful implementation of care for the chronically ill patient across his or her lifetime. While consumers state that they are more comfortable and feel less stigmatized when receiving mental health services in a primary care setting, primary care practices are not uniformly good at incorporating mental health services into their sites with co-location and collaborative arrangements.

Taylor-Brown and McDaniel make the point that there needs to be extensive research focused on the impact of providing care to individuals with chronic mental health conditions as well as the needs to caregivers who support them. Women predominantly acting as primary caregivers turn out to be at risk for secondary mental health problems. It is also now known that caregivers often care for more than one family member. Several trends are likely to increase demand on caregiving men in the future.

On the educational side, the authors suggest that the practice environment of family medicine needs to foster greater provider readiness to detect and treat mental disorders and to facilitate referral to mental health specialists for consultation when needed. The majority of specialty mental health care in this country is currently delivered through managed care carve outs rather than through integrated health systems, and efforts need to be made to improve primary care and mental health collaborations.

Taylor-Brown and McDaniel emphasize the biopsychosocial model as a framework for all professionals delivering comprehensive care to the chronically ill. It advocates early involvement of family members in patient care. Efforts need to be focused on the collaborative family healthcare envisioned as a cooperative relationship between patients, family members and their teams and even healthcare team members need training in this approach.

Section II: The Mental Health Caregiving Context

Beardslee and Gladstone. In this chapter, Bill Beardslee and Tracy Gladstone review mental health promotion and mental illnesses prevention work over the past three decades. The review references documented progress in the prevention of mental illness. Founding of the Society for Prevention Research and its *Journal of Prevention* reflects the growing interest in this field.

Throughout their chapter, Beardslee and Gladstone stress one of the crucial issues in prevention, which is to develop a partnership with families and to move away from the expert and patient model, recognizing that the ultimate theme of prevention work is to strengthen the resources within the individual, the family, and the community. Their groundbreaking prevention research with families and depression is an outstanding illustration of how to build prevention into a modern medical approach to caregiving.

In terms of future directions, the authors remark that community and family members with the proper training and support can do many interventions otherwise done by healthcare professionals. They stress the need to encourage the aim of understanding child and family development and using this as a basis of practice. They also stress the need to orient mental healthcare professionals to look beyond simple diagnostic models and to embrace more developmental models and their attendant translational issues. There is a crying need for more research on the basic science of prevention, and the authors of this chapter bring this point home.

Finally, Beardslee and Gladstone stress that there needs to be much more work on how to incorporate prevention intervention approach in federal, state, and local policy.

Motes and Smith. Patricia Motes and Chaundrissa Smith address caregiving efforts designed to promote positive mental health outcomes for children and adolescents. They describe the system of care philosophy that envelopes public sector caregiving for child and adolescent mental health. Motes and Smith note that within this caregiving approach, the significance of family caregivers, cultural competency, and community-based interventions are emphasized. The efficacy of caregiving efforts within a system of care is discussed in light of practice issues, research on child and family outcomes, and the education and training of caregivers. The chapter concludes with a look at policy issues and implications for the future of caregiving and child and adolescent mental health.

Myers and Harper. In their chapter, Jane Myers and Melanie Harper focus on the intersection between midlife developmental issues and caregiving. Because most caregivers are in this middle phase of life, it is particularly critical to understand how midlife developmental and social issues influence, and are influenced by, their caregiving activities. The discussion is grounded in theories of adult development as well as contextual and transition theories. The authors conclude that "midlife caregivers need both social-emotional and instrumental support to deal first with issues of midlife, second with issues of caregiving, and finally with the special issues related to caregiving during the midlife period."

Smith and Milano. In this chapter, Tom Smith and Mary Milano stress that most Americans are involved in an organized expression of faith that can produce spiritual supports within them and provide significant resiliency when they are facing illness. With this in mind, the authors contend it is important for caregivers to recognize the central place spirituality plays in the lives of many of their patients as well as in the lives of themselves and their colleagues.

Taking the spiritual history and incorporating spiritual beliefs into caregiving are practical ways to provide value for both patient and caregiver, suggest Smith and Milano. They conclude that faith communities are not maximizing their ability to strengthen the lives of family caregivers who can benefit from spiritual engagement in these communities. They also suggest that researchers have found links between health and spirituality including lower rates of depression and improved compliance with care. Those who are more spiritual also apparently have a more active coping style that allows them to deal with their illnesses more positively. More research in these areas will be required.

Section III: Local, State, and National Issues Effecting Caregivers and Mental Health Caregiving

English, de Voursney, and Enomoto. In their chapter on caregiving and mental health policy, Mike English (now deceased), David de Voursney, and Kana Enomoto explain the disconnect between the evidence on caregiver burden and efficacy, and the lack of support for reimbursement for caregiving activities. They suggest that the best way to frame the policy argument for an expanded caregiver support policy is as "helping families to help themselves." "Because informal caregiving is valuable and effective," they conclude, "it should be considered an essential component of the public health system."

Schachter and Holland. In their chapter, Sherry Schachter and Jimmie Holland focus their attention on expectations society now has of caregivers in the climate of managed care. Patients increasingly remain at home with chronic conditions and become a major burden, both to the family and the primary caregiver. How does the caregiver expect to manage clinic visits, doing minor medical procedures at home while also maintaining the home and the household jobs that go with it? This is made more complicated by the "graying of America," with more caregivers who are seniors and who may have chronic illnesses themselves. In this context, when those who have been cared for pass away, the surviving family member faces grief associated with loss and often does not have their counseling needs met. Policymakers at the federal, state, and local level must realize that this is an increasing burden in our society that will only get worse over the next few decades. At the same time, clinicians need to be diligent to monitor the family members with complicated grief and to make available appropriate resources such as bereavement support groups.

Schachter and Holland note that hospitals must be cognizant of the need of discrete populations and be sensitive to cultural, racial, and ethnic issues including religious beliefs and customs. Information clearing houses and training organizations will increasingly be needed as future caregiving in our society increases.

In terms of the future, Schachter and Holland advocate that professional caregivers should stay in touch with family caregivers after a significant loss. They suggest that bereavement support groups, senior citizen centers, and community centers collaborate with local hospice and home care facilities and long term care facilities to offer help, support, and information to family caregivers in languages other than English.

The authors also suggest that healthcare professionals need more education so that they can better care for their own personal psychological needs and acknowledge their feelings about mortality and loss experience. They also need more education to improve communication skills about end of life care.

Crocco and Eisdorfer. Elizabeth Crocco and Carl Eisdorfer provide an overview of research in the area of caregiving. The chapter reviews the extensive body of research documenting the prevalence and demographics of caregiving, the impact of caregiver burden on physical and mental health , and the specific psychological, demographic, cultural, and social risk factors for caregiver depression. They recommend that future research focus on better understanding the specific factors placing caregivers at risk, as well as working to develop interventions that can prevent or mitigate these potential adverse effects of caregiving.

Book Summary

Lollar and Talley. In the summary chapter on mental health caregiving issues, Don Lollar and Ronda Talley discuss the wide range of issues presented in this book. Critical themes that emerge from the authors' discussions focus progressively from environmental and cultural issues through policy, practices, and systems.

Lollar and Talley note that across all chapters the issue of preparation of professionals emerged. While most chapters in the book focus on mental health and family caregiving, parts of numerous chapters address the mental health of providers—professional caregivers. The authors advocate for coherent assessment and intervention in the care triad of care recipient, family caregiver, and professional caregiver as they work together to help each other plan and implement service and support plans that will optimize life experiences for all parties.

Conclusions

Throughout the book, major themes regarding the issues involved in providing quality care to individuals with mental health challenges are highlighted. Attention is devoted to each issue in terms of current practice, policy, research, and education and training. In addition, the authors answered the questions of what is needed in the future to better support those individuals who are challenged with mental health disabilities as well as those who are living each day with suboptimal mental health. This latter group is sometimes described as the walking wounded; they can function at some level, but they do not enjoy a life of satisfaction or fulfillment. This latter group is one whose needs are often unaddressed, but whose mental health status manifests itself in poor quality of life, awkward or nonexistent social relationships, and the emergence of physical illnesses. Thus, not only do the walking wounded suffer, their mental and physical illnesses place a burden on society through increased medical costs, decreased work productivity, and marginalized social relationships and community engagement. And quite importantly, caring for these individuals extracts an emotional and physical toll on the loved ones who witness their unhappiness.

We are living in time when medical science is offering new promise for the treatment of mental health problems. From a scientific perspective, it is a time of hope. However, stigma regarding the diagnosis, treatment, and care of individuals who have mental and behavioral problems still exists. Former First Lady Rosalynn Carter has battled this sigma since the 1970s, first as a governor's wife, then in her role as presidential wife. She has continued her advocacy for those who suffer from mental illness for over four decades and she specifically has recognized the challenges facing those who love and care for someone with a mental illness. Due to her work and the bravery of many high-profile individuals who have publically disclosed their diagnoses and treatments with the world, the stigma of mental illness has started to fade.

We are not there yet; we are not to the point where more individuals consider a mental health issue on par with a heart or lung problem than not. But we are moving in the right direction. As awareness of the biologically based factors that contribute to mental illness increases and as more individuals acknowledge their struggles and treatment without shame, public acceptance will follow. As medical science continues to accelerate in its discovery of promising new approaches to pharmaceutical options, real progress can be made. Combining new therapeutic behavioral treatments with pharmaceutical ones show great promise in alleviating the life difficulties and real suffering of individuals with mental health challenges.

However, we would be remiss if we did not recognize the contributions and needs of those who care for individuals with mental health challenges. At times, caregiving can be a lonely, isolating, depressing, and demanding job. Caregivers are vulnerable to having existing mental health problems exacerbated by the demands of care or developing mental health issues triggered by their caregiving duties. Even when the caregiver chooses to provide the care and loves the individual they are caring for, their status as a caregiver puts them at an increased risk of developing mental health problems when compared to individuals who do not caregive.

This book is for you—those of you facing each day often uncertain of exactly what the day will bring, but knowing that you are needed in order to enhance the life of an individual with mental health challenges. We know you are there. We thank you for what you are doing. And we know you need support, too, in your role as caregiver. We hope that this book acknowledges the job you do, that you find its contents meaningful and relevant, and that it offers you hope for the future.

References

Agency for Healthcare Quality. (2013). Partners in health: Mental health, primary care and substance use inter-agency collaboration tool kit, 2nd Edition. http://www.ibhp.org/uploads/file/IBHPIinteragency%20Collaboration%20Tool%20Kit%202013%20.pdf. Accessed 11 September 2013.

Aneshensel, C. S., Pearlin, L. I., & Schuler, R. H. (1993). Stress, role captivity, and the cessation of caregiving. *Journal of Health and Social Behavior, 34*(1), 54–70.

Berg-Weger, M., Rubio, D. M., & Tebb, S. (2001). Strengths-based practice with family caregivers of the chronically ill: Qualitative insights. *Families in Society, 82*(3), 263–272.

Carter, R., & Golant, S. (1999). Helping someone with mental illness: A compassionate guide for family, friends, and caregivers. New York: Three Rivers.

Carter, R., Golant, S. K., & Cade, K. E. (2010). Within our reach: Ending the mental health crisis. New York: Rodale.

Center for Mental Health Services. (2006). Mentally healthy aging: A report on overcoming stigma for older Americans. (DHHS Pub. No. [SMA] 05–3988). (2005). Rockville: Center for Mental Health Services, Substance Abuse and Mental Health Services Administration. http://www.mentalhealth.samhsa.gov/media/ken/pdf/SMA05-3988/aging_stigma.pdf and http://www.mentalhealth.samhsa.gov/publications/allpubs/sma05-3988/findings.asp. Accessed 2 May 2006.

Centers for Disease Control and Prevention (CDC). (2001). Mental illness surveillance among adults in the United States. *Morbility and Mortality Weekly Report (Supplement), 60*(03), 1–32.

Centers for Disease Control and Prevention (CDC). (2013). Mental health surveillance among children—United States, 2005–2011. *Morbility and Mortality Weekly Report, 62*(02), 1–35.

Family Caregiver Alliance. (2006). California caregiver resource centers: A 20-year partnership in caring. San Francisco: California Department of Mental Health. http://www.caregiver.org/caregiver/jsp/content_node.jsp?nodeid=973. Accessed 18 May 2006.

Horowitz, A. (1985). Family caregiving to the frail elderly. In C. Eisdorfer (Ed.), *Annual review of gerontology and geriatrics* (Vol. 5, pp. 194–246). New York: Springer.

Metlife & National Alliance for Caregiving. (2006). 2006 MetLife Foundation family caregiver awards program. Retrieved from http://www.asaging.org/asav2/caregiver/index.cfm?CFID=12644792&CFTOKEN=19400852#definition.

Montgomery, R. J. V., Gonyea, J., & Hooyman, N. (1985). Caregiving and the experience of subjective and objective burden. *Family Relations, 34,* 19–26.

New Freedom Commission on Mental Health. (2003). Achieving the promise: Transforming mental health care in America. Final report (DHHS Pub. No. SMA-03–3832). Rockville: U.S. Department of Health and Human Services. http://www.mentalhealthcommission.gov/reports/Finalreport/toc_exec.html. Accessed 1 May 2006.

Nijboer, C., Triemstra, M., Tempelaar, R., Sanderman, R., & van den Bos, G. A. M. (1999). Determinants of caregiving experiences and mental health of partners of cancer patients. *Cancer, 86*(4), 577–588.

Schumacher, K., Stewart, B., Archbold, P., Dood, M., & Dibble, S. (2000). Family caregiving skill: Development of the concept. *Research in Nursing & Health, 23*, 191–203.

Seltzer, M. M., & Li, L. W. (2000). The dynamics of caregiving: Transitions during a three-year prospective study. *Gerontologist, 40*(2), 165–178.

Substance Abuse and Mental Health Services Administration, U.S. Department of Health and Human Services. (2013). Behavioral health treatment needs assessment toolkit for states (HHS Publication No. SMA13–4757). Rockville: Substance Abuse and Mental Health Services Administration, U.S. Department of Health and Human Services.

Talley, R. C., & Crews, J. E. (Eds.). (2013). *The multiple dimensions of caregiving and disability*. New York: Springer.s

Thompson, K. (2003). US Department of HHS, 2002, 2004, 2005. Stigma and public health policy for schizophrenia. *The Psychiatric Clinics of North America, 26*(1), 273–294.

U.S. Department of Health and Human Services. (1999). Mental health: A report of the Surgeon General—Executive summary. Rockville: U.S. Department of Health and Human Services, Substance Abuse and Mental Health Services Administration, Center for Mental Health Services, National Institutes of Health, National Institute of Mental Health. http://www.surgeongeneral.gov/library/mentalhealth/home.html. Accessed 16 March 2006.

U.S. Department of Health and Human Services. (2000). Healthy people 2010: Conference edition: Chap. 18. Mental health and mental disorders. Washington: U.S. Department of Health and Human Services. http://www.mentalhealth.samhsa.gov/features/hp2010/18Mental.asp. and http://www.mentalhealth.samhsa.gov/features/hp2010/objectives.asp Accessed May 17 2006.

U.S. Department of Health and Human Services. (2001a). Mental health: Culture, race, and ethnicity: A supplement to mental health: A report of the Surgeon General. http://www.mentalhealth.samhsa.gov/cre/toc.asp. Accessed 4 Apr 2006.

U.S. Department of Health and Human Services. (2001b). Report of the surgeon general's conference on children's mental health: A national action agenda. Washington: U.S. Department of Health and Human Services. http://www.hhs.gov/surgeongeneral/topics/cmh/childreport.htm. Accessed 16 May 2006.

U.S. Department of Health and Human Services. (2004). Community integration for older adults with mental illnesses: Overcoming barriers and seizing opportunities. (DHHS Pub. No. [SMA] 05–4018). Rockville: Center for Mental Health Services, Substance Abuse and Mental Health Services Administration. http://www.mentalhealth.samhsa.gov/publications/allpubs/sma05-4018/. Accessed 19 Apr 2006.

U.S. Department of Health and Human Services. (2005). Family guide to systems of care for children with mental health needs. http://www.mentalhealth.samhsa.gov/publications/allpubs/sma-4054/. Accessed 1 May 2006.

World Health Organization (WHO). (2011). Mental health: A state of well-being. Geneva: World Health Organization. http://www.who.int/features/factfiles/mental_health/en/indexhtml. Accessed 3 June 2013.

Part I
Developmental Issues in Mental Health Caregiving

The Impact of Caregiving on Physical and Mental Health: Implications for Research, Practice, Education, and Policy

Diane L. Elmore

Family caregivers have played a significant role in our society since the beginning of time. Each year, the demand for caregiving affects millions of American families from all socioeconomic, ethnic, and educational backgrounds. Today, family caregivers play an essential role in our system of care by providing a significant proportion of our health and long-term care for the chronically ill, disabled, and aging. Feinberg et al. (2011) estimated that the economic value of services provided by family caregivers was US$ 450 billion in 2009.

Although caregiving has always been important, there are several factors that have increased the need for family caregivers in our society. First, improvements in health care, nutrition and education over the last several decades, have resulted in increased life expectancy and a subsequent growth in the aging population in the U.S. In fact, those 65 and older are now the fastest growing segment of the U.S. population (U.S. Census Bureau 2011). As more and more Americans live longer lives, we are experiencing an increased need for caregivers. Today, almost half of older adults require some help with their personal care and daily needs, and family members and loved ones are providing the bulk of this care.

Next, older Americans are not only the recipients of care, but are also often caregivers themselves. Grandparents or other relatives caring for children are sometimes referred to as "kinship caregivers." Kinship care families are growing, with 1 in 11 children residing in kinship care at some point before the age of 18, and specifically, 1 in 5 black children spending time in kinship care at some point in their childhood (The Annie E. Casey Foundation 2012). According to the U.S. Census Bureau (2012), 2.7 million grandparents were the primary caregivers of one or more of their grandchildren in 2010. In addition, many Americans are caring for both children and older adult parents at the same time. These individuals are often identified as belonging to the "sandwich" generation, pulled between the caregiving needs of their dependents across the lifespan.

D. L. Elmore (✉)
National Center For Child Traumatic Stress, UCLA/Duke University,
NCCTS—Duke University, 411 West Chapel Hill Street,
Suite 200, 27701 Durham, NC, USA
e-mail: delmore@apa.org

R. C. Talley et al. (eds.), *The Challenges of Mental Health Caregiving*,
Caregiving: Research • Practice • Policy, DOI 10.1007/978-1-4614-8791-3_2,

Finally, over the last several decades, the needs and rights of members of the disability community have been highlighted, bringing to the forefront the importance of humane and consumer-driven care for individuals living with disabilities and chronic conditions. As such, many individuals with disabilities have moved from institutional care to community-based settings, where they often prefer to reside. This focus on community-based living has increased the need for both professional and family caregivers to assist persons with disabilities and chronic disease to maintain their independence in the community.

Although caregiving can be a rewarding opportunity for many family caregivers, this labor of love can put individuals at risk for substantial stressors, including financial, physical, and psychological hardship. Research indicates that caregivers may put their own health and well-being at risk while assisting loved ones (Burton et al. 1997; Tang and Chen 2002). The strain of caregiving demands has been linked to poor health outcomes including depression, physical illness, anxiety, and poor sleep habits (Schulz et al. 1997). On the other hand, there is also evidence that suggests that caregiving, if not overly strenuous, can actually be associated with mental health benefits to the caregiver (Beach et al. 2000).

This chapter will provide an overview of the relationship between physical health, mental health, and caregiving. Lessons learned from relevant research, clinical practice, education and training, and public policy will be highlighted. In addition, implications and opportunities for future directions in each of these areas will be offered.

The Connection Between Physical and Mental Health

In preparation for a discussion of the relationship between physical health, mental health, and caregiving, it is first important to provide a brief overview of the relationship between physical and mental health, sometimes referred to as the mind–body connection. According to Brower (2006), the notion that the mind and body are intimately connected has existed for centuries. Over time, a strong body of research has developed, indicating that our functioning as human beings results from an integration of the biological, psychological, and social factors in our lives (Uvnas-Moberg et al. 2005). According to Ray (2004), this biopsychosocial approach suggests that our thoughts are a function of our brain, and therefore, changes in our thoughts result in subsequent changes in our brain and body. Ray (2004) further explains that in the biopsychosocial model, it is "the neurotransmitters, hormones, and cytokines that act as messenger molecules carrying information between the nervous, endocrine, and immune systems."

Stress is a state of intensive mind–body activity that occurs in the context of stressful life events. The individual seeks physiological stability in the face of stress-induced change. This process is called allostasis. This balance, however, comes at the cost of metabolic wear and tear, referred to as allostatic loading. When allostatic loading is persistent or excessive, vulnerability to disease increases (McEwen 1998).

The research literature provides examples of the way in which health and disease are influenced by biological, psychological, and social interactions, and subsequent allostatic loading that may occur. According to Chesney et al. (2005), positive emotions can have a beneficial impact on health and well-being. For example, higher levels of optimism are suggested to be associated with lower levels of stress and depression (Brissette et al. 2002), reduced risk of illness, more rapid recovery from illness, and utilization of fewer sick days following a significant life event (Kivimaki et al. 2005). In contrast, research indicates that negative psychological emotions and states such as anger and depression can be associated with poor health outcomes, including increased mortality (Chesney et al. 2005).

Caregiving Research

There is an increasing body of research regarding the relationship between caregiving, physical health, and mental health. Although the literature in this area is still emerging, there currently exists significant evidence to support the potential for both positive and negative health effects of caregiving (Beach et al. 2000). The next section provides an overview of some of the research related to the physical and mental health consequences of caregiving, highlights research regarding stress and caregiver health, identifies methodological challenges in the caregiving literature, and outlines future directions for caregiving research.

Physical and Mental Health Consequences Associated with Caregiving

Research suggests that caregivers, or a subgroup of caregivers, are at risk for negative physical health effects, which may emerge over time as care demands increase (Schulz and Beach 1999; Schulz et al. 1997). Caring for a loved one may often include assistance with activities of daily living (ADLs) such as bathing, dressing, eating, and transferring. These caregiving tasks can put a great deal of strain on a caregiver's physical health. Research suggests that caregivers may experience direct and indirect physical health consequences, including deficits in antibody responses to vaccination (Glaser et al. 2000), higher levels of stress hormones (Gallagher-Thompson et al. 2006; Vitaliano et al. 2003), and poorer sleep quality (Brummet et al. 2006).

Additional research indicates that caregiving also can have significant consequences on the mental health of caregivers. Studies suggest that, when compared to their noncaregiving counterparts, caregivers report higher levels of stress/distress, depression, emotional problems, and cognitive problems (Brehaut et al. 2004; Douglas and Daly 2003). Additional research indicates that caregivers may also experience lower levels of subjective well-being and self-efficacy (Pinquart and Sorensen 2003), higher negative affect, and poorer levels of social support (Brummet et al. 2006). As explained above, evidence suggests that the physical and mental health consequences of caregiving are intimately linked (Cannuscio et al. 2002).

The Role of Chronic Stress in Caregiver Health

According to Ray (2004), stress occurs when there is an imbalance in the environmental demands placed on an individual and the individual's ability (or perceived ability) to cope with these demands. It is easy to see how this imbalance can result in caregiver stress.

Stress can play a significant role in the physical and mental health of caregivers. Vitaliano et al. (2003) identifies two pathways by which chronic stress can impact caregiver health. One pathway suggests that chronic stress leads to psychosocial distress and increases in stress hormones. The other pathway links chronic stress to risky health behaviors (e.g., substance abuse, poor nutrition, sedentary lifestyle) that are often associated with physical and mental health problems (Vitaliano et al. 2003).

A great deal of evidence suggests that chronic stress can result in a variety of physical and mental health challenges, including increased risk of metabolic syndrome (Chandola et al. 2006), immune dysregulation, increased risk for disease, delayed wound healing, and premature aging (Robles et al. 2005).

Specifically, caregivers who experience stress and strain in care provision appear to have the greatest physical and psychological health effects of all caregivers, including symptoms of depression, anxiety; inadequate time for sleep, self-care, and other health related activities (Schulz et al. 1997; Schulz and Beach 1999); and an increased risk of infection (Kiecolt-Glaser et al. 2003). Further evidence has identified caregiving as an independent risk factor for mortality among strained caregivers, who had a 63 % greater chance of death within four years when compared to noncaregivers (Schulz and Beach 1999). These mortality rates were highest among those who already had disease and next highest in those caregivers with subclinical disease (Schulz and Beach 1999).

Physical and Mental Health Benefits Associated with Caregiving

While caregiving can be stressful and have a variety of negative physical and mental health consequences, evidence suggests that the role of a family caregiver can also result in health benefits for some. According to Wight et al. (1998), caregiving can be an enriching and life enhancing experience, thereby creating a positive impact on caregiver health. Evidence suggests that some individuals derive benefits from their role as caregiver, including improved mental health, increased closeness to their loved one, and a sense of satisfaction related to fulfilling this important duty

(Beach et al. 2000; Kramer 1997). In addition, research indicates that caregivers who continue to fulfill social roles outside their duty as caregivers often report better health (Wight et al. 1998).

A growing area of investigation, sometimes referred to as "positive psychology," has a great deal of relevance to understanding and promoting the physical and mental health of caregivers. This area of research suggests that psychosocial factors (e.g., social support) and positive emotional states (e.g., optimism) can act as protective factors against illness (Hooker et al. 1992; Kivimaki et al. 2005). Billings et al. (2000), identify mood as "an important psychophysiological pathway between coping and health." In their study of caregivers of patients with HIV/AIDS, they further explain that those who maintained a positive emotional state displayed fewer negative health consequences, thus supporting the value of positive affect as a protective factor for both physical and mental health problems during stressful situations (Billings et al. 2000).

Evidence is emerging to suggest that providing social support may also be a confounding variable in analyzing the possible health effects of religious and spiritual behavior. Such research suggests that there may be health benefits associated with helping others when the helper is not overwhelmed by the effort (Post 2005). Some of this information comes from research regarding the association between volunteerism and health. A study by Oman et al. (1999) revealed that older adults who volunteered for two or more organizations had a 63 % lower mortality risk than nonvolunteers during the 5-year study period. While the effect dropped to 44 % after controlling for age, sex, physical mobility, exercise, health habits, social support, and psychological status, the result was still highly significant. Further analyses of these data revealed that being helpful was more important to health than exercise and weekly religious service attendance and only slightly less important than not smoking.

Methodological Challenges in the Caregiving Literature

Although many efforts have been made to understand both the positive and negative consequences of caregiving on health, significant limitations in the literature make it difficult to draw precise hypotheses regarding the physical health effects of caregiving (Dew et al. 1998). Of particular concern are a variety of methodological weaknesses that are present in the caregiving literature. According to Schulz et al. (1997), problems exist in the sampling strategy for many caregiver studies because caregiver subjects are often recruited from support groups, health and social service agencies, or through solicitation of those suffering from the burdens of caregiving. These studies, which utilize samples of individuals who have already self-identified their distress, may not produce results that are representative of the greater caregiver community.

Others, including Beach et al. (2000), suggest that another problem with data from caregiving studies is that caregivers are often treated as a homogeneous group, rather than recognizing that caregivers face varying levels of intensity of caregiving stressors. In particular, as we look at health outcomes among those providing care, it may be important to further study the relationship between the intensity of care provided and subsequent health consequences. Some evidence suggests that a dose response exists in caregiving, in which those who provide more burdensome care may be at greater risk for negative health consequences (Burton et al. 1997; Spector et al. 2002).

Additionally, Dew et al. (1998) suggest the need for longitudinal studies in this area, as the impact of caregiving on health may take time to become evident. Although longitudinal studies can be more difficult and time-consuming to conduct, such investigations may yield data that provide a more complete picture of the relationship between caregiving and health.

Future Directions in Caregiving Research

While some important efforts have been made to understand the relationship between caregiving and physical and mental health, much empirical work is still necessary. Future directions in caregiving research should include a continued investigation of the important role of stress on caregiver health. Relatedly, much work is still needed to identify and understand the positive characteristics and factors that appear to promote health and mediate negative health outcomes.

Future studies must employ rigorous methodologies in order to accurately understand the impact of caregiving on physical and mental health. Efforts should be made to recruit caregivers from a variety of backgrounds and settings in order to ensure that representative samples are obtained. In addition, attention should be paid to understanding the differences and unique characteristics of caregivers. Researchers should attempt to study these differences and their relation to health outcomes to assist us in developing interventions that target the specific individual and collective needs of caregivers. Finally, when possible, caregivers and their families should be followed over time, in order to attempt to understand the long-term progression of health in this population. Continued careful and consistent research can bring us closer to understanding the true nature of the connection between caregiving and health, and assist in keeping family caregivers physically and mentally healthy and productive.

Clinical Practice Issues in Caregiving

Much attention has been paid to reducing the physical and mental health burden faced by caregivers; however, there is still significant work to be done in the development and evaluation of effective clinical interventions, education, and training (Whittier et al. 2003; Zarit et al. 1987). Although a variety of clinical and psychoeducational interventions are utilized to address the needs of caregivers, little empirical evaluation of such programs has been done. What evaluation has been conducted has often been inconclusive. In addition, many caregivers are unable or unwilling to use interventions because of logistical issues, cost, and discomfort in using resources outside of their family network (Czaja and Rubert 2002). This section will provide an overview of some of the current issues and future directions in clinical practice to address the health and well-being of family caregivers.

Identifying Caregivers in Need

One of the first steps to reduce the burden of caregiving and promote health among caregivers must be to develop effective practices to identify those in need. According to Schulz and Beach (1999), primary care providers who work with older adults residing in the community are well positioned to identify caregivers at risk for negative outcomes. This would also be true of health care providers who care for individuals with disabilities and chronic diseases across the lifespan. These frontline professionals can help to recognize caregivers at risk or in need and guide them to appropriate care and resources.

Health Promotion and Disease Prevention

Evidence suggests that caregivers may neglect their own health care needs, resulting in negative health outcomes (Tang and Chen 2002). According to Burton et al. (1997), caregiving is associated with time limitations for exercise, rest and recuperation, and failure to remember to take prescription medications. Caregivers are often so focused on the needs of their care recipients that they have limited time available to care for themselves.

Because the work of caregiving can place individuals at risk for a variety of physical and mental health problems, clinical interventions should focus on changing health behaviors that enhance caregiver vulnerability (Burton et al. 1997). In addition to providing information and education regarding health risks, interventions are needed to educate caregivers about the importance of health promotion and prevention activities. Evidence suggests that caregivers may benefit from such direct health promotion interventions (Castro et al. 2002). Therefore, comprehensive interventions should focus on education regarding the health risks of caregiving and information related to health promotion and prevention, as well as direct training and engagement in behaviors that can maintain health and prevent disease. Clearly, health care professionals are well-suited to engage caregivers in such a dialogue. Unfortunately, evidence suggests that health professionals often fail to encourage disease prevention and health promotion among caregivers (Jackson and Cleary 1995). Because of the critical role that members of the health care community play as front line contacts and health experts, it is critical that they be engaged in efforts to encourage and promote healthy lifestyles among family caregivers.

Integrated Care for Care Recipients and Caregivers

The relationship between the family caregiver and the care recipient plays a central role in the lives of both of these individuals as well as the family unit as a whole. Raina et al. (2005) suggest that family functioning is a central component of the physical and psychological health of caregivers. This notion is supported by evidence that reveals an association between poor family functioning and high levels of caregiver burden (Tremont et al. 2006).

Unfortunately, many of the clinical interventions provided in our health care system today are focused on either the patient/care recipient or the caregiver alone. This individualized model often fails to recognize the important connected relationship between the caregiver and their loved one. Although collaborative intervention models have been proposed, little evaluation of such interventions has been completed. It will be important for those who are treating the caregiver and the care recipient together to evaluate such programs and share their findings.

As interventions to address caregiver health are developed and implemented, it is essential that caregivers, care recipients, and the family as a whole be considered and addressed. Schulz and Beach (1999) suggested the importance of utilizing intervention models and treatment approaches that focus on the needs of caregivers and their care recipients as a unit; while Raina et al. (2005) called on health care providers to use interventions that support the family as a whole.

Helping Caregivers to Manage Behavior Problems

Behavior problems, sometimes associated with cognitive impairment, can be a troubling and stressful issue for many caregivers (Goode et al. 1998). In a study with families caring for children with chronic disease, Raina et al. (2005) found that the physical and psychological health of caregivers was strongly associated with child behavior. Similar findings have also been supported in research with caregivers of older adults with dementia (Zarit et al. 1987). It is clear that these day-to-day behavioral battles take their toll on the well-being of the caregiver and the care recipient. Therefore, it is suggested that providing caregivers with training in management strategies to address difficult behaviors may potentially help change health outcomes among caregivers (Raina et al. 2005).

Respite Care

While the work of family caregivers is truly heroic, no one person can provide the sole care for a family member alone. In order to maintain good physical and mental health, caregivers need appropriate breaks and down time. Respite care is a service that temporarily relieves a family member of his or her caregiving duties. Evidence suggests that caregivers who receive respite care report improved physical and emotional health (Theis et al. 1994). In addition, respite care may make it possible for individuals in need of care to remain in the home and avoid or delay institutional placement (Theis et al. 1994). However, many caregivers struggle with their need or desire to take time out from caring for their loved one. Some caregivers hesitate to leave their family member for any extended period of time, due to feelings of guilt or anxiety regarding the patient's care in their absence. Today, it is unknown what proportion of health care and social service providers share information, education, and resources with caregivers regarding the benefits of respite care. However, health care and social service providers are ideally positioned to educate and inform caregivers about respite care. A variety of important clinical and educational/training interventions could be provided around the respite care issue. Such psychoeducational interventions should focus on the health benefits of respite care while facilitating discussion regarding the feelings of anxiety and guilt that caregivers often feel associated with leaving their loved one in the care of another.

Future Directions in Clinical Practice

Future directions in clinical practice to address the physical and mental health of family caregivers would benefit from the use of a public health approach. Such an approach would focus on prevention, early intervention, and physical and mental health promotion among caregivers. These efforts should incorporate the knowledge from the literature related to the connection between physical and mental health and work to promote the health of the mind and body together. The clinical health care community has typically treated the mind and the body separately (Brower 2006). As previously explained, research indicates that psychosocial factors and affective states can influence the physical and mental health of caregivers. This evidence may be helpful in guiding and informing new interventions that directly address a caregiver's emotional state in hopes of promoting physical and mental health. Future prevention and intervention efforts should incorporate attempts to understand a caregiver's personality traits, mood, and the meaning that they attach to their own health as a way of understanding, promoting, and improving caregiver health.

Education and Training Related to Caregiving

Significant shortcomings exist in the level of education and training available to family caregivers regarding the relationship between health and caregiving. Evidence suggests that family caregivers often report feeling unprepared for their caregiving duties (Family Caregiving and Public Policy 2003).

According to Schmall (1995), caregiver education and training have the potential to improve self-efficacy, confidence, and family relationships and reduce stress and feelings of guilt. Toseland and Smith (2001) identify a variety of ways to educate and train family caregivers, including single session community workshops and forums, lecture series and discussions, support groups, psychoeducational and skill-building groups, individual counseling, family counseling, care coordination/management, and technology-based interventions. While a variety of these models are currently being utilized, the research literature fails to definitively identify the most effective methods for educating and training caregivers (Toseland and Smith 2001).

Similar limitations in education and training exist in the health care arena. Health professionals from a variety of disciplines often lack the education and training necessary to appropriately identify, treat, and refer family caregivers with physical and mental health needs.

Future Directions in Education and Training

Future directions in education and training must focus on two important areas. First, such initiatives must be available to all family caregivers to promote and maintain their own physical and mental health, as well as the health of care recipients. Additional investigation is necessary to identify the most effective educational models for the diverse needs of family caregivers. Next, efforts must be made to educate and train the health care workforce to meet the physical and mental health needs of caregivers. In addition, because many care recipients and family caregivers are older adults, particular attention should focus on increasing the capacity of the geriatric health workforce. Such education and training opportunities should be available to those currently training in the health professions, as well as those already in the health workforce, through continuing professional education opportunities.

Family Caregiving and Public Policy

A variety of caregiving issues have made their way to the national policy debate in recent years, resulting in the creation of local, state, and federal programs and initiatives to ease the physical, psychological, and financial burden of family caregivers. While these programs are assisting some, the availability, accessibility, and quality of these initiatives varies significantly across the country. Feinberg (1997) identified four primary public policy approaches in the U.S. to address the needs of family caregivers, including direct services, financial incentives and compensation, the cash-and-counseling model, and employer-based mechanisms. This section will provide an overview of some of the primary federal policy initiatives for family caregivers and discuss the potential impact of these policies on the physical and mental health of caregivers.

Direct Services for Family Caregivers

Direct services for family caregivers include a variety of supports that assist and complement the role of the caregiver. There are several important federal programs related to services for family caregivers, including the National Family Caregiver Support Program, the Lifespan Respite Care Program, and the Department of Veterans Affairs (VA) Caregiver Support Services.

One of the largest federal programs established to directly assist family caregivers with services and supports is the National Family Caregiver Support Program (NFCSP), which was signed into law in 2000 as part of the Older Americans Act amendments. In an effort to recognize and support the heroic efforts of family caregivers, this program was established to provide information to caregivers about available services; assist caregivers in gaining access to supportive services; offer individual counseling, organization of support groups, and caregiver training; provide respite care for temporary relief from caregiving responsibilities; and assist with supplemental services to complement the care provided by caregivers (Administration on Aging 2004). Eligible individuals are family caregivers who provide care for individuals age 60 or older; family caregivers who provide care for individuals with Alzheimer's disease and related disorders, regardless of age; grandparents and other relative caregivers (not parents) 55 years of age or older providing care to children under age 18; or grandparents and other relative caregivers (not parents) 55 years of age or older providing care to adults age 18–59, with disabilities, to whom they are related by blood, marriage, or adoption.

In order to meet the needs of the American Indian, Alaska Native, and Native Hawaiian family caregiving communities, the federal government also established the Native American Caregiver Support Program (NACSP). This program is significantly smaller, however provides similar services to those of the NFCSP.

Both the NFCSP and the NACSP are administered by the Administration on Aging (AoA) within the U.S. Department of Health and Human Services (HHS) and are available to family caregivers of older adults and grandparents and kinship caregivers of children. Although the NFCSP and the NACSP services and supports are an important step in the right direction to help caregivers, the programs have been unable to assist all of the family caregivers in need in our country. Because the primary mandate of these two programs focuses on addressing the needs of caregivers of older adults, many of those who care for persons outside of this age category are not covered under these programs.

One of the most frequently requested direct services by caregivers nationwide is respite care (National Alliance for Caregiving and AARP 2009). Respite provides a much needed break for family caregivers from their daily care duties. Research suggests that respite care is associated with improved physical and mental health outcomes among caregivers (Theis et al. 1994). Unfortunately, across the country many family caregivers are unable to locate, access, or afford quality respite care. In addition, many caregiving families are hesitant to take advantage of the limited available resources, as they are concerned about leaving their loved ones with staff members who may be untrained or inadequately trained to complete the caregiving tasks in their absence.

In 2006, the Lifespan Respite Care Program (LRCP) was established by Congress to bring together federal, state, and local resources and funding streams to help support, expand, and streamline the delivery of planned and emergency respite services while also providing for the recruitment and training of respite workers and caregiver training and empowerment (Administration on Aging 2012). Through this AoA-administered program, grants have been distributed to states and the District of Columbia to improve the availability and quality of respite services across the lifespan.

Another group of caregivers who have recently received the attention of federal policymakers are family caregivers of our nation's military service members and veterans. In May 2010, a federal caregiving initiative was established by Congress, which authorizes the VA to offer several services and supports for approved family caregivers of veterans wounded since 9/11. Among the authorized services are monthly stipends, travel expenses, access to health care insurance, mental health services and counseling, comprehensive VA caregiver training, and respite care (U.S. Department of Veterans Affairs 2012).

Of course, such existing policy initiatives address only some of the needs of the diverse population of family caregivers. Many caregivers are increasing in age and facing their own subsequent chronic health problems. Today, a large proportion of the caregiver community is made up of aging spouses, adult children, and grandparents. These individuals are caring for their loved ones while managing their own chronic diseases and health conditions. The growing numbers of grandparents and other aging family members who are raising young relatives often need support and assistance as well. Grandparents, in particular, may face many health challenges along with significant social struggles as they care for the next generation. Grandparents and other relatives often encounter unnecessary barriers in raising the children in their care. These include difficulties in navigating the educational and health care systems, maintaining appropriate housing, obtaining affordable legal services, and accessing a variety of federal benefits and services, including physical and mental health care.

Several federal legislative initiatives have been proposed in recent years to address the growing needs of grandparents and other kinship caregivers. These initiatives would assist kinship caregivers in navigating their way through existing programs and service systems. By supporting grandparents and other kinship caregivers with their caregiving duties and in their efforts to obtain vital social and health resources, such policies may help to reduce stressors and improve the health and well-being of members of this growing caregiving population.

Financial Incentives and Compensation for Family Caregivers

Although much of family caregiving is unpaid, it is not without cost. Research confirms that economic concerns can contribute to the overall burden of many family caregivers (Grunfeld et al. 2004). Food, medicines, and other caregiving necessities place added strain on the already tight family budgets of many caregivers. In addition, because of their responsibilities at home, some caregivers have difficulty finding or holding jobs, thus making financial burdens even more serious. Many caregiving families struggle to stay afloat and often find themselves in the difficult situation of choosing between using their limited resources to pay for their own health and social service needs or the care and treatment of their loved ones. This financial burden may be associated with increased stress and poorer physical and mental health outcomes.

A variety of financial incentives and compensation have been developed to assist family caregivers with the economic costs of caregiving. These initiatives include direct payments and tax incentives for family caregivers (Feinberg 1997). Several federal legislative initiatives have been proposed to ease some of the financial burden on family caregivers. Because financial burdens can be extremely stressful, it is hoped that the enactment of such financial incentives and compensation initiatives will not only ease the financial burden of caregiving, but may also have a positive secondary impact on the health of caregivers. Reducing economic pressures may help to reduce some of the stress faced by caregivers, which may consequently reduce negative health outcomes.

Family Caregiving and Consumer Direction

Consumer direction is an approach that arose out of the move from institutional care for individuals with disabilities to home- and community-based alternatives (Doty 2000). Home- and community-based services provide Medicaid beneficiaries with the option of receiving services in their own home or community, rather than in institutional settings. These programs serve a variety of targeted populations, including individuals with physical and/or intellectual disabilities and those living with mental illness. Such initiatives allow states to offer a variety of unlimited services including a combination of standard medical services and nonmedical services. Standard services include but are not limited to: case management, homemaker services, home health aide, personal care, adult day health services, habilitation, and respite care (U.S. Department of Health and Human Services 2012).

One innovative model of consumer direction is the Cash and Counseling model, which provides "a flexible monthly allowance to recipients of Medicaid personal care services or home and community based services" (Cash and Counseling 2005). The program allows consumers to make a variety of decisions regarding their care, such as who they hire to meet their caregiving needs, including relatives (Foster et al. 2003). Evaluations of this model reveal that family caregivers who participated were less likely to report high levels of physical, emotional, and financial strain, and reported that their caregiving role was less burdensome on their job performance and social lives (Foster et al. 2003). While the Cash and Counseling and the consumer directed approach may not be right for everyone, such models provide a promising option for many consumers and family caregivers in need of physical, emotional, and financial support and flexibility.

Employer-Based Mechanisms to Support Family Caregivers

Because many family caregivers remain in the workforce, several employment-based policy initiatives have been developed to support family caregivers. One of the most significant federal initiatives is the Family and Medical Leave Act (Public Law 103-3), which was signed into law in 1993. This law allows full-time employees to take up to 12 weeks of unpaid leave annually to care for an ill family member or a new baby (Feinberg 1997). While this initiative took an important step in the right direction, it does not cover all workers/worksites and is not useful to those who cannot afford unpaid leave.

In addition to the federal initiatives, many individual employers provide a variety of supports, including flexible work schedules, telecommuting, family leave (preferably paid), exercise facilities/wellness programs/or club memberships at reduced cost, avoidance of mandated overtime, and minimizing required transfers, but when they are necessary, assistance with elder care resources (Neal and Wagner 2001). These resources can ease caregiver stress and burden, in hopes of improving and maintaining caregiver health.

Future Directions in Caregiving Policy

Although several important policy initiatives have been enacted in recent years to directly and indirectly address the health and well-being of family caregivers, additional legislative and implementation work remains. Of the federal programs and demonstrations that have been established to assist states in helping family caregivers, some eligibility restrictions continue to limit the proportion of family caregivers who may receive services. In addition, funding levels for many programs "fall far short of their needs" (Alzheimer's Association and National Alliance for Caregiving 2004).

It is clear that there is much work to be done in the advocacy arena at the local, state, and federal levels to address the growing needs of family caregivers. According to Family Caregiving and Public Policy (2003), it is time for a national policy that addresses the growing needs of family caregivers. In order to make the physical and psychological health of caregivers a national policy priority, future directions in caregiving policy must include collaboration among caregivers, care recipients, advocacy organizations, health care providers, professional organizations, and local, state, and national organizations. These entities must reach out to policymakers in a unified manner to share their message and urge legislators to act. While important public policy initiatives have been proposed, significant action and follow-through is needed to transform policy proposals into enacted and appropriately implemented laws that protect and improve the health and well-being of our family caregivers, and those for whom they care.

References

Administration on Aging. (2004). About NFCSP. http://www.aoa.gov/prof/aoaprog/caregiver/overview/overview_caregiver.asp.

Administration on Aging. (2012). Lifespan Respite Care Program. http://www.aoa.gov/AoARoot/AoA_Programs/HCLTC/LRCP/index.aspx.

Alzheimer's Association and National Alliance for Caregiving. (2004). Families care: Alzheimer's caregivers in the United States 2004. http://www.alz.org/Resources/FactSheets/Caregiverreport.pdf.

Beach, S. R., Schulz, R., Yee, J. L., & Jackson, S. (2000). Negative and positive health effects of caring for a disabled spouse: Longitudinal findings from the caregiver health effects study. *Psychology and Aging, 15*(2), 259–271.

Billings, D. W., Folkman, S., Acree, M., & Moskowitz, J. T. (2000). Coping and physical health during caregiving: The roles of positive and negative affect. *Journal of Personality and Social Psychology, 79,* 131–142.

Brehaut, J. C., Kohen, D. E., Raina, P., Walter, S. D., Russell, D. J., Swinton, M., et al. (2004). The health of primary caregivers of children with cerebral palsy: How does it compare with that of other Canadian caregivers? *Pediatrics, 114,* 182–191.

Brissette, I., Scheier, M. F., & Carver, C. S. (2002). The role of optimism and social network development, coping, and psychological adjustment during a life transition. *Journal of Personality and Social Psychology, 82,* 102–111.

Brower, V. (2006). Mind–body research moves towards the mainstream. *European Molecular Biology Organization Reports, 7*(4), 358–361.

Brummet, B. H., Babyak, M. A., Siegler, I. C., Vitaliano, P. P., Ballard, E. L., Gwyther, L. P., et al. (2006). Association among perception of social support, negative affect, and quality of sleep in caregivers and noncaregivers. *Health Psychology, 25*(2), 220–225.

Burton, L. C., Newsom, J. T., Schulz, R., Hirsch, C. H., & German, P. S. (1997). Preventive health behaviors among spousal caregivers. *Preventive Medicine, 26,* 162–169.

Cannuscio, C. C., Jones, C., Kawachi, I., Colitz, G. A., Berkman, L., & Rimm, E. (2002). Reverberation of family illness: A longitudinal assessment of informal caregiving and mental health status in the nurses' health study. *American Journal of Public Health, 92*(8), 1305–1311.

Cash and Counseling. (2005). About us. http://www.cashandcounseling.org/about.

Castro, C. M., Wilcox, S., O'Sullivan, P., Baumann, K., & King, A. C. (2002). An exercise program for women who are caring for relatives with dementia. *Psychosomatic Medicine, 64,* 458–468.

Chandola, T., Brunner, E., & Marmot, M. (2006). Chronic stress at work and the metabolic syndrome: Prospective study. *British Medical Journal, 332,* 521–525.

Chesney, M. A., Darbes, L. A., Hoerster, K., Taylor, J. M., Chambers, D. B., & Anderson, D. E. (2005). Positive emotions: Exploring the other hemisphere in behavioral medicine. *International Journal of Behavioral Medicine, 12*(2), 50–58.

Czaja, S. J., & Rubert, M. P. (2002). Telecommunications technology as an aid to family caregivers of persons with dementia. *Psychosomatic Medicine, 64,* 469–476.

Dew, M. A., Goycoolea, J. M., Stukas, A. A., Switzer, G. E., Simmons, R. G., Roth, L. H., et al. (1998). Temporal profiles of physical health in family members of heart transplant recipients: Predictors of health change during caregiving. *Health Psychology, 17*(2), 138–151.

Doty, P. (2000). The federal role in the move toward consumer direction. *Generations, 24,* 22–27.

Douglas, S. L., & Daly, B. J. (2003). Caregivers of long-term ventilator patients: Physical and psychological outcomes. *Chest, 123*(4), 1073–1081.

Family Caregiving and Public Policy (2003). Principles for Change. http://www.thefamilycaregiver.org/pdfs/Principles.pdf.

Feinberg, L. (1997). Options for supporting informal and family caregivers: A policy paper. San Francisco: American Society on Aging.

Feinberg, L., Reinhard, S. C., Houser, A., & Choula, R. (2011). Valuing the invaluable: 2011 update—The growing contributions and costs of family caregiving. http://assets.aarp.org/rgcenter/ppi/ltc/i51-caregiving.pdf.

Foster, L., Brown, R., Phillips, B., & Carlson, B. L. (2003). *Easing the burden of caregiving: The impact of consumer direction on primary informal caregivers in Arkansas* (Document No. PR03-110). Princeton: Mathematica Policy Research, Inc. http://www.mathematica-mpr.com/publications/PDFs/easingburden.pdf.

Gallagher-Thompson, D., Shurgot, G. R., Rider, K., Gray, H. L., McKibbin, C. L., Kraemer, H. C., et al. (2006). Ethnicity, stress, and cortisol function in Hispanic and non-Hispanic white women: A preliminary study of family dementia caregivers and noncaregivers. *American Journal of Geriatric Psychiatry, 14*(4), 334–342.

Glaser, R., Sheridan, J. F., Malarkey, W. B., MacCallum, R. C., & Kiecolt-Glasser, J. K. (2000). Chronic stress modulates the immune response to a pneumococcal pneumonia vaccine. *Psychosomatic Medicine, 62,* 804–807.

Goode, K. T., Haley, W. E., Roth, D. L., & Ford, G. R. (1998). Predicting longitudinal changes in caregiver physical and mental health: A stress process model. *Health Psychology, 17*(2), 190–198.

Grunfeld, E., Coyle, D., Whelan, T., Clinch, J., Reyno, L., Earle, C. C., et al. (2004). Family caregiver burden: Results of a longitudinal study of breast cancer patients and their principle caregivers. *Canadian Medical Association Journal, 170*(12), 1795–1801.

Hooker, K., Monahan, D., Shifren, K., & Hutchinson, C. (1992). Mental and physical health of spouse caregivers: The role of personality. *Psychology and Aging, 7*(3), 367–375.

Jackson, D. G., & Cleary, B. L. (1995). Health promotion strategies for spousal caregivers of chronically ill elders. *Nurse Practitioner Forum, 6,* 10–18.

Kiecolt-Glaser, J. K., Preacher, K. J., MacCallum, R. C., Atkinson, C., Malarkey, W., & Glaser, R. (2003). Chronic stress and age-related increases in the proinflammatory cytokine IL-6. *Proceeding of the National Academy of Sciences, 100*(15), 9090–9095.

Kivimaki, M., Vahtera, J., Elovainio, M., Helenius, H., Singh-Manoux, A., & Pentti, J. (2005). Optimism and pessimism as predictors of change in health after death or onset of severe illness in family. *Health Psychology, 24*(4), 413–421.

Kramer, B. J. (1997). Gain in the care giving experience: Where are we? What next? *Gerontologist, 37,* 218–232.

McEwen, B. S. (1998). Protective and damaging effects of stress mediation. *New England Journal of Medicine, 338,* 171–179.

National Alliance for Caregiving and AARP. (2009). Caregiving in the U.S. http://www.caregiving.org/data/Caregiving_in_the_US_2009_full_report.pdf.

Neal, M. B., & Wagner, D. L. (2001). Working caregivers: Issues, challenges and opportunities for the aging network (Issue Brief for National Family Caregiver Support Program). Washington, DC: Administration on Aging.

Oman, D., Thoresen, C. E., & McMahon, K. (1999). Volunteerism and mortality among the community-dwelling elderly. *Journal of Health Psychology, 4,* 301–316.

Pinquart, M., & Sorensen, S. (2003). Differences between caregivers and noncaregivers in psychological health and physical health: A meta-analysis. *Psychology and Aging, 18*(2), 250–267.

Post, S. G. (2005). Altruism, happiness and health: It's good to be good. *International Journal of Behavioral Medicine, 12,* 66–67.

Raina, P., O'Donnell, M., Rosenbaum, P., Brehaut, J., Walter, S. D., Russell, D., et al. (2005). The health and well-being of caregivers of children with cerebral palsy. *Pediatrics, 115*(6), 626–636.

Ray, O. (2004). How the mind hurts and heals the body. *American Psychologist, 59*(1), 29–40.

Robles, T. F., Glaser, R., & Kiecolt-Glaser, J. K. (2005). Out of balance: A new look at chronic stress, depression, and immunity. *Current Directions in Psychological Science, 14*(2), 111–115.

Schmall, V. L. (1995). Family caregiver education and training: enhancing self-efficacy. *Journal of Case Management, 4*(4), 156–162.

Schulz, R., & Beach, S. R. (1999). Caregiving as a risk factor for mortality: The caregiver health effects study. *Journal of the American Medical Association, 282*(23), 2215–2219.

Schulz, R., Mittelmark, M., Burton, L., Hirsch, C., & Jackson, S. (1997). Health effects of caregiving: The caregiver health effects study: An ancillary study of the cardiovascular health study. *Annals of Behavioral Medicine, 19*(2), 110–116.

Spector, W. D., Shaffer, T. J., Hodlewsky, R. T., De La Mare, J. J., & Rhodes, J. A. (2002). *Future directions for community-based long-term care health services research: Expert meeting summary, June 20–21, 2000* (AHRQ Publication No. 02-0022). Rockville: Agency for Healthcare Research and Quality.

Tang, Y. Y., & Chen, S. P. (2002). Health promotion behaviors in Chinese family caregivers of patients with stroke. *Health Promotion International, 17*(4), 329–339.

The Annie E. Casey Foundation. (2012). Stepping up for kids: What government and communities should do to support kinship families. http://www.aecf.org/KnowledgeCenter/~/media/Pubs/Initiatives/KIDS%20COUNT/S/SteppingUpforKids2012PolicyReport/SteppingUpForKidsPolicyReport2012.pdf.

Theis, S. L., Moss, J. H., & Pearson, M. A. (1994). Respite for caregivers: An evaluation study. *Journal of Community Health Nursing, 11*(1), 31–44.

Toseland, R. W., & Smith, T. (2001). *Supporting caregivers through education and training* (Issue Brief for National Family Caregiver Support Program). Washington: Administration on Aging.

Tremont, G., Davis, J. D., & Bishop, D. S. (2006). Unique contribution of family functioning in caregivers of patients with mild dementia. *Dementia and Geriatric Cognitive Disorders, 21*(3), 170–174.

U.S. Census Bureau. (2011). The older population: 2010. http://www.census.gov/prod/cen2010/briefs/c2010br-09.pdf.

U.S. Census Bureau. (2012). Grandparents day 2012: Sept 9. http://www.census.gov/newsroom/releases/archives/facts_for_features_special_editions/cb12-ff17.html.

U.S. Department of Health and Human Services. (2012). Home & community-based services 1915 (c). http://www.medicaid.gov/Medicaid-CHIP-Program-Information/By-Topics/Long-Term-Services-and-Support/Home-and-Community-Based-Services/Home-and-Community-Based-Services-1915-c.html.

U.S. Department of Veterans Affairs. (2012). Services for family caregivers of post-9/11 veterans. http://www.caregiver.va.gov/support_benefits.asp.

Uvnas-Moberg, K., Arn, I., & Magnusson, D. (2005). The psychobiology of emotion: The role of the oxytocinergic system. *International Journal of Behavioral Medicine, 12*(2), 59–65.

Vitaliano, P. P., Zhang, J., & Scanlan, J. M. (2003). Is caregiving hazardous to one's physical health? A meta-analysis. *Psychological Bulletin, 129*(6), 946–972.

Whittier, S., Coon, D., & Aaker, J. (2003). *Caregiver support interventions* (Research Brief No. 10). Washington: National Association of State Units on Aging.

Wight, R. G., LeBlanc, A. J., & Aneshensel, C. S. (1998). AIDS caregiving and health among midlife and older women. *Health Psychology, 17*(2), 130–137.

Zarit, S. H., Anthony, C. R., & Boutselis, M. (1987). Intervention with caregivers of dementia patients: Comparison of two approaches. *Psychology and Aging, 2*(3), 225–232.

Cultural Considerations in Caring for Persons with Mental Illness

Brent E. Gibson

Most of the growth in the U.S. population over the next 50 years will take place among those currently categorized as racial and/or ethnic minorities (Doucet and Hamon in press; He and Hobbs 1999). Although diversity is not new to the USA, its many complexities, and the ongoing changes in the population, present challenges to researchers, educators, social and mental health service providers, and policy makers. Many of the challenges arise from differences between dominant American culture (White, middle-class, protestant, heterosexual) and the many competing cultures within the USA that are associated with minorities, such as racial, ethnic, religious, sexual, and social class categories. These other cultures are considered "competing" because their very existence is juxtaposed against the many pressures—social, medical, economic, religious—of dominant American culture to assimilate. Indeed many of the institutions established by the dominant culture, such as schools, hospitals, and the mass media, facilitate/encourage/demand (both implicitly and explicitly) assimilation of diverse members of society. However, assimilation is not desired by many minority group members. Therefore, they resist the pressures of the dominant culture and aim to survive within contested and marginalized space. The competition between dominant and nondominant cultures is not only for limited resources, but also for a claim to right personhood—to the ability to view the world through a different cultural lens without being labeled *other, wrong, ignorant, misfit, crazy* (Appiah 2005).

An important area for us to examine the challenging dynamics of culture, concerns caregiving for persons with mental illness. The following chapter provides such an examination by covering three interrelated topics: (a) culturally based illness meanings, (b) family caregivers' experiences of burden and reward, and (c) culturally

B. E. Gibson (✉)
Research Institute on Aging, Jewish Home Lifecare, 120 W. 106th Street, New York, NY 10025, USA
e-mail: bgibson@jewishhome.org

Arlene R. Gordon Research Institute of Lighthouse International, 111 East 59th Street, New York, NY 10022-1202, USA
e-mail: bgibson@lighthouse.org

R. C. Talley et al. (eds.), *The Challenges of Mental Health Caregiving*, Caregiving: Research • Practice • Policy, DOI 10.1007/978-1-4614-8791-3_3,

competent formal service provision for persons with mental illness and their families. Research, policy, education/training, and practice in the extant literature related to these three topics is reviewed, and recommendations for future directions are made.

We must begin with some definitions. Indeed definitions and meanings are at the heart of this chapter. If the authors and readers of this chapter have divergent definitions and meanings of key concepts used throughout, the intended messages are unlikely to be communicated effectively, which, we argue later, is often the case in communication between different cultural groups. First, we borrow from Dilworth-Anderson and Gibson (2002) and define culture as an ever changing "set of shared symbols, beliefs, and customs that shapes individual and/or group behavior (Levine 1974; Ogbu 1993, p. S56)." Culture is learned through ongoing interactions and experiences with group members and provides guidelines for all of life's activities through perceptions of group members' expectations (Goodenough 1999).

Second, we use ethnicity to refer to specific group membership on the basis of shared history among people. Such shared history can include country or geographic region of origin, language, religion, race, etc. Although heterogeneity exists within ethnic groups, ethnic group members often share many aspects of culture with one another. The degree to which ethnic group members share culture depends on how broad the ethnic category is. For example, ethnic categorization based only on shared language (e.g., Hispanic) obviously will include a more culturally heterogeneous group of people than more specific categorization based on additional factors (e.g., Mexican-American Catholics).

Third, we define race as a socially and culturally constructed category based on phenotypic characteristics and perceived ancestry. Although phenotypes have a genetic component, racial categorization is based on social, not genetic criteria (Brodwin 2005). Thus, race is ascribed to individuals by larger social groups and, as remains true today, has been used historically in the USA to distinguish members of the dominant, majority group from members of subordinate, minority groups. Since they lack any sound scientific biological basis, race categories continue to be problematic in research, policy, and practice. However, as powerful social constructs, we must continue to examine their influence on group and individual behavior among both minority and majority racial categories. Race provides an even more crude proxy for culture than does ethnicity. For example, Black race in the USA can be assigned to people who were born in the USA, are the descendents of slaves brought from West Africa in the 1600s, 1700s, and 1800s, and whose ethnicity is often referred to as African-American. Also, Black race can be assigned to people whose skin is brown and who were or were not born in the USA, but whose families immigrated from Cuba, Haiti, Nigeria, Brazil, etc. (note that people racially categorized as White also live in and immigrate from these countries and usually share more culturally with their Black countrymen than their White counterparts in the USA). Ethnicity may be captured by combining a country of origin and "American" (e.g., Cuban-American). The Black people from these various countries differ culturally from one another as well as from African-Americans. However, the effects of being Black in the USA (especially among those born in the USA) may confer similar risks across these groups for experiencing the pernicious effects of racism (e.g., discrimination, poverty, mental illness; U.S. Department of Health and Human Services [HHS] 2001). Therefore, it is important to attend to the effects of race, ethnicity, and culture and to disentangle their effects whenever possible.

We use the term "ethnoracial" to denote recognition of the importance of both ethnicity and race in shaping people's experiences. As illustrated above, ethnoracial group can be more culturally meaningful than racial or ethnic categories alone. For example, ethnoracial categorization as Black Hispanic may be more useful than Black or Hispanic alone, whereas Black, Cuban-American may be more useful still.

Finally, we borrow from medical anthropology (Kleinman 1980; Kleinman et al. 1978) and define illness meanings as ways of understanding peoples' experiences of illnesses and their attendant symptoms. Illness meanings are socially constructed through interactions with others in the family, community, and larger social systems. Therefore, illness meanings are deeply embedded in both cultural and situational contexts, and their analysis is inherently an analysis of culture. Illness meanings reflect the cultural community's level of acceptable recognition of, interpretation of, and response to an illness (Chrisman and Kleinman 1983). Thus, illness meanings, as reflections of cultural beliefs, can profoundly affect how individuals, communities, and service providers approach and treat illnesses. Evidence is quite clear from cross-cultural research that the expression (Barrio et al. 2003), course (Vaughn and Leff 1976), and effective treatment (Jenkins 1988) of mental illnesses are bound by culture as opposed to being universal, biomedically bound processes (Good 1997).

Current Status

Culturally Based Illness Meanings

Research

Medical anthropologists laid the foundation for studying cultural meanings related to mental illness through ethnographic research (Fabrega 1989; Good 1997; Kleinman 1980, 1988). Although research in this area has become more multidisciplinary, anthropology continues to lead the way, as reflected in the content of journals such as *Culture, Medicine and Psychiatry*. For example, in 1999, a special issue was published containing articles written from a multidisciplinary project headed by Dr. Sue Levkoff (of Harvard Medical School) that addressed caregiving experiences and illness meanings that different ethnoracial groups assigned to symptoms of dementia exhibited by family members (Hinton et al. 1999). Gibson (2001) and Dilworth-Anderson and Gibson (2002) used data from that project to discuss the ways in which illness meanings affect family caregiving decisions and outcomes and families' interactions with formal service providers. Taken together, findings from the project indicate that culture shapes the recognition of symptoms and the meaning that family members assign to symptoms of illness. These illness meanings then influence the decisions that family members make regarding care provision, their appraisals of burden related to caregiving, and the specific stress-related outcomes they experience (Dilworth-Anderson and Gibson 2002; Fox et al. 1999; Gibson 2001; Hinton and Levkoff 1999). Others have reported similar findings regarding illness meanings and the influence of culture on dementia caregiving (e.g., Gaines 1989; Gallagher-Thompson et al. 2003; Yeo and Gallagher-Thompson 1996).

Another relevant area of research regarding illness meanings involves the identification of "culture bound syndromes" (American Psychiatric Association 1994). Researchers have identified specific sets of symptoms categorized by cultural group members as conditions that may not exist in other cultures. For example, among various Hispanic cultures within the USA (and in their countries of origin, e.g., Mexico and Puerto Rico), a mental illness called *nervios* has been identified (Guarnaccia et al. 1992; Jenkins 1988). Symptoms of *nervios* may mirror those associated with schizophrenia, depression, bipolar disorder, or anxiety disorder within the mainstream U.S. psychiatric community. However, within some Hispanic cultural contexts, these symptoms point clearly to *nervios* (Guarnaccia et al. 1992). This is but one example of the cultural nature of illness definitions, and it illustrates that all illnesses—whether identified by the DSM-IV, traditional healers, or laypersons—are culturally bound syndromes. Gaines (1992) provided an extensive cultural critique of the U.S. system for mental illness diagnosis (through DSM-III) and concluded that it represents a cultural nosology based in U.S. ethnopsychology. Thus, the U.S. system is no less cultural than any other. The dominant system within the USA simply privileges specific types of knowledge (e.g., Western biomedical, scientific) while excluding other types of knowledge (e.g., spiritual, holistic, traditional). This acknowledgement is central to understanding informal and formal care provision for persons with mental illness, because it can facilitate breaking down barriers of cultural misunderstanding.

Acknowledging that the dominant nosology (the latest DSM) is a reflection of a culturally based ethnopsychology does not require abandoning it because of its inherent cultural biases. However, it requires recognition that other culturally based ethnopsychologies exist that are no less relevant to understanding and treating mental illness among their adherents. Thus, the dominant system does not lead its followers to *The Truth*. For example, Morey (1991) examined taxonomies as "collections of hypothetical constructs" (p. 289) and wrote, "The DSM is one perspective that has generated a fair amount of internal validity research (as noted by Widiger et al. 1991), but its theoretical basis is somewhat muddled. There is clearly a need for research on alternatives" (p. 292). The difficulty is to avoid privileging one way of knowing over all others, and, in doing so, letting go of the power that stems from being part of the dominant system. As more researchers acknowledge that the dominant nosology (the latest DSM) is a reflection of a culturally based ethnopsychology, the knowledge produced by their work will be less culturally biased, their attempts to include minority group members in their studies will be made easier, and their results will demonstrate understanding of various cultural perspectives.

Practice

Given the above discussion of cultural illness meanings, one aspect of culturally competent service provision for persons with mental illness and their families is the acknowledgment of numerous valid cultural systems for understanding mental illness. This allows practitioners to abandon their traditional position as owners and purveyors of knowledge and begin to learn about their clients' cultural and contextual systems. Thus, taking the first step (acknowledgement of other valid systems) can lead to additional cultural competence (learning specific cultural beliefs and illness meanings). The issue of power was mentioned earlier and is important to consider with respect to practitioners. There is a differential in power by the very nature of the practitioner–client (or patient) relationship, because the practitioner serves as a resource that the client/patient needs. This preexisting power differential is not inherently problematic. However, when practitioners couple this preexisting power differential with the power that comes from practicing a dominant system and therefore hold up their knowledge as *The Truth*, then differing cultural systems for understanding mental illness (and their adherents) are labeled as *other, dysfunctional, baseless* (Freire 1997). In doing so, practitioners maintain their (and the dominant culture's) power within society through oppression, and minority clients/patients are not well served (Pitner and Sakamoto 2005). The distrust that exists between practitioners and minority clients/patients is strengthened, and disparities in mental health outcomes persist.

Education/Training

Most programs training the next generation of researchers, practitioners, and policy makers with respect to mental illness caregiving now include some coverage of culture and its influence on people's experiences of various illnesses. However, such coverage is typically peripheral or complimentary to the core curriculum. Unfortunately, failure to fully integrate cultural content throughout the curriculum leaves students believing it represents a specialty topic that does not apply to all people and all illness experiences. Additional marginalization occurs when special topics courses are provided exclusively by instructors of ethnoracial or other minority backgrounds. In these cases, students may receive the unintended message that issues of culture are important to minority group members because of personal agendas but are not important to mainstream White people. Furthermore, making minority group members responsible for teaching others about topics such as racism, discrimination, and oppression couches these issues with minority group members as if these problems are specifically theirs to tackle. Programs that use a more integrated model, whereby issues of culture are infused throughout the curriculum, are increasing. However, such changes are hampered by the lack of additional resources necessary to implement curricular and faculty change, lack of specific training in culture among existing faculty, and continued shortage (although it is increasing) of empirical data regarding best practices for teaching cultural material.

Policy

At the national level, progress has been made in recognizing that cultural beliefs shape illness meanings and responses to different treatment approaches. The publication of Surgeon General Satcher's supplemental report, *Mental Health: Culture, Race, and Ethnicity* (U.S. DHHS 2001), was groundbreaking in its recognition (at the Federal level) of the importance of these issues for eliminating mental health disparities across racial and ethnic groups in the USA. Furthermore, it provided an "important road map for Federal, State, and local leaders to follow in eliminating disparities in the availability, accessibility, and utilization of mental health services" (HHS 2001, p. iii). This document has been critical in shaping programs at state and local levels for the development of culturally competent services.

Family Caregivers' Experiences of Burden and Reward

Research

A large body of evidence exists regarding the stresses and burdens associated with providing care for ill loved ones. Within this larger body of research are numerous studies that address the negative effects of caregiving for persons with dementia or other serious mental illnesses (Baronet 1999; Dilworth-Anderson et al. 2002; Good 1997; Ohaeri 2003). This research has clearly demonstrated that caregiving can take a physical, emotional, and financial toll on caregivers. Much of this work has centered on objective and subjective burden and depressive symptoms among caregivers. Although there is some inconsistency across studies, African-American caregivers have tended to report less subjective burden and fewer depressive symptoms when compared to European-American and Hispanic caregivers. Unfortunately, few studies exist that compare caregivers from other groups.

Stueve et al. (1997) found that Black caregivers of adults with mental illness perceived less burden in the caregiving role than White caregivers, whereas there was no difference in perceived burden between Hispanic caregivers and White caregivers. Horwitz and Reinhard (1995) found that although Black parents caring for their adult children with serious mental illness reported equivalent caregiving duties, they reported less subjective burden than their White counterparts. In addition, Black adults caring for their siblings with serious mental illness reported more caregiving duties and less subjective burden than their White counterparts. However, in her review of the caregiver burden literature, Baronet (1999) found four other studies that did not demonstrate a significant difference in subjective burden between different ethnoracial groups of caregivers of persons with serious mental illness. Similarly, in their review of studies of care provision of dependent elders (mostly due to dementia) that attended to issues of race, ethnicity, and culture, Dilworth-Anderson et al. (2002) found that some studies demonstrated differences in burden between ethnoracial groups while others did not. These inconsistencies seem to stem from differences in methods and sampling, but there may be additional cultural issues that should be addressed. Fox et al. (1999) conducted an in-depth qualitative analysis of burden among African-American families caring for elders with dementia. This analysis provided a compelling critique of studies reporting that African-American caregivers experience less burden than White caregivers (or other ethnoracial groups). They argue that existing social gerontological literature ignores some of the most pertinent cultural factors (e.g., occupational segregation and institutional racism) related to burden among African-American caregivers, and that common measures of caregiving burden are inadequate.

Caregiving reward, or positive aspects of caregiving, has received far less attention than burden and negative effects of caregiving. However, despite a number of limitations, this area of study has been increasing in volume and sophistication in recent years (Kramer 1997). Studies of caregiving reward have shown that it represents a separate dimension from burden, with many caregivers reporting both burden and reward, and both effect caregiver well-being (Grant et al. 1998; Martire et al. 2004; Riedel et al. 1998; Tarlow et al. 2004). This area of research is particularly important because it shifts focus from caregiving being solely a negative and burdensome experience to the more realistic view of caregiving as a complex process involving positives and negatives simultaneously. Greater attention to positive aspects of caregiving may uncover additional points on which to focus various interventions. For example, cognitive-behavioral interventions can focus on ways to help caregivers reframe their experiences as fulfilling in the face of challenges.

Practice

Effective treatment of people with severe mental illness is the first step in helping to reduce burden among their family caregivers. Research has consistently shown that among family caregivers, "the most important predictors of burden are problematic behaviour, disability and the severity of symptoms" (Ohaeri 2003, p. 457) of the care recipients. However, since no treatments have been shown to be completely effective for people suffering from a particular mental illness, additional strategies are needed in order to reduce burden among family caregivers. First, practitioners should view family members as their most important resource for effectively treating mentally ill patients. Often, due to miscommunication and cultural misunderstandings, practitioners and family members perceive themselves in opposition with each other. Practitioners are too quick to see family members' actions as undermining the patient's treatment without fully understanding the cultural or familial meanings motivating such actions. On the other hand, family members are too quick to dismiss treatment strategies as nonsensical or ineffective. Becoming partners with families in helping people recover from serious mental illnesses requires practitioners to work with families to develop treatment plans as opposed to prescribing what family members must do for their ill relatives to get better. In addition, such partnerships necessitate the inclusion of the ill person to the degree that he/she can participate. If practitioners, patients, and family members start out on the same page with respect to treatment strategies and goals, there is greater likelihood for compliance by all parties. Finally, we recognize that many families are filled with problems that make engagement with them difficult for practitioners. However, to ignore these systemic family problems is to ignore the social context that can facilitate or impede recovery from mental illness. In short, failure to address the family context leads to treatment failure. For caregivers, burden may stem not from caregiving per se but from systemic family dysfunction.

Second, attention should be paid to reducing both objective and subjective burden among family caregivers. In intervention work with family caregivers of persons with dementia, much attention has been given to reducing objective burden through providing assistance with care tasks (e.g., personal care assistants to help bathe patients or adult daycare to provide supervision of the care recipient and respite for the caregiver). However, such assistance, while obviously valuable to caregivers—most report satisfaction—has had little demonstrable effect on reducing subjective burden among family caregivers. Therefore, more work is needed in developing strategies to reduce subjective burden. A promising area for future intervention work concerns psychotherapeutic approaches aimed at improving the quality of the relationship between caregivers and care recipients. Some of this can happen through culturally appropriate psychoeducational approaches aimed at improving caregivers' knowledge about illnesses. For example, helping a caregiver understand that some difficult behaviors are symptoms of the care recipient's illness, rather than an intentional attempt by the care recipient to upset the caregiver, can affect the way the caregiver appraises the relationship. However, psychoeducational approaches can only go so far. Due to the history and ongoing nature of family relationships, individual and/or family therapy may be necessary in order for relational patterns and cognitive appraisals to change. The family systems approach to understanding and treating mental illness within families provides a powerful theoretical perspective for improving relationship quality and reducing subjective burden (Eisdorfer et al. 2003; Minuchin 1974; Minuchin and Fishman 1981; Szapocznik et al. 1994).

Policy

At the local level, policies that encourage and support family engagement in the treatment process are critical to improving the well-being of both caregivers and care recipients. Unfortunately, without adequate funding, such policies cannot be implemented. Current levels of funding for most local, public mental health centers are inadequate even for basic diagnosis and individual treatment of persons with severe mental illnesses. Therefore, as models of best practice, culturally competent, family-centered, individualized treatment approaches will require significantly more funding by government agencies. Dixon et al. (1999) found that of 44 states in the USA that provided information, 32 (73 %) did not have a policy regarding support services for families of persons with severe and persistent mental illness. Although 35 (80 %) of the states reported providing funding for such family support services, most of them provided funding for family-to-family programs sponsored by the National Alliance for the Mentally Ill (NAMI), and the states reported limited funding ranging from US$ 11,500 to US$ 150,000 for the past year. Dixon et al. attributed that funding to the strong advocacy and grassroots efforts of NAMI. Finally, these researchers found that only three states (not named in the report) funded the types of psychoeducational programs for families that have been rigorously tested and shown to significantly improve outcomes for mentally ill persons and their families (see McFarlane et al. 1995).

Cultural Competence

Research

Very little research examines the efficacy of specific aspects of culturally competent mental health service provision to individuals and families. Experimentally controlled intervention trials are even less common. However, several important studies have been conducted. The Resources for Enhancing Alzheimer's Caregiver Health (REACH) project demonstrated the efficacy of several intervention approaches with diverse groups of dementia caregivers at six study sites across the USA. Site-specific findings were reported in a special section of a 2003 issue of *The Gerontologist.* For example, Eisdorfer et al. (2003) found that for most of the Cuban-American and European-American caregivers at the Miami site, a combination of family therapy and computer-assisted telephone technology led to reductions in depressive symptomatology when compared to caregivers in control conditions. However, there were some complex interactions that led to differences in treatment efficacy by treatment type, ethnicity, and the specific caregiver–care recipient relationship (e.g., Cuban-American wives of persons with dementia in the minimal intervention control group showed the greatest reduction in depressive symptoms when compared to their counterparts in the targeted intervention groups). Such complexities point to the importance of being able to tailor interventions to the needs and preferences of specific groups, not only by ethnicity, but also by gender and relationship to the person in need of care. Similar evidence of such differences by gender and ethnoracial groups were provided by Snowden (2001), who compared the effects of social embeddedness on the psychological well-being of African-American and White adults. He found that for African-American men, social involvement was more strongly related to psychological well-being than it was for White men. However, no such difference existed between African-American women and White women. Thus, increasing social embeddedness among African-American men may have more profound effects on their well-being than it would on the well-being of White men and women or African-American women.

The REACH project yielded a number of important findings that go beyond the scope of this chapter. However, taken together, they highlight several important points. First, the needs of caregivers are often broad and require multidimensional or multicomponent interventions. Schulz et al. (2003) indicated that REACH II, the second generation of REACH, which is currently underway, would test a standard, multicomponent intervention across the same ethnoracial groups of caregivers as REACH. However, the intervention will have flexibility to be tailored to specific needs of caregivers. Thus, although the same components will be available to all caregivers, the "dosing" of each component will be individualized through a needs assessment process.

Such attention to multiple needs, and differing degrees of attention to each need, requires a shift for practitioners who work primarily with persons exhibiting acute symptoms of major disorders. Although caregivers across ethnoracial groups tend to exhibit elevated levels of depressive symptoms when compared to noncaregivers, most do not experience major depression. Thus, specific interventions aimed at treating populations with major depression are ineffective and inappropriate for the majority of caregivers. Second, interventions must be tailored not only to address cultural differences, but also to address gender and relationship to patient differences (as discussed earlier). Third, as Sue and Zane (1987) suggested, therapist credibility, both ascribed and achieved, and gift-giving (perceived gains, such as hope, from the therapist by the client/patient) must be established early in treatment to prevent early termination of treatment. Eisdorfer et al. (2003) reported that the caregivers who dropped out of their intervention study had significantly higher baseline levels of depressive symptoms. Thus, it is possible that those most in need of intervention dropped out early. It is impossible to know why these caregivers dropped out, but Sue and Zane made a strong case for focusing on credibility and gift-giving as keys to culturally competent practice.

To date, no intervention studies on the scale of REACH have been conducted with various ethnoracial groups of caregivers of persons with severe mental illnesses other than dementia. Instead, smaller controlled trials of interventions (usually focusing on one ethnoracial minority group at a time) have taken place with these caregivers. Such projects have usually involved the caregivers as part of a treatment protocol for a person with schizophrenia (e.g., Chien and Chan 2004; Lau and Zane 2000). In addition, numerous studies have been conducted that involve mostly White European or European-American caregivers and their mentally ill or demented relatives. These studies have demonstrated the efficacy of psychoeducational, multifamily, and family-to-family interventions on the well-being of both family caregivers and their ill relatives (Dixon et al. 2001; Sörensen et al. 2002).

Practice

As discussed in the first section of this chapter, we believe a starting point for cultural competence is acknowledging that multiple *valid* worldviews exist. Development of critical consciousness is one path to reaching such an acknowledgement and developing cultural competence (Pitner and Sakamoto 2005). Pitner and Sakamoto described critical consciousness as a cognitive and affective process that takes place at both individual and structural levels:

> Cognitively and affectively, critical consciousness involves the process of continuously reflecting on and examining how our own biases, assumptions, and cultural worldviews affect the ways we perceive diversity and power dynamics at a personal level. At a structural level, critical consciousness requires relinquishing professional power to partner with the client. (p. 685)

Pitner and Sakamoto also focus on how the personal (identity) and structural (power) threats/challenges that accompany the development of critical consciousness can be pitfalls to working effectively with diverse clients (e.g., cognitive load and anxiety can lead to stereotyping). Therefore, we recommend that practitioners be aware of these pitfalls and recognize how their own anxiety related to cultural challenges may lead them to biased, prejudicial, racist behavior. Close professional training supervision in the early development of critical consciousness is a must.

Once the ongoing process of critical consciousness is established and multiple systems of knowing are acknowledged, we further suggest three other culture-general competencies: (a) "scientific mindedness," (b) seeing the individual within context, and (c) consultation/referral. We also propose four culture-specific competencies (those that can be useful for application to a particular group or individual). These are (a) language, (b) worldviews, (c) illness meanings, and (d) norms, values, beliefs, and practices.

Culture-General Competencies First, scientific mindedness is a term used by Sue (1998) referring to "therapists who form hypotheses rather than make premature conclusions about the status of culturally different clients, who develop creative ways to test hypotheses, and who act on the basis of acquired data" (p. 445). This process, as in research, can help a practitioner avoid treating assumptions and preconceptions as fact. Second, seeing the individual within context refers to recognizing the unique individuality of clients as well as the shared cultural context within which they live. Such recognition requires practitioners to avoid broad-brush application of cultural characteristics (i.e., stereotyping) to individuals based on their racial, ethnic, or cultural group memberships. Obviously, not all members of particular groups believe, think, or act the same. Being able to recognize when shared cultural characteristics are applicable to an individual and when they are not (what Sue 1998, called "dynamic sizing") is critical when dealing with ethnoracial minorities as well as nonminorities. Finally, a well-developed skill (and collegial network) for consultation and referral is necessary for all practitioners, but is of particular importance for those serving diverse populations. Figuring out when consultation with, or referral to, another practitioner with more cultural expertise for a given client can make a huge difference for clients and practitioners alike. When practitioners perceive themselves to be culturally competent in general, it may be hard for them to admit they need help with a client presenting cultural challenges. For any given practitioner, cultural competence will vary across groups; it is not a matter of having it or not.

Culture-Specific Competencies First, language is an unavoidable topic in a practice treating diverse groups. When a practitioner and client do not share the same native language(s), the practitioner must assess the client's proficiency in the language which he intends to use. When the client's proficiency is low, referral to a practitioner who shares a native language with the client is preferred. When this is not possible, a well-qualified translator should be sought. With the exception of gathering basic intake information, this should not be a family member. A well-qualified translator is one who is proficient in the language of the patient, has sufficient cultural knowledge to interpret culturally nuanced language, and sufficient practice knowledge to facilitate specific service to the client. Second, knowledge of a cultural group's specific worldviews is necessary for meeting clients "where they are." Worldviews reflect broad ways of seeing and understanding the world, which (much like cultures) shape our experiences and interpretations of them. A collectivist orientation to social life and the mind-body-spirit connection are examples of parts of one's worldview. If the practitioner does not recognize his client's worldview, it may be necessary to gain such knowledge directly from the client.

Third, knowledge and understanding of cultural illness meanings can facilitate work with ethnoracially and culturally diverse clients. As discussed in an earlier section, clients may have various expressions, descriptions, and understandings of their illness symptoms. The importance of understanding the culture-specific nature of the meaning applied to illness symptoms cannot be overstated. Differences in illness meanings may be quite obvious when comparing two very different cultures. However, when comparing less culturally distinct groups within the USA (e.g., African-Americans and White European-Americans), differences in illness meanings may be subtle and nuanced (see Dilworth-Anderson and Gibson 2002, for an example addressing illness meanings of dementia related symptoms). Finally, knowledge of other specific cultural norms, values, beliefs, and practices of clients is necessary for adequate service to them. Some of this knowledge, as with the other culture-specific competencies, can be gained through personal experience, research and practice literature, or consultation with cultural experts. However, much of it can and should be gained through interaction with clients and their families, for they are the only true experts regarding their specific cultural frames.

Education/Training

Although there is little empirical evidence for how best to teach the cultural competencies listed earlier, basic agreement seems to have been reached in the counseling literature that the three major domains outlined in Sue et al. (1982) position paper —awareness of values and beliefs, cultural/multicultural knowledge, and cultural/multicultural skills,—are important to target in training culturally competent mental health care providers. Kim and Lyons (2003) pointed to combinations of didactic methods ("intellectual exercises such as reading, writing, and Socratic discussions" [p. 401]) and experiential methods (getting to know people from different cultures, role play, and simulations of racism and discrimination) in order to facilitate learning in both the cognitive and affective domains.

In recent years, several measures of cultural competence for mental health care providers have been developed and tested. Kocarek et al. (2001) compared the Multicultural Counseling Awareness Scale: Form B (MCAS), the Multicultural Awareness-Knowledge-and-Skills Survey (MAKSS), and the Survey of Graduate Students' Experiences with Diversity (GSEDS) and assessed their psychometric properties. Despite some concerns regarding specific subscales or individual items, they found all three measures demonstrated adequate validity and internal consistency for use in assessing multicultural competence among mental health care providers and trainees. Additional work with these measures is needed in order to determine which specific training practices are most effective in the development of cultural competence. One limitation of these measures is that all three rely on self-report. Therefore, after taking classes in multicultural counseling, it is possible that respondents can identify the competencies they should have and whether they have them or not. More time-intensive forms of assessment (e.g., direct supervision of clinical interactions) are necessary to determine the degree to which individuals are able to practice cultural competence.

Policy

Great strides recently have been made in policies that impact mental health practitioners' level of cultural competence. In March 2002, the American Psychological Association's Committee on Accreditation (2002) issued new standards for education and training programs in professional psychology that included requirements for recruitment and retention of diverse groups of faculty and students and curricula to ensure cultural competence among graduates. These standards had to be met by all programs under review beginning in 2003. The Liaison Committee for Medical Education followed suit in September of 2003 (Liaison Committee for Medical Education 2003) with similar standards applied to the accreditation of medical schools. Of course, these medical school standards impact general practitioners (who care for many of the nation's mentally ill people) as well as psychiatrists (who have specialized training in the treatment of mental illness). Lu and Primm (2006) provided an excellent review of policy development over the past 10 years, and they made recommendations for how psychiatrists can continue to contribute to meeting the ultimate goals of these policies: elimination of mental health disparities in the USA. The Commission on Accreditation of Marriage and Family Therapy Education has implemented similar standards to those mentioned earlier, as have most other accrediting bodies for mental health and social service professionals. It is too soon to judge the full impact of requiring cultural diversity and cultural competency training among the programs training most of the nation's mental health service providers, but the impact certainly should be felt. The policies mandate what, for many years, have been suggestions or aspirational goals for culturally competent practice.

Future Directions

Although some minor recommendations were made throughout this chapter, the following section outlines several key recommendations for future cultural considerations in caring for persons with mental illness. First, knowledge from caregiving research using samples from different illness categories (e.g., dementia and schizophrenia) should be integrated. Despite many congruent findings and conceptual overlaps, caregiving research across illnesses is currently divided. Second, measurement issues related to burden and depression have been discussed in the context of culture. We suggest in-depth investigation of the congruence of underlying constructs and their operationalization across groups. Third, more information is needed regarding ways to tailor interventions to specific groups. Finally, we recommend a strong public relations campaign on behalf of people suffering from mental illness and their families. Such a campaign requires the voices of researchers, practitioners, educators, and policy makers.

Integration of Knowledge across Illnesses

It is important to recognize the similarities and differences between care provision for someone with dementia and someone with some other serious mental illness such as schizophrenia (Biegel and Schulz 1999). However, it is also important for researchers examining these different types of caregiving to borrow from one another. In this way, they can better understand what is common across caregivers for ill relatives and what is common only to those caring for relatives with specific illnesses. This is an area in which the study of illness meanings can be quite useful. In addition, continued theoretical work is needed in caregiving research that moves beyond and enhances stress and coping/stress process models. For example, taking a life span (Baltes 1987) or life course (Elder 1998) on developmental perspective can provide a broad theoretical framework for understanding caregiving of different types. These perspectives focus on the history and timing of disordered symptoms, which can have a profound impact on family, community, and professional involvement (Cook et al. 1997; Pickett et al. 1995).

Measurement Issues: Burden and Depression

Fox et al.'s (1999) critique of social gerontological studies of burden among African-American caregivers (discussed in an earlier section), coupled with inconsistent findings across other studies, point to the need for studies of burden to focus on the ways in which burden may be experienced and expressed differently across cultural groups. The continued application of measures developed and standardized using

White populations and held against the study of other ethnoracial groups is inappropriate. Furthermore, although they are important, reporting psychometric properties such as Cronbach's alpha coefficients and convergent validity (with other measures developed and standardized with White, middle class Americans) are insufficient to demonstrate that measures should be applied across diverse cultural groups. Instead, already established measures must be examined for content validity and concurrent validity in addition to reliability and convergent validity. Triangulation using qualitative and quantitative data can be useful in these processes.

Although Schulze and Rössler (2005) indicated that several measures recently have been validated across cultural groups, more work is needed in the development of measures using diverse samples and diverse cultural perspectives. Measures developed with attention to cultural differences have great potential for broad application. However, it is important to continue to recognize the difficulties inherent in such broad application (e.g., constructs that exist within one cultural group and not another). Thus, separate measures may be needed for each group being studied.

Of course, this can cause great difficulty in interpreting outcomes across groups. Current methods are dependent upon the equivalence of measures. To the degree that equivalence across cultural groups is impossible, research methods may need to shift. At the very least, researchers must recognize that mean differences between ethnoracial groups on a single measure (even when controlling for other factors) may be reflective of cultural differences in the underlying construct. In addition, such differences may emerge due to differences in responses to the measure or expression of the phenomenon in question.

The following illustrates cross-cultural challenges when studying depressive symptoms. As with burden, inconsistent findings have been reported with respect to depressive symptoms across ethnoracial groups of caregivers of elders with dementia. Some studies find significantly more depressive symptoms among White caregivers than among African-American caregivers, whereas others find no significant differences between these two ethnoracial groups (Dilworth-Anderson et al. 2002). There are several equally plausible interpretations for the findings of significant differences. The most common interpretation of such differences is that there is some cultural factor (e.g., religiosity, experience with adversity, social support) that protects African-American caregivers from depression; thus, the differences reflect a true difference in the underlying construct of depression (which is assumed to be the same construct between the two groups). Another interpretation is that African-American caregivers and White caregivers exhibit some systematic differences in the ways in which they report depressive symptoms, which essentially leads to underreporting by African-American caregivers or overreporting by White caregivers. Note that this interpretation still relies upon the assumption that the underlying construct of depression is the same between the two groups. Finally, an interpretation that has not been offered in the extant literature comparing African-American and White caregivers is that the underlying construct of depression is different between the two groups. Thus, mean differences on a measure of depressive symptomatology between the two groups actually reflect culturally based differences in the underlying construct of depression.

Finally, it is probable that all three of the aforementioned interpretations are correct to some degree (despite incongruent assumptions). That is: (a) the two groups experience different levels of depressive symptoms due to the influence of cultural factors; (b) the two groups differ systematically in their reporting of depressive symptoms; and (c) the two groups differ in depressive symptoms because the underlying cultural construct of depression differs between them. Therefore, it is important to attend to all three (and other) potential interpretations (and their underlying assumptions) instead of continuing to assume measurement equivalence across groups.

Anthropologists have presented strong evidence that depression is not a universal construct exhibited and experienced across various cultural groups. Kleinman and Good (1985) wrote:

> The claim that cross-cultural studies of depression provide significant challenge to contemporary theories and research methods rests first on the argument that dysphoria and depressive illness vary in important ways across cultures. If there are significant variations, the validity of the psychiatric conception of depression as a universal disorder is called into question, and social and cultural variables take on particular importance for understanding the sources of differences. (p. 37)

This argument takes us back to the importance of studying illness meanings and the ways in which culture shapes the expression, experience, and course of mental illness. With respect to translation and cross-cultural adaptation of research instruments, van Widenfelt et al. (2005) commented:

> To date, the most common assumption in health research appears to be that culture has only a minimal impact on the construct being measured, and therefore the way a construct is defined and operationalized in one culture can be applied directly in another culture (Herdman et al. 1997, p. 136)

Too often this assumption is false. More multidisciplinary efforts are needed for the cross-cultural development of assessment instruments that contain a common set of items relevant to the various cultures of interest (what van Widenfelt et al. called the "parallel approach") and instruments that contain culture-specific items (what van Widenfelt et al. called the "simultaneous approach"). Hsueh et al. (2005) provided an excellent example through their translation and validation of Picot's Caregiver Rewards Scale from the original English version to a Chinese version, which contained a different final set of items (due to cultural differences) than the original version.

Tailoring Interventions

The consistency of findings regarding the positive effects of psychoeducational, multifamily, and family-to-family interventions on the well-being of both family caregivers and their ill relatives (Dixon et al. 2001; Sörensen et al. 2002) supports their continued use across ethnoracial groups. However, much more research is needed to determine how such interventions should be tailored to meet the needs of diverse groups of caregivers. Bae and Kung (2000) proposed a specific intervention for Asian-American caregivers that includes a psychoeducational workshop and psychotherapeutic family session. However, they discussed how these interventions can be infused with cultural meaning and how Asian-American cultural nuances can be recognized and appropriately addressed during the interventions. More work needs to be done in the area of tailoring interventions to diverse groups of caregivers and their ill family members.

REACH and REACH II are leading the way with respect to dementia caregiving, but caregiving for persons with other serious mental illnesses must be addressed as well. Modification and testing of the REACH interventions for use with diverse families of persons with schizophrenia, major depression, or bipolar disorder could prove beneficial. There is no need to start from scratch when it comes to family interventions for various disorders.

Public Relations Campaign

Research findings and policies related to caring for persons with serious mental illnesses can provide a roadmap for effective care for diverse groups, but politicians and the general public must be willing to provide the fuel behind these efforts. Therefore, researchers and practitioners must be active participants in the political discourse regarding effective mental health services across diverse groups. Furthermore, we are responsible for messages sent to consumers and the general public about the importance of mental health services—including the costs of providing the best, most effective services as well as the costs of continuing to provide services that are substandard.

Over the last 50 years, great strides have been made in the USA to destigmatize persons and families dealing with mental illness. We have de-hospitalized a population of mentally ill persons with great hope for their return to successful lives among us in the community. The time has come for another large-scale public relations effort on behalf of people with mental illness. Far too many individuals and families dealing with mental illness are suffering tremendously, and a disproportionate number of those continuing to suffer are from ethnoracial minority groups and/or those living in poverty in the USA. Our society will prosper only to the degree to which we facilitate people's rise from poverty, recovery from illness, and movement from places of marginalization and oppression to places of acceptance and right personhood.

References

American Psychiatric Association. (1994). *Diagnostic and statistical manual of mental disorders (4th ed.)*. Washington, DC: American Psychiatric Association.

American Psychiatric Association, Committee on Accreditation. (2002). *Guidelines and principles for accreditation of programs in professional psychology*. www.apa.org/ed/G&P2.pdf.

Appiah, K. A. (2005). *The ethics of identity*. Princeton: Princeton University Press.

Bae, S. W., & Kung, W. W. M. (2000). Family intervention for Asian Americans with a schizophrenic patient in the family. *American Journal of Orthopsychiatry, 70*(4), 532–541.

Baltes, P. B. (1987). Theoretical propositions of life-span developmental psychology: On the dynamics between growth and decline. *Developmental Psychology, 23*(5), 611–626.

Baronet, A. M. (1999). Factors associated with caregiver burden in mental illness: A critical review of the research literature. *Clinical Psychology Review, 19*(7), 819–841.

Barrio, C., Yamada, A. M., Atuel, H., Hough, R. L., Yee, S., Berthot, B., et al. (2003). A tri-ethnic examination of symptom expression on the positive and negative syndrome scale in schizophrenia spectrum disorders. *Schizophrenia Research, 60*(2–3), 259–269.

Biegel, D. E., & Schulz, R. (1999). Caregiving and caregiver interventions in aging and mental illness. *Family Relations, 48*(4), 345–354.

Brodwin, P. (2005). Introduction: Genetic knowledge and collective identity. *Culture, Medicine and Psychiatry, 29*(2), 139–143.

Chien, W. T., & Chan, S. W. C. (2004). One-year follow-up of a multiple-family-group intervention for Chinese families of patients with schizophrenia. *Psychiatric Services, 55*(11), 1276–1284.

Chrisman, N. J., & Kleinman, A. (1983). Popular health care, social networks, and cultural meanings: The orientation of medical anthropology. In D. Mechanic (Ed.), *Handbook of health, health care, and the health professions* (pp. 569–590). New York: The Free Press.

Cook, J. A., Cohler, B. J., Pickett, S. A., & Beeler, J. A. (1997). Life-course and severe mental illness: Implications for caregiving within the family of later life. *Family Relations, 46,* 427–436.

Dilworth-Anderson, P., & Gibson, B. E. (2002). The cultural influence of values, norms, meanings, and perceptions in understanding dementia in ethnic minorities. *Alzheimer Disease and Associated Disorders, 16,* S56–63.

Dilworth-Anderson, P., Williams, I. C., & Gibson, B. E. (2002). Issues of race, ethnicity, and culture in caregiving research: A twenty-year review. *Gerontologist, 42,* 237–272.

Dixon, L., Goldman, H., & Hirad, A. (1999). State policy and funding of services to families of adults with serious and persistent mental illness. *Psychiatric Services, 50*(4), 551–553.

Dixon, L., McFarlane, W. R., Lefley, H., Lucksted, A., Cohen, M., Falloon, I., et al. (2001). Evidence-based practices for services to families of people with psychiatric disabilities. *Psychiatric Services, 52*(7), 903–910.

Doucet, F., & Hamon, R. R. (in press). A nation of diversity: Demographics of the United States of America and their implications for families. In B. Sherif-Trask & R. R. Hamon (Eds.), *Cultural diversity and families: Expanding perspectives*. Thousand Oaks: Sage.

Eisdorfer, C., Czaja, S. J., Loewenstein, D. A., Rubert, M. P., Argüelles, S., Mitrani, V. B., et al. (2003). The effect of a family therapy and technology-based intervention on caregiver depression. *Gerontologist, 43,* 514–531.

Elder, G. A. (1998). The life course as developmental theory. *Child Development, 69,* 1–12.

Fabrega, H. (1989). On the significance of an anthropological approach to schizophrenia. *Psychiatry, 52,* 45–65.

Fox, K., Hinton, W. L., & Levkoff, S. (1999). Take up the caregiver's burden: Stories of care for urban African American elders with dementia. *Culture, Medicine, and Psychiatry, 23,* 501–529.

Freire, P. (1997). *Pedagogy of the oppressed (2nd ed.)*. New York: Continuum.

Gaines, A. D. (1989). Alzheimer's disease in the context of Black (Southern) culture. *Health Matrix, 6,* 33–38.

Gaines, A. D. (1992). From DSM-I to III-R; voices of self, mastery and the other: A cultural constructivist reading of U.S. psychiatric classification. *Social Science and Medicine, 35*(1), 3–24.

Gallagher-Thompson, D., Haley, W., Guy, D., Rupert, M., Argüelles, T., Zeiss, L. M., et al. (2003). Tailoring psychological interventions for ethnically diverse dementia caregivers. *Clinical Psychology: Science and Practice, 10*(4), 423–438.

Gibson, B. E. (2001). *Dementia caregiving among four ethnic groups: Illness meanings and the stress process*. Unpublished Master's Thesis, University of North Carolina at Greensboro, Greensboro.

Good, B. J. (1997). Studying mental illness in context: Local, global, or universal? *Ethos, 25*(2), 230–248.
Goodenough, W. H. (1999). Outline of a framework for a theory of cultural evolution. *Cross-Cultural Research, 33,* 84–107.
Grant, G., Ramcharan, P., McGrath, M., Nolan, M., & Keady, J. (1998). Rewards and gratifications among family caregivers: Towards a refined model of caring and coping. *Journal of Intellectual Disability Research, 42*(1), 58–71.
Guarnaccia, P. J., Parra, P., Deschamps, A., Milstein, G., & Argiles, N. (1992). Si dios quiere: Hispanic families" experiences of caring for a seriously mentally ill member. *Culture, Medicine, and Psychiatry, 16,* 187–215.
He, W., & Hobbs, F. (1999). *The emerging minority marketplace: Minority population growth: 1995–2050.* Washington: U.S. Department of Commerce, Minority Business Development Agency. http://www.mbda.gov/documents/mbdacolor.pdf.
Herdman, M., Fox-Rushby, J., & Badia, X. (1997). 'Equivalence' and the translation and adaptation of health-related quality of life questionnaires. *Quality of Life Research, 6*(3), 237–247.
Hinton, W. L., & Levkoff, S. (1999). Constructing Alzheimer's: Narratives of lost identities, confusion, and loneliness in old age. *Culture, Medicine, and Psychiatry, 23,* 453–475.
Hinton, W. L., Fox, K., & Levkoff, S. (1999). Introduction: Exploring the relationships among aging, ethnicity, and family dementia caregiving. *Culture, Medicine, and Psychiatry, 23,* 403–413.
Horwitz, A. V., & Reinhard, S. C. (1995). Ethnic differences in caregiving duties and burdens among parents and siblings of persons with severe mental illness. *Journal of Health and Social Behavior, 36,* 138–150.
Hsueh, K. H., Phillips, L. R., Cheng, W., & Picot, S. J. F. (2005). Assessing cross-cultural equivalence through confirmatory factor analysis. *Western Journal of Nursing Research, 27*(6), 755–771.
Jenkins, J. H. (1988). Ethnopsychiatric interpretations of schizophrenic illness: The problem of nervios within Mexican-American families. *Culture, Medicine and Psychiatry, 12,* 301–329.
Kim, B. S. K., & Lyons, H. Z. (2003). Experiential activities and multicultural counseling competence training. *Journal of Counseling & Development, 81*(4), 400–408.
Kleinman, A. (1980). *Patients and healers in the context of culture.* Berkley: University of California Press.
Kleinman, A. (1988). *Rethinking psychiatry: From cultural category to personal experience.* New York: Free Press.
Kleinman, A., & Good, B. J. (1985). Introduction to Part I. In A. Kleinman & B. J. Good (Eds.), *Culture and depression: Studies in the anthropology and cross-cultural psychiatry of affect and disorder* (pp. 37–42). Berkley: University of California Press.
Kleinman, A., Eisenberg, L., & Good, B. (1978). Culture, illness, and care: Clinical lessons from anthropologic and cross-cultural research. *Annals of Internal Medicine, 88,* 251–258.
Kocarek, C. E., Talbot, D. M., Batka, J. C., & Anderson, M. Z. (2001). Reliability and validity of three measures of multicultural competency. *Journal of Counseling & Development, 79*(4), 486.
Kramer, B. J. (1997). Gain in the caregiving experience: Where are we? What next? *Gerontologist, 37*(2), 218–232.
Lau, A., & Zane, N. (2000). Examining the effects of ethnic-specific services: An analysis of cost-utilization and treatment outcome for Asian American clients. *Journal of Community Psychology, 28*(1), 63–77.
Levine, R. A. (1974). Parental goals: A cross-cultural view. *Teachers College Record, 76*(2), 226–239.
Liaison Committee on Medical Education. (2003). *Functions and structure of a medical school: Standards for accreditation of medical education programs leading to the M.D. degree.* www.lcme.org/functions2003september.pdf.
Lu, F. G., & Primm, A. (2006). Mental health disparities, diversity, and cultural competence in medical student education: How psychiatry can play a role. *Academic Psychiatry, 30*(1), 9–15.

Martire, L. M., Schulz, R., Mulsant, B. H., & Reynolds III, C. F. (2004). Family caregiver functioning in late-life bipolar disorder. *American Journal of Geriatric Psychiatry, 12*(3), 335–336.

McFarlane, W. R., Lukens, E., Link, B., Dushay, R., Deakins, S. A., Newmark, M., et al. (1995). Multiple-family groups and psychoeducation in the treatment of schizophrenia. *Archives of General Psychiatry, 52,* 679–687.

Minuchin, S. (1974). *Families and family therapy*. Cambridge: Harvard University Press.

Minuchin, S., & Fishman, C. (1981). *Family therapy techniques*. Cambridge: Harvard University Press.

Morey, L. C. (1991). Classification of mental disorder as a collection of hypothetical constructs. *Journal of Abnormal Psychology, 100*(3), 289–293.

Ogbu, J. (1993). Variability in minority school performance: A problem in search of an explanation. In E. Jacob, & C. Jordan (Eds.), *Minority education: Anthropological perspectives* (pp. 83–111). Norwood: Ablex.

Ohaeri, J. U. (2003). The burden of caregiving in families with a mental illness: A review of 2002. *Current Opinions in Psychiatry, 16,* 457–465.

Pickett, S. A., Greenley, J. R., & Greenberg, J. S. (1995). Off-timedness as a contributor to subjective burdens for parents of offspring with severe mental illness. *Family Relations, 44,* 195–201.

Pitner, R. O., & Sakamoto, I. (2005). The role of critical consciousness in multicultural practice: Examining how its strength becomes its limitation. *American Journal of Orthopsychiatry, 75*(4), 684–694.

Riedel, S., Fredman, L., & Langenberg, P. (1998). Associations among caregiving difficulties, burden, and rewards in caregivers to older post-rehabilitation patients. *Journals of Gerontology: Psychological Sciences, 53*(3), P165–174.

Schulz, R., Burgio, L. D., Burns, R., Eisdorfer, C., Gallagher-Thompson, D., Gitlin, L. N., et al (2003). Resources for Enhancing Alzheimer's Caregiver Health (REACH): Overview, site-specific outcomes, and future directions. *Gerontologist, 43*(4), 514–520.

Schulze, B., & Rössler, W. (2005). Caregiver burden in mental illness: Review of measurement, findings and interventions in 2004–2005. *Current Opinion in Psychiatry, 18,* 684–691.

Snowden, L. R. (2001). Social embeddedness and psychological well-being among African Americans and Whites. *American Journal of Community Psychology, 29*(4), 519–536.

Sörensen, S., Pinquart, M., & Duberstein, P. (2002). How effective are interventions with caregivers? An updated meta-analysis. *Gerontologist, 42*(3), 356–372.

Steuve, A., Vine, P., & Struening, E. L. (1997). Perceived burden among caregivers of adults with serious mental illness: Comparison of Black, Hispanic, and White families. *American Journal of Orthopsychiatry, 67,* 199–209.

Sue, S. (1998). In search of cultural competence in psychotherapy and counseling. *American Psychologist, 53,* 440–448.

Sue, S., & Zane, N. (1987). The role of culture and cultural techniques in psychotherapy: A critique and reformulation. *American Psychologist, 42,* 37–45.

Sue, S., & Chu, J. Y. (2003). The mental health of ethnic minority groups: Challenges posed by the supplement to the Surgeon General's report on mental health. *Culture, Medicine and Psychiatry, 27*(4), 447–465.

Sue, D. W., Bernier, J. E., Durran, A., Feinberg, L., Pedersen, P., Smith, E. J., et al. (1982). Position paper: Cross-cultural counseling competencies. *Counseling Psychologist, 10,* 45–52.

Szapocznik, J., Scopetta, M. A., Ceballos, A., & Santisteban, D. (1994). Understanding, supporting and empowering families: From microanalysis to macrointervention. *Family Psychologist, 10*(2), 23–27.

Tarlow, B. J., Wisniewski, S. R., Belle, S. H., Rubert, M., Ory, M. G., & Gallagher-Thompson, D. (2004). Positive aspects of caregiving: Contributions of the REACH project to the development of new measures for Alzheimer's caregiving. *Research on Aging, 26*(4), 429–453.

U.S. Department of Health and Human Services (HHS). (2001). *Mental health: Culture, race, and ethnicity—A supplement to mental health: A report of the surgeon general*. Rockville: U.S. Department of Health and Human Services, Substance Abuse and Mental Health Services Administration, Center for Mental Health Services.

van Widenfelt, B. M., Treffers, P. D. A., de Beurs, E., Siebelink, B. M., & Koudijs, E. (2005). Translation and cross-cultural adaptation of assessment instruments used in psychological research with children and families. *Clinical Child and Family Psychology Review, 8*(2), 135–147.

Vaughn, C., E., & Leff, J. (1976). The influence of family and social factors on the course of psychiatric illness. *British Journal of Psychiatry, 129,* 125–137.

Yeo, G., & Gallagher-Thompson, D. (Eds.). (1996). *Ethnicity and the dementias*. Washington: Taylor & Francis.

Chronic Illness and Primary Care: Integrating Mental Health and Primary Care

Susan Taylor-Brown, Tziporah Rosenberg and Susan H. McDaniel

Caring for members who are chronically ill is an expected but stressful component of family life. Family caregivers play a vital but largely invisible role in patient care, both in terms of their individual efforts and as members of the labor force (Jacobs 2006; Levine 1999). Levine (2004) reports that over 27 million Americans now provide vital long-term home health care for relatives and loved ones—everything from dispensing medication and operating medical equipment, to assisting with physical therapy and personal hygiene, to making sure the bills are paid. They receive no pay for this work, little training, and little respect or support from the health care system. While illness can result in increased intimacy, family members commonly face health risks, financial burdens, emotional strain, mental health problems, workplace issues, retirement insecurity, and lost opportunities (Feinberg et al. 2005). Treating chronic illness is a natural and central component of primary health care, focusing on the full spectrum of life stage issues from infancy through death. Thus, it is the ideal venue for addressing how chronic health conditions affect the entire family.

S. Taylor-Brown (✉)
Department of Pediatrics, Golisano Children's Hospital,
University of Rochester, School of Medicine & Dentistry, PO Box 671,
Rochester, NY 14642, USA
e-mail: Susan_Taylorbrown@URMC.Rochester.edu

Department of Family Medicine, University of Rochester Medical Center,
601 Elmwood Ave, Box PSYCH, Rochester, NY 14642, USA

T. Rosenberg · S. H. McDaniel
Department of Family Medicine, University of Rochester Medical Center,
601 Elmwood Ave, Box PSYCH, Rochester, NY 14642, USA
e-mail: tziporah_rosenberg@urmc.rochester.edu

Department of Psychiatry, University of Rochester Medical Center,
601 Elmwood Ave, Box PSYCH, Rochester, NY 14642, USA

S. H. McDaniel
e-mail: SusanH2_McDaniel@URMC.Rochester.edu

R. C. Talley et al. (eds.), *The Challenges of Mental Health Caregiving,*
Caregiving: Research • Practice • Policy, DOI 10.1007/978-1-4614-8791-3_4,

Introduction to Primary Care: Chronic Medical Illness

The prevalence of chronic illness is increasing across the lifespan for a variety of reasons, foremost being the increased survival rate of children with chronic illness coupled with the increased survival of elderly individuals with multiple chronic health conditions. Greater longevity for those dealing with chronic illness coupled with decreased hospital stays has resulted in lengthier periods of family caregiving than was previously typical. Over time the cumulative effects of age coupled with multiple chronic conditions lead to functional deficits resulting in disability. When a person becomes disabled, the need for and intensity of caregiving increases. A family's ability to care for the affected family member may therefore be compromised due to this increased intensity and duration of care. The stresses inherent in caring for someone with chronic conditions are distinct from those inherent in caring for family members with acute illnesses. When dealing with chronic conditions, depending upon severity, family members may serve as the primary caregiver for the ill person from the time of diagnosis until his/her death. While the level of care required to support chronically ill individuals varies over time, overall demands are frequently ongoing, complex, and exhausting. In the case of a child with chronic health concerns, for example, caregiver responsibilities may begin at birth, a situation that deeply and permanently affects family life. An infant with multiple chronic conditions may require a lifetime of assistance, and parents are transformed into deliverers of high-tech care, often times performing painful medical procedures.

Overall, family members provide 70–80 % of all in-home care to older people with chronic illness, and it is predominantly women (i.e., mothers, daughters, daughters-in-laws, wives, and granddaughters) who provide the majority of this support (National Alliance for Caregiving and American Association of Retired Persons (NAC and AARP) 2009). In fact, mothers remain the primary caregivers of both the young and the old. Of course, some men also serve as primary caregivers; husbands frequently provide care for wives with disabilities (Bengtson et al. 1996; Russell 2001). It is the growth of the oldest-old that commonly creates strain for the middle-aged adults who provide care. The average American woman can expect to spend 18 years caring for an older family member compared to 17 years caring for her children (Pavalko and Artis 1997). Changes in family life—including an upswing in single-parent households, the movement of women into the work force and public policies that emphasize family-focused care while requiring women to work outside of the home—are challenging a family's ability to care for members who are chronically ill. In addition, women caregivers are more likely than their male counterparts to give up employment, modify their work schedules, or forgo promotions or career development opportunities, to accommodate their care responsibilities (Pavalko and Artis 1997). Currently, our society mostly avoids recognizing these challenges and provides very few supports to successfully care for individuals with chronic conditions.

This chapter begins with a case example that illustrates the many challenges of family caregiving in the midst of other developmental challenges. It then reviews what

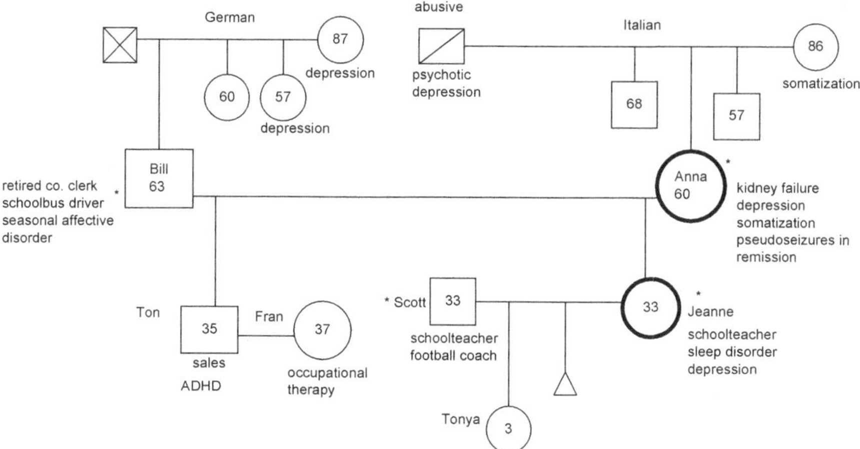

Fig. 1 Caregiving and chronic illness in one family

is known about the impact on the caregiver's mental health of caring for someone who has a chronic condition. Emphasis is given to the impact of chronic illness, multiple health problems, multiple loss issues, and "complicated caregiving." Suggestions are offered regarding changes needed in education and training and practice and policy for improved care.

Case Illustration

Anna,[1] 55, presented regularly to her primary care doctor, Dr. PC. This was no surprise, given her list of health problems: kidney failure, hypothyroidism, hypertension, depression, and somatization. Dr. PC collaborated with a psychiatrist in treating Anna's depression. In the past year, Anna periodically experienced blackouts. Both her psychiatrist and her primary care doctor referred her to a neurologist to rule out epileptic seizures. After 10 days in the hospital being monitored and tested for electrical seizures, results were conclusive; Anna's seizures were non-electrical, or psychogenic, in nature. The neurologist suggested that Anna was under considerable family stress related to caregiving, and referred her to Dr. FT for family therapy. The following story emerged in the first session.

Anna was the primary caregiver for her father who suffered from a psychotic depression from the age of 30 (See Fig. 1). When depressed, Anna's father physically abused Anna's mother and was emotionally abusive to his sons and daughter. Soon after high school, both sons left home to attend college in another state and never

[1] This family is an actual case treated by Dr. McDaniel and her primary care colleagues. While the patients have given their permission for their story to be told, the names and some identifying features have been changed to protect their anonymity.

returned. Anna's father was hospitalized in a psychiatric state hospital when he was in his 40s and died there 20 years later. While Anna's mother rarely visited her husband, Anna felt it was her duty as a good Italian-American, Catholic daughter and did so every Sunday afternoon until her father died.

Anna's mother had a history of chronic medical problems and somatization disorder. Regardless of the severity of her illnesses (and they were usually mild), Anna's mother experienced them as life-threatening and dramatically asked Anna for help. Anna dutifully performed whatever tasks her mother requested but increasingly resented these chores. In the meantime, Anna, in her mid-20s, married Bill, who fell hard for this pretty, warm, caring woman. His family was German-American and not very expressive. Bill's father had died during a medical procedure during Bill's late adolescence and was unable to see or validate Bill's success as a man. Bill's mother and a younger sister had a history of depression. Bill himself was a "man's man" who had considerable difficulty with his own son's attention deficit disorder and need for medical intervention. Bill never attended a medical appointment with either his wife or his son.

The first family therapy session included Anna, Bill, their 30-year-old son Tony, and their 28-year-old daughter Jeanne. The adult children still lived in their family home. The referring neurologist stopped in for 15 min of the session to describe what he found during Anna's hospitalization and why he made the referral. It soon became clear that Anna was both symptomatic—having regular psychogenic seizures in addition to her other medical problems—and the primary caretaker of her mother, her husband, and her adult children. She was bending, if not breaking, under the strain. Dr. FT gave the family a homework assignment that tested the children's ability to take care of some of their own chores (such as doing the laundry) and to treat their mother with more respect. Somewhat to Anna's surprise, her children immediately changed their behavior because they were worried about their mother.

Given this mix of medical and mental health problems, Dr. FT asked Dr. PC if he would like to see this couple with her. The two doctors work at the same Primary Care Center, and Dr. PC felt that it was such an interesting and labor-intensive case that it was worth dedicating extra time to this conjoint treatment. His primary focus was on Anna's psychogenic seizures. Dr. FT hypothesized that alleviating Anna's caregiver burden might ameliorate these symptoms. In addition, Drs. FT and PC focused on the couple's relationship, recognizing that current or historical abuse is often associated with somatoform disorders. As the couple sessions continued, a history of emotional abuse by Bill emerged that was associated with the winter months. An assessment of Bill revealed a diagnosis of seasonal affective disorder. His abusive behavior came to a halt over time through a combination of (1) antidepressant medication for Bill, (2) continued work on the transgenerational aspects of the case (such as Bill's desire for his father's approval and Anna's resentment of her mother's attention-seeking behavior), and (3) behavioral prescriptions for the couple regarding their marriage. Anna's psychogenic seizures evaporated when Bill's emotional abuse stopped.

The next focus of treatment was on Jeanne who became engaged to Scott and developed a mild sleep disturbance just before their wedding. In discussing the issues with Drs. FT and PC, it became clear that Jeanne was replicating her parents' marriage (or the first 30 years thereof). Jeanne was anxious for good reason, and, when she became anxious, her sleep suffered. She was determined to go through with the marriage, however, and made it clear that premarital counseling was not something in which she or her fiancé was interested. Some brief relaxation techniques got her through a beautiful wedding. The family placed bets on when, during the week before the wedding, Anna's mother would be hospitalized as they had become accustomed to her somatizing during important events that were focused on someone other than herself. Drs. FT and PC were somewhat surprised when the family's bets turned out to be accurate.

The next few years were relatively quiet for this family. Anna and Bill did very well in their marital therapy, and Anna's symptoms moved to the background. Jeanne got married, was successful as a teacher, had a daughter and a son and became pregnant with her third child. Tony became engaged and planned his own wedding. Then Anna's kidney functioning deteriorated, and with it came increased depression and an increase in a variety of somatic symptoms. Faced with a decision to start hemodialysis, Anna asked her older brother if he would donate his kidney to her and was crushed when he refused "because his wife would not allow it." Family dynamics continued to play out when Jeanne told Anna that her husband would not allow her to donate a kidney because of their young children. Tony told his mother he would donate a kidney, but Anna was highly ambivalent about taking a kidney from her son. She started hemodialysis and struggled with severe, recurring depression. Bill had learned how to deal with Anna's illness far better than he had in earlier years, and he attended every doctor visit with his wife and provided her with much support. Jeanne became her mother's primary confidant, and the transgenerational caregiving cycle began again, this time with Jeanne at the hub.

Jeanne had an unremarkable pregnancy the third time around. However, she developed severe postpartum insomnia, and came to see Drs. FT and PC together. They brought in Scott and confirmed their earlier impression that this marriage repeated many of the same patterns as those seen in Anna and Bill's early relationship. Jeanne was the primary caregiver to her parents, her husband, and now her three young children. Scott was busy coaching basketball, teaching, and playing sports himself and was therefore relatively unavailable. Some of Jeanne and Scott's treatment involved having Bill talk to Scott about what he had learned over the years that he wished he had known early in his marriage. It also involved bringing Tony into the situation so that Jeanne had help in caring for her mother and her own family. At this time, Tony was married, but did not yet have children of his own.

This case illustrates a number of points that are common among family caregivers:

- Women are usually the primary caregivers.
- Women are often caring for multiple generations at the same time.
- The patterns of caregiving repeat across generations.
- Caregivers often become sick and are notoriously bad at caring for themselves.
- Collaborative care, involving primary care clinicians and family-oriented mental health professionals, can provide primary care treatment and secondary prevention.

Relationship of Caregiving with Mental Health and Primary Care for Chronic Medical Illness

Caregiving is an expected part of family life. Parents care for children as they develop and equally at the other end of the life spectrum, family members care for the elderly. As noted by Carol Levine (1999), there is a mental health component in every caregiving experience:

> Caregivers are at risk for mental and physical health problems themselves. Exhausted caregivers may become care recipients, leading to a further, often preventable, drain on resources. Does my managed-care company realize, for instance, that during the past year it paid more for my stress-related medical problems than for my husband's medical care?. (p. 1590)

By and large, we do not fully understand the impact on the family unit of caring for someone with a chronic condition. Parents caring for children with chronic illness experience unique stressors related to the child's behavior and caregiving demands (Raina et al. 2005). Family caregivers are largely invisible both as individuals and in terms of their contributions to the labor force (Levine 1999). Dr. Jack Medalie described the concept of the "hidden patient" to capture the role a caregiver plays in the life of the chronically ill member:

> In any family in which there is an individual with an acute and life-threatening or chronic and long-term illness or disease, the caregiver (usually the spouse, the oldest daughter, or sometimes the whole family unit) is under considerable stress. Unless this caregiver receives sufficient support from the family and/or others, coping mechanisms will fail and the caregiver will develop overt or covert signs of illness. (1999, p. 174)

We have too little information regarding the impact of caregiving on the primary caregiver's mental and physical health . However, the available information strongly supports the need for more attention to the plight of caregivers. In this regard, it is helpful to distinguish between "objective" and "subjective" burdens that caregivers experience (Bengtson et al. 1996). *Objective burden* refers to the instrumental care demands, while the *subjective burden* refers to the feelings aroused in caregivers. These feelings are highly individual; what is challenging for one caregiver may not adversely affect another. Bass et al. (1996) report that feelings of burden are related primarily to the availability of external resources and social supports, not to the severity of the illness.

Caregivers experience higher morbidity and mortality than age-matched noncaregivers. In a landmark study assessing health problems of caregivers, Schulz and Beach (1999) reported that, over a four-year period, caregivers over 65 who were experiencing emotional strain were 63 % more likely to die than age matched non-caregivers. Caregivers suffer higher rates of multiple physical illnesses, depression, and anxiety than noncaregivers (McDaniel et al. 2005). As people are living longer, a growing number of families have three or four generations of family members for which to provide care. More and more of the "young old" (aged 65–80) are caring for their "old old" (those over 80) parents. Of course, many of the "young old" have their own chronic conditions.

Caregivers who experience mental health issues related to caring for someone with chronic illness have difficulty getting their needs met. Mental health problems and illnesses are real and disabling conditions that are experienced by one in four Americans (Kessler, Chiu, Demler, and Walters 2005). Yet mental health continues to be highly stigmatized and the majority of people experiencing mental conditions fail to receive care. The first ever Surgeon General's report on mental health was published in 1999. The following year, a supplement was released that examined mental health disparities affecting racial and ethnic minorities. Mistrust of traditional mental health services keep many from seeking care (DHHS 2000). At the same time, caregiving should not be cast solely in a negative light. There are many benefits and growth-enhancing aspects to caring for a loved one. While the majority of theoretical perspectives on caregiving have neglected to take positive experiences into consideration (Biegel et al. 1991), there is a growing interest in assessing the positive aspects of caregiving for the caregiver, the patient, and the family (Jacobs 2006; Kramer 1997). The stress of family caregiving depends as much upon the meaning and satisfaction derived by the family member as the actual work involved (McDaniel et al. 2005). The emotional, physical, and financial costs related to caregiving deserve further study.

Status of Caregiving and Primary Care: Chronic Medical Illness

Policy

The "graying" of the US population is raising concerns about the public costs and burdens of family caregiving (Hooyman and Gonyea 1999). Currently, the USA does not have a coherent long-term care policy (Graham 1999; Levine 1999). Caregivers remain largely invisible in the social and political fabric of the country. Based upon 1997 data, there are 25 million unpaid informal caregivers in the USA, who get little from the system in return for the estimated \$ 196 billion a year in labor they provide (Arno et al. 1999). This estimated figure was recently revised in 2004 to \$ 306 billion of care based upon an estimate of 28.9 million caregivers at \$ 9.92/h (Becker 2006). Similar trends are noted in the UK with Newman (2006) reporting that, carers save the economy £ 57 billion/year.

No one would disagree that the family is the unit of care in today's society. There is a long social, cultural, and religious tradition that dictates that families are the central providers of health care. The problem is not that public policy looks first to families, but that it generally looks only to families and fails to support those who do accept this responsibility (Levine 1999). Services for the chronically ill patient are inadequately reimbursed, limiting the development and efficacy of family-based care. The American health care system provides financial incentives and rewards for curative care while ignoring the day-to-day needs involved in keeping the chronically ill at home. Custodial care is not reimbursed while acute high-tech care is. The American health care system offers little in the way of institutional support for families who are burdened with caregiving (Koren 1986). Policy makers have not yet found a way to support family members who do choose to become caregivers.

There is a growing awareness that many members of the labor force have caregiving responsibilities. These caregivers are performing a vital function for society by retaining the chronically ill in community settings that are less costly than institutional care options. Individual states are incorporating caregiver support services into their programs by increasing funding of home and community-based services (HCBS), with policy makers interested in learning more about forward-looking practices in caregiver support that will bolster a family's ability to provide care at home (Fox-Grage and Gibson 2006). Currently, eight states have active bills that include some form of paid family leave for workers who need and want to keep their jobs while providing care for family members (Greene 2006). Family members jeopardize their own health and financial well-being by providing long-term care that is not perceived as a shared, community responsibility.

Contemporary caregivers face unique challenges. The devolution of the federal government's role in caring for society's vulnerable members, coupled with state and local governments' inadequate responses, results in a diminishing safety net and women carrying a disproportionate burden in providing long term care. Smeeding (1998) notes that:

> The locus of responsibility for costs, above and beyond those which the federal government decides it can afford, will be shifted to other parties: lower levels of government (states and localities) in the case of AFDC and Medicaid and thence to individuals and their families. (p. 26)

Social welfare reform also places women at a disadvantage. Temporary Assistance for Needy Families (TANF) regulations with work requirements are not supportive of caregivers. Who will care for the chronically ill while the caregiver is at work? These issues are not unique to our country. In cross-cultural studies among Western cultures, American, Australian, Canadian, and British caregivers report similar problems of isolation and unmet financial and other needs (Schofield et al. 1998). Scandinavian countries, in contrast, do assume some community responsibility for care (Levine 1999).

The current policy debates about Medicare and Medicaid illustrate the progressive shift in responsibility from the federal government to state and local governments, and ultimately to affected families. Generally, out-of-home care is supported more than in-home care. Medicaid continues to show a strong institutional bias with more than 45 % of the $ 125 billion spent on long-term care in 2011 going to nursing homes and institutions. Fragmentation of services and inequities prevail in the current market-driven health care economy (Levine 1999).

Furthermore, most health insurance policies fail to cover many of the equipment costs required for home health care (e.g., health care aides, disposable supplies, and therapies). Such necessities may actually be deemed "not medically necessary" in addition to other expenses that are not being adequately covered. Insurance may also offer only partial coverage for high-tech supplies. For example, in 2002, a wheelchair cost $ 3,700 while the insurance company paid only $ 500, leaving the family with a significant bill.

As health care policy has shifted to a market-driven model, the growing interest in cost containment creates an environment wherein the needs of caregivers are considered too extensive and cannot be met. This is exacerbated by the progressive double-digit increases in the cost of health care coverage, the net effect being that the family bears the burden of care.

States are playing a growing role in financing support services for caregivers. Some states are incorporating caregiver support services into programs that serve older people, while other states have a separate program for caregiver support (Fox-Grage and Gibson 2006). Families are challenged to find existing service in different service systems from health care to community based services. Fox-Grage and Gibson (2006) report emerging trends that support family caregivers including assessing the caregiver, consumer direction in family caregiver support services, and collaborations between the aging network and the health care system. Family caregivers are the backbone of community-based long-term care and too often the lack of coordination between the aging network and the health care system adversely affects the family caregiver's ability to care for a loved one at home.

Efforts to achieve parity for mental health services have resulted in federal legislation, however have yet to be fully realized and implemented. As the debate over equal coverage continues, primary care providers are one of the key providers of care for caregivers who experience the stresses and strains related to providing chronic care. Primary care providers serve an important function for these families by assisting them in coping with and adapting to the demands of the caregiver role.

Practice

From the cradle to the grave, family caregivers provide clinical observations, direct care case management, and a full range of other services (Houlihan 1987; Jacobs 2006; Maletta and Hepburn 1986). While providers view family members as care managers, they do not consistently involve them in care planning (Levine 1999). Family involvement in the care of an individual with a chronic condition varies across primary care settings. In pediatrics, it is assumed that the parents are the caregivers, while for adult patients, some practices integrate family members providing care while others involve them inconsistently, if at all.

Dissatisfaction with earlier treatment models that specifically exclude family members has led to a family consumer movement in medical care. Emerging first in pediatrics, involving parents of children with special health care needs (CSHCNs), family-centered care positions families as integral members of the treatment team. The US Public Health Service, the Maternal and Child Health Bureau (MCHB), and Congressional action have all confirmed that services for CSHCN should be family-centered, community-based, comprehensive, coordinated, and culturally competent (Hutchins and McPherson 1991). The consumer movement has spread to encompass caregivers across the lifespan, including those who care for the elderly. Family concerns about the adequacy and safety of care has also been validated by the Institute of Medicine report (Kohn et al. 2002). Efficient collaborative family-centered models that include health-care institutions, providers, the workplace, and patients and their families need to be implemented to significantly improve quality of care, reduce direct and indirect costs, improve productivity, and enhance family well-being (Bloch 1993).

In primary care, interdisciplinary team members, who have diverse orientations toward the patient and his/her family, work together to treat chronic illness. The team employs clinical approaches ranging from the traditional medical model to family-centered care to the collaborative family healthcare model. The traditional medical model views patients as the recipients of care while families maintain a passive role in care decisions. By contrast, the collaborative family healthcare model envisions a collaborative relationship between patients, family members, and the healthcare team (Campbell and McDaniel 2000). A family conference can be a useful format for exploring the complex caregiving issues involved in chronic health conditions. In the family-centered approach, a practitioner solicits family members' perspectives on how the patient is doing and how the caregiver is doing in providing care. This approach recognizes that the caregiver's concerns may adversely affect the ability to provide long-term care for the patient. Many family-oriented primary care clinicians provide care for the patient's extended family, including family caregivers, as their physical and psychological health can seriously impact the health, well-being, and living situation of the elder (McDaniel et al. 2005).

As noted earlier, a caregiver may experience adverse health and mental health conditions related to providing care for the chronically ill. The following checklist reflects those factors that have been found to increase caregiver burden (Houlihan 1987; McDaniel et al. 2005). It can be used to evaluate or monitor a patient and his/her caregivers. No one factor should be seen necessarily as predicting an unmanageable situation, but taken together the factors may be able to assess or predict the degree of burden (Table 1).

In the case as Anna described earlier, her mother was highly dependent on her. Anna felt guilty about her anger and resentment toward her mother, they had a history of conflict; Anna had her own history of illness—including periods of depression, she had little personal time away from caregiving, she had little respite from other family members in taking care of her mother, there were other family problems—especially with regard to her marriage, and her son also had problems requiring caregiving. In sum, at the time of her referral for family therapy, Anna was experiencing symptoms of her own related to significant caregiving burden.

The existing literature focuses on the care of one family member and usually describes a dyadic relationship (e.g., a parent caring for a child or a spouse caring for a spouse). However, families like Anna's, or those with genetic conditions or HIV-affected families, for example, frequently have two or more family members coping with disease. For many families as well, the need to provide care to multiple family members occurs because ill members are in the same age cohort.

Table 1 Predicting the burden of family caregivers. (McDaniel et al. 2005)

Caregiver burden increases when
The patient
Is demented and/or disruptive
Is highly dependent on the caregiver
The caregiver
Feels guilty about his/her anger and resentment towards the patient
Has had a conflictual relationship with the patient prior to patient's illness
Does not understand much about the patient's problems or condition
Has his/her own illness and/or disability
Is depressed, isolated, or lonely
Has poor relationships with other family members
Has little personal time away from caregiving
The family
Denies the patient's diagnosis
Leaves most of the caregiving to one person
Is in conflict
Has few financial resources
Has conflictual relationships with the medical providers
The community does not have
Adult day care programs or respite care
Family psychoeducation and support groups
Psychological and family therapy services

Case Illustration

Mrs. Paul, 60 years old, cared for her husband throughout his three-year battle with colon cancer. A colostomy was performed, the cancer staged, and for the next 3 years, Mr. Paul was engaged in a complex combination of radiation and chemotherapy treatments complimented by palliative care. During this time, he continued to work, as his health allowed. During the last 2 months of Mr. Paul's life, the medical treatment regimen was curtailed and he received in-home hospice care until his death. As she became her husband's primary caregiver, Mrs. Paul's life was dramatically altered. Her three adult children commuted home, as often they were able, from their respective jobs in other cities. The majority of Mr. Paul's care was delivered at a comprehensive cancer center 6 h from his home, while the local hospital provided interim care. As a result, the family had to deal with two separate oncology care teams as well as the primary care team.

A month before Mr. Paul was diagnosed, Mrs. Paul's father was also diagnosed with colon cancer. Mrs. Paul commuted regularly to Florida to help her mother care for her ailing father until his death. Soon after her father's death, Mrs. Paul's maternal uncle (with whom she was very close) and her uncle's wife died within 6 months of each other. Simultaneously, Mrs. Paul's mother developed Alzheimer's disease. On the day of Mrs. Paul's husband's death, her mother was hospitalized in an intensive care unit following major abdominal surgery. Subsequently, her mother suffered a heart attack followed by a series of transient ischemic attacks and was hospitalized and then transferred to a tertiary care center for open heart surgery. After the surgery, she was transferred to a rehabilitation facility in another city. During this time, Mrs. Paul's mother received care in institutions that were 7 h drive from Mrs. Paul's home. Currently, Mrs. Paul's mother is located nearby in a nursing home, but her condition continues to deteriorate.

Mrs. Paul has not had a break in complex caregiving functions in over 4 years in addition to the multiple losses that she has experienced. It appears that "complicated caregiving" might more accurately capture the realities of caregivers like Mrs. Paul, who are caring for more than one family member simultaneously. These complicated caregiving roles impose great physical and emotional demands on the caregiver. Complicated grieving describes the occurrence of closely timed losses that result in an individual being challenged to address the loss issues from multiple deaths (Doka 1989, 2000). As evidenced in this case, the challenges of complicated caregiving are influenced by the related challenges of complicated grieving. As a person experiences losses and deaths that occur close together, coping and adaptation skills are strained. The balance between caregiver needs and those of ill family members is difficult to maintain, and the resulting fallout may result in the need for institutional care of a family member. Many families experience such simultaneous care demands (McDaniel SH, Doherty WJ and Hepworth J, 2014).

While the need for family-oriented approaches is, therefore, widely called for, few primary care providers are able to deliver this model of care in today's managed care environment (McDaniel et al. 2005). Further, many practitioners have not been trained to address nor are they exposed to integrated mental health and primary care service models of practice. Custodial care is generally not valued as a focal point of healthcare delivery despite the fact that it is integral to the successful implementation of care for individuals with chronic conditions across the lifespan (Levine 1999). In addition, models of primary care practice do not uniformly incorporate the provision of on-site mental health services. Currently, there is no general measure that delineates primary care physician (PCP)/mental health practitioner (MHP) care patterns or collaboration for a particular provider or primary care site (Gerdes et al. 2001). Researchers have suggested the need to specify the nature of the PCP/MHP relationship in order to explain outcome variance. In addition, mental health services are generally not readily available to ethnic and racial minorities (DHHS 1999).

Education and Training

While collaborative relationships between primary care providers and mental health providers should play a central role in the assessment and care of the mental health of caregivers, primary care practitioners have varying levels of training in addressing the mental health needs of caregivers. The importance of collaboration between primary care and mental health care providers is well recognized (Kates et al. 1997). Primary care providers serve as the gatekeeper for mental health services that may be greatly beneficial to the caregiver.

There are unique differences between primary care mental health services and traditional mental health services (Frank et al. 2004). The primary distinction is that primary care mental health services are provided on site versus traditional mental health services where the provider refers a patient to an outside agency. Consumers report being more comfortable and feeling less stigmatized when receiving mental health services at a primary care setting (Kates et al. 2000). Primary care providers generally have easy access to caregivers and can facilitate the delivery of mental health care to them.

The education and training of primary care providers varies in its emphasis on addressing mental health issues in the primary care setting. Providers' comfort with and training in regard to addressing mental health issues vary considerably across subspecialties. Equally important is the primary care provider's preparation in functioning as a member of an interdisciplinary team. It appears that the culture, training and practice environment of family medicine also fosters greater provider readiness to detect and treat mental disorders and to refer caregivers to mental health specialists for consultation (Gerdes et al. 2001). However, a large proportion of mental health care (this number is closer to about a third (20 states or so still have/use carve-outs)) in this country is currently delivered through managed care carveouts rather than through integrated health systems (Frank and Garfield 2007; Gerdes et al. 2001). Mental health carveouts unfortunately present organizational, financial, and communication barriers to collaboration (Yuen et al. 1999). There needs to be full integration between primary care and mental health service delivery systems.

Family-centered care is one of the principles of best practices for CSHCN, and Congress has emphasized the importance of family-centered care. Families are the recognized experts in the care of their children. Patterson and Hovey (2000) acknowledge:

> There are excellent training curricula in schools of medicine, nursing, public health, social work, and education; continuing education programs for existing professionals; an increased number of consumer conferences and organizations to keep parents apprised of their rights and to develop their savvy as advocates; and federal and state legislation to guarantee needed resources. (p. 238)

Mental health professionals (psychologists, social workers, and nurses) benefit from an enhanced understanding of team dynamics and collaborative practice models due to their in-depth training. The biopsychosocial model provides a framework for all professionals delivering comprehensive care to the chronically ill. This model is widely used in medicine, social work, psychology, and nursing, and advocates for early involvement of family members in patient care (McDaniel et al. 2005). Providers need to recognize that they have attitudes and biases toward the aged, the chronically ill, and the disabled that they must examine and assess for their impact on the provider's delivery of care (McDaniel et al. 2005). It is also critical that MHP collaborators develop collaboration implementation strategies sensitive to specific provider specialties and cultures (Campbell and McDaniel 2000; McDaniel et al. 1995), and collaborative efforts that depend both on organizational care patterns and personal relationships among providers.

Research

There has not been extensive research done regarding the impact on a caregiver's mental health in providing care for an individual with chronic conditions, to date, the majority have focused on deleterious effects. Positive aspects of caregiving on the caregiver's mental health deserve assessment. Donelan et al. (2002) study of informal caregivers reported that their caregiver experiences had a positive influence on their life and their relationships with those they care for; 71 % reported an improved relationship with the care recipient, and 89 % said that the person expressed appreciation. Further assessment of both positive and negative effects of caregiving on mental health is needed. Some family members may find it very rewarding while others experience it differently. We do have knowledge in select areas, including children and elderly family members with chronic conditions; an emerging area is caring for someone as they are dying.

Three decades of epidemiological and clinic-based studies of children with chronic conditions (Cadman et al. 1995; Raina et al. 2005; Silver et al. 1995; Thompson and Gustafson 1996) have reported that mothers predominantly act as primary caregivers and that they are at risk for secondary mental health problems. Mothers with chronically ill children, with the highest levels of perceived stress, were apt to have shorter telomere length, indicative of premature aging at the cellular level on average of at least one decade of additional aging, compared to low stress mothers (Ebel et al. 2004). Raina et al. (2005), found that the physical and psychological health of caregivers of children with cerebral palsy, who were primarily mothers, was strongly influenced by child behavior and caregiving demands.

A randomized clinical trial of a community-based family support intervention for mothers of children with chronic illness found that mothers in the intervention group had less anxiety (Ireys et al. 2001). Family support intervention in this study improved mental health status of the mothers. Less is known about the effects on fathers or grandparents who are increasingly raising their grandchildren.

Studies also indicate that the popular notion of American families abandoning their elderly parents is largely a myth (Brody 1985). Most elderly are cared for in the community, not in nursing homes. About two out of three older persons in the community (67 %) rely solely on informal help, mainly from wives and adult daughters (Stone 2000). A family member accompanied 26 % of elderly patients in the Direct Observation of Primary Care study (Medalie et al. 1998), and the vast majority of individuals with chronic conditions are cared for in the home rather than in institutional settings. Brown et al. (2003) found that mortality was significantly reduced for individuals who provided instrumental support to friends, relatives, and neighbors along with individuals who reported providing emotional support to their spouse. Unfortunately, the researchers did not quantify the amount of caregiving provided in their operational definition of instrumental support.

In caring for the elderly, the vast majority of research has centered on the experience of the female caregiver. Husbands are severely under-represented in interventions designed for caregiver support (Russell 2001; Toseland and Rossiter 1989). However, several trends are likely to put increasing demands on caregiving men (Kaye and Applegate 1990). Men experience less physical and emotional stress, tend to use outside assistance better and do not use support groups (Russell 2001). Male and female caregivers utilize different supports, and interventions should be designed with this in mind (Kramer 1999; Russell 2001). In addition, Kramer (2000) reports that interventions should be designed with couples in mind as opposed to focusing on individual caregivers.

Family caregivers often have their lives turned upside down in caring for their loved one (Fisher 1998). Caregivers have poorer mental health outcomes than their peers (Williamson et al. 1998). Covinsky et al. (2003) studied a range of characteristics of a large, geographically and ethnically diverse population of caregivers of patients with moderate or advanced dementia and noted that a third of the more than 5,000 caregivers reported six or more symptoms of depression. Haley (1997) reported that caregivers of Alzheimer's patients experience two to three times greater levels of depression as those in their age group. About 46–79 % of caregivers are clinically depressed with more women providing caregiving and acknowledging being depressed (Cohen 1990; Family Caregiver Alliance 2000; Mohamed, Rosenheck, Lyketsos, and Schneider, 2010). Elderly caregivers who experience mental and emotional strain related to caregiving are more likely to have higher mortality rates than their noncaregiving counterparts (Schulz and Beach 1999). Cooper et al. (2003) found a differential rate of family caregiver acceptance of antidepressant medication with significantly lower acceptance among African-American and Hispanic caregivers than non-Hispanic Caucasians.

Research also indicates that caregivers often care for more than one family member. For example, in many families, the reality of HIV disease is that more than one family member is infected. One or both parents as well as one or more of the children may be HIV infected. In these families, children often function as caregivers for their parents and siblings. These children remain largely outside the purview of the HIV care providers. The children assume adult roles prematurely. As a result, little is known about their reality, and few services are extended to HIV-affected youth caring for other family members. The stigma of HIV disease further isolates them from community support (Itin et al. 2004).

Practice interventions for caregivers include psychoeducational interventions to alleviate caregiver stress. Interventions to assist caregivers have tended to be individualistic in nature, e.g., counseling, education, and/or support groups versus systemic change (Hooyman and Gonyea 1999). Such interventions can help in a number of ways, e.g., knowledge about available resources, coping strategies, connection to other caregivers, and ways to address stress in other parts of caregivers' lives. Yet research suggests that the overall stress of caregiving is not reduced (Abel 1991; Smith et al. 1991). Similarly, support groups for caregivers focus on individual competence without altering structurally based gender inequities in care responsibilities; nor do they necessarily serve to increase the funding and development of appropriate, accessible, and affordable services (Abel and Nelson 1990; Hooyman and Gonyea 1999). The United Hospital's Fund Family Caregiving Grant initiative, which awarded funds to seven New York hospitals to design and implement programs to assist family caregivers is one of the first of its kind and provides a good range of models for health care institutions interested in providing this kind of help (Levine

2004). Levine initiated a project, *Inventing the Wheel*, aimed at improving interactions between healthcare providers and family caregivers (Becker 2006). Community resources are being developed to support family caregivers.

Caring for someone as they are dying, adds another dimension to the caregiver's role. Family members become the untrained, untutored carers who so willingly shoulder immense responsibilities, doing something they have never done before, every action, every day colored by the knowledge that soon they will lose the one they love (Doyle 1994; Jacobs 2006). Caregiving at the end of life is characterized by difficulty, uncertainty, and a frequent lack of support from the health care system (Zuckerman 2004). With death comes grieving, exacerbating the caregiver's burden. In recent years, the World Health Organization has recognized the health and well-being of family caregivers in their concept of palliative care (Sepulveda et al. 2002). Despite this, Osse et al. (2006) reported that family caregiver's needs are rarely assessed systematically.

As noted earlier, family-centered care envisions the family as the unit of care, taking into account not only the needs of the identified patient, but the caregiver's needs as well. Unfortunately, a family-centered approach to the care of chronic conditions remains largely outside of mainstream primary care. Focus groups at the United Hospital Fund report that family members lack basic information about the patient's diagnosis, prognosis, and treatment plan; potential medicinal side effects; and whom to call when problems arise (Levine 1998). Perhaps as a consequence, clinicians have difficulties with family members regarding acute care decision-making (Levine and Zuckerman 1999), while family members want increased communication respectful of their roles in the patient's life. Fear and anxiety may also complicate the learning of new tasks, e.g., operating a feeding tube.

Future Directions

Policy Reform

Caregiving is an important societal function and should be recognized as such. Policy makers are beginning to recognize the critical role families play in the provision of long-term care and are addressing family-related matters that historically were thought to be too private for a public response (Feinberg 1997). As the numbers of chronically ill family members increase, existing care gaps will tend to increase. Is caring for the chronically ill primarily the family's responsibility? Are there ways to develop collective solutions addressing the underlying structural factors (Hooyman and Gonyea 1999)? Today, the care of the chronically ill is still considered primarily the responsibility of individual families. The gaps in care and support for the chronically ill and their caregivers are creating a need for reevaluation, and a groundswell of public support. The trajectory of current managed care is in direct conflict with efforts to increase familial support. The National Family Caregiver Support Program created a paradigm shift that incorporates the explicit inclusion of family caregivers of long-term care reform (Feinberg and Newman 2004).

Callahan (1994) argued that, for treatment of chronic conditions, the emphasis should be on care, not cure. In caring for the chronically ill, care options should support community-based models of care that are less costly than institutional care. Current social policies provide few financially feasible options to institutional care (Kramer 2000). Long-term care in the community by family members is assumed to be preferable to institutionalization (Hooyman and Gonyea 1999), but policies have focused on the dependent individual, not on those who provide care (Osterbusch et al. 1987). Existing long-term care policies are based on the social welfare model where government interventions are provided as a last resort. The Nationally Family Caregiver Support Program provides respite, information, and referral and counseling through local Agencies on Aging is beginning to address some of these shortcomings. Implementation of this program varies widely from state to state. Whittier et al. (2005) examined the scope and range of resources for family caregivers from the perspective of Area Agencies on Aging (AAA) and reported a need for enhanced efforts to improve the service network for supporting family caregivers.

Reform is needed on a number of fronts. There needs to be a lifespan approach that incorporates culturally competent care that is accessible in a variety of venues, e.g., the patient's home, doctors' offices, neighborhood health centers, clinics, and hospitals. It is evident that both patients and caregivers benefit from mental health services in coping with a chronic condition, and not just the patient. Parity for mental health care coverage was passed through federal legislation in 2008, although, mental health remains stigmatized. Health and mental health services are differentially available to racial and ethnic groups (AHRQ, 2005). Health care reform efforts should consider reimbursing family health care with a preventive orientation and relational-centered mental health services on the same basis as physical care (Rolland 1993).

It is clearly inadequate to assess only the individual who needs care and there is growing emphasis on systematically assessing the needs of caregivers. In the absence of a unified federal policy, states are selectively responding to the challenges of caregiving. California, Massachusetts, Minnesota, Pennsylvania, and Washington have taken the lead in developing plans that assess the needs of the family caregivers to guide the development of services (Fox-Grage and Gibson 2006). Partnerships are emerging between the aging services networks and area health care systems to enhance the support available to caregivers. This shift to a more family-centered perspective in assessing needs and delivering services appears to be a promising approach for increasing the well-being of both individual care recipient and family caregivers (Fox-Grage and Gibson 2006).

Beyond parity of health and mental health benefits, there are concerns about where mental health services are delivered. As noted previously, racial and ethnic minorities are reluctant to access traditional mental health services. The US Surgeon General has recommended that mental health be integrated into primary care settings to increase access to care (DHHS 1999). The supplement noted that many minority individuals prefer to receive mental health care in primary care settings (DHHS 2000). Paid services frequently complement and strengthen informal care provided by family caregivers (Litwak et al. 1994). Thus, it seems reasonable to provide supports that will assist family members in continuing to provide care within their homes. This approach appears to be cost-effective and more favorable on a multitude of levels as institutional care is the most costly care option. Long-term care requires a more expansive focus that incorporates the needs of caregivers utilizing a lifespan approach. The long-term costs associated with not only the care for the chronically ill but also the long-term effects on the mental and physical health of the caregivers will be significantly greater if changes are not made to the current mode of providing care to our chronically ill.

As a consequence of cost containment efforts, families are transformed into caregivers with little preparation or financial support (Levine 2004). Services for caregivers require increased financial support in both health care funding and social security. Restructuring Medicare can help to meet the long-term needs of the elderly and disabled, as well as address the creation of a more flexible range of options for home and community-based care (Cassell et al. 1999). The ongoing decline in government support of public funding for the provision of long-term care in the community is a major threat to our ability to accomplish community-based care. Hooyman and Gonyea (1999) call for the modification of the Social Security System to recognize the economic value of years devoted to caregiving, e.g., a caregiver wage or attendant allowance. There is bipartisan support for legislation providing a tax-credit of $ 3000/year for caregivers as well as caregiver support grants for states. However, legislative enactment is being held hostage by politics (Levine 2000). Caring for dependent relatives is socially important work that must be supported with public resources and shared by both men and women (Sipla and Simon 1993). A critical challenge is to ensure that family support is an explicit objective of all federal and state long-term care policies and programs (Feinberg 2004).

Practice

Family caregivers are essential members of the health care team (McDaniel et al. 2005). The collaborative family healthcare (CFH) model envisions a collaborative relationship between patients, family members, and the healthcare team (Campbell and McDaniel 2000; McDaniel, Doherty, and Hepworth, 2013). Families and health care team members need training in this approach. The CFH approach fosters innovation by changing how services are delivered and what services are available to meet the needs of caregiving members. As McDaniel et al. (2005) advocate, family-oriented clinicians need to monitor patients and their caregivers in order to continually assess and attempt to reduce the burden of care. Routine visits provide an opportunity for this ongoing evaluation, as the caregiving burden is usually shouldered unevenly by family members and may change over the course of prolonged illness.

Men and women alike need support in their caregiving roles, and caregivers benefit from connection with community supports that help families to function most effectively. Where possible, providers should support the use of natural help systems rather than relying exclusively on professionals (Hooyman and Gonyea 1999).

Levine (2003) advises physicians to ask patients about their caregiving responsibilities, treat caregiver depression, or make appropriate referrals and provide information about community resources. Given that caregiving roles vary among ethnic and racial groups, education needs to occur within the cultural context of the caregiver's beliefs and values. In particular, there need to be adequate community services available that are culturally appropriate. Family-centered care models and feminist practice models position families and service providers as partners in tailoring services to best serve the chronically ill individual and his/her caregivers. The practitioner involved in a true advocacy role would focus on quality of care issues at both the individual family level and at the system level (Challis 1994).

Rather than wait until a family asks for help, which almost always happens when they are in crisis (Family Caregiver Alliance 1990), scheduling predictable, preventive contacts with a health care professional can help both caregivers and patients diffuse problems (Altilio and Rigogliso 2004). Family members benefit when clinicians assess the health and functioning of family caregivers, even when these family members are not the clinician's patients (McDaniel et al. 2005). The American Medical Association's (2006) Caregiver Self-Assessment Tool is a simple checklist that can be used to initiate a conversation about depression. Parks and Novielli (2000) note that family physicians can have a significant impact on the health and well-being of caregivers. However, given the current climate, this is rarely the reality, but can be a vision for the future. We are hopeful that family medicine practitioners and other primary care practitioners who care for individuals with chronic conditions will also consider the physical and mental health needs of their patients' caregivers.

Education and Training

As previously noted, we gain a very different perspective when we view a chronically ill person, not in isolation, but as an integral member of an extended family. Levine (1999) notes that "the attitudes, behavior and decisions of specific individuals make the system work or fail for me" (p. 1587). She provides direction for the training and preparation of health care providers who work with chronically ill individuals and their families.

While population health may potentially trigger a return to more limiting, less effective models of care and education, it also affords the opportunity to reevaluate what the medical profession considers to be essential to its work (Saba 2000). All faculties responsible for training health professionals should critically review the drive for cost-containment under managed care. The biomedical model does not tell the complete story regarding a person's health status. Since chronic conditions are longstanding, practitioners and their patients will benefit from more holistic training that incorporates the family into the treatment team. Altilio and Rigoglioso (2004) call for expanded advocacy by the health care team to ensure that patients and their families obtain benefits, discharge planning, and education and support.

Research from a Family-Centered Perspective

Building on the earlier discussion, future research efforts would benefit from a more rigorous conceptualization of caregiving coupled with an expansive assessment of health indicators utilizing multidimensional outcome indicators (George and Gwyther 1986; Kramer 1997). Caregiving has a positive impact on the caregiver's wellbeing and a greater understanding of this will be useful in designing interventions to facilitate coping and adaptation.

While children are not expected to be caregivers, in reality, they often are. These children, acting as caregivers for their parents and/or siblings, deserve study, as more information is needed about the realities of youthful caregiving. Specific to HIV/AIDS, more information is needed regarding the combined impact of caregiving and the unfortunate reality of AIDS-related deaths on the development of HIV-affected youth (Itin et al. 2004). Levine et al. (2005) analyzed two national studies (from 1998 to 2004) and reported that young adults aged 18–25 years who are caregivers for ill, elderly, or disabled family members or friends make up to 12 and 18 % of the total number of adult caregivers who had a variety of unmet needs in caring for another person. Many of these young adult caregivers were men and they may have unique needs.

Caregiving should be seen as a risk factor when assessing the caregiver's medical and mental health. The health of the caregiver also affects the ability to keep the affected family member within the community. Beyond assessing the impact on the family member who takes on the role of primary caregiver, one needs to evaluate the impact of this caregiver's role on other family members. For example, how are siblings impacted when one child either becomes chronically ill (Fanos 1996) or takes on the role of caregiver?

Future intervention studies designed to reduce caregiver stress need to incorporate both a couple and a family focus. Caregivers identify and want to talk about the positive aspects of caring for a loved one (Donelan et al. 2002; Kramer 1997; Russell 2001). Caregiving experiences and outcomes influence the total family's functioning and well-being, not just that of the identified caregiver.

In summary, the roles, education and training, and combined collaborative efforts of caregivers, primary care providers, and mental health providers, all need to be taken into consideration when dealing with chronic medical illness. The financial, physical, and emotional disparities fall greatly on those family members, typically women, who are providing the in home care and often times not only for the chronically ill family member but also for others as well. Future research needs to continue to explore both the positive, as well as the negative, impacts on family members caring for their chronically ill relatives. In addition, the burdens placed on such individuals need to be lessened by creating greater services for these families to support them financially, physically, and emotionally in this growing segment of our aging society.

Acknowledgement Preparation of this paper was supported in part by a grant from Project on Death in America.

References

Abel, E. (1991). *Who cares for the elderly? Public policies and the experiences of adult daughters*. Philadelphia: Temple University Press.

Abel, E., & Nelson, M. (1990). *Circles of care: Work and identity in women's lives*. Albany: State University of New York Press.

Agency for Healthcare Research and Quality. (2005). National healthcare disparities report. http://archive.ahrq.gov/qual/nhdr05/nhdr05.htm

Altilio, T., & Rigoglioso, R. (2004). Social workers, the health care team, and caregiver advocacy. In C. Levine (Ed.), *Always on call* (pp. 149–165). Nashville: Vanderbilt Press.

American Medical Association Caregiver Self-Assessment Tool (2006). http://www.ama-assn.org/ama/pub/physician-resources/public-health/promoting-healthy-lifestyles/geriatric-health/caregiver-health/caregiver-self-assessment.page. Retrieved August, 2013.

Arno, P., Levine, C., & Memmott, M. (1999). The economic value of informal caregiving. *Health Affairs*, *18*(2), 182–188.

Bass, D., Noelker, L., & Rechlen, L. (1996). The moderating influence of service use on negative caregiving consequences. *Journal of Gerontology. Series B, Psychological Sciences and Social Sciences*, *51*, S121–131.

Becker, C. (2006, Oct. 23). In search of respect. *Modern Healthcare*, *36*(42), 30–33.

Bengtson, V., Rosenthal, C., & Burton, C. (1996). Paradoxes of families and aging. In R. Binstock & L. George (Eds.), *Handbook of aging and the social sciences* (4th ed., pp. 253–282). San Diego: Academic.

Biegel, D., Sales, E., & Schulz, R. (1991). *Family caregiving in chronic illness: Alzheimer's disease, cancer, heart disease, mental illness, and stroke*. Newbury Park: Sage.

Bloch, D. (1993). The "full-service" model: An immodest proposal. *Family Systems Medicine*, *11*, 1–9.

Brody, E. (1985). Parent care as a normative family stress. *Gerontologist*, *26*, 19–29.

Brown, S., Nesse, R., Vinokur, A., & Smith, D. (2003). Providing social support may be more beneficial than receiving it: Results from a prospective study of mortality. *Psychological Science*, *14*(4), 320–327.

Cadman, D., Rosenbaum, P., Boyle, M., & Offord, D. (1995). Children with chronic illness: Family and parent demographic characteristics and psychosocial adjustment. *Pediatrics*, *87*, 884–889.

Callahan, D. (1994). Setting limits: A response. *Gerontologist*, *34*, 393–398.

Campbell, T., & McDaniel, S. (2000). Consumers and collaborative healthcare. *Families, Systems, and Health*, *18*, 133–136.

Cassell, E., Besdine, F., & Siegel, L. (1999). Restructuring Medicare for the next century: What will beneficiaries really need? *Health Affairs (Millwood)*, *18*(1), 118–131.

Challis, D. (1994). Case management: A review of UK developments and issues. In M. Titterton (Ed.), *Caring for people in the community: The new welfare* (pp. 91–112). London: Jessica Kingsley.

Cohen, D., Luchins, D., Eisdorfer, C., Paveza, G., Ashford, J., Gorelick, P., et al. (1990). Caring for relatives with Alzheimer's disease: The mental health risks to spouses, adult children and other family caregivers. *Behavior, Health, and Aging*, *1*(3), 171–182.

Cooper, L. A., Gonzales, J. J., Gallo, J. J., Rost, K. M., Meredith, L. S., Rubenstein, L. V., & Ford, D. E. (2003). The acceptability of treatment for depression among African-American, Hispanic, and white primary care patients. Medical Care, *41*(4), 479–489.

Covinsky, K. E., Newcomer, R., Fox, P., Wood, J., Sands, L., Dane, K., & Yaffe, K. (2003). Patient and caregiver characteristics associated with depression in caregivers of patients with dementia. *Journal of General Internal Medicine, 18*(12), 1006–1014.

Doka, K. (1989). *Disenfranchised grieving*. New York: Lexington Books.

Doka, K. (2000). *Living with grief*. New York: Hospice Foundation of America.

Donelan, K., Hill, C., Hoffman, C., Scoles, K., Feldman, P., Levine, C., et al. (2002). From the field: Challenged to care: Informal caregivers in a changing health system. *Health Affairs, 21*(4), 222–225.

Doyle, D. (1994). *Caring for a dying relative*. Oxford: Oxford Press.

Ebel, E., Blackburn, E., Lin, J., Dhabar, F., Adler, N., Marrow, J., et al. (2004). Accelerated telomere shortening in response to life stress. *Proceedings of the National Academy of Sciences, 101*(49), 17312–17315.

Family Caregiver Alliance. (1990). *Who's taking care? A profile of California's of brain impaired adults*. San Francisco: Author.

Family Caregiver Alliance. (2000) *California's caregiver resource center system annual report, FY 1999–2000*. San Francisco: Family Caregiver Alliance.

Fanos, J. (1996). *Living with sibling loss*. Mahwah: Lawrence Earlbaum Associates.

Feinberg, L. (1997). *Options for supporting informal and family caregiving*. San Francisco: American Society on Aging.

Feinberg, L. (2004). Caregiving on the public policy agenda. In C. Levine (Ed.), *Always on call* (pp. 193–207). Nashville: Vanderbilt Press.

Feinberg, L., & Newman, S. (2004 Dec). A study 10 states since passage of the national family caregiver support program: Policies, perceptions, and program development. *Gerontologist, 44*(6), 760–769.

Feinberg, L., Newman, S., & Fox-Grage, W. (2005, April). Family caregiver support services: Sustaining unpaid family and friends in a time of public fiscal constraint (Research report). http://www.aarp.org/research/housing-mobility/caregiving/fs112_hcbs.html. Accessed August 2013.

Fisher, I. (1998, June 7). Families providing complex medical care, tubes and all. *The New York Times*, p. 1.

Fox-Grage, W., & Gibson, M. (2006, March). In-brief: Ahead of the curve: Emerging trends and practices in family caregiver support (Research report). Information, resources, and assistance in long-term care. http://www.aarp.org/research/longtermcare/resources/inb120_caregiver.html. Accessed August 2013.

Frank, R., McDaniel, S., Bray, J., & Heldring, M. (2004). *Primary care psychology*. Washington, DC: American Psychological Association.

Frank, R. G., & Garfield, R. L. (2007). Managed behavioral health care carve-outs: Past performance and future prospects. *Annual Review of Public Health, 28*, 303–320.

George, L., & Gwyther, L. (1986). Caregiver well-being: A multidimensional examination of family caregivers of demented adults. *Gerontologist, 26*, 253–S59.

Gerdes, J., Yuen, E., Wood, G., & Frey, C. (2001). Assessing collaboration with mental health providers: The primary care perspective. *Families, Systems, & Health, 19*(40), 429–443.

Graham, J. (1999, January 17). Halfway measures. *Chicago Tribune*.

Greene, K. (2006, July 25). Calls mount for caregiver paid leave. *Wall Street Journal*, D.2.

Haley, W. (1997). The family caregiver's role in Alzheimer's disease. *Neurology, 48*(55 Suppl 6), S25–29.

Hooyman, N., & Gonyea, J. (1999). A feminist model of family care: Practice and policy directions. *Journal of Women and Aging, 11*(2/3), 149–169.

Houlihan, J. (1987). Families caring for frail and demented elderly: A review of selected findings. *Family Systems Medicine, 5*, 344–356.

Hutchins, V., & McPherson, M. (1991). National agenda for children with special needs: Social policy for the 1990s through the 21st century. *American Psychologist, 46*, 141–143.

Ireys, H., Chernoff, R., DeVet, K., & Young, K. (2001). Maternal outcomes of a randomized controlled trial of a community based support program for families of children with chronic illnesses. *Archives Pediatric Adolescent Medicine, 155*, 771–777.

Itin, C., McFeaters, S., & Taylor-Brown, S. (2004). Family Unity Camp for HIV affected families: Creating a family-centered and community building context for interventions that facilitate coping with HIV/AIDS related losses. In J. Berzoff & P. Silverman (Eds.), *End of life care textbook for social workers*. New York: Columbia University Press.

Jacobs, B. (2006). *The emotional survival guide for caregivers—Looking after yourself and your family while helping an aging parent*. New York: Guilford.

Kates, N., Craven, C., Bishop, J., Clinton, T., Kraftcheck, D., LeClair, K., et al. (1997). Shared mental health care in Canada. *Supplement to Canadian Journal of Psychology, 42*, 8.

Kates, N., Crustolo, A., Farrar, S., & Nikolaou, L. (2000). Integrating health services into primary care: Lessons learnt. *Families, Systems, & Health, 19*, 5–12.

Kaye, L., & Applegate, J. (1990). Men as elder caregivers: Building a research agenda for the 1990s. *Journal of Aging Studies, 4*, 289–298.

Kohn, L., Corrigan, J., & Donaldson, M. (Eds.). (2002). *To err is human: Building a safer health system* (Institute of Medicine Report). Washington, DC: National Academy Press.

Koren, M. J. (1986). Home care: Who cares? *New England Journal of Medicine, 314*, 917–920.

Kramer, B. (1997). Gain in the caregiving experience: Where are we? What next? *Gerontologist, 37*(2), 232.

Kramer, B. (1999). Caregiving as a life course transition among older husbands: A prospective study. *Gerontologist, 39*(6), 658–666.

Kramer, B. (2000). Husbands caring for wives with dementia: A longitudinal study of continuity and change. *Social Work, 25*(2), 97–107.

Levine, C. (1998). *Rough crossings: Family caregivers' odysseys through the health care system*. New York: United Hospitals Fund.

Levine, C. (1999). The loneliness of the long-term caregiver. *New England Journal of Medicine, 340*(20), 1587–1590.

Levine, C. (2000, Aug./Sept.). Night shift. *Ms.*, 42–46.

Levine, C. (2003). Depression in caregivers of patients with dementia: A greater role for physicians. *Journal of Geriatric Internal Medicine, 18*, 1058–59.

Levine, C. (2004). *Always on call: When illness turns families into caregivers* (rev. & expanded ed.). Knoxville: Vanderbilt University Press.

Levine, C., & Zuckerman, C. (1999). The trouble with families: Toward an ethic of accommodation. *Annals of Internal Medicine, 130*, 148–152.

Levine, C., Hunt, G., Halper, D., Hart, A., Lautz, J., & Gould, D. (2005). Young adult caregivers: A first look at an unstudied population. *American Journal of Public Health, 95*(11), 2071–2075.

Litwak, E., Jessop, D., & Moulton, H. (1994). Optimal use of formal and informal systems over the life course. In E. Kahana, D. Biegel, & M. Wykle (Eds.), *Family caregiving across the lifespan*. Thousand Oaks: Sage.

Maletta, G., & Hepburn, K. (1986). Helping families cope with Alzheimer's: The physician's role. *Geriatrics, 41*, 81–88.

McDaniel, S., & Cole-Kelly, K. (2003). Gender, couples, and illness: A feminist analysis of medical family therapy. In L. Silverstein & T. J. Goodrich (Eds.), *Feminist family therapy* (pp. 267–280). Washington, DC: American Psychological Association.

McDaniel, S., Campbell, T., & Seaburn, D. (1995). Principles for collaboration between health and mental health providers in primary care. *Family Systems Medicine, 31*, 283–298.

McDaniel, S., Campbell, T., Hepworth, J., Lorenz, A., & Shore, B. (2005). Anticipating loss: Healthcare for older persons and their family caregivers. *Family-oriented primary care* (2nd ed.; pp. 242–260). New York: Springer.

McDaniel, S. H., Doherty, W. J., & Hepworth, J. (2013). Caregiving, end of life, and loss. In *Medical family therapy and integrated care* (pp. 255–273). Washington, D.C.: American Psychological Association.

McDaniel, S. H., Doherty, W. J. & Hepworth, J. (2014). *Medical family therapy and integrated care*, 2nd Ed. Washington, D.C.: American Psychological Association Publications.

Medalie, J. (1999). *Patients and doctors: Life-changing stories from primary care*. Madison: University of Wisconsin Press.

Medalie, J., Zyzanski, S., Langa, D., & Stange, K. (1998). The family in family practice: Is it a reality? *Journal of Family Practice, 46*(5), 390–396.

Mohamed, S., Rosenheck, R., Lyketsos, C. G., & Schneider, L. S. (2010). Caregiver burden in Alzheimer disease: Cross-sectional and longitudinal patient correlates. *American Journal of Geriatric Psych, 18*(10), 917–927.

National Alliance for Caregiving and AARP (2009). Caregiving in the U.S.: A focused look at those caring for someone age 50 or older. Washington, D.C.: National Alliance for Caregiving and AARP.

Newman, D. (2006, June 16). Ensuring carers receive care too. *General Practitioner*, p. 64.

Osse, B., Vernooij-Dassen, M., Schade, E., & Grol, R. (2006). Problems experienced by the informal caregivers of cancer patients and their needs for support. *Cancer Nursing*, *29*(5), 378–388.

Osterbusch, S., Keigher, S., Miller, B., & Linsk, N. (1987). Community care policies and gender justice. *International Journal of Health Services*, *17*, 217–232.

Parks, S., & Novielli, K. (2000, December 15). A practical guide to caring for caregivers. American Family Physician, *62* (12). http://www.aafp.org/afp/2000/1215/p2613.html. Accessed August 2013.

Patterson, J. M., & Hovey, D. L. (2000). Family-centered care for children with special health needs: Rhetoric or reality. *Families, Systems & Health: The Journal of Collaborative Family Health Care*, *18*(2), 237–251.

Pavalko, E., & Artis, J. (1997). Women's caregiving and paid work: Casual relationships in late mid-life. *Journal of Gerontology. Series B, Psychological Sciences and Social Sciences, 52*, S170–179.

Raina, P., O'Donnell, M., Rosenbaum, P., Brehaut, J., Walter, S., Russell, D., et al. (2005). The health and well-being of caregivers of children with cerebral palsy. *Pediatrics*, *115*(6), 1755.

Rolland, J. (1993). *Families, illness and disability*. New York: Basic Books.

Russell, R. (2001). In sickness and in health: A qualitative study of elderly men who care for wives with dementia. *Journal of Aging Studies*, *15*, 351–367.

Saba, G. (2000). Preparing healthcare professionals for the 21st century: Lessons from Chiron's cave. *Families, Systems, & Health*, *18*(3), 356–364.

Schofield, H., Booth, S., Hermann, H., Murphy, B., Nankervis, J., & Singh, B. (1998). *Family caregivers: Disability, illness and aging*. St. Leonards, Australia: Allen & Unwin.

Schulz, R., & Beach, S. (1999). Caregiving as a risk factor for mortality: The caregiver health effects study. *Journal of the American Medical Association*, *282*(23), 2215–2219.

Sepulveda, C., Marlin, A., Yoshida, T., & Ullrich, A. (2002). Palliative care: The World Health Organization's global perspective. *Journal of Pain Symptom Management*, *24*(2), 91–96.

Silver, E., Ireys, H., Bauman, L., & Stein, R. (1995). Psychological outcomes of a support intervention in mothers of children with ongoing health conditions: The Parent-to-Parent Network. *Journal of Community Psychology*, *25*, 249–264.

Sipla, J., & Simon, B. (1993). Home care allowances for the frail elderly: For and against. *Journal of Sociology and Social Welfare*, *20*, 119–134.

Smeeding, T. (1998). Reshuffling responsibility in old age: The United States in comparative perspective. In J. Gonyea (Ed.), *Resecuring Social Security and Medicare: Understanding privatization and risk* (pp. 24–36). Washington, DC: Gerontological Society of America.

Smith, G., Smith, M., & Toseland, R. (1991). Problems identified by family caregivers in counseling. *Gerontologist*, *31*, 15–22.

Stone, R. (1999). Long-term care: Coming of age in the 21st century. In J. Olson & K. Bogenschneider (Eds.), *Wisconsin family impact seminars briefing report: Long-term care-state policy perspectives* (pp. 3–11). Madison: University of Wisconsin-Madison School of Human Ecology.

Stone, R. (2000). *Long-term care for the elderly with disabilities: Current policy, emerging trends, and implications for the twenty-first century*. New York: Milbank Memorial Fund.

Thompson, R., & Gustafson, K. (1996). *Adaptation to chronic illness*. Washington, DC: American Psychological Association.

Toseland, R., & Rossiter, C. (1989). Group interventions to support family caregivers: A review and analysis. *Gerontologist*, *29*, 438–445.

US Department of Health and Human Services. (1999). *Mental health: A report of the Surgeon General*. Washington, DC: Author.

US Department of Health and Human Services. (2000). *Mental health: A report of the Surgeon General* (Supplement). Washington, DC: Author.

US Department of Health and Human Services. Administration on Aging. (2013) State and area agencies on aging. http://www.aoa.gov/AOARoot/AoA_Programs/OAA/How_To_Find/Agencies/Agencies.aspx. Accessed Aug 2013.

Whittier, S., Scharlach A., & Dal Santo, T. (2005). Availability of caregiver support services: Implications for implementation of the National Family Caregiver Support Program. *Aging Social Policy, 17* (1) 45–62.

Williamson, G., Shaffer, D., & Schulz, R. (1998). Activity restriction and prior relationship history as contributors to mental health outcomes among middle-aged and older spousal caregiver. *Health Psychology, 17*(2), 152–62.

Yuen, G., Gerdes, J., & Waldfogel, S. (1999). Linkages between primary care physicians and mental health specialists. *Families, Systems, and Health, 17*, 285–308.

Zuckerman, C. (2004). Til death do us part: Family caregiving at the end of life. In C. Levine (Ed.), *Always on call* (pp. 176–189). Nashville: Vanderbilt Press.

Further Reading

AARP, 601 E St., NW, Washington, DC 20049, Phone: 1–800-424-3410. http://www.aarp.org/cargive/home.html.

A portrait of informal caregivers in America, 2001: Caregivers are a population at risk. http://www.facct.org/facct=/site/facct/facct/hom.

Alzheimer's Association, Find Your Chapter. http://www.alz.org.

Caregiver-Information.com. http://www.caregiver-information.com.

Chronic Conditions: Making the Case for Ongoing Care, (2002 Dec.). *Chronic care chartbook.* A joint project of Johns Hopkins University and The Robert Wood Johnson Foundation estimates that 9.4 million caregivers of all ages were providing at least 24 hours of care per week in the US in 1998. More detailed statistics are on the website: www.partnershipforsolutions.org.

Eldercare Online. http://www.ec-online.net.

Fraidin, L., Glajchen, M., & Portenoy, R. (2000). *The caregiver resource directory: A practical guide for family caregivers.* Available from The Department of Pain Medicine and Palliative Care, Beth Israel Medical Center, First Avenue at 16th St., NY, NY 10003. http://www.stoppain.org.

Generations United, a national coalition dedicated to intergenerational policy, programs, and issues. http://www.gu.org/.

Grandparent Caregiver Law Center, Brookdale Center on Aging of Hunter College, 275 State St. Albany, NY 12210 Phone: (518) 434-4571. http://www.brookdale.org/gpc/.

Living with Advanced Lung Disease and *Living with Advanced Congestive Heart Failure*. Produced by the RAND Center to Improve Care of Dying. www.medicaring.org.

The Families and Health Care Project. United Hospital Fund. http://www.uhfnyc.org/.

US Administration on Aging—Caregiver Resources. http://www.aoa.dhhs.gov/caregivers/default.htm.

United Hospital Fund. http://www.uhfnyc.org/.

Part II
The Mental Health Caregiving Context

Mental Illness Prevention and Promotion

William R. Beardslee and Tracy R. G. Gladstone

The research discussed in this paper is based on the Preventive Intervention Project at the Judge Baker Children's Center, Boston. This research has been conducted with the support of NIMH Grant RO1MH48696, The William T. Grant Foundation, and a Faculty Scholar Award of the William T. Grant Foundation to Dr. Beardslee.

There has been a remarkable growth of high quality empirical studies in the prevention of mental illness and the promotion of mental health over the past three decades. A series of reports (Institute of Medicine (IOM) 1994; National Advisory Mental Health Council Workgroup 2001; Beardslee & Gladstone 2004) has documented progress in the prevention of mental illness. More recently, the Institute of Medicine issued two new reports, one focused entirely on the prevention of emotional and behavioral disorders in youth (National Research Council and Institute of Medicine 2009a) and another with a specific focus on parental depression (National Research Council and Institute of Medicine 2009b). This progress has occurred through the definition of a set of rigorous standards for the conduct of research in prevention (e.g., testing of theoretically driven hypotheses, use of valid assessment instruments, blind assessment of subjects separate from intervention delivery, evaluation of outcomes over the long term, etc.), primarily using randomized trial designs. Yet, against the backdrop of successfully conducted prevention trials and efforts to promote mental health, virtually nothing has been written about the needs of caregivers who engage

W. R. Beardslee (✉)
Judge Baber Children's Center, Principal Investigator, TEAMS,
Children's Hospital, 53 Parker Hill Avenue, Boston, MA, USA
e-mail: william.beardslee@childrens.harvard.edu

Children's Hospital Boston, 21 Autumn Street, Boston, 02115 MA, USA

T. R. G. Gladstone
Director, Robert S. and Grace W. Stone Primary Prevention Initiatives,
Wellesley Centers for Women, Wellesley College, 106 Central Street,
Wellesley, 02481 MA, USA
e-mail: tgladsto@wellesley.edu

R. C. Talley et al. (eds.), *The Challenges of Mental Health Caregiving*,
Caregiving: Research • Practice • Policy, DOI 10.1007/978-1-4614-8791-3_5,

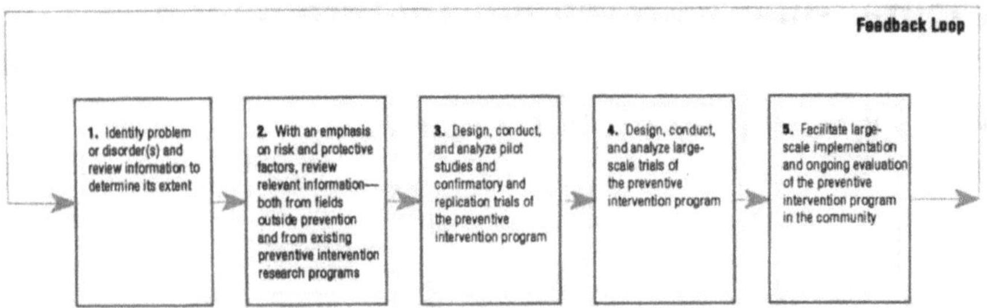

Fig. 1 The preventive intervention research cycle. (Institute of Medicine 1994)

in prevention and health promotion and, in particular, what kinds of special supports they need. Caring for caregivers in prevention settings is absolutely essential to the success of preventive intervention efforts to date and will be even more important if such efforts are to be widely implemented in large-scale programs.

Efforts at Prevention and Health Promotion

Typically, preventive interventions move through an orderly sequence of stages based first on the identification of risk and resilience, on more detailed knowledge of protective resources and vulnerability factors, through pilot studies, efficacy trials, effectiveness trials, and finally through large scale programs (see Fig. 1).[1] Each of these phases influences one another. Perhaps the most successful program to follow this model over the last half century has been Head Start. Similar large-scale efforts have been employed in smoking prevention.

A wide range of prevention strategies used at different points across the life span have shown considerable merit. These programs adopt a public health approach, and we believe that addressing large scale public health issues is essential if we have to address the prevention of mental health concerns (Institute of Medicine 1994; National Research Council and Institute of Medicine 2009a; World Health Organization 2004). For example, during pregnancy and early in the life of the developing child, high quality interventions focused on improving the mental and physical health of both the child and the mother are quite efficacious. The Nurse Home Visitation Program has shown effects on both mothers and developing children some fifteen years after implementation (Olds et al. 1997; Olds et al. 2007). Similarly, there is excellent evidence about the value of high quality daycare (Berrueta-Clement et al. 1984). These approaches provide support for the broader programmatic initiatives such as Head Start and Early Head Start. As children move through the life span into adolescence, empirically based trials have shown promising results, including

[1] The National Advisory Mental Health Council Workgroup on Child and Adolescent Mental Health Intervention Development and Deployment. *Blueprint for change: Research on child and adolescent mental health*. Washington, D.C.: 2001.

approaches for drug abuse prevention and community wide approaches to antisocial behavior (Hawkins et al. 2008; Hawkins et al. 1992). The value of social skills training, particularly for those at high risk for conduct or interpersonal difficulties, has repeatedly been demonstrated for both grammar and high school students as well (Institute of Medicine 1994; National Research Council and Institute of Medicine 2009a).

Many organizations are now promoting and supporting prevention efforts. The founding of the Society for Prevention Research and its journal, *Prevention*, reflect a growing interest in prevention. In addition, the World Federation for Mental Health has made prevention of mental illness a priority.

Health promotion has a much longer history than prevention. There has been some success in integrating basic public health principles with medical and educational practices. Recent evidence about the value of diet, exercise, smoking cessation, and control of alcohol use in adults has emphasized the value of community-wide approaches to health promotion (Institute of Medicine 1994; National Research Council and Institute of Medicine 2009a). Within pediatrics, the need for regularly scheduled health promotion and well-child visits is well established. Interestingly enough, one of the recent recommendations from the Surgeon General's conference to set an agenda for child mental health was that there should be a similar yearly assessment of the child's psychological and emotional needs (U.S. Dept. of Health and Human Services 2001).

In this presentation, we will first discuss obstacles to prevention and health promotion efforts. We will then relate these obstacles to the need for caregiver support. Subsequently, we will discuss our work on the prevention of depression, illustrating one prevention approach, and we will outline our approach to addressing caregiver needs. Finally, we will outline future directions and provide some concluding remarks. We recognize that our approach is limited, but we believe it illustrates some key principles. In this chapter, we will focus on programs for children and their families and on the staff who work in these programs (i.e., professional caregivers). We recognize the great value of lay and family caregivers and believe that many of the issues we discuss (e.g., lack of support in caring for very ill people) pertain to these individuals, too. We also recognize the important role of professional and family caregivers in the care of chronic mentally ill adults and in the rehabilitation of adults in psychiatric inpatient and outpatient settings. However, to cover all these areas would be beyond the scope of a relatively short chapter.

Obstacles to Preventive Interventions and Health Promotion

Presently, there is a bias among researchers, policy makers, and practitioners toward clinical programs rather than toward prevention. This bias presents obstacles to the implementation of prevention programs. Five characteristics of preventive interventions set them apart from clinical programs, although clinical programs have much in common with prevention programs, and often the same individual delivers both prevention services and clinical services. These characteristics form the core of prevention efforts and also pose difficulties for those supporting caregivers in prevention.

First, preventive intervention is inherently interdisciplinary. It is very difficult to demonstrate the prevention of a serious mental illness over time. The randomized trial designs used to evaluate prevention programs require the enrollment of large numbers of subjects who by definition are not all ill and, therefore, will not change much with the initial delivery of the preventive intervention (Institute of Medicine 1994). Thus, intense, powerful interventions are needed. These often involve multiple domains of intervention drawn from different disciplines simultaneously. Unfortunately, there is a lack of support and training for those working within one particular discipline to employ prevention approaches that require working collaboratively with other disciplines and in settings other than those used for clinical care.

Second, the focus of preventive interventions differs from the focus of clinical care. For clinicians, the primary focus is taking care of someone who comes in with an illness and asks for care. Very often, clinicians' time is consumed by clients in crisis. Prevention requires a very different focus, that is, building strengths and resources that will be useful to the child and the family, 1, 2, 5, and 10 years down the line. When faced with the dilemma of whether to care for someone acutely ill or to focus on prevention, clinicians inevitably will focus on the alleviation of acute suffering and the treatment of current diagnosable illness in the moment of clinical presentation, and rightly so. But to do only this often neglects preventive intervention efforts and does not serve the best interests of the clinician or the child over the long term. We must provide the necessary infrastructure support so that clinicians will be able to focus on the long-term needs of the child, and so that they are rewarded for taking such action.

Third, clinicians are trained in pathology-based models. Yet, the science of understanding healthy child development is the basis for preventive interventions (Beardslee 2000). More generally, understanding health requires the same discipline and spirit of scientific inquiry as pathology, yet far less time is spent either in empirical research or training in clinical disciplines. There is growing awareness of the need for strength-based approaches across the life span in the development of preventive interventions and health promotion (Maton et al. 2002), yet these are often not part of clinical programs.

Fourth, there is a profound societal bias against taking care of the long-term needs of children. Due to the historical absence of national health insurance, incentives for prevention are not nearly as strong in the United States as they are in countries that have national health insurance. Furthermore, even for those with insurance coverage, if a large number of individuals enrolled in a prepaid health plan turn over in a given year, there are no incentives to offer care that might influence the long-term future of the child. The solution to this problem will require systems change. Consideration of prevention in the United States or in any other setting requires supporting health care for all children and their families (Beardslee et al. 2011). The passage of health care reform has already focused attention on prevention, and this focus is likely to expand.

Finally, prevention involves considering large scale public health and public risk factors that often fall outside the domain of a single discipline. For example, risk factors such as exposure to violence have a large impact on the occurrence of depression and yet, those who treat depression generally are neither trained nor believe they have the resources to address ways of reducing violence.

Caring for Caregivers

Attention to the needs of caregivers in prevention requires much further study and the development of both programs and policies to support prevention efforts. Despite differences, one key overlap between prevention and clinical care is that staff in both endeavors is often engaged in very taxing and difficult maneuvers to care for families who face multiple adversities. These, in turn, often stir up feelings and reactions within staff. Attention to the needs of staff is crucially important, often in a group setting. We know from experience in the care of patients with cancer or AIDS that staff members benefit from opportunities to come together and talk about what they encounter and what it stirs up in them.

Unfortunately, to date limited research has focused on improving support and preventing burnout among mental health caregivers. Overall, positive functioning among caregivers, and/or decreased difficulties with burnout, have been associated with administrators who are considerate and friendly with their staff, perceived support from supervisors, reassurance of worth and guidance from supervisors, and peer cohesion and support from colleagues (Leiter and Harvie 1996; Maslach et al. 2001). Informal contacts with colleagues have been found to be particularly helpful to mental health caregivers. In fact, Reid et al. (1999) found that work colleagues were a vitally important source of support for most staff, but that they were most helpful in informal rather than formal support group settings. Staff supervision was reportedly quite helpful, but less than informal support from colleagues. Reid et al. found that more formal psychodynamic staff groups were not well received.

Given the dearth of literature addressing the needs of caregivers, in the following, we offer some reflections based on our own experience in caring for caregivers in a preventive program. We began our support for caregivers in prevention by providing groups for staff members offering preventive services because of Dr. Beardslee's work with staff groups in clinical settings. In particular, Dr. Beardslee and his colleague, Dr. David DeMaso, found that staff groups were helpful for front line caregivers who were dealing with very difficult professional and personal issues because they were working with children with very severe, often life-threatening illnesses, including childhood cancer and brain and spinal cord injuries (Beardslee and DeMaso 1982). In working on a neonatal unit in which about 20 % of the youngsters died before leaving the unit, Beardslee and DeMaso found that having a regular space and time to talk about the feelings engendered in taking care of these very ill children was crucial in order for nurses and other frontline caregivers to function effectively. Such groups offered emotional support, provided an opportunity for people to talk through what they were experiencing and to come to consensus about the mission, and to sort out the personal reactions. Moreover, caregivers struggled with the twin poles of over-involvement and under-involvement. Often, for example, young caregivers would attend the funerals of children they cared for and talk about it. More experienced caregivers would be deeply involved with families and were also able to pace themselves and provide guidance and support to younger caregivers. Also, there were many issues about the systems in which these caregivers worked that were not always working well (i.e., excessive over-time, bureaucratic barriers to care), and being able to talk this through was crucially important. While these programs primarily centered on medical care, the same issues have arisen in developing programs to care for mentally ill patients.

In starting our prevention efforts, we found that these same principles applied to prevention approaches. Caregivers needed to make sense and meaning of terrible difficulties faced by children and their families in order to help them. Prevention often involves, for example, working with groups that have been disadvantaged, are quite poor, or are victimized by violence. An approach that allows the staff to get together, talk about these experiences and find a common ground proved to be as important in prevention as it had been in clinical care.

Prevention of Depression in Children

The area of the prevention of depression has received considerable attention (Beardslee and Gladstone 2001; Gladstone and Beardslee 2009; Munoz et al. 2012), and it is one of the areas most frequently recommended for further prevention efforts. In developing prevention efforts for depression, it is important to understand that there are large, important nonspecific risk factors (e.g., risk factors for depression and for other disorders), as well as risk factors that are specific to depression. Major nonspecific risk factors for depression include exposure to violence or poverty; a major specific risk factor for depression is the presence of first-degree relatives with depression (Gladstone et al. 2011; Yoshikawa et al. 2012). In the Institute of Medicine's report, the risk factors for depression were outlined (see Table 1).[2]

Also, the prevention of depression can be a byproduct of attention to other risk factors. For example, Rick Price et al. (Price et al. 1992, 2002) began developing a jobs-retraining program. As their work evolved, they found that rapid re-employment with a good job was a significant protective factor for depression. Put another way, they found that those who did not become re-employed were at great risk for depression. Similar work by Ricardo Munoz et al. (1995) has indicated the value of a preventive approach for those at risk for depression because of minority status in a general practice. Dr. Sheppard Kellam et al. (1991), in the study of various interventions with children, including one that enhanced reading, showed that those who learned to read had fewer symptoms of depression.

[2] Day Dell Publishing Group, Inc., 1997.

Table 1 Risk factors for the onset of depression. (Institute of Medicine 1994 (modified))

Risk Factors for the Onset of Depression
Having a parent or other close biological relative with a mood disorder
Having a severe stressor such as a loss, divorce, marital separation, unemployment, job dissatisfaction, a physical disorder such as a chronic medical condition, a traumatic experience, or a learning disorder in children
Having low self-esteem, a sense of low self-efficacy, and a sense of helplessness and hopelessness
Being female
Living in poverty
Historical trauma

In the prevention of depression in children, a number of different approaches have merit. Seligman et al. used a classroom-based approach for youngsters with depressive symptomatology (Brunwasser et al. 2009; Seligman 1995), and Clarke, Garber, et al. used a cognitive behavioral approach specifically targeting children of depressed parents who are also manifesting symptoms, first in a single site (Clarke et al. 2001) and then in a four-site replication study that showed substantial preventive effects on episodes of depression, first at nine months (Garber et al. 2009), and then at 33 months (Beardslee et al. in press). Our own approach was a public health prevention approach for families based on increasing understanding (Beardslee et al. 1997a; Beardslee Wright et al. 1997b). Like many prevention approaches, all three of these approaches are built on the principles of enhancing resilience. Seligman's work (Seligman et al. 1995) was built on an understanding of resilience and optimism as an antidote to depression. In work by Clarke, Garber, et al. (Clarke et al. 2001; Garber et al. 2009), a cognitive behavioral approach was offered aimed at cognitive restructuring in order to strengthen the cognitive capacity of the individual. As clearly mentioned below, our own work grew directly from the study of resilient youth whose parents were depressed.

The Preventive Intervention Project: Our Approach

To address the problem of the prevention of depression in children at risk, we devised and tested two manual-based strategies: a clinician-based strategy, and a lecture-based program. Both approaches were designed to enhance the resilience and strength of families coping with parental depression. Based on quantitative analysis of resilient youths of depressed parents (Beardslee and Podorefsky 1988) and also on wide-ranging open-ended interviews, three main characteristics of resilience were identified. First, youngsters who were resilient were deeply involved in extracurricular and school activities and were very much active, in contrast to their parents. The capacity to accomplish age-appropriate developmental tasks is a crucial aspect of resilience and is often threatened by the presence of parental depression because youngsters either don't understand what is going on or don't feel free to leave home. Second, resilient youth were involved deeply in human relationships. These youngsters were deeply committed to friends, family, and extended family. Third, resilient youth possessed the quality of self-understanding. These youngsters described their understandings of themselves and of the illness of their parents as crucial in their being able to deal with their parents' illness. They said knowing that their parents' illness had a name, that it was an illness, and that they were free to go on with their own lives was absolutely critical in their ability to cope.

We devised our prevention intervention strategies for use with a wide range of practitioners from many different disciplines, and we tried to incorporate the core principles of resilience. We provided direct information to parents about resilience, about depression, and about ways to obtain treatment for depression for both parents and children. In our clinician-facilitated approach, we utilized six sessions during which clinicians met with the parent(s) to obtain a history, provided psychoeducational information about depression, met with the children, worked again with parents to prepare for a family meeting, and then assisted parents in conducting a family meeting during which all aspects of depression were discussed and parents were able to talk with children about ways to promote their health. In our lecture approach, we delivered the same information in a two-session group lecture format without children present.

The Preventive Intervention Project: Findings

We demonstrated consistently that both interventions are safe, feasible, do not harm people, and result in sustained behavior and attitude changes in the parents (Beardslee et al. 1997a; Beardslee et al. 1997b). In later analyses following all the families through 2.5 years (Beardslee et al. 2003) and 4.5 years (Beardslee et al. 2007) post-intervention, we found sustained gains from both forms of intervention with the greater gains in parent change in the clinician centered intervention. We also showed a gradual reduction in levels of children's depressive symptoms, and we found both parents and children reported better family functioning. Perhaps most surprisingly, the greater the amount of change that the parents made in response to the intervention, the greater the increase in children's understanding of parental illness. This finding suggests that the interventions increase positive interactions between parents and children (Beardslee et al. 2003; Beardslee et al. 2007).

From our work, we came to understand that depression profoundly disrupts the family's ability to talk together and to make meaning of raising their children (Beardslee 2002). When they understood depression as an illness, they were able to build the resilience of their kids and have some hope; families were able to make meaning of the illness, fit it into a context, and often find their way back to religious faith and to their communities. We also learned that many families eventually took on the capacity to talk together without any intervention from us. We called this process "the emergence of the healer within." After an initial conversation about depression and resilience, families often had many conversations and applied the same strategies to many other issues. In this sense, the parents were caregivers for themselves, their spouses, and for their children. We found that many parents were convinced that they had irrevocably damaged their children. We showed them that they had not, and that there was much that could be done. Over time, we found that parents could learn to be effective parents despite depression, and that they were able to move beyond depression and re-enter the communities and neighborhoods in which they lived. Many found that their religious faith was crucial in dealing with depression. We called this process "making peace and moving on."

The best way to reach families was to provide ways to enhance strengths and resilience in their children. But to get there, families had to go on a journey, and the journey often involved making sense of terrible illnesses and experiences. This orientation that tries to build resources within a family so that they are able to carry on without the constant intervention of a skilled clinician is an important part of prevention.

The Preventive Intervention Project: Partnership with Families

One of the crucial issues in prevention, we learned, is to develop a partnership with families, to move away from the expert and patient model, and to recognize that the ultimate aim of prevention work is to develop the resources and strengths within the individual, the family, and the community. This has been reflected to some extent in the community mental health movement through the empowerment movement and through the recognition that those who have suffered with mental illness in their family members should be part of the governing structure in community boards. Very little has been written about how to get caregivers to engage in a paradigm shift such that they move away from models based on diagnosis and expert treatment and move toward partnerships; yet, this is more and more recognized as essential in prevention work. Most who now are engaged in work with communities or families would endorse a position that says we must find resources within and must make use of processes that are started by preventive interventions and are then self-sustaining. Yet, how this occurs, and how this new orientation can best be facilitated, has received almost no systematic clinical, research, or policy attention.

It is important to note that prevention and health promotion go hand in hand with treatment. They are inseparable. In our work with families, we were dealing with parents who had painful, recurrent illnesses and were trying to prevent illness in their children. We believed that prevention required doing whatever the family needed, and this certainly included maintaining quality treatment for the depressed family member.

It is also important to remember that when exposed to very different adversities (e.g., bereavement, victimization by violence), family members need to talk through and make sense of these experiences before they can move forward and develop new strategies. But timing of intervention is of crucial importance. We recognized that the multiple responsibilities of family members (i.e., caring for children, caring for one another, providing income) sometimes confuse the process of engaging in recovery from the process of developing new strategies that promote family health. We thus learned that it was very important to engage with families at a time when they were not in crisis and had the time and energy to devote to making sense of things. It is important to note that prevention takes place at a different point than does clinical care, which more likely occurs when families are in crisis.

The Preventive Intervention Project: Addressing Caregiver Needs

Our work with the professionals conducting our clinician-facilitated preventive intervention highlighted the importance of attending to caregivers who are focusing on prevention and health promotion. Many caregivers in the professions and in the community are called upon to treat some family members while simultaneously developing prevention for other family members. In simplest terms, this means assisting families in making meaning of the difficulties posed by the illness, and in making arrangements to strengthen non-ill family members so that they are not overcome by adversity. For caregivers who emphasize health promotion and prevention, this dual role can stir up significant feelings that must be addressed so that they can be effective in their care giving role.

Just as we discovered that a narrative approach was helpful in really understanding what went on with families, we also found that such a strategy was very useful in understanding what our prevention staff actually did that was helpful (Beardslee 2002). From the beginning, our efforts as a staff were shared. Our prevention team met weekly and discussed every family that we were working with at length, talking about what would go on in the next session, trying to strategize about how to offer the best prevention. The same kinds of meetings were also beneficial for our team of assessors, who, like the clinical preventionists, were viewed as very helpful. Assessors were trained to take care of clinical emergencies and to provide support for families. The families experienced us as a coordinated and integrated team working together to help them, and this strengthened our prevention approach. Moreover, our staff meetings provided a vital way for caregivers to refresh themselves, think clearly, and to come to a common agenda.

The staff group model proved a crucial part of supporting frontline preventionists by letting caregivers support one another while engaging in a very difficult endeavor. Very often, the families' stories stirred up many feelings and concerns in staff members. Also, there was great uncertainty about what to do to help families when they were faced with the recurrence of a painful and impairing illness like depression. Staff members needed to support families as they struggled to determine what type of intervention was required (e.g., hospitalization). Just as importantly, they needed to support one another. When we took our work into an inner city neighborhood in Boston and engaged primarily with single parent women of the non-dominant culture, we found it was even more important for the staff to meet together and talk (Podorefsky et al. 2001). The level of exposure to violence and life disruption was profound. For example, in one of the families we worked with, the mother experienced depression because her 17 year-old son had been murdered. After his death, she simply stopped reading, stopped being part of the community, and even withdrew from church. Gradually, she resumed these activities. Our ability to talk together as a staff about how horrifying this was, made our ability to help, we think, much greater. Similarly, staff meetings and discussion was very helpful when we adapted our interventions for Latino families, using bicultural and bilingual assessors in an open trial (D'Angelo et al. 2009).

As ours was the first family-based prevention, we were able to engage in best practices, and we gave staff members considerable freedom to intervene with families on their own terms (e.g., at times, they chose to meet them in their homes). Inevitably, caregivers became guides and supporters for the families in a whole set of ways other than simply providing information about depression and resilience. Our staff was comprised of skilled clinicians. When we stopped to look at what we were doing as a staff, we were inevitably confronted with gross inequities and difficulties in the health care system. When we were working in a middle class setting with people with health insurance, often it was very difficult to get care. When we were working in the inner city, it was even more difficult. We concluded that there was a need for reformation so that health care was available to all and that there was equal coverage for mental and physical illness. Thus, a crucial component of staff work in prevention is to understand how systems work to help families, and to understand how to advocate for families when systems do not work. Moreover, the acknowledgement that the systems were dysfunctional helped preventionists see what they could do and what they could not do with individual families.

Staff meetings also enabled us to work together to rethink our professional orientations. Together, we went through the process of learning how to add to our usual clinical orientations (i.e., cognitive-behavioral, psychodynamic, family systems, neurobiological) a preventive, strength-based approach. Finally, we found that meeting regularly and going over the preventive interventions strengthened them.

The Preventive Intervention Project: Challenges for Caregivers

One of the most frustrating experiences for caregivers occurs when efforts at prevention fail. Caregivers often feel betrayed or confused when, despite their best efforts, the illness recurs in a parent, a child develops depression, or a family is unable to implement the tools of the intervention. This is a time when caregivers need additional assistance. Often family members, as well as the staff that works with the family, blame themselves. Feelings of guilt or inadequacy only compound their frustration at an already difficult time and impede everyone's ability to help. The family of the depressed person needs to be reminded that depression can be an intractable illness that sometimes fails to respond to even the best efforts of caregivers and the most advanced treatments currently known to science. In many cases, it is appropriate to reassure caregivers that, despite the frustrating circumstances, their efforts have still been beneficial. Combating the sense of hopelessness at these times is crucial. Caregivers need reassurance that attempts to build resilience are not attempts to encourage fixed traits, and that someone who appears unable to bounce back from adversity at one point may well show resilient traits at another time or in different circumstances. Finally, caregivers need a safe place where they can talk openly about their feelings.

The particular needs of caregivers when a family does not do well are illustrated in the following three family situations. The P. family initially appeared to benefit greatly from the Preventive Intervention Project. The mother's goal in the intervention was to protect her three adolescent daughters from suffering the same legacy of lifelong dysthymia she had suffered. Both parents worked actively with us to promote resilient characteristics in the children, encouraging the girls in outside interests such as sports, and holding family meetings to discuss concerns. When the middle daughter left home to attend college, she inexplicably became depressed. The parents had a hard time understanding why this happened. They blamed themselves for failing to instill sufficient resilient characteristics in their daughter. The staff working with the family also felt discouraged when this seemingly poster family for the Preventive Intervention Project suddenly encountered difficulties.

Even the best prevention programs cannot always prevent illness. In the case of this family, there were a number of other stressful events (academic struggles, a potentially serious medical diagnosis in a sibling) that probably triggered the episode. The most important task initially in working with the parents was to reassure them that they had not done something wrong. Just as some physically fit people go on to develop cardiovascular disease, many offspring of depressed parents (and non depressed parents) do develop depression. Fortunately, this family demonstrated many strengths that enabled them to address the girl's needs. The girl, through her familiarity with the project, recognized her symptoms and sought help right away. Family members were able to support one another and communicate openly. Project staff identified a therapist conveniently located to the girls' college. With these additional supports, the girl was able to recover and resume classes after a short time. Staff members were able to provide this support to the P. family because they understood that the girl's illness did not reflect a failure of staff efforts, they were able to share their frustration with one another, and they had the opportunity to think together strategically about what could be accomplished.

For the S. family, the steady bombardment of stressful life events never allowed them the time to benefit fully from the intervention. This family had fewer emotional resources and, like many families that live in poverty, multiple life stressors. Originally from an Asian country, they lived in relative isolation from family and other sources of support. Furthermore, they came from a culture where mental illness is viewed with great shame. The mother suffered from severe medication resistant depression, and the oldest child in the family was already showing troubling symptoms at age 11. As professional caregivers, our aim was to help them access services for their child and develop a shared understanding of events that was less focused on guilt and blame. At the same time, we needed to adapt our approach so that it was relevant to the experiences, strengths, and cultural issues of this family (Podorefsky et al. 2001). Despite our best efforts, the mother's condition deteriorated to the point that she required multiple hospitalizations. Our efforts to get the child involved in treatment and to access school services were stymied when the family decided to send the child back to Asia to be raised by extended family. Under the strain of so many adverse circumstances, the marriage dissolved. Nonetheless, we were able to continue with the family and work with the father, the mother, and the children over the years that followed. Eventually, all family members developed a considerable understanding of depression. Again, this was possible only as the prevention staff came to see that these were real and important prevention goals, even though they were more limited than originally thought.

Family C. is a single parent family who has been quite invested in the Preventive Intervention Project. Ms. C.'s intent was to learn how to talk with her son (G.) about her own issues of depression so that she could educate him about it, but not frighten or burden him. By all accounts, she was quite successful, and she believed the project had a positive effect on her and on her son. She applied the educational component of our project quite successfully. Not only did she use our principles about prevention and resiliency in regard to depression, but she was able to generalize them to other problematic areas of her family's life as well, of which there were many. At times of crisis, she requested and received additional time with our clinical staff. She always came for her yearly assessment meetings, making scheduling of these a priority in her busy life, and using these meetings as a time to reflect back on and sometimes reinterpret the events of the past year. At various times this family was exemplified by our research staff as one who really took full advantage of what our project had to offer.

Unfortunately, G. had a rocky adolescence marked by poor school performance (he has been diagnosed with a learning disability), legal problems, and finally a diagnosis of depression. What is heartening is the fact that Ms. C., by her own admission very worried about her son, was able to cope with his diagnosis quite well. She saw to it that he received appropriate mental health services and continued to advocate for his needs at school. Nonetheless, for the caregivers who worked with this family over the past 8 years, the son's continuing difficulties were quite disappointing.

All of these families were extremely draining for caregivers and illustrate the need for staff support when providing care to a family. In the Preventive Intervention Project, there is a support system built into the design of the study. In fact, there are at least three members of our assessment team working with each family, so that each assessor always has colleagues with whom to seek a second opinion, share the burden of obtaining additional help for the family and, most important, give vent to their frustration and sadness. Likewise, the clinicians had a strong support network with weekly staff meetings where information about each family was shared and discussed, and where ample support was available for each caregiver.

As researchers, our relationships with our research participants and our roles as caregivers are different than traditional patient/therapist relationships. However, it is no less difficult for us when things don't turn out as we hoped, despite everyone's best efforts. The nagging questions of "Could I have done more?" "Could we have seen this coming sooner?" "Could we have tried something different?" are always playing in the background, despite the fact that we are working within the parameters of a research protocol. The support received from other members of the research team at these times is invaluable. Group meetings with other members of the research team enable the caregiver to see the strengths and positive changes made by the family as a result of his/her "caregiving," despite the family's ongoing struggles with depression.

Lee Schorr (1997) has written about the characteristics of quality interventions and preventions across an array of successful programs (Table 2).[2] We believe that providing support for caregivers enables them to engage in these actions. We believe that many of these characteristics are important for caregivers in other domains covered in this volume.

While the issues in either lay caregiving situations or family caregiving situations are somewhat different, it is our belief that provision of adequate support to the caregiver, recognition of a vital role of the caregiver, and consideration of prevention efforts for families when one member is identified as ill are principles that apply to other situations as well.

Future Directions

We have several recommendations for future directions on caregivers in health promotion and prevention.

a. *Practice.* Particular care needs to be given to how to implement a preventive intervention in different disciplines. As one example, many interventions devised in health care settings undoubtedly will find their greatest use in schools. Many interventions done by health care professionals can be done by community and family members with the proper training and support. How to bring this about needs much more attention. Particularly in mental health, we need to encourage the aim of understanding fundamental positive child and family development and use this as the basis for practice. We need to orient health care professionals working in mental health to move beyond simple mechanistic, diagnostic models and to embrace much more fluid developmental models. We need to emphasize the translation of work devised in one setting to another setting, and we need to focus on the dominant effects of race, class, and ethnicity on the transposition of interventions from one setting to another. As interventions developed in one setting are applied to new settings, it is essential that we recognize different levels of support available to caregivers in varied settings, and make certain that across practice settings, caregivers receive the support they need. When we moved our intervention from a middle class setting into the inner city, we found there was great interest in resilience and health promotion, yet very little was written about how to do this, and about how to support caregivers in this endeavor. Much more needs to be done.
b. *Education and Training.* We believe that, precisely because prevention is inherently interdisciplinary and is often based in the community rather than in hospitals, education and training are often quite uneven. We need to think creatively about how to put education and training in prevention and in caregiver support more fully within the curriculum. We believe that training in empirically validated, manual-based prevention models should be a part of the training of psychiatrists, psychologists, social workers, and public health specialists. In addition, training is needed in systems of care, or the effects of neighborhood on development, as well as in social class and other potent risk factors (e.g., exposure to violence).

Table 2 Characteristics of quality interventions and preventions across an array of successful programs

	Current Status	Future Directions
Practice	A wide range of prevention strategies used at different points across the life span have shown considerable merit. For example, during pregnancy and early in the life of the developing child, interventions focused on improving mental and physical health for both the child and the mother are quite efficacious.	Particular care needs to be given to how to implement a preventive intervention in different disciplines. As one example, many interventions devised in health care settings undoubtedly will find their greatest use in schools.
	Presently, there is a bias among researchers, policymakers, and practitioners toward clinical programs rather than toward prevention. This bias presents obstacles to the implementation of prevention programs.	Particularly in mental health, we need to encourage the aim of understanding fundamental positive child and family development and use this as a basis for practice.
	Because of the interdisciplinary nature of prevention approaches, it is often difficult for those trained and working within one particular discipline to embrace them.	We need to orient health care professionals working in mental health to move beyond simple mechanistic, diagnostic models and to embrace much more fluid developmental models.
	Very often, clinicians' time is consumed by clients in crisis. When faced with the dilemma of whether to care for some acutely ill or to focus on prevention, clinicians inevitably will focus on the alleviation of acute suffering in the moment of clinical presentation, and rightly so. To do this often neglects preventive intervention efforts and does not serve the best interests of the clinician or the child.	We need to emphasize the translation of work devised in one setting to another setting, and we need to focus on the dominant effects of race, class, and ethnicity on the transposition of interventions from one setting to another.
	Staff in both prevention and clinical care are often engaged in very taxing and difficult maneuvers to care for families who face multiple adversities. Staff benefit from opportunities to come together and talk about what they encounter and what it stirs up in them.	
Research	There has been remarkable growth of high quality empirical studies in the prevention of mental illness and the promotion of health over the past three decades. Yet, against the backdrop of successfully conducted prevention trials and efforts to promote health, virtually nothing has been written about the needs of caregivers who engage in prevention and, in particular, what kinds of special supports they need.	We certainly need more research on the basic science of prevention. The NIMH report, Blueprint for Change (2001), documents a valuable set of strategies for research that is needed in the future, both at the molecular and basic science level and at the implementation level.
		We need to empower people in prevention to think about building partnerships with families so that families can ultimately do things on their own; and we need research on ways to support caregivers so that they are able to achieve this goal.

Table 2 (continued)

	Current Status	Future Directions
Education/ Training	Clinicians are trained in pathology-based models. Yet, the science of healthy child development is the basis for preventive interventions.	We need to think creatively about how to put education and training prevention more fully within the curriculum.
	Training of clinicians often does not involve training in prevention and yet, if not introduced from the beginning, then prevention almost always does not seem to trainees as important as clinical care.	Training in empirically validated, manual-based prevention models should be part of the training of psychiatrists, psychologists, social workers, and public health specialists.
	In some disciplines, there is a strong intellectual bias against multidisciplinary interventions and a great deal of interest in single interventions from a single intellectual framework. Prevention involves considering domains outside of the usual domains of a given discipline.	Training is needed in systems of care, on the effects of neighborhood on development, as well as in social class and other potent risk factors.
	Precisely because prevention is inherently interdisciplinary and is often based in the community rather than in schools or hospitals, education and training are often quite uneven.	All too often, both in health care and in teaching, we have trained young people who enter the field, work under very difficult circumstances, and then burn out after a year or two. We need to think about ways to support these people at every level.
Policy/ Advocacy	Many organizations are now promoting and supporting prevention efforts. The founding of the Society for Prevention Research and its journal, Prevention, also reflect a growing interest in prevention.	The basic science of preventive intervention is the study of healthy child, adolescent and adult development. The only perspective that makes sense is a systemic ecological perspective as advocated by Bronfenbrenner (1979). We need to look carefully at how interventions at different levels can have effects.
	There is a profound societal bias against taking care of the long-term care needs of children. That is, because of the historical absence of national health insurance, incentives for preventions are not nearly as strong as they are in countries that have national health insurance.	We need to determine ways that the infrastructures can support preventionists' and families' difficult but rewarding task of engaging together in prevention. We need to think systematically about how people can influence the practice of preventive intervention.
	From a policy point of view, there is little systematic integration of prevention and health promotion at either state or local levels, although this varies a great deal.	We need to far more fully engage in broad-based support for prevention and for caregivers engaged in prevention.

c. *Research.* We certainly need more research on the basic science of prevention. The NIMH report, *Blueprint for Change* (2001), documents a valuable set of strategies for research that is needed in the future, both at the molecular and basic science level and at the implementation level. In addition, we currently spend very little time focusing on the dilemmas of caregivers trying to do prevention while taking care of ill families. We have spent very little time focused on the particular dilemmas of caregivers in different cultural settings. We need to empower people in prevention to think about building partnerships with families, so that families can ultimately do things on their own. And we need research on ways to support caregivers so that they are able to achieve this goal.
d. *Policy.* From a policy point of view, there is little systematic integration of prevention, health promotion, and caregiver support at either state or local levels, although this varies a great deal. For example, when we wrote the Institute of Medicine report, it was very difficult to get a sense of what funds were being spent on prevention at the federal level because it was poorly categorized. This was particularly true of empirical work. We need much more work on how to incorporate preventive intervention approaches from a policy point of view at the federal, state, and local levels. Similarly, it was very difficult to find family centered care as opposed to individual centered care. This, too, needs major attention.
e. *Infrastructure Support.* Support of caregivers to undertake difficult prevention maneuvers with families is critical to the success of strength-based preventive intervention projects and has largely been neglected. We need a much greater focus on understanding what the key elements are that provide support to staff on the front lines. We need to determine what level of administrative time and fiscal support is necessary to enable caregivers to stay with families over the long-term and to remain active preventionists.

Concluding Remarks

What is stirred up inside a caregiver confronted with someone in great pain? In prevention, we are asking caregivers to think about the long-term future, to think about positive strategies, and then to think about all the family—mother, father, children, and all their interrelationships. Focusing on the family level is a much more difficult, and much more rewarding, task than focusing on individuals. We need to determine ways that the infrastructures can support preventionists' and families' difficult but rewarding task of engaging together in prevention.

We need to think systematically about how policy can influence the practice of preventive intervention. All too often, both in health care and in teaching, we have trained young people who have entered the field, work under very difficult circumstances (e.g., in inner city schools), and then burn out after a year or two. We need to think about ways to support these people at every level. Finally, at the heart of our prevention efforts is the belief that we must assume responsibility for the long-term future of children.

In order to devise programs that have long-term effects, we must devise strategies that allow preventionists to stay active with families over a number of years and to maintain their own and the families' hopes and optimism. This is crucial for the future of prevention efforts and indeed for the strengthening and preserving of America's families in the years to come. We must also be mindful of the need for fundamental systems reform. In particular, we must strengthen the public health infrastructure to support prevention and achieve health care for all, and we must encourage responsibility for the long-term care of children and their caregivers in the context of their schools, homes, and neighborhoods.

References

Beardslee, W. R. (2000). Prevention of mental disorders and the study of developmental psychopathology: A natural alliance. In J. Rapoport (Ed.), *Childhood onset of "adult" disorder: What can it tell us*? (pp. 233–354). Washington: American Psychiatric Press.

Beardslee, W. R. (2002). *Out of the darkened room: Protecting the children and strengthening the family when a parent is depressed*. New York: Little, Brown and Company.

Beardslee, W. R., Brent, D. A., Weersing, V. R., Clarke, G. N., Porta, G., Hollon, S. D., ... Garber, J. (in press). Prevention of depression in at-risk adolescents: Longer-term effects. *Journal of the American Medical Association Psychiatry*.

Beardslee, W. R., & DeMaso, D. R. (1982). Staff groups in a pediatric hospital: Content and coping. *American Journal of Orthopsychiatry, 52,* 712–718.

Beardslee, W. R., & Gladstone, T. R. G. (2001). Prevention of childhood depression: Recent findings and future prospects. *Biological Psychiatry, 49,* 1101–1110.

Beardslee, W. R., & Gladstone, T. R. G. (2004). Prevention of risks for mental health problems: Lessons learned in examining the prevention of depression in families. In H. Remschmidt, M. Belfer, & I. Goodyer (Eds.), *Facilitating pathways: Care, treatment and prevention in child and adolescent mental health*, (245–254). New York: Springer Medizin Verlag Berlin Heidelberg.

Beardslee, W. R., & Podorefsky, D. (1988). Resilient adolescents whose parents have serious affective and other psychiatric disorders: The importance of self- understanding and relationships. *American Journal of Psychiatry, 145,* 63–69.

Beardslee, W. R., Salt, P., Versage, E. M., Gladstone, T. R. G., Wright, E. J., & Rothberg, P. C. (1997a). Sustained change in parents receiving preventive interventions for families with depression. *The American Journal of Psychiatry, 154,* 510–515.

Beardslee, W. R., Wright, E., Salt, P., Drezner, K., Gladstone, T. R. G., Versage, E. M., et al. (1997b). Examination of children's responses to two preventive intervention strategies over time. *Journal of the American Academy of Child and Adolescent Psychiatry, 36,* 196–204.

Beardslee, W. R., Gladstone, T. R. G., Wright, E. & Cooper, A. B. (2003). A family-based approach to the prevention of depressive symptoms in children at risk: Evidence of parental and child change. *Pediatrics, 112,* e119–131.

Beardslee, W. R., Wright, E., Gladstone, T. R. G. & Forbes, P. (2007). Long-term effects from a randomized trial of two public health preventive interventions for parental depression. *Journal of Family Psychology, 21,* 703–713.

Beardslee, W. R., Chien, P. L. & Bell, C. C. (2011). Prevention of mental disorders, substance abuse, and problem behaviors: A developmental perspective. *Psychiatric Services, 62,* 247–254.

Berrueta-Clement, J. R., Schwienhart, L. J., Barnett, W. S., Epstein, A. S., & Weikart, D. P. (1984). *Changed lives: The effects of the perry preschool program on youths through age 19*. Ypsilanti: High/Scope Press.

Brunwasser, S. M., Gillham, J. E. & Kim, E. S. (2009). A meta-analytic review of the penn resiliency program's effect on depressive symptoms. *Journal of Consulting and Clinical Psychology, 77,* 1042–1054.

Clarke, G. N., Hornbrook, M., Lynch, F., Polen, M., Gale, J., Beardslee, W., O'Connor, E. & Seeley, J. (2001). A randomized trial of a group cognitive intervention for preventing depression in adolescent offspring of depressed parents. *Archives of General Psychiatry, 58,* 1127–1134.

D'Angelo, E., Llerena-Quinn, R., Shapiro, R., Colon, F., Rodriguez, P., Gallagher, K. & Beardslee, W. R. (2009). Adaptation of the preventive intervention program for depression for use with predominantly low-income Latino families. *Family Process, 48,* 269–291.

Garber, J., Clarke, G. N., Weersing, V. R., Beardslee, W. R., Brent, D. A., Gladstone, T. R. G., DeBar, L. L., Lynch, F. L., D'Angelo, E., Hollon, S. D., Shamseddeen, W., & Iyengar, S. (2009). Prevention of depression in at-risk adolescents: A randomized controlled trial. *Journal of the American Medical Association, 301,* 2215–2224.

Gladstone, T. R. G. & Beardslee, W. R. (2009). The prevention of depression in children and adolescents: A review. *The Canadian Journal of Psychiatry, 54,* 212–221.

Gladstone, T. R. G., Beardslee, W. R. & O'Connor, E. E. (2011). The prevention of adolescent depression. *Psychiatric Clinics of North America, 34,* 35–52.

Hawkins, J. D., Catalano, R. F., & Miller, J. Y. (1992). Risk and protective factors for alcohol and other drug problems in adolescence and early adulthood: Implications for substance abuse prevention. *Psychological Bulletin, 112,* 64–105.

Hawkins, J. D., Brown, E. C., Oesterle, S., Arthur, M. W., Abbott, R. D. & Catalano, R. F. (2008). Early effects of communities that care on targeted risks and initiation of delinquent behavior and substance use. *Journal of Adolescent Health,* 43, 15–22.

Institute of Medicine. (1994). *Reducing risks for mental disorders: Frontiers for preventive intervention research.* Washington: National Academy Press.

Kellam, S. G., Werthamer-Larson, L., Dolan, L. J., Brown, C. H., Mayer, L. S., Rebok, G. W., et al. (1991). Developmental epidemiologically based preventive trials: Baseline modeling of early target behaviors and depressive symptoms. *American Journal of Community Psychology, 19,* 563–584.

Leiter, M. P., & Harvie, P. L. (1996). Burnout among mental health workers: A review and a research agenda. *International Journal of Social Psychiatry, 42,* 90–101.

Maslach, C., Schaufeli, W. B., & Leiter, M. P. (2001). Job burnout. *Annual Review of Psychology, 52,* 397–422.

Maton, K., Schellenbach, C., Leadbeater, B., & Solarz, A. (2002). *Investing in children, youth, families, and communities: Strengths-based research and policy.* Washington: American Psychological Association.

Munoz, R. F., Ying, Y., Bernal, G., Perez-Stable, E. J., Sorensen, J. L., Hargreaves, W. A., et al. (1995). Prevention of depression with primary care patients: A randomized controlled trial. *American Journal of Community Psychology, 23,* 199–222.

Munoz, R. F., Beardslee, W. R. & Leykin, Y. (2012). Major depression can be prevented. *American Psychologist, 67,* 285–295.

National Advisory Mental Health Council Workgroup on Child and Adolescent Mental Health Intervention Development and Deployment. (2001). *Blueprint for change: Research on child and adolescent psychiatry.* Washington: Author.

National Research Council and Institute of Medicine. (2009a) Prevention committee. *Preventing mental, emotional, and behavioral disorders among young people: Progress and possibilities.* Washington: National Academies Press.

National Research Council and Institute of Medicine. (2009b) *Depression in parents, parenting, and children.* Washington: National Academies Press.

Olds, D. L., Eckenrode, J., Henderson, C. R., Kitzman, J., Powers, J., Cole, R., Sidora, K., Morris, P., Pettitt, L. M. & Luckey, D. (1997). Long-term effects of home visitation on maternal life course and child abuse and neglect. *Journal of the American Medical Association, 278,* 637–643.

Olds, D. L., Sadler, L. & Kitzman, H. (2007). Programs for parents of infants and toddlers: Recent evidence from randomized trials. *Journal of Child Psychology and Psychiatry, 48,* 355–391.

Price, R. H., van Ryn, M., & Vinokur, A. D. (1992). Impact of a preventive job search intervention on the likelihood of depression among the unemployed. *Journal of Health and Social Behavior, 33,* 158–167.

Price, R. H., Choi, J. N., & Vinokur, A. D. (2002). Links in the chain of adversity following job loss: How financial strain and loss of personal control lead to depression, impaired functioning, and poor health. *Journal of Occupational Health Psychology, 7,* 302–312.

Podorefsky, D. L., McDonald-Dowdell, M., & Beardslee, W. R. (2001). Adaptation of preventive interventions for a low-income, culturally diverse community. *Journal of the American Academy of Child and Adolescent Psychiatry, 40,* 879–886.

Reid, Y., Johnson, S., Morant, N., Kuipers, E., Szmukler, G., Bebbington, P., et al. (1999). Improving support for mental health staff: A qualitative study. *Social Psychiatry and Psychiatric Epidemiology, 34,* 309–315.

Schorr, L. B. (1997). *Common purpose: Strengthening families and neighborhoods to rebuild America.* New York: Doubleday Dell Publishing Group, Inc.

Seligman, M. E. P., Reivich, K., Jaycox, L., & Gillham, J. (1995). *The optimistic child: A proven program to safeguard children against depression and build lifelong resilience.* New York: HarperPerrenial.

United States Department of Health and Human Services. (2001). *Mental health: Culture, race and ethnicity—a supplement to mental health: A report of the Surgeon General.* Rockville: Author.

World Health Organization. (2004). *Prevention of mental disorders: Effective interventions and policy options: Summary report.* Geneva: Author.

Yoshikawa, H., Aber, J. L & Beardslee, W. R. (2012). The effects of poverty on the mental, emotional, and behavioral health of children and youth. *American Psychologist, 67,* 272–284.

Systems of Caregiving: The Promotion of Positive Mental Health Outcomes in Children and Adolescents

Patricia Stone Motes and Chaundrissa Oyeshiku Smith

Promoting mental health and preventing mental disorders in children and adolescents is critical to the overall health of our country. Recent epidemiological data suggest that between 9 and 13 % of children and adolescents have significant functional impairments at home, at school, with peers, and within the community (U.S. Department of Health and Human Services [HHS] 1999). This estimate would indicate that about six to nine million children in the USA suffer from a major mental illness. Successful efforts in promoting mental health for children and adolescents require attention from a range of caregiving systems, including mental health, education, juvenile justice, child welfare, developmental disabilities, substance abuse, and the primary care sector.

This chapter addresses the core caregiving efforts designed to promote positive mental health outcomes for children and adolescents. Specifically, this chapter describes the system of care philosophy that largely drives public sector caregiving for child and adolescent mental health. Within this caregiving approach, the significance of family caregivers, cultural competency, and community-based interventions are emphasized. The efficacy of caregiving efforts within a system of care is discussed in light of practice issues, research on child and family outcomes, and the education and training of caregivers. The chapter concludes with a look at policy issues and implications for the future of caregiving and child and adolescent mental health.

P. S. Motes (✉)
Division of Policy and Research on Medicaid and Medicare,
Institute for Families in Society, University of South Carolina,
1600 Hampton Street, Suite 524, Columbia, SC 29208, USA
e-mail: pmotes@mailbox.sc.edu; tricia.motes@gmail.com

C. O. Smith
Department of Psychiatry and Behavioral Sciences,
Emory University School of Medicine, Atlanta, USA
e-mail: csmit33@emory.edu

R. C. Talley et al. (eds.), *The Challenges of Mental Health Caregiving*,
Caregiving: Research • Practice • Policy, DOI 10.1007/978-1-4614-8791-3_6,

Systems of Caregiving

The promotion of positive mental health outcomes for children and adolescents with significant emotional and behavioral disorders is complex and requires support and intervention across multiple caregiving systems. Thus, addressing the mental health needs of these children and adolescents has traditionally meant navigating many different systems. Historically, family caregivers have had to contend with mental health care that was characterized by fragmentation, overly restrictive services, inappropriate care, high costs, and poor outcomes (Knitzer 1982; Wagner 1995). In 1982, Knitzer brought attention to the challenges of family caregivers and the systemic problems related to mental health services for children and adolescents when she published *Unclaimed Children*. Knitzer pointed out that children were not only critically underserved but also inappropriately served. Her work exposed significant gaps in services for children in need of special education, mental health services, and child welfare services. The study pointed out the lack of comprehensive systems of care for children, adolescents, and their families. Knitzer's publication is generally credited with leading the efforts to reform child mental health services toward community-based integrated systems of care.

The Child and Adolescent Service System Program (CASSP) was a pioneering reform effort advocating a comprehensive approach to coordinating and delivering child and adolescent services across multiple service providers through a "system of care" (see Stroul and Friedman 1986). In response to Knitzer's national study in 1982, Congress appropriated funds in 1984 to address the needs of children who were "unclaimed" by the public agencies responsible to serve them. Thus, this federally funded effort was established largely as a recognition that the public sector needed to become more integrated in order to fully and efficiently meet the multiple and changing needs of children and adolescents with mental health needs. Stroul and Friedman defined this approach as a "system of care" based on principles and values that included coordinated services, cultural competency, and community-based care, with family caregivers as integral to the decision-making in planning and delivery of services to their children.

The CASSP system integrates a philosophy concerning service delivery to children and their families. The actual service delivery is expected to differ on the basis of the unique strengths and needs of the families and communities. Its framework is based on three core values: child-centered and family-focused care, community-based care, and culturally competent care. Further, the fundamental values of this system of care are supported by ten principles that describe the optimal nature of the system of care. (See Table 1 for guiding principles within the system of care framework.)

Building on the values and principles of CASSP, other reform efforts followed: Robert Wood Johnson Foundation Mental Health Services for Youth, the Anne E. Casey Children's Mental Health Initiative for Urban Youth, and the Children's Services program sponsored by the Center for Mental Health Services. The *National Agenda for Achieving Better Results of Children and Youth with Serious Emotional Disturbance* (U.S. Department of Education [DOE] 1994), developed for the Office

Table 1 Guiding principles within the system of care framework. (Stroul and Freidman 1986, p. 17)

Guiding principles within the system of care framework	
1	Children with emotional disturbances should have access to a comprehensive array of services that address their physical, emotional, social, and educational needs.
2	Children with emotional disturbances should receive individualized services in accordance with the unique needs and potentials of each child and guided by an individualized service plan.
3	Children with emotional disturbances should receive services within the least restrictive, most normative environment that is clinically appropriate.
4	The families and surrogate families of children with emotional disturbances should be full participants in all aspects of the planning and delivery of services.
5	Children with emotional disturbances should receive services that are integrated, with linkages between child-serving agencies and programs and mechanisms for planning, developing, and coordination services.
6	Children with emotional disturbances should be provided with case management or similar mechanisms to ensure that multiple services are delivered in a coordinated and therapeutic manner and that they can move through the system of services in accordance with their changing needs.
7	Early identification and intervention for children with emotional disturbances should be promoted by the system of care in order to enhance the likelihood of positive outcomes.
8	Children with emotional disturbances should be ensured smooth transitions to the adult service system as they reach maturity.
9	The rights of children with emotional disturbances should be protected, and effective advocacy efforts for children and adolescents with emotional disturbances should be promoted.
10	Children with emotional disturbances should receive services without regard to race, religion, national origin, sex, physical disability, or other characteristics, and services should be sensitive and responsive to cultural differences and special needs.

of Special Education and Rehabilitative Services, also builds on these same principles through seven specific targets that address the need for culturally competent, community-based, family-focused, comprehensive, and collaborative approaches to planning and service delivery. (See Table 2 for targets for National Agenda.)

Families: Integral to the System of Care

The CASSP framework for community-based caregiving systems has significantly shifted the roles and expectations of families of children and youth with emotional and behavioral problems. Historically, families were largely disregarded as important caregivers. Early mental health efforts either viewed families as nonexistent or saw them as the causal pathways for their children's difficulties; currently, families are more and more regarded as essential partners in the care of their children (e.g., Epstein et al. 1998; Knitzer et al. 1993). Surgeon General Satcher (Conference on Children's Mental Health 2000) stated that while the responsibility for children's mental health

Table 2 Targets of the national agenda for achieving better results for children and youth with serious emotional disturbance. (U.S. Department of Education 1994)

Targets of the National Agenda	
1	Expand positive learning opportunities and results
2	Strengthen school and community capacity
3	Value and address diversity
4	Collaborate with families
5	Promote appropriate assessment
6	Provide ongoing skill development and support
7	Create comprehensive and collaborative systems

is dispersed across multiple child-serving systems, families are the primary systems in caregiving for children and youth with emotional and behavioral disorders (U.S. Public Health Service 2000). Families are now often involved individually in the care of their own children and involved in policy and systemic issues through advocacy organizations (e.g., National Alliance for the Mentally Ill and Federation of Families for Children's Mental Health).

Attention to families as decision makers is an integral principle in the community-based systems of care philosophy. However, this movement toward families as significant partners in caregiving has not occurred without concerns and issues to be addressed. Friesen and Stephens (1998) point out that the effort to involve families in the caregiving system has largely occurred at a rate faster than what research and practice have been able to accommodate. Essentially, families have moved into multiple roles (i.e., service recipients, partners in intervention, service providers, advocates and policy makers, and evaluators and researchers) in supporting this caregiving system without the needed research and practice guidelines being put in place (see later sections of this chapter for a fuller discussion of these issues).

The centrality of family in children's development is presented by Friesen and Stephens (1998) through a discussion of "family as context." In examining the role of the caregiver and family as context, the authors point out the important roles families play in the ecology of their children's lives. One significant aspect of this contextual relationship is the link between the parent's behavior and emotions and the children's mental health outcomes.

The link between the family system and child and adolescent mental health outcomes has been extensively examined. Such research has often led to the view that parents are partly, if not fully, responsible for their child's mental health condition (Friesen and Stephens 1998). However, the reciprocal influence of youth mental health on parental caregiving behaviors must also be recognized, in that youth with emotional disorders may provide added stress to a caregiver (Suarez and Baker 1997), possibly affecting their caregiving behaviors (Early et al. 2002). Natural support systems are often reduced for families of children with emotional and behavior disorders because of stigma, embarrassment, or simply because caregivers have too little energy to reach out to others. Parents typically report that limited social supports decrease their quality of life (Crowley and Kadzin 1998). Parents of children with emotional and behavioral problems also report feeling less competent, more depressed, worried, tired, and as having more spousal and familial problems than other parents (Farmer et al. 1997).

From a practice perspective, Modrcin and Robison (1991) further highlight the reciprocal interactions between parents and children who have serious emotional and behavioral disorders. Among the issues highlighted are the lack of preparation for parenting a child with mental illness, the constant adaptations to the unique child-rearing challenges, and the loss and grief of recognizing that the dreams for their child's future are not likely to be realized. These issues are clearly important in establishing an effective context for therapeutic intervention that facilitates family participation.

Family processes including poor parental monitoring and discipline (Dishion and McMahon 1998), inadequate family management (Hawkins et al. 1992), marital conflict (Downey and Coyne 1990; Lindahl and Malik 1999), and parenting behaviors (Lewinsohn et al. 1994) have been linked to child and adolescent mental health outcomes. Conversely, positive familial processes such as social support from family (McCabe et al. 1999; Wills et al. 1992), strong familial attachments (Resnick et al. 1997), and parental warmth (McCabe et al. 1999) have been associated with positive mental health outcomes. The current research largely anchored by an ecological framework offers links between family behavior and children and youth outcomes and shapes a focus on prevention and intervention, rather than a focus on blame and guilt.

According to Knitzer et al. (1993), family participation in caregiving promotes an increased focus on families, the provision of services in natural settings, greater cultural sensitivity, and a community-based system of care. Family-focused and strengths-based service delivery is critical in the successful implementation of a system of care (Dunst et al. 1994).

Cultural Competency

A value central to the system of care philosophy is that of cultural competence. Developing a culturally competent system of care that provides services consistent with the culture of diverse families is viewed as a developmental process occurring along a continuum, for systems as well as individual caregivers (Cross et al. 1989). Cultural competence has been defined as a set of congruent behaviors, attitudes, and policies that enable a system, agency, or individual caregivers to work effectively in cross-cultural situations. It is further defined as having five essential elements: valuing diversity, ongoing cultural self-assessment by systems and caregivers, understanding the dynamics of difference when cultures interact, ongoing development of knowledge related to diverse cultures, and adapting service delivery practices to reflect an understanding of cultural diversity (Cross et al. 1989).

The current mental health system is not well equipped to meet the needs of diverse children and families. The Surgeon General's report on mental health (HHS 1999) points out that there are numerous barriers to diverse groups receiving mental health services (e.g., differences in help seeking behaviors, lack of trust of the mental health system, stigma of mental illness, cost for services, bias of caregivers in diagnosis and treatment). Ample data support the relationship between underutilization of mental health services and poverty for minority children and families, although the data are less clear for cultural differences and underutilization. There are limited assessment procedures and interventions that specifically address cultural differences. A clear need exists for increased attention to culturally appropriate treatment services to ensure that services are not only used but are *useful* to diverse families and their children.

Placing cultural competence as a priority for a system of care ensures that cultural issues are integrated into all aspects of practice (e.g., program planning and program implementation), research, and training. Cultural competency requires caregivers to be aware of and respectful to the values, beliefs, traditions, customs, parenting styles, and other culturally specific family interactions. Caregivers must also partner with diverse communities and work in concert with the natural support systems of these communities (Greenbaum 1998; Kretzman and McKnight 1993).

Community-Based Interventions

The current framework for caregiving in support of improved metal health outcomes for children, adolescents, and their families is guided by a shift from institutional to community-based interventions. Based on an ecological perspective, the CASSP model focuses on the interactions of multiple factors in determining individual behavior. The model is guided by principles designed to ensure that the strengths and uniqueness of emotionally and behaviorally disturbed children and their families are valued.

Significant theoretical and empirical data supports an ecological perspective as an overarching strategy in addressing the needs of children and youth with serious emotional and behavioral disturbance (Bronfenbrenner 1979; Dunst et al. 1988; Hawkins and Catalano 1992; Henggeler and Borduin 1990). An ecological framework focusing on outcomes for children, youth, and their families bridges interventions across settings, links interventions to changes in environments and systems, alters processes in the system by involving multiple change agents, and conceptualizes child, youth, and family functioning in terms of interactions between and among broader social environments, rather than solely in terms of individual performance (Motes et al. 1999). An ecological framework, supported by cultural competent practices, encourages caregiving to occur in natural and everyday settings. School-based services and home-based services are primary community-based interventions that support this system of care model.

School-Based Services

Through the school system, 70–80 % of children and adolescents receive mental health services (Burns et al. 1995). Schools will likely continue to play instrumental roles in treating children's mental health needs (Miller et al. 2002) and offer an opportunity to promote positive mental health outcomes (Holtzman 1992).

School-based services are family oriented and are easily accessible to families. These services are found to be efficient, effective means of providing low-stigmatizing support to families and children because of the universal nature of schools and the central focus on academic and social competence. The school serves as the entry point for services, but the service provision is integrated across the home, school, neighborhood, and larger community.

School-based programs can offer treatment at an early point to children and youth who are already exhibiting significant emotional disturbance and assist school staff (e.g., teachers and counselors) in working with these children. School programs also have many opportunities to assist children, adolescents, and their families at times of crisis and to prevent relatively minor, potentially transient problems from becoming serious, persistent disorders (Petersen et al. 1993). Schools have the capacity to provide support to parents and siblings (e.g., Dryfoos 1990) and to assist troubled (e.g., depressed) youth who often are not otherwise identified (Adelman et al. 1993).

Home-Based Services

Like school-based services, a portal for entry for this community-based intervention is through the home, because these services are consistent with the resources and needs of the unique family situation. Home-based services, also known as family preservation services and in-home services, have three major goals. These goals are to protect the integrity of the family and prevent unnecessary out-of-home placements; to facilitate a community-based support system for the family; and to build the strengths and competencies of the family to address the future needs of its family members (Stroul 1988).

Efficacy of Caregiving in Systems of Care

Practice: Expanded Caregiver Roles

Service delivery in systems of care has been more shaped by philosophy, values, and principles than by research support for practice guidelines. Both the CASSP system of care model (see Table 1) and the National Agenda (see Table 2) have provided the primary guidance to practice within systems of care. While both initiatives lay out several principles and targets that directly influence caregiving practice, there are three areas that appear to have significantly expanded the "how" of caregiver roles concerning children and adolescents with mental health needs. These areas are family partnership, interagency collaboration, and case management services.

Family Partnership

In systems of care, the importance of family partnership with other service providers and full family participation in all aspects of planning and delivery of services, as respectively indicated by the National Agenda and the CASSP model, is clearly a priority. Friesen and Stephens (1998) present many of the practice issues that relate to family partnership within systems of care. They point out that while families continue to be recipients of care (e.g., parent training, individual therapy, respite care), the process of receiving services has been significantly shaped by the involvement of families in service delivery teams. Service teams are more broadly addressing the needs of the full family, not simply the child or adolescent identified for treatment. Partnership practice requires professionals to reconcile their own expertise with that of families and balance the roles of sharing power and retaining professional responsibility. In expanded caregiving practice, family members as service providers challenge organizations to address issues of ethics, compensation, and other organizational structures that may support and/or hinder family partnership.

There are some emerging research data that offer support to the practice of family partnership in systems of care. Family involvement in planning services has caused families to feel that their children's mental health needs are being met (DeChillo et al. 1994). Family involvement in services has also resulted in family members feeling empowered in their children's treatment (Curtis and Singh 1996; Thompson et al. 1997). Additionally, research points to improved coordination of services with greater parental participation (Koren et al. 1997). While practice efforts adapt and move forward to support expanded family roles, there is clearly a need for more research and professional training to help anchor the practice of family partnerships in systems of care.

Interagency Collaboration

Interagency collaboration is in many ways the cornerstone of the system of care model; it is a strategy designed to reduce fragmentation and duplication of services provided by multiple agencies. CASSP principle 5 specifies that services should be "integrated, with linkages between child-serving agencies and programs" (Stroul and Freidman 1986, p. 17). The process of collaboration in order to meet the mental health needs of children, adolescents, and their families can take many forms. However, consistent with the system of care models, collaboration typically centers on individualized planning that is family centered, community based, and culturally competent. Interagency collaboration further requires commitment to a structure that distributes power and shares resources.

Interagency collaboration is the key to the delivery of comprehensive services to children and their families within a system of care. Successful collaborations have resulted in improved services to children and their families through gaining access to resources, identifying gaps in services, and avoiding duplication of services

(Hochberg 1993). Collaborative efforts also allow organizations to share information with each other and help streamline bureaucratic procedures (Hochberg 1993). However, there are important challenges to community collaborations: inadequate funding, resistance by key organizations, and turf issues (Floyd 2007).

Case Management

Case management is another significant service delivery component within the system of care model. In fact, case management is specified as a mechanism to "ensure that multiple services are delivered in a coordinated and therapeutic manner" (Stroul and Freidman 1986, p. 17; CASSP, principle 6). Case management is a model or process for service delivery, not a treatment intervention per se. One widespread approach to case management is termed "wraparound." This comprehensive case management approach develops an individualized plan that focuses interventions on the strengths of youth and their families; family participation is key to wraparound services. Individualized planning for the youth and family occurs with a focus on strengths and resources across multiple life domains. Typically, the wraparound planning process includes both nontraditional supports (e.g., extended family members, respite caregivers) and traditional services designed to flexibly address the full continuum of services (Eber and Nelson 1997).

There is fairly limited research on case management services, especially wraparound services. However, according to the Surgeon General's mental health report, there is evidence that case management is an effective service delivery practice for addressing the needs of youth with serious emotional disturbances.

Research: Child and Family Outcomes in Systems of Care

The CASSP system of care framework has facilitated the development and implementation of practices and programs aimed at improving the level of service to children with emotional disturbances and their families. A proliferation of programs exists, with many of them maintaining strategies that coincide with the targets of the National Agenda. While the goals of these programs are to provide the most comprehensive services to children and families and ultimately produce improved mental health outcomes, empirical evidence is limited that supports these objectives.

The task of conducting rigorous empirical investigations of the system of care frameworks is daunting. These complexities are rooted in the very nature of the system of care framework. For example, creating comprehensive and collaborative systems necessitates utilizing several agencies whose techniques and strategies may be extremely dissimilar. This may prove difficult, especially when there is a need to implement experimental investigations with fidelity, which often requires practitioners to be trained in a standard protocol of treatment (e.g., manual treatment) and provide evidence that the intervention was actually executed (Burns and Friedman 1990).

Although this standard of fidelity is common in research trials, the real-world application of this system of care framework within countless communities across the USA has been unable to meet such rigorous standards. However, these limitations do not imply that research investigations of the system of care framework are nonexistent. Several system of care programs have examined various processes and outcomes associated with this philosophy. Some research endeavors have looked at broader issues related to the system of care framework such as cost effectiveness (Skiba and Nichols 2000), reductions of out-of-home placements (Eber et al. 1996), or consumer satisfaction with services (Bickman 1996).

Investigations of system of care programs have also used a variety of methodologies. Some investigations have utilized quantitative data collection methods, whereas many others have relied on qualitative or anecdotal assessments of system of care services based on information received from stakeholders (McLaughlin et al. 1997). These data may be useful in understanding the process of system of care programs. However, these findings may be insufficient in providing relevant information on the effectiveness of system of care programs as a mechanism for producing improved mental health outcomes for children with emotional disturbances. The past decade has produced an increase in research studies that have attempted to support the need for outcome-oriented investigations of system of care programs. This research has focused on multiple outcome levels. Among these outcome domains are the system infrastructure, service delivery, and child and family outcomes (Center for Mental Health Services 1997). This section will discuss selected program efforts that embody the system of care philosophy as they apply to the domain of child and family outcomes.

The Linkages to Learning (LTL) program has been implemented at elementary school sites in Montgomery County, Maryland (Leone et al. 1996). The program has attempted to integrate educational, health, mental health, and social services at selected after-school programs (Leone et al. 1996). Fox et al. (1999) and Leone et al. (2002) reported the effectiveness of this program on child socioemotional and academic outcomes based on longitudinal data collected over a 4-year period from students receiving LTL services at their school and students attending a matched control school. Parents of children within the LTL program reported significantly fewer negative behaviors (i.e., internalizing and externalizing) over time, although at baseline, the children attending the LTL school were exhibiting higher levels of negative behaviors than their controlled counterparts. The LTL program also appeared to have an impact on children's academic outcomes. Within the LTL school, some children were not actively receiving LTL services. However, students who were receiving services maintained significantly higher math scores than those students who were not receiving services. Although child outcomes are often viewed as foremost within the system of care framework, it is also imperative that families of these children are positively impacted. LTL reported trends toward favorable outcomes for family members as well. LTL families showed significant improvements in family cohesion that were not found for control families. Additionally, LTL parents exhibited lower levels of depression over time, whereas control families maintained their existing depression levels.

Programs that utilize wraparound systems have been identified as being central to the system of care concept (Winters and Pumariega 2001). Wraparound efforts serve children and families with emotional and/or behavioral disorders (Eber et al. 1996) through assisting communities to develop individually based services for the care of these children (McGinty et al. 2001). Outcomes for the wraparound process have been evaluated in Vermont (Yoe et al. 1996) and Illinois (Eber et al. 1996). Yoe et al. (1996) evaluated outcomes for 40 youth who received wraparound services and found significant decreases in youth problem behaviors, externalizing and internalizing behaviors, and abuse-related behaviors after 12 months. Wraparound approaches have also shown promise in decreasing out-of-home placements (Eber et al. 1996) and increasing community-based living arrangements (Yoe et al. 1996) among the youth who were served. However, these findings are limited because they are solely based on the outcomes of youth participating in wraparound services without a comparison or control group. As a result, whether the outcomes are due solely to the wraparound services is unknown.

The results of these previously mentioned efforts are encouraging, although they must be interpreted with caution because of small sample sizes or a failure to have a control or comparison group. Duchnowski et al. (2002) noted the challenge of identifying comparison groups at the community level. Bickman and colleagues (1996, 2000) have attempted to account for these methodological limitations through a program demonstration project in Fort Bragg, North Carolina. This quasi-experimental evaluation implemented a comprehensive health care system within a military community, replacing the existing traditional services, and compared the outcomes to two other military communities in which traditional services continued. Several long-term individual-level outcomes were evaluated for youth receiving services. Clinically significant differences were not found between youth receiving system of care services and comparison youth at 12 months (Bickman 1996), 18 months (Hammer et al. 1997), or 5 years (Bickman et al. 2000). Furthermore, the cost of implementation of the Fort Bragg project was much greater than in the traditional settings. Favorable findings were shown in terms of greater access to services, consumer satisfaction in regards to services, and less use of patient hospitalization and residential treatment.

These previous examples of outcome evaluations have provided preliminary insight into the research status of programs adopting the system of care philosophy. Similar to other treatment mechanisms aimed at providing services to children and families with mental health needs, a gap exists between linking research to practice. This is particularly of concern considering the widespread development and proliferation of system of care programs across the nation. Although empirically validated treatments have been recognized under the umbrella of system of care, such as multisystemic therapy (Henggeler et al. 1994), it is imperative that additional attempts are made to further validate the system of care framework as a viable means to achieve outcomes for children with emotional disturbances and their families.

Publications have been produced identifying programs as "best practices" or "effective" in system of care, although they have not been rigorously tested. It may be that these programs are identified because of their embodiment of the system of care philosophy rather than empirical evidence that they are effective. An appeal has been made for integrating more evidence-based interventions into the system of care framework (Kutash et al. 2002) in order to generate the desired improvements in youth mental health outcomes. It is imperative that this integration becomes a reality in order for effective interventions to impact the mental health outcomes for youth and their families. This collaboration necessitates adaptations by both sides. That is, researchers must be willing to adapt to the concerns of those within the naturalistic settings, whereas practitioners within these settings must be willing to adhere to evidence-based practices (Hoagwood et al. 2001). However, both groups must remain cognizant that programming cannot be developed under the premise that "one size will fit all," and programs will need to be adapted to fit the unique needs of a school or community (McLaughlin et al. 1997).

The obstacles to conducting rigorous experimental investigations may be limiting the incorporation of evidence-based practices within the system of care. Many evidence-based interventions are often conducted under ideal conditions, in which the needs of a client and the techniques of a practitioner are highly controlled. Burns and Friedman (1990) noted that clinical trials, which occur frequently to assess treatment effectiveness in psychotherapeutic settings, are virtually nonexistent in examining programs that adhere to the system of care philosophy. Concern often arises when these rigorous conditions are applied to "real-world" settings, in which clients may present several mental health concerns or whose concerns do not fit the evidence-based treatment protocol. It is unknown whether the evidence-based interventions that are currently available can meet the demands of the public sector's mental health needs. Increased collaboration between researchers and community-based mental health agencies is necessary for interventions to be developed, implemented, and evaluated for their utility. These partnerships may assist in decreasing the current gap that exists between researchers and practitioners, allowing for these entities to work together for the goal of promoting positive mental health outcomes. Ultimately, these collaborations can assist in the development of rigorous clinical trials within naturalistic settings.

Education and Training: Support for Practice and Research

The philosophy of system of care recognizes that although families are central to the mental health development of youth, a multitude of additional individuals serve as caregiving resources. A number of professionals, such as psychologists, nurses, special education professionals, and social workers provide services for children with serious emotional disturbance and their families (Kutash and Duchnowski 1997). These persons play a significant role influencing mental health outcomes. Surprisingly, some may have limited training and preparation to do so. As such, there has been an increasing emphasis on improving the quality of training for practitioners working with issues concerning youth mental health (Hanley and Wright 1995). In addition to training efforts supporting practice, training efforts must to be linked to the growing research based on evidence-based interventions that lead to positive outcomes for children, youth, and their families (see previous section).

Schools are often faced with managing youth's mental health issues. However, teachers are largely trained to emphasize academic achievement (Waxman et al. 1999). Roeser and Midgley (1997) surveyed approximately 200 teachers and found that nearly all teachers (99 %) believed that the mental health concerns of their students were "somewhat" to "very much" part of their roles as teachers. Two-thirds of the teachers reported feeling "somewhat to very overwhelmed" by their students' mental health needs. However, these teachers also reported that the challenges they face in the classroom related to their students' mental health concerns were not discussed in their teacher training courses. Roeser and Midgley (1997) recommend that educator training programs incorporate teaching methods for teachers to assist youth with their mental health needs. Furthermore, schools can provide teachers with support (i.e., information and resources) to assist their students.

Among all possible caregiving resources, mental health professionals receive the most extensive training in treating mental health problems in children and adolescents. Recommendations have been made (e.g., LaGreca and Hughes 1999; Mayes 1999) that outline the skills, competencies, and training requirements for clinicians who primarily work with youth and families. Some of these guidelines include: (1) an understanding of early childhood and special education principles, (2) an ability to conduct assessments of children and their caregiving environments, (3) maintenance of collaborative and interprofessional skills, and (4) knowledge of prevention, family support, health promotion, and social issues affecting children, youth, and families (LaGreca and Hughes 1999; Mayes 1999).

Although these guidelines have been disseminated, it is imperative that they become incorporated into training programs curricula. This implementation is necessary because of the disparity that continues to exist between the training that mental health professionals receive (i.e., curriculum and approaches) and the actual needs of individuals for whom the mental health sector serves (Duchnowski and Friedman 1990). Mental health professionals may feel ill prepared to meet the challenges of public populations because training programs have failed to address these guidelines. Increased collaboration between academic settings and the mental health sector to encourage the development of effective mental health interventions may assist in reducing the gap between training programs and real-world application (Duchnowski and Friedman 1990). Furthermore, these partnerships may promote the utilization of evidence-based services with real-world applicability.

The stigma associated with mental health professionals has contributed to primary care professionals serving as "de facto" mental health providers (Olson et al. 2001). However, fewer than 5 % of primary care pediatricians surveyed by Olson et al. had received training in dealing with mental health problems in youth, specifically depression. This same survey found that although 90 % of pediatricians felt that it was their responsibility to recognize depression in their youth patients, only 25 % felt responsible for treating the disorder. Primary care professionals attributed their limited ability to diagnose and treat youth mental health disorders to training limitations and insufficient knowledge of the treatment of depression (Olson et al. 2001) as well as of the Diagnostic and Statistical Manual (American Psychiatric Association 1994). Treatment recommendations to increase primary care professionals' ability to serve as caregiving agents in treating mental health disorders in youth involve increased consultations with mental health professionals, improving primary care professionals' diagnostic capabilities, and increased utilization of the child and adolescent version of the Diagnostic and Statistical Manual for Primary Care (American Academy of Pediatrics 1996). Recently, there has been increased interest in assessing the effectiveness of primary care professionals in treating youth mental health and behavioral disorders. For example, the evidence-based, multilevel Triple P-Positive Parenting Program (Sanders 1999) maintains intervention strategies in which primary care professionals provide brief consultation to parents in order to increase positive parenting skills and promote positive youth mental health.

Within the context of professionals serving as caregiving resources to youth with mental health needs, there is additional concern regarding preparation in collaboratively working with families, another limitation within the current status of training programs (Jivanjee and Friesen 1997). Practitioners trained to work primarily with children and adolescents must develop additional skills and competencies supportive of partnership practice (e.g., collaborative family efforts across diverse cultures). Of significance is the ability to work with family members "whose values, culture, attitudes, and behaviors are different from the practitioner, and finding an appropriate balance between sharing power and retaining professional responsibility" (Friesen and Stephens 1998 p. 245).

The development and use of evidence-based interventions in training programs and real-world practice needs to be a shared responsibility between researchers, academics, practitioners, and family members. The challenge to developing a system of care that promotes positive outcomes for children, adolescents, and their families is the development of "best practices" based on research findings, supported by education and training programs.

Conclusion

The promotion of positive mental health outcomes for children and adolescents with significant emotional and behavioral disorders is complex and requires support and intervention across multiple caregiving systems. These caregiving efforts have been shaped primarily by a system of care framework, especially the leadership of CASSP and the National Agenda. This framework lays out policy guidelines that call for comprehensive systems of care, focusing on integration across multiple child-serving organizations. Within this framework, families are viewed as central to the ecology of their children's lives and thus central to the system of caregiving. Further, the framework focuses on community-based interventions (e.g., home and school) that are delivered in culturally competent ways.

The system of care framework is based on both theoretical and empirical research regarding the usefulness of ecologically oriented services for both prevention and intervention to promote social, behavioral, and developmental outcomes for children and adolescents. Research studies specific to the system of care framework find some support for the system of care as a viable approach to fostering an infrastructure and service delivery process in support of improved child and adolescent outcomes (e.g., access to services, reduction in institutional care), although such research efforts are hampered by many methodological shortcomings. However, there is less evidence that interventions within the system of care are significantly bettering mental health outcomes for children than those offered outside a system of care. Although this finding is troubling, it is perhaps more a statement about the status of evidence-based programs in real-world settings than an indictment of the system of care framework. Essentially, there are fairly limited evidence-based programs, although the number is growing, such as Promoting Alternative Thinking Strategies (PATHS) (Greenberg et al. 1998) and Multisystemic Therapy (Henggeler et al. 1998), but these programs are largely absent from the specific research on systems of care. When such interventions are included within systems of care, positive outcomes for children and adolescents and their families are realized. In many instances, these research-based programs have not been translated into interventions that can be readily applied in real world settings of systems of care. As more evidence-based programs are developed with appropriate training curricula (e.g., manual interventions), they should be integrated into systems of care, including practice, education, and training programs. These changes should significantly impact child and family outcomes.

The caregiving practice has been shaped as a partnership with families, within a service delivery system based on interagency collaboration and coordination of multiple services (e.g., case management). However, as this chapter points out, there is a huge gap between practice, research, and training. Policies to anchor the systems of care framework must require the integration of more evidence-based interventions. Describing programs as "best practices" or "effective" because they embody the principles of the system of care is not acceptable. The goal of the system of care is not to see its principles in action, but rather to see better mental health outcomes for children, adolescents, and their families.

References

Adelman, H. S., Barker, L. A., & Nelson, P. (1993). A study of a school-based clinic: Who uses it and who doesn't? *Journal of Clinical Child Psychology, 22,* 52–59.

American Academy of Pediatrics. (1996). *The classification of child and adolescent mental diagnoses in primary care: Diagnostic and statistical manual for primary care, child and adolescent version*. Elk Grove Village, IL: American Academy of Pediatrics.

American Psychiatric Association. (1994). *Diagnostic and statistical manual of mental disorders* (4th ed.). Washington: American Psychiatric Association.

Bickman, L. (1996). Implications of a children's mental health managed care demonstration evaluation. *Journal of Mental Health Administration, 23,* 107–117.

Bickman, L., Lambert, W.E., Angrade, A.R., Penaloza, R.V. (2000). The Fort Bragg continuum of care for children and adolescents: Mental health outcomes over 5 years. *Journal of Consultation and Clinical Psychology, 68,* 710–716.

Bronfenbrenner, U. (1979). *The ecology of human development: Experiements by nature and design*. Cambridge: Harvard University Press.

Burns, B., & Friedman, R. (1990). Examining the research base for child mental health services and policy. *Journal of Mental Health Administration, 17,* 87–98.

Burns, B., Costello, E.J., Angold, A., Tweed, D., Stangl, D., Farmer, E.M., Erkanli, A. (1995). Children's mental health service use across service sectors. *Health Affairs, 14,* 147–159.

Center for Mental Health Services. (1997). *Annual report to Congress on the evaluation of the comprehensive community mental health services for children and their families program, 1997.* Atlanta: Macro International Inc.

Cross, T., Bazron, B., Dennis, K., & Isaacs, M. (1989). *Towards a culturally competent system of care: A monograph on effective services for minority children who are severely emotionally disturbed.* Washington: CASSP Technical Assistance Center, Georgetown University Child Development Center.

Crowley, M. J., & Kazdin, A. E. (1998). Child psychosocial functioning and parent quality of life among clinically referred children. *Journal of Child and Family Studies, 7,* 233–251.

Curtis, W. J., & Singh, J. J. (1996). Family involvement and empowerment in mental health service provision for children with emotional and behavioral disorders. *Journal of Child and Family Studies, 5,* 503–517.

DeChillo, N., Koren, P. E., & Schultze, K. H. (1994). From paternalism to partnership: Family and professional collaboration in children's mental health. *American Journal of Orthopsychiatry, 64,* 564–576.

Dishion, T. J., & McMahon, R. J. (1998). Parental monitoring and the prevention of child and adolescent problem behavior: A conceptual and empirical formulation. *Clinical Child and Family Psychology Review, 1,* 61–75.

Downey, G., & Coyne, J. C. (1990). Children of depressed parents: An integrative review. *Psychological Bulletin, 108,* 50–76.

Dryfoos, J. G. (1990). *Adolescents at risk: Prevalence and prevention.* New York: Oxford University Press.

Duchnowski, A. J., & Friedman, R. M. (1990). Children's mental health: Challenges for the nineties. *Journal of Mental Health Administration, 17,* 3–12.

Duchnowski, A. J., Kutash, K., & Friedman, R. M. (2002). Community-based interventions in a system of care and outcomes framework. In B. J. Burns & K. Hoagwood (Eds.), *Community treatment for youth: Evidence-based interventions for severe emotional and behavioral disorders* (pp. 16–37). New York: Oxford University Press.

Dunst, C. J., Trivette, C., & Paget, A. (1994). *Supporting and strengthening families.* Cambridge: Brookline Books.

Dunst, C. J., Trivette, C. M., & Deal, A. G. (1988). *Enabling and empowering families: Principles and guidelines for practice.* Cambridge: Brookline Books.

Early, T. J., Gregorie, T. K., & McDonald, T. P. (2002). Child functioning and caregiver well-being in families of children with emotional disorders: A longitudinal analysis. *Journal of Family Issues, 22,* 374–391.

Eber, L., & Nelson, C. M. (1997). Integrating services for students with emotional and behavioral needs through school-based wraparound planning. *American Journal of Orthopsychiatry, 67,* 385–395.

Eber, L., Osuch, R., & Redditt, C. A. (1996). School-based applications of the wraparound process: Early results on service provision and student outcomes. *Journal of Child and Family Studies, 5,* 83–99.

Epstein, M. H., Kutash, K., & Duchnowski, A. (1998). Outcomes for children and youth with emotional and behavioral disorders and their families: Programs and evaluation best practices. Austin: Pro-Ed Inc.

Farmer, E. M. Z., Burns, B. J., Angold, A., & Costello, E. J. (1997). Impact of children's mental health problems on families: Relationships with service use. *Journal of Emotional and Behavioral Disorders, 5,* 230–238.

Floyd, A. (2007). Collaboratives: Avenues to build community capacity. In P.S Motes & P. Hess (Eds.) *Collaborating with community-based organizations through consultation and technical assistance.* New York: Columbia University Press.

Fox, N., Leone, P., Rubin, K., Oppenheim, J., Miller, M., & Friedman, K. (1999). *Final report on the linkages to learning program and evaluation at Broad Acres Elementary School*. Washington: U.S. Department of Education.

Friesen, B. J., & Stephens, B. (1998). Expanding family roles in the system of care: Research and practice. In M. R. Epstein, K. Kutask, & A. J. Duchnowski (Eds.), *Outcomes for children and youth with behavioral and emotional disorders and their families: Programs and evaluation, best practices* (pp. 231–259). Austin: Pro-Ed Inc.

Greenbaum, S. D. (1998). The role of ethnography in creating linkages with communities: Identifying and assessing neighborhoods' needs and strengths. In M. Hernandez & M. R. Isaacs (Eds.), *Promoting cultural competence in children's mental health services* (pp. 119–132). Baltimore: Paul H. Brookes.

Greenberg, M. T., Kusche, C., & Mihalic, S. F. (1998). *Blueprints for violence prevention: Promoting alternative thinking strategies*. Boulder: University of Colorado, Institute of Behavioral Science, Center for the Study and Prevention of Violence.

Hammer, K. M., Lambert, E. W., & Bickman, L. (1997). Children's mental health in a continuum of care: Clinical outcomes at 18 months for the Fort Bragg Demonstration. *Journal of Mental Health Administration, 24,* 465–471.

Hanley, J. H., & Wright, H. (1995). Child mental health professionals: The missing link in child mental health reform. *Journal of Child and Family Studies, 4*(4), 383–388.

Hawkins, J. D., & Catalano, R. F. (1992). *Communities that care: Action for drug abuse prevention* (1st ed.). San Francisco: Jossey-Bass.

Hawkins, J., Catalano, R., & Miller, J. (1992). Risk and protective factors for alcohol and other drug problems in adolescence and early adulthood: Implications for substance abuse prevention. *Psychological Bulletin, 112,* 64–105

Henggeler, S. W., & Borduin, C. M. (1990). *Family therapy and beyond: A multisystemic approach to treating the behavior problems of children and adolescents*. Pacific Grove: Brooks/Cole.

Henggeler, S. W., Mihalic, S. F., Rone, L., Thomas, C., & Timmons-Mitchell, J. (1998). *Blueprints for violence prevention, book six: Multisystemic therapy*. Boulder: Center for the Study and Prevention of Violence.

Henggeler, S. W., Schoenwald, S. K., Pickrel, S. G., Rowland, M. D., & Santos, A. B. (1994). The contribution of treatment outcome research to the reform of children's mental health services: Multisytemic family therapy as an example. *Journal of Mental Health Administration, 21,* 229–239.

Hoagwood, K., Burns, B. J., Kiser, L., Ringeisen, H., & Schoenwald, S. K. (2001). Evidence-based practice in child and adolescent mental health services. *Psychiatric Services, 52*(9), 1179–1189.

Hochberg, M. R. (1993). *Building villages to raise our children: Staffing*. Cambridge: Harvard Family Research Project.

Holtzman, H. (1992). *School of the future*. Austin: American Psychological Association and Hogg Foundation for Mental Health.

Jivanjee, P. R., & Friesen, B.J. (1997). Shared expertise: Family participation in interprofessional training. *Journal of Emotional and Behavioral Disorders, 5,* 205–211.

Knitzer, J. (1982). *Unclaimed children: The failure of public responsibility to children and adolescents in need of mental health services*. Washington: Children's Defense Fund.

Knitzer, J., Steinberg, Z., & Fleisch, B. (1993). *At the schoolhouse door: An examination of programs and policies for children with behavioral and emotional problems*. New York: Bank Street College of Education.

Koren, P., Paulson, R. W., Kinney, R. F., Yatchmenoff, D. K., Gordon, L. J., & DeChillo, N. (1997). Service coordination in children's mental health: An empirical study from the caregiver's perspective. *Journal of Emotional and Behavioral Disorders, 5*(3), 162–172.

Kretzman, J. P., & McKnight, J. L. (1993). *Building communities from the inside out: A path toward finding and mobilizing a community's assets*. Evanston: Northwestern University, Center for Urban Affairs and Policy Research, Neighborhood Innovations Network.

Kutash, K., & Duchnowski, A. J. (1997). Create comprehensive and collaborative systems. *Journal of Emotional and Behavioral Disorders, 11,* 66–75.

Kutash, K., Duchnowski, A. J., Sumi, W. C., Rudo, Z., & Harris, K. M. (2002). A school, family, and community collaborative program for children who have emotional disturbances. *Journal of Emotional and Behavioral Disorders, 11,* 66–75.

LaGreca, A. M., & Hughes, J. N. (1999). United we stand, divided we fall: The education and training needs of clinical child psychologists. *Journal of Clinical Child Psychology, 28,* 435–447.

Leone, P. E., Evert, R.J., & Friedman, K. (2002). Building linkages to learning through community partnerships. In B. Algozzine & P. Kay (Eds.), *Preventing problem behaviors* (pp. 126–141). Thousand Oaks: Corwin.

Leone, P., Lane, S., & Arllen, N., & Peter, H. (1996). School-linked services in context: A formative evaluation of Linkages to Learning. *Special Services to the Schools, 11,* 119–133.

Lewinsohn, P. M., Roberts, R. E., Seeley, J. R., Rohde, P., Gotlib, I. H., & Hops, H. (1994). Adolescent psychopathology: II. Psychosocial risk factors for depression. *Journal of Abnormal Psychology, 103,* 302–315.

Lindahl, K. M., & Malik, N. M. (1999). Linking marital conflict and children's adjustment: The role of triadic family processes in Anglo and Hispanic families. *Journal of Clinical Child Psychology, 28,* 12–24.

Mayes, L. C. (1999). Addressing mental health needs of infants and young children. *Child and Adolescent Psychiatric Clinics of North America, 8,* 209–224.

McCabe, K. M., Clark, R., & Barnett, D. (1999). Family protective factors among urban African American youth. *Journal of Clinical Child Psychology, 28*(2), 137–150.

McGinty, K., McCammon, S. L., & Koeppen, V. P. (2001). The complexities of implementing a wraparound approach to service provision: A view from the field. *Journal of Family Social Work, 5,* 95–110.

McLaughlin, M. J., Leone, P. E., Meisel, S., & Henderson, K. (1997). Strengthen school and community spirit. *Journal of Emotional and Behavioral Disorders, 5,* 15–23.

Miller, D. N., DuPaul, G. J., & Lutz, J. G. (2002). School-based psychosocial interventions for childhood depression: Acceptability of treatments among school psychologists. *School Psychology Quarterly, 17,* 78–99.

Modrcin, M. J., & Robison, J. (1991). Parents of children with emotional disorders: Issues for consideration and practice. *Community Mental Health Journal, 27,* 281–293.

Motes, P. S., Melton, G., Pumariega, A., & Simmons, W. W. (1999). Ecologically-oriented school-based mental health services: Implications for service system reform. *Psychology in the Schools, 36,* 391–401.

Olson, A. L., Kelleher, K. J., Kemper, K. J., Zuckerman, B. S., Hammond, C. S., & Dietrich, A. J. (2001). Primary care pediatricians' roles and perceived responsibilities in the identification and management of depression in children and adolescents. *Ambulatory Pediatrics, 1,* 91–98.

Petersen, A. C., Compas, B. E., Brooks-Gunn, J., Stemmler, M., Ey, S., & Grant, K E. (1993). Depression in adolescence. *American Psychologist, 48,* 155–168.

Resnick, M. D., Bearman, P. S., Blum, R. W., Bauman, K. E., Harris, K. M., Jones, J., et al. (1997). Protecting adolescents from harm: Findings from the National Longitudinal Study on Adolescent Health. *Journal of the American Medical Association, 278*(10/September 10), 823–832.

Roeser, R., & Midgley, C. (1997). Teachers' views of issues involving students' mental health. *Elementary School Journal, 98,* 115–133.

Sanders, M. R. (1999). Triple P-Positive Parenting Program: Towards an empirically validated multilevel parenting and family support strategy for the prevention of behavior and emotional problems in children. *Clinical Child and Family Psychology Review, 2,* 71–90.

Skiba, R. J., & Nichols, S. (2000). What works in wraparound programming. In M. P. Kluger, G. Alexander, & P. A. Curtis (Eds.), *What works in child welfare* (pp. 23–32). Washington: CWLA.

Stroul, B. A. (1988). *Series on community-based services for children and adolescents who are severely emotionally disturbed, Vol. I: Home-based services.* Washington: CASSP Technical Assistance Center, Georgetown University Child Development Center.

Stroul, B., & Freidman, R. (1986). *A system of care: Children and youth with severe emotional disturbance.* Washington: Georgetown University Child Development Center, National Technical Assistance Center for Children's Mental Health.

Suarez, L. M., & Baker, B. L. (1997) Child externalizing behavior and parents' stress: The role of social support. *Family Relations, 46,* 373–381.

Thompson, R. W., Ruma, P. R., Brewster, A. L., Besetsney, L. K., & Burke, R. V. (1997). Evaluation of an Air Force child physical abuse prevention project using the reliable change index. *Journal of Child and Family Studies, 6,* 421–434.

U.S. Department of Education. (1994). *National agenda for achieving better results for children and youth with serious emotional disturbance.* Washington: Office of Special Education Programs.

U.S. Department of Health and Human Services. (1999). *Mental health: A report of the Surgeon General, executive summary.* Rockville: U.S. Department of Health and Human Services, Substance Abuse and Mental Health Services Administration, Center for Mental Health Services, National Institutes of Health, National Institute of Mental Health.

U.S. Public Health Service. (2000). *Report of the Surgeon General's conference on children's mental health: A national action agenda.* Washington: Department of Health and Human Services, 2000.

Wagner, M. M. (1995). Outcomes for youths with serious emotional disturbance in secondary school and early adulthood. *Critical Issues for Children and Youth, 5,* 90–112

Waxman, R. P., Weist, M. D., & Benson, D. M. (1999). Toward collaboration in the growing education-mental health interface. *Clinical Psychology Review, 19*(2), 239–253.

Wills, T. A., Vaccaro, D., & McNamara, G. (1992). The role of life events, family support, and competence in adolescent substance abuse: A test of vulnerability and protective factors. *American Journal of Community Psychology, 20*(3), 349–374.

Winters, N. C., & Pumarieaga, A. J. (2001). Systems of care for children and adolescents with serious emotional difficulties. In V. H. Booney & A. J. Pumariega (Eds.), *Clinical assessment of child and adolescent behavior* (pp. 513–532). New York: Wiley.

Yoe, J., Santarcangelo, S., Atkins, M., & Burchard, J. (1996). Wraparound care in Vermont: Program development, implementation, and evaluation of a statewide system of individualized services. *Journal of Child and Family Studies, 5,* 22–39.

Midlife Concerns and Caregiving Experiences: Intersecting Life Issues Affecting Mental Health

Jane E. Myers and Melanie C. Harper

Midlife Concerns and Caregiving Experiences: Intersecting Life Issues

> Using data from the National Survey of Families and Households, I have determined that a significant proportion (about 16 %) of the U.S. adult population engages in in-household or out-of-household caregiving for a disabled family member or friend at any given time. Caregiving rates peak during the midlife years (ages 35–64) for both women and men. Caregiving also continues at relatively high rates into young old age. (Marks 1996).

> Midlife—the years between 30 and 70, with 40–60 at its core—is perhaps the least studied and most ill-defined of any period in life. It abounds with changing images and myths—the "midlife crisis," the "change of life," the "empty nest syndrome," and many more. But we have little documentation and less understanding of what really happens, biologically or psychologically, during this extended period of time (MacArthur Foundation n. d.).

These two quotes are illustrative of core aspects of caregiving as well as midlife, and reflect the intersection of these phenomena in the lives of many individuals. Consistent with the quote from the John D. and Catherine T. MacArthur Foundation Research Network on Successful Midlife Development, Brim (1992) noted that midlife is "the last uncharted territory in human development" (p. 171). Lachman (2001), in the introduction to her seminal *Handbook of Midlife Development*, underscored the complexity of the midlife period and the disparate perspectives that must be reconciled if we are to achieve an accurate understanding of the experience of development in the middle years. She suggested that the only way to truly understand

J. E. Myers (✉)
Department of Counseling & Educational Development,
The University of North Carolina at Greensboro, 217 Curry Building,
Greensboro, NC 27402-6171, USA
e-mail: jemyers@uncg.edu

M. C. Harper
St. Mary's University, San Antonio, TX 78228, USA
e-mail: mharper@stmarytx.edu

R. C. Talley et al. (eds.), *The Challenges of Mental Health Caregiving*,
Caregiving: Research • Practice • Policy, DOI 10.1007/978-1-4614-8791-3_7,

midlife is to incorporate multiple perspectives, and to recognize "the vast range of possibilities and variations by historical period, timing of events in the life course, gender, culture, race, ethnicity, and social class" (p. xviii).

Caregiving is one experience that transcends or perhaps permeates the multiple perspectives required to understand midlife experiences. The fact that families are the frontline of care, and that one in four households includes a caregiver, has been well established (National Alliance for Caregiving & AARP 1997). Among those who provide care, persons in midlife predominate (Marks 1996). At any time, approximately 20 % of midlife women and 14 % of midlife men provide care to relatives and friends who are ill or have disabilities. Caregiving during the middle years is so common that Brody (1985) defined it as a normative midlife experience, a definition recently challenged by Putney and Bengtson (2001), and Cavanaugh (1998) explained it as a normative "life event challenge" (p. 131). To get a further understanding of caregiving in midlife, it is first necessary to understand midlife and the normative developmental processes and experiences of this period of life.

In this chapter, common midlife changes and experiences are described, followed by a review of theoretical perspectives that contribute to an understanding of individual psychological and emotional responses in the middle years. This information provides a foundation for examining caregiving in midlife, including the dynamics of caregiving experiences, the needs of caregivers, and the resources available to address those needs. The chapter concludes with a summary of what is known about caregiving in midlife and a discussion of policies, programs, and resources required to meet the needs of midlife caregivers now and in the future.

Midlife: Physical, Psychological, and Social Processes

People in midlife have been variously referred to as being in the "command" or "power" generation, as they occupy positions of power and authority in most societies, and as the "sandwich" generation, squeezed in the middle between their adolescent children striving to reach independent adulthood and their aging parents becoming potentially dependent. The middle years of the life span, called "middlescence" by some, is seen as similar to adolescence in being a time fraught with challenges, turmoil, and crisis. Popular language tells us both that "life begins at 40" and one is "over the hill at 40". Sorting out the mythology of what midlife is all about requires consideration of the physical, psychological, and social processes and changes of this challenging developmental period.

Physical Change in Midlife

The physical changes attributed to midlife begin much earlier, actually in the 20s, but become visible or noticeable around the age of 40 for most people. These include wrinkling and sagging of the skin due to loss of subcutaneous fat, the development of "age spots" due to changes in skin pigmentation, and thinning as well as graying of the hair. Height begins to decrease and weight tends to increase. Both bone density and muscle strength begin to decline, with concomitant decreases in energy. Declines in all body systems are evident, especially vision and cardiovascular efficiency.

Although rates of accidents as well as infectious illnesses decline in midlife, rates of chronic disease increase. These diseases are characterized by slow onset and long duration. For women, the most frequent chronic disorders are arthritis, hypertension, and sinus problems, while for men the most common are hypertension, arthritis, and hearing impairments (Santrock 2002). Both men and women experience declines in sexual functioning. For men the climacteric is very gradual and subtle; for women, menopause can range from a nonevent passage to a life-changing physical and biomedical condition (Huffman and Myers 1999).

The physical changes of midlife are universal, gradual, decremental, and highly variable in timing and overt manifestation across individuals. Some, such as declines in energy, can be mediated by lifestyle choices (e.g., exercise), while others, such as graying hair, can be masked though not reversed (e.g., through the use of hair dyes and cosmetics). For many, the most significant impact of physical change is reflected in psychological responses, rather than physical functioning per se.

Psychological Aspects of the Midlife Experience

The awareness of physical change and decline confronts people in midlife with the reality that they are no longer young. Additional life and family changes, such as the aging of parents and the ascendance of adolescent children to adulthood, contribute to this growing awareness of the life span, and the fact that one's life is now half over. Turmoil, anxiety, and fears related to growing older are not uncommon, and as a consequence about a fourth of persons over the age of 35 report experiencing a midlife crisis (Wethington 2000). A researcher in the MIDMAC study, the largest study ever conducted on midlife, Wethington reports that more than half of those who report having a midlife crisis actually experience stressful life events instead due to their awareness of the aging process, and the feeling that life might be passing them by, as well as challenging situations and events, such as job transitions, that require a response based on the new awareness of personal aging. She also noted, contrary to popular mythology, a lack of gender differences in the experience of crisis during this period of the life span.

Transcending all aspects of change in midlife, and integral to understanding personal responses to change, is a new conception of the meaning of time and mortality; in fact, the hallmark of the midlife transition is a shift in time perspective (Jacques 1967, cited in Papalia et al. 2002). Where once life was viewed as infinite, midlife carries a new awareness of one's mortality and the finite nature of the life span. This new awareness stimulates a reevaluation of life goals and often an urgency to set and achieve new goals (Jung 1966; Neugarten 1977). Decisions related to relationships, such as marriage, and vocations, are made in the context of this new awareness of time left to live, and new beliefs in one's ability to achieve satisfaction and success in meeting life goals with only a limited amount of available time. Relatedly, persons in midlife often experience a general mellowing in response to life events, understanding that things tend to work out given sufficient time, combined with a renewed sense of meaning concerning the importance of various life events (Vaillant 1989).

Questions concerning the meaning of life and death, or existential concerns about one's purpose in life, are often viewed as the core of the midlife transition and reflect the spiritual challenges of the middle years. Paproski (2001), following qualitative analysis of interviews with 7 women and 3 men between 47 and 63 years of age in British Columbia, concluded that spirituality plays a significant role in the developmental processes of midlife by helping people cope with challenges and losses and revise their values and identity as a consequence. Although the findings of Paproski's study were limited further by the racial and ethnic homogeneity of participants (9 of the participants were Caucasian and 1 participant was Asian), the findings support the premise that for at least some adults, spiritual examination and development provide a foundation for the examination and resolution of existential concerns during the midlife transition.

As children reach adulthood and the demands of parenting diminish, persons in late midlife may experience a greater sense of freedom relative to their time, and goals once delayed as secondary to parenting and careers may now acquire new meaning. Moreover, earnings peak in the middle years and adult children leave home, resulting in more flexible income for many people. This new sense of free time combined with prospects of retirement creates demands for learning to use leisure time effectively (Kelly 1996; McGuire 2000). Avocational pursuits postponed during childrearing years and new opportunities for creative use of free time now become possible and desirable.

In contrast to the thought of midlife as the generation in "command," Lowenthal et al. (1975) reported that the changes of midlife and beyond are more stressful than those of any other period of the life span, due to physical declines and a loss of roles and sense of personal power. These losses occurring as opportunities for reaching expectations (such as raising children or achieving a certain level of professional success or personal competence) seem to diminish, in marked contrast to the growth and expansion of earlier adulthood when all dreams still feel possible. They postulated that midlife adults experience the most stress and the least sense of control due to their inability to delay or prevent the aging process. In particular, these researchers noted that midlife women experience the greatest challenges to adjustment and the most maladjustment, reflected in the fact that depression peaks in midlife, especially for women. In addition to personal processes of aging, many of the sources of stress in midlife are due to changing social aspects of life.

Social Aspects of Midlife

Social aspects of midlife are as variable across individuals as are physical changes. Midlife is a time for changes related to the meaningful use of time, including work, leisure, and planning for retirement. Additional social changes revolve around family relationships and dynamics, including parental loss and grandparenting.

Although job satisfaction increases steadily throughout the adult life span, middle-aged workers today face challenges due to factors such as the globalization of economies, rapid changes in technology combined with the creation and elimination of whole classes of occupations, downsizing of organizations, and the option of early retirement (Avolio and Sosik 1999). Midlife career changes have become increasingly common, stimulated at times by corporate decisions constituting forcible change. For others, change represents the opportunity for new directions and the achievement of new goals (Moen and Wethington 1999). In either case, a sense of urgency may exist relative to midlife career change, as the individual recognizes that only a finite amount of time exists in which one can obtain training for, employment in, and advancement across a new career path.

Alternately, midlife carries the certainty that one is approaching retirement and hence there is a need to plan for one's lifestyle in the later years. Kim and Moen (2001) underscored the changing nature of retirement in relation to longevity and economic transformations. Based on a trend at the end of the twentieth century toward retirement in the fifth decade of life, combined with increases in longevity, they suggested, "retirement is no longer the upper boundary of midlife, as men and women face an extended postretirement phase of activity and vitality" (p. 489). Although the recent rise in the minimum age for receiving full Social Security benefits and the reduction in retiree health benefits offered by many employers might reverse the trend toward earlier retirement, in 2004 there seemed to be a continued steady decline in involvement in the labor force after the age of 55 (Purcell 2005). Timing of, attitudes toward, and reasons for exit from the labor force (i.e., voluntary retirement, forced retirement, and disability) vary by gender (Dentinger and Clarkberg 2002; Purcell 2005; Szinovacz et al. 2001), race, and ethnicity (Flippen and Tienda 2000; Szinovacz et al. 2001). For women, who may enter the labor force later than men, the opportunity to retire may not occur until later in life due to fewer years of service and lower income (Dietz et al. 2003). Although participation in the labor force during the past decade has remained fairly constant for midlife and older men, for midlife and older women, participation in the labor force has increased (Purcell 2005). As midlife adults prepare for and possibly enter retirement, activity revolves around social relationships, which, for persons in midlife, "have probably never been more dynamic—or more complicated" (Antonucci et al. 2001, p. 571).

Social relationships in midlife include friendship, community, and work relationships, as well as family and intergenerational family relationships. All of these relationships may be sources of comfort as well as stress (Antonucci et al. 2001). For example, midlife is a time when the divorce rate increases and new relationships between individuals and members of blended families are negotiated. Putney and Bengtson (2001) summarized existing research on midlife families and identified four key themes or issues: (1) family caregiving and the competing role demands experienced by persons in midlife; (2) the increasingly longer dependency of adult children; (3) family solidarity and/or conflict and the impact on well-being of family members; and (4) kinkeeping, or the maintenance of strong family ties, most often a task assumed by women. Of increasing significance is the new role of grandparenting, which in itself is among the most variable of social roles during the midlife years.

From a traditional perspective, grandparenting provides a source of biological renewal and continuity, as well as emotional fulfillment (Sanders and Trygstad 1993). Some individuals adopt a grandparenting style that is fun and interactive, others choose a more formal role in which the older family member is a source of wisdom and family history, while others choose a distant role that may include benevolence but is characterized by infrequent intergenerational contact (Neugarten and Weinstein 1964). Younger grandparents tend to be more involved in multiple social roles and both less satisfied with and less invested in grandparenting roles, leading Burton and Bengtson (1985) to conclude that "the experience of grandparenting may be most strongly related to timing and family intergenerational dynamics" (p. 62). A notable exception is the significant increase in the numbers of grandchildren living with grandparents, a number which has doubled in the last two decades. This phenomenon is discussed later, following a review of major theories of midlife development that provide a context for understanding the impact of grandparenting as a caregiving role in midlife.

Theoretical Perspectives on Midlife Development

Staudinger and Bluck (2001) hypothesized that the scarcity of research on midlife is due to the fact that there is "no clear demarcation of midlife, at least not as clear as the ones for childhood as the beginning and old age as the end of life" (p. 4). Chronological age is far less useful in predicting the behavior of adults than of children, and subjective reports of middle age status tend to be a more reliable indicator than age of navigation through the middle years (Neugarten and Datan 1996). That said, there is a general agreement about the ages that constitute midlife, and thus a variety of theories that purport to explain this developmental period. For purposes of discussion, these theories can be grouped according to views of midlife in the context of life span development, theories of adult development, and theories that emphasize context and transition as explanatory of developmental processes.

Life Span Theories

Traditional approaches to development emphasized the critical nature of childhood with little change occurring in adulthood or later life (Santrock 2002). In contrast, life span theories emphasize the changing nature of development over the life span, and suggest that change occurs through sequential stages that are more or less linear and hierarchical. Erikson (1963) proposed that development occurs through eight psychosocial stages, each confronting the individual with a central crisis that must be faced and resolved. In midlife, the central crisis is defined as *generativity versus stagnation*. Generativity allows the adult to achieve a sense of immortality by leaving something of value to the next generation, while stagnation, or self-absorption, occurs when the person lacks or fails to fulfill a desire to leave behind a legacy. According to this theory, adults in midlife are primarily concerned with making a positive and lasting impact on their maturing adolescent children.

Havinghurst (1974) proposed seven life span stages based on learning theory and postulated a handful of tasks to be learned in each sequential stage. The tasks of midlife include achieving adult social and civic responsibilities, establishing and maintaining an economic standard of living, assisting teenage children to become responsible adults, developing leisure time pursuits, relating to one's spouse as a person, accepting the physiological changes of middle age, and adjusting to aging parents. Similar to Erikson, Havighurst proposed that the successful accomplishment of tasks in each stage was necessary for positive developmental progression across the life span.

More recently, Baltes (2000) defined the life span perspective as incorporating seven major components. These include the beliefs that development is lifelong, multidimensional, multidirectional, plastic, and contextual. In addition, the study of development is multidisciplinary and involves growth, maintenance, and regulation. These beliefs are reflected in a variety of current theories of adult development.

Theories of Adult Development

Adult development theories attempt to explain observed changes in behavior, cognition, and affect across the three periods of adult life: young adulthood (20–40 years), middle adulthood (40–65 years), and late adulthood (ages 65+; Papalia et al. 2002). Three theories that are particularly salient for understanding midlife include those of Jung (1966), Neugarten (1977), and Levinson (1978).

Jung observed that midlife is a time for two significant psychological changes: increased introspection and an increased need for balance. The first change involves increased interiority, or greater concern with one's inner life. Consistent with this change, Jung viewed midlife as a period of significant spiritual growth in preparation for later life, with diminishment on the personal ego and a growing awareness of the presence of a higher power in the universe. The second change is reflected in a variety of behaviors, notably efforts to develop more balance in one's gender identity. Thus, people experience "greater autonomy over choices and roles than is offered by the unitary, society-driven, sex-role orientation of the young" (Staudinger and Bluck 2001, p. 11). Jung also suggested that midlife is a time when extraversion and introversion become more balanced, with greater concern directed toward internal experiencing rather than external demands.

Neugarten (1977) also emphasized the greater interiority of midlife adults, attributing this to the replacement of the biological clock of childhood with the psychological and social clocks of adulthood. She noted that the changing view of time experienced in the middle years (i.e., seeing life no longer as time since birth but as time left to live) permits midlife adults to develop a sense of their own life cycle. This new sense permits comparisons with others along an expected continuum of stereotypical social goals (i.e., family and occupational accomplishments) as well as more in-depth examination of one's personal goals and priorities. The transitions of midlife result in greater maturity and a more significant sense of purpose in creating positive outcomes for oneself and others.

Levinson (1978) also examined the interaction of biological and social influences in adulthood, and particularly in midlife, through studies of 40 men between 35 and 45 years of age who lived between Boston and New York. The men were evenly divided among four occupations (hourly workers, executives, academic biologists, and novelists), were primarily Caucasian (only 12 % were identified as Black), and were mostly well educated (70 % had completed college). Following extensive biographical interviews with the men, Levinson proposed that young adulthood is a time for establishing an identity, defining an occupational dream and career, developing an intimate relationship, and starting a family. In midlife, a time when men have typically achieved the goals of young adulthood, a search for meaning in life takes precedence over achievement. Midlife crisis occurs as men attempt to reorder their priorities, with greater emphasis on relationships and less on careers. Midlife crisis typically occurs during the transition into midlife, which requires that one come to terms with or resolve four major conflicts that have existed since adolescence: being young versus being old, being destructive versus being constructive, being masculine versus being feminine, and being attached to others versus being separated from them.

Longitudinal research by Helson (1992) with 88 mostly upper-middle-class White graduates of Mills College, a private women's college in California, suggests that women experience a different progression of stages in adulthood than those proposed by Levinson to explain the development of men. Helson found that the women, who were studied between their college graduation (1958–1960) and their mid-50s, experienced turmoil in their early 40s, however, crisis appeared at other times in their lives also, such as during early marriage and parenting. Women may experience struggles for independent identity in work and family during young adulthood, and in early midlife, common developmental themes include put-downs and barriers to success in the workplace and abandonment by partners as consequences of independence and assertiveness at home and at work. One later midlife theme is overload, which can result from difficulties and changes in relationships with partners, children, and parents, multiple roles, and economic strain.

Schaie's (2000) meta-analyses of longitudinal studies focused on the charting of adult cognitive development patterns. Schaie found that chronic diseases, environmental circumstances, and psychological characteristics during midlife, along with genetic characteristics, were predictors of cognitive functioning in later life. Caregiving during midlife could affect these predictors, as caregiving has been associated with poorer subjective health and changes in activities (National Alliance for Caregiving & AARP 2004). Thus, caregiving may affect cognitive development years after caregiving responsibilities end.

Contextual and Transition Theories

The complexity of individual development has led to a recent emphasis on context as the foundation for understanding human functioning as well as growth and change. Sociocultural contexts include the environment or setting, culture, ethnicity, and gender (Santrock 2002). These contexts are embedded in Bronfenbrenner's (2000) ecological theory. In this system theory, five environmental systems affect and are affected by the individual. These include the microsystem, mesosystem, exosystem, macrosystem, and chronosystem. The microsystem, or the setting in which one lives, includes family, peers, school, and neighborhood. The mesosystem involves relationships between various microsystems. The exosystem includes external contexts such as the government, that have an affect on individuals, and the macrosystem represents the attitudes and ideologies of one's culture. The chronosystem is comprised of patterns of changes and transitions over the life course. Although caregiving may be viewed as primarily existing in the microsystem, the interrelationships between that microsystem and the other systems form a more complete context for the individual's experience of caregiving. For example, the level of support for and facilitation of the caregiver role by other family members, friends, the workplace, social and religious organizations, and governmental agencies can affect the individual's stress related to and satisfaction with caregiving. Similarly, cultural attitudes toward caregiving and past experiences with changing relationships, work transitions, and caregiving (possibly even as a child observing a parent transitioning to the caregiver role) can yield a personal environment of confidence and acceptance or hesitance and reluctance as the midlife adult encounters new caregiving opportunities or demands.

Schlossberg et al. (1995) defined transitions as "any event, or non-event, that results in changed relationships, routines, assumptions, and roles. Transitions often require new patterns of behavior" (p. 27). Consistent with other adult development theorists (e.g., Levinson), Schlossberg, Walters, and Goodman go on to describe adult development not in terms of linear age-related stages and tasks, but rather in terms of life events to which the individual must adapt. The adaptation process requires an evaluation of the type and context of the transition, the assets and liabilities of the individual, and resources for support and coping. Transitions occur over time, with the process of adaptation sometimes requiring months or years.

The changes of midlife are among the most significant of the adult life span, and thus, they result in an extended period of adjustment, or transition individually as well as collectively. There is general consensus that the ultimate focus of change in midlife is internal, and external demands from families, peers, employers, and others may create conflicts that accentuate the challenges of the midlife period. Central to the present discussion is the role of caregiver, which often has its onset during the challenging and sometimes tumultuous midlife decades.

Caregiving in Midlife: Intersections and Interactions

Similar to the normative developmental challenges of midlife, caregiving is a singularly complex and multifaceted phenomenon. Although caregiving has both positive and negative consequences, responses of caregivers are primarily explained in terms of stress, burden, and negative comorbid physical and mental health outcomes (e.g., Gallagher-Thompson et al. 1998; Haug et al. 1999; Vitaliano et al. 1997). Models purporting to explain both the positive and negative outcomes of caregiving experiences are primarily based in literature on stress and coping (e.g., Pearlin et al. 1990; Schulz and Salthouse 1999). Significant midlife issues that can also be explained in this context include the gendered nature of the caregiving experience, cultural variations in caregiving, and grandparenting as caregiving. Each of these issues is explored below, followed by a brief review of the literature addressing interventions to help midlife caregivers cope with the multiple stresses of providing care.

Gendered Nature of Caregiving

Women, the traditional kinkeepers in most societies, bear the brunt of caregiving duties (Stone et al. 1987). Moreover, the nature of the caregiving experience differs for men and women, consistent with a gender-based division of labor (Connell et al. 2001). Men are most likely to arrange services or care management while women are more likely to provide hands-on and personal care (Neal et al. 1997). Women caregivers on average provide more hours of caregiving than men caregivers, and women provide over twice as much care as men for individuals who need the highest levels of care (National Alliance for Caregiving & AARP 2004). Although most midlife caregivers are employed, caregivers providing the highest level of care, which requires more than 40 hours a week of caregiving, are more likely to be employed part-time or retired than caregivers who have lesser responsibilities in their caregiving roles. Possibly, to support different approaches to caregiving or because of the added demands of caring for persons with greater needs, women tend to retire more quickly and men more slowly when faced with caregiving responsibilities (Dentinger and Clarkberg 2002). Early retirement and other common work accommodations such as reduced hours of work, adjustments to work schedules, and refusal of career enhancing opportunities can affect women's long-term financial situations by reducing career growth, salary, and retirement income (MetLife Mature Market Institute 1999). This long-term financial impact can increase women caregivers' risk for poverty later in life. Most studies report that women also experience higher levels of depression than men do when placed in caregiving roles (Yee and Schulz 2000); however, Baronet (1999), following an extensive review of the literature on caregiver burden, concluded that gender is unrelated to either objective or subjective burden. Findings from a 2003 national survey of 6,139 adults in the USA, however, indicate that persons who provide the highest levels of caregiving subjectively experience greater levels of emotional stress, physical strain, and financial burden than persons who provide lower levels of caregiving (National Alliance for Caregiving & AARP). Considering that women provide a disproportionate amount of higher-level caregiving than men and are more likely than men to feel that they have had no choice but to take on caregiving responsibilities, women are more likely to experience a sense of greater burden from their increased caregiving responsibilities.

Almost two-thirds of adult women are now employed outside the home, leaving women less available for caregiving duties. Thus, gender differences in patterns and consequences of caregiving are becoming more of a source of family conflict (Neal et al. 1997). The addition of the caregiver role for women adds to the already challenging tasks of midlife. Most midlife women caregivers are married or live with a partner and work, and most younger midlife caregivers (35–49 years of age) have children under the age of 18 (National Alliance for Caregiving & AARP 2004). For about 30 % of midlife caregivers, their caregiving role is multiplied by providing care to more than one recipient. With the average duration of the caregiving role estimated at 4.3 years and 17 % of older midlife adults (50–64 years of age) reporting that they have been providing care for more than 10 years, added caregiver roles can affect much of midlife. The multiple roles engaged in by women in midlife, combined with the normative physical, psychological, and social challenges of midlife development, combine to make women in midlife a population at risk for both physical and mental illnesses in response to overwhelming and often conflicting sources of stress.

Logsdon and Robinson (2000) underscore the importance of social support in helping women cope with caregiving stress, however, they also explain a number of significant barriers that prevent women from receiving support. These include a lack of adequate alternate care providers, over-involvement in caregiving roles leading to shrinkage of one's social support system, and a lack of comfort in asking for or receiving assistance. In addition, women are socialized to believe that caregiving duties can be performed without assistance. Such beliefs vary across cultures and contribute to cultural and ethnic differences in caregiving outcomes (Connell et al. 2001).

Cultural Variations in Caregiving

Cultural beliefs and values affect decision making across the life span. For example, the meaning of terms such as dependence and aging, notions of health and illness, and perceptions of the roles of males and females and persons of differing ages vary across cultures (Olson 2001). Beliefs about help-seeking behaviors and the appropriateness of nonfamily care also vary across persons of differing cultural and ethnic backgrounds. As a consequence, informal or family caregivers may experience inordinate stressors due to cultural beliefs about the nature of care provision and the singular role of family care to persons in need.

"For groups that stress collectivism, interdependence, and close family ties, dependency of frail elderly parents is an expected and accepted phase of the family life cycle" (Olson 2001, p. 7). In these cultures, frail older individuals move in with younger family members, and multigenerational households, with the stresses attendant to blended families, are common. The kinkeepers in these situations are most often midlife women, who provide at least three times as many hours providing care as other family members, while simultaneously attempting to care for young and adolescent children, maintain intimate relationships with spouses, and maintain employment to garner needed economic resources for the family. What differs for those of low socioeconomic status and many ethnic minorities is that women frequently lack a spouse to share at least some of the duties of economic sustenance as well as care provision (Putney and Bengtson 2001).

Ethnicity has been found to be an important background variable affecting the relationship between stress and caregiver well-being (Haley et al. 1996). African-American caregivers, for example, are more likely to report having a network of extended family to help in care provision and thus report less caregiving stress than do Caucasian caregivers. Korean-American caregivers, while reporting higher levels of family ties, also report greater depression, anxiety, and burden (Connell et al. 2001).

Further, the effects of religiosity on caregiver well-being are mediated by ethnicity (Wykle and Segall 1991). This relationship helps to explain the differences in subjective burden reported by African-American families when indices of objective burden (e.g., restriction of social activity) are the same for these individuals and Caucasian families (Haley et al. 1995). For additional information on the impact of culture and ethnicity in caregiving, see Chap. 3.

Grandparenting as Caregiving

By the late 1990s, 5.5 % of children under age 18 lived in homes maintained by their grandparents, a 44 % increase over the preceding decade, representing over 2.5 million households (Fuller-Thompson and Minkler 2001). This caregiving commitment is primarily long term in nature, with 56 % of grandparents providing care for more than 3 years, and one in five for more than 10 years. A partial explanation for this burgeoning phenomenon is increases in teen childbearing, which have resulted in a "compression of generations" wherein young grandmothers are raising both their children and their grandchildren (Bengtson 2001). Additional reasons include the high rate of divorce, an explosion in the prison population making parents unavailable to their children, increases in the number of women using crack cocaine, and increases in AIDS (Glass and Honeycutt 2002).

The consequences of the caregiving role for grandparents can be positive as well as negative. On the positive side, grandparents may feel needed and enjoy relationships with their grandchildren; on the negative side, they need to deal with a variety of personal losses, including loss of freedom, relationships with adult children, peer groups, leisure activities, and employment (Heywood 1999). Fuller-Thompson and Minkler (2001) analyzed data from the 1992–1994 National Survey of Families and Households and found that caregiving grandparents have 50 % higher odds of having activities of daily life (ADL) limitations; in addition, caregiving grandparents were more likely to rate their health lower and to report higher levels of depressive symptomatology. Higher levels of stress—financial, social, emotional, and relationship stress—are reported by grandparents when addictive, illegal, or unethical, or neglectful behaviors of children are the impetus for caregiving (Giarrusso et al. 2000). Younger grandparents and low family cohesion are also associated with higher levels of stress (Sands and Goldberg-Glen 2000), along with substance abuse and behavior problems of grandchildren (Glass and Honeycutt 2002).

Limited available research suggests "there appear to be both subcultural and/or ethnic differences in the experiences of custodial grandparents... (Cultural differences)... influence the mental health, role satisfaction, and role meaning of grandparents raising grandchildren who are experiencing emotional or behavioral difficulties, either arising from the divorce of or abuse by their parents or related to difficulties in adjusting to their grandparents who must now raise them" (Toledo et al. 2000, p. 108). Most cross-cultural research has focused on African-American grandparents in comparison to Caucasians, in part because of the higher incidence of custodial grandparenting in this population. African-American grandparents report feelings of being discounted by providers and isolated from support systems, and depend heavily on their faith beliefs for strength and consolation (Baird et al. 2000). Additional information on grandparent caregiving may be found in *Intergenerational Caregiving* (Talley, Henkin, and Butts [Eds.], this series).

Interventions for Midlife Caregivers

Not surprisingly, anxiety surrounding both the possibility and the reality of caregiving affects midlife caregiving families before, during, and after the end of caregiving experiences. Understanding and alleviating the negative effects of caregiving requires attention to both physical and mental challenges, to antecedents as well as consequences of the caregiving role, and to factors that can mediate and/or moderate these consequences. Moreover, successful interventions require consideration of the extended impact of caregiving on all members of the family system, not just the front-line care provider (Knight and McCallum 1998; Zarit et al. 1998). Three widely used types of intervention include respite care, support groups and counseling, and family interventions. Additionally, interventions that address specific immediate needs of caregivers should be developed or integrated more effectively into existing programs, and governmental policies should be reviewed to identify modifications that can help support caregivers and the persons for whom they provide care.

Respite care provides a "time out" for caregivers by providing an alternate means of assistance to care recipients for a short period of time, lasting from a few hours to a few days. McNally et al. (1999) conducted a review of 29 studies of respite care and concluded that "respite intervention has neither a consistent or enduring beneficial effect on carers' well-being" (p. 1). These authors underscored the need for a more "carer-centered" (p. 1) approach to the respite care experience.

The strong relationship between social support and caregiver subjective burden has given rise to an emphasis on support groups for caregivers as a means of reducing perceived stress. Research on the efficacy of support groups is equivocal. For example, using a delayed-treatment control group design, Schwiebert and Myers (1994) found no differences in caregiver burden as a result of support group participation, however, there was a significant increase in coping resource effectiveness for 51 midlife caregivers who participated in a structured group experience. Roberts et al. (2000) conducted a systematic review of literature on services and models of care for dementia caregivers, and did not even include support groups based on an earlier conclusion by Lavoie (1995) that support groups simply do not work. In contrast, Roberts et al. (2000) found that individual, supportive counseling in Canada was effective in reducing the number of nursing home placements, particularly at the early stages of dementia, and was instrumental in increasing psychosocial adjustment to care recipient's illnesses among caregivers with poor coping skills. Rabins (1998) also noted the importance of early intervention among high risk (i.e., dementia) caregivers, suggesting that emotional and social care early in the disease process may prevent the development of physical as well as emotional problems.

Gallagher-Thompson et al. (1998) reported that 75 % of caregivers feel that caregiving makes them feel useful; possible positive feelings include contributing to feelings of self-worth, confidence, and companionship. However, anger, frustration, and other symptoms of caregiver distress are predominant emotions. Family-based interventions are needed to help midlife caregivers cope effectively with stress and the many challenges of role definition and redefinition when the physical and/or mental well-being of loved ones declines (Cavanaugh 1998; Knight and McCallum 1998; Zarit et al. 1998).

Interventions that address specific immediate needs of caregivers should be developed or integrated more effectively into existing programs. In interviews with 1,247 caregivers in the USA, 67 % of the caregivers reported that they needed help or wanted information about at least one of the 14 listed items (National Alliance for Caregiving & AARP 2004). The most frequently cited items were "finding time for myself" (35 %), "keeping the person I care for safe at home" (30 %), "managing my emotional and physical stress" (29 %), and "balancing my work and family responsibilities" (29 %). Additional frequently reported needs were, identifying "easy activities I can do with the person I care for" (27 %), learning "how to talk with doctors and other health care professionals" (22 %), and "making end-of-life decisions" (20 %). Although the least cited need was "finding non-English language educational materials" (5 %), only about 14 % of the caregivers identified themselves as ethnic minorities (Hispanic, Latino, or other), making this a concern for nearly one-third of ethnic minority caregivers. Thus, interventions should target specific needs identified by caregivers, and these interventions should be delivered in the languages spoken and read by the caregivers. Designing interventions to meet caregiver needs, however, is not enough. Interventions must also be designed for convenient access from trusted sources.

When asked where they would look for information to help them with some aspect of caregiving, the caregivers most frequently cited the Internet (29 %), a doctor

(28 %), and a family member or friend (15 %; National Alliance for Caregiving & AARP 2004). Although the Internet is not a handy resource for everyone and not all Web sites contain accurate information, for caregivers who may be bound to home by their caregiving responsibilities, the Internet may provide an especially accessible means for gathering information and maintaining connection with and support from others. Many Web sites (e.g., www.alzfdn.org, www.cancer.org, and www.caregiving.org) already provide extensive information about caring for people with specific illnesses and caregiving in general. However, few Web sites (e.g., www.aarp.org, www.caregiver.org, and www.caregiving.com) provide interactive interventions, such as chats, listservs, and opportunities for questions to be answered by experts through e-mail, which can enable caregivers to access personalized information or experience real time connection and support. Adding interactive resources to existing Web sites or links to Web locations that provide interactive resources may provide caregivers who feel isolated by their caregiving and their other roles with new avenues for connection and support. These avenues may increase the social support that isolated caregivers need, especially women caregivers, who may need social support in order to cope with caregiving stress.

In addition to increasing Web-based interventions and their visibility, raising the awareness of doctors concerning the importance of providing care and direction to their patients' caregivers may help caregivers receive the support they need. Instead of just being responsive to caregiver questions, doctors could initiate discussions about common caregiving concerns and offer information about resources that can assist caregivers with their individual needs. Outreach in the community to educate the general population about caregiver needs and how best to support caregivers could help caregivers receive the support they need from family members and friends and from their workplaces. By designing interventions that are flexible enough to meet the unique needs of individual caregivers and making those interventions available through sources that caregivers trust and view as easily accessible, more caregivers may recognize that support is available and utilize that support.

Governmental policies should be reviewed to identify modifications that can help support caregivers and the persons for whom they provide care. Considering that caregivers view keeping the person they care for safe at home as a major concern (National Alliance for Caregiving & AARP 2004), one way to support the immediate needs of caregivers is to initiate and support governmental policies that could assist with safe and adequate long-term care within the home. Policies that could assist in relieving worries about not being able to continue to provide adequate in-home care could reduce caregiver stress and allow caregivers to redirect energy to self-care and caregiving. Although most of the concerns identified by caregivers are immediate concerns, initiating policies that protect caregivers later in life after caregiving ceases may be more important in the long term for caregivers. At the time of caregiving, the career and financial sacrifices that caregivers make may seem reasonable or necessary, but in the long term, these sacrifices may lead to poverty and hardship during old age, particularly for women caregivers who may have entered the labor force later in life, who may not earn as much as their male counterparts, and who may retire earlier in response to the greater demands of higher-level caregiving. Policies that reduce the future negative financial consequences of career sacrifices for caregiving (for example, Social Security credits for caregiving work and paid compensation for providing care that would be community-based if not provided by family members) would honor the valuable contributions of caregivers to communities, ease caregiver stress concerning the future, and reduce the poverty that can occur in old age due to earlier years of caregiving. Policy review should focus on satisfying both the immediate needs of caregivers and the future needs resulting from sacrifices associated with caregiving. Review of governmental policies, the development and assessment of new interventions that address specific immediate needs of caregivers, and the integration of policy changes and new interventions in existing programs would provide additional support for caregivers and the persons for whom they provide care.

Future Directions

A brief review of three significant caregiving issues—gender, culture, and grandparenting—underscores the serious and complex nature of caregiving issues for midlife adults. Caregiving is a gendered experience that varies across cultures, and increasingly incorporates and changes traditional conceptions of the role of grandparents. In addition to the stresses associated with each issue, the developmental tasks of midlife create an intersecting and interacting constellation of experiences and life challenges. From a developmental perspective, persons in midlife experience new freedoms and physical, psychological, and social changes that result in greater interiority and greater concern with establishing personally determined goals and priorities for the second half of life. The demands of caregiving inhibit the search for personal meaning that is so clearly a hallmark of the midlife transition. Clearly, the well-being of midlife caregivers is threatened and they comprise a population at risk. Multiple foci of intervention are needed, including alleviation of distressing symptomology, prevention of dysfunctional outcomes, and enhancement of caregiver wellness. Primary, secondary, and tertiary interventions are needed, with the locus of involvement including the individual, family, care providers, and community.

Midlife caregivers need both social–emotional and instrumental support to deal first with issues of midlife, second with issues of caregiving, and finally with the special issues related to caregiving during the midlife period and managing the later life consequences of assuming the caregiver role. The design of intervention programs in all areas requires a more extensive knowledge base of the needs of midlife caregivers than now exists. Meta-analytic studies of demographics, normal developmental issues, stressors, caregivers, and interventions need to be conducted with a specific focus on the midlife years. Comparisons across age groups with younger and older caregivers and comparisons within the midlife group on factors such as age, gender, marital status, urban–rural dwelling, role commitments, and ethnicity need to be conducted. As new cohorts reach middle and later life, new studies need to be conducted to verify the nature and extent of cohort differences in the experience of midlife as well as of caregiving during this time period.

Of particular importance are studies that discriminate the etiology of negative health and mental health symptoms for midlife caregivers to determine the variance in outcomes due to normative midlife issues and to the stress of caregiving. For example, given that depression rates for women peak in midlife, to what extent are depressive symptoms a reaction to developmental challenges of this period versus to the involvement of midlife women in caregiving roles? Accurate information in relation to these questions is essential for the development of timely and effective interventions, both proactive and reactive in nature.

Accurate information regarding the intersection of midlife and caregiving issues is also necessary for policy makers as a basis for informed decision making. Family leave policies have been instrumental in allowing family members latitude to attend to caregiving needs. At the same time, family leave increases economic burdens on families and thus contributes to stress that leads to negative caregiver responses. Additional means of providing respite to families are needed, based on research that identifies needs as well as model programs addressing these needs. Family caregivers are tremendous resources to communities and save large amounts of money that otherwise would be committed to community care for dependent persons of all ages. Policies that support the needs of midlife caregivers, especially caregiving grandparents, will enable continued informal caregiving in spite of the enormous stresses associated with caregiving roles during the otherwise demanding middle adult years.

References

Antonucci, T. C., Akiyama, H., & Merline, A. (2001). Dynamics of social relationships in midlife. In M. E. Lachman (Ed.), *Handbook of midlife development* (pp. 571–598). NY: Wiley.

Avolio, B. J., & Sosik, J. J. (1999). A life span framework for assessing the impact of work on white-collar workers. In S. L. Willis & J. D. Reid (Eds.), *Life in the middle: Psychological and social development in middle age* (pp. 249–274). San Diego: Academic Press.

Baird, A., John, R., & Hayslip, B. (2000). Custodial grandparenting among African Americans: A focus group perspective. In B. Hayslip & R. Goldberg-Glen (Eds.), *Grandparents raising grandchildren: Theoretical, empirical, and clinical perspectives* (pp. 125–144). NY: Springer.

Baltes, P. (2000). Life-span developmental theory. In A. Kazdin (Ed.), *Encyclopedia of psychology* (pp. 52–57). Washington, DC: American Psychological Association/Oxford University.

Baronet, A. M. (1999). Factors associated with caregiver burden in mental illness: A critical review of the research literature. *Clinical Psychology Review, 19,* 819–841.

Bengtson, V. L. (2001). Beyond the nuclear family: The increasing importance of multigenerational relationships in American society. *Journal of Marriage and the Family, 63,* 1–16.

Brim, G. (7. Dec 1992). Commentary. *Newsweek*, p. 52.

Brody, E. M. (1985). Parent care as normative family stress. *Gerontologist, 25,* 19–29.

Bronfenbrenner, Y. (2000). Ecological theory. In A. Kazdin (Ed.), *Encyclopedia of psychology* (pp. 129–133). Washington, DC: American Psychological Association/Oxford University.

Burton, L. M., & Bengtson, V. L. (1985). Black grandmothers: Issues of timing and continuity. In V. L. Bengtson & J. F. Robertson (Eds.), *Grandparenthood* (pp. 61–78). Beverly Hills: Sage.

Cavanaugh, J. C. (1998). Caregiving to adults: A life event challenge. In I. H. Nordhus, G. R. VandenBos, S. Berg & P. Fromholt (Eds.), *Clinical geropsychology* (pp. 131–136). Washington, DC: American Psychological Association.

Connell, C. M., Janevic, M. R., & Gallant, M. P. (2001). The costs of caregiving: Impact of dementia on family caregivers. *Journal of Geriatric Psychiatry and Neurology, 14,* 179–187.

Dentinger, E., & Clarkberg, M. (2002). Informal caregiving and retirement timing among men and women. *Journal of Family Issues, 23,* 857–879.

Dietz, B. E., Carrozza, M., & Ritchey, P. N. (2003). Does financial self-efficacy explain gender differences in retirement saving strategies? *Journal of Women and Aging, 15,* 83–96.

Erikson, E. (1963). *Childhood and society*. NY: Norton.

Flippen, C., & Tienda, M. (2000). Pathways to retirement: Patterns of labor force participation and labor market exit among the pre-retirement population by race, Hispanic origin, and sex. *Journal of Gerontology: Social Sciences, 55,* 14–S27.

Fuller-Thompson, E., & Minkler, M. (2001). America's grandparent caregivers: Who are they? In B. Hayslip & R. Goldberg-Glen (Eds.), *Grandparents raising grandchildren: Theoretical, empirical, and clinical perspectives* (pp. 3–22). NY: Springer.

Gallagher-Thompson, D., Coon, D. W., Rivera, P., Powers, D., & Zeiss, A. M. (1998). Family caregiving: Stress, coping, and intervention. In M. Hersen & V. B. Van Hasselt (Eds.), *Handbook of Clinical Geropsychology*. NY: Plenum Press.

Giarrusso, R., Feng, S., Silverstein, M., & Marenco, A. (2000). Primary and secondary stressors of grandparents raising grandchildren: Evidence from a national survey. *Journal of Mental Health and Aging, 6,* 291–310.

Glass, J. C., & Honeycutt, T. L. (2002). Grandparents parenting grandchildren: Extent of situation, issues involved, and educational implications. *Educational Gerontology, 28,* 139–161.

Haley, W. E., West, C. A. C., Wadley, V. G., Ford, G. R., White, F. A., Barrett, J. J., et al. (1995). Psychological, social, and health impact of caregiving: A comparison of Black and White dementia family caregivers and noncaregivers. *Psychology and Aging, 10,* 540–552.

Haley, W. E., Roth, D. L., Coleton, M. I., Ford, G. R., West, C. A., Collins, R. P., et al. (1996). Appraisal, coping, and social support as mediators of well-being in Black and White family caregivers of patients with Alzheimer's disease. *Journal of Consulting and Clinical Psychology, 64,* 121–129.

Haug, M. R., Ford, A. B., Stange, K. C., Noelker, L. S., & Gaines, A. D. (1999). Effects of giving care on caregivers' health. *Research on Aging, 21*(4), 515–538.

Havinghurst, R. J. (1974). *Developmental tasks and education*. NY: Mackay.

Helson, R. (1992). Women's difficult times and the rewriting of the life story. *Psychology of Women Quarterly, 16,* 331–347.

Heywood, E. M. (1999). Custodial grandparents and their grandchildren. *Family Journal Counseling and Therapy for Couples and Families, 7,* 367–372.

Huffman, S., & Myers, J. E. (1999). Counseling women in midlife: An integrative approach to menopause. *Journal of Counseling & Development, 77,* 258–266.

Jacques, E. (1967). The mid-life crisis. In R. Owen (Ed.), *Middle age* (pp. 22–36). London: BBC.

Jung, C. G. (1966). *Two essays on analytic psychology. In Collected works* (Vol. 7). Princeton: Princeton University Press.

Kelly, J. R. (1996). Leisure. In J. Birren (Ed.), *Encyclopedia of gerontology* (Vol. 2) (pp. 19–30). San Diego: Academic Press.

Kim, J., & Moen, P. (2001). Moving into retirement: Preparation and transitions in late midlife. In M. E. Lachman (Ed.), *Handbook of midlife development* (pp. 487–527). New York: Wiley.

Knight, B. G., & McCallum, T. J. (1998). Psychotherapy with older adult families: The contextual, cohort-based maturity/specific challenge model. In I. H. Nordhus, G. R. VandenBos, S. Berg & P. Fromholt (Eds.), *Clinical geropsychology* (pp. 313–328). Washington, DC: American Psychological Association.

Lachman, M. E. (2001). *Handbook of midlife development*. NY: Wiley.

Lavoie, J. P. (1995). Support groups for informal caregivers don't work! Refocus the groups or the evaluations. *Canadian Journal of Aging, 14,* 580–603.

Levinson, D. (1978). *The seasons of a man's life*. New York: Knopf.

Logsdon, M. C., & Robinson, K. (2000). Helping women caregivers obtain support: Barriers and recommendations. *Archives of Psychiatric Nursing, 14,* 244–248.

Lowenthal, M. F., Thurnher, M., & Chiriboga, D. (1975). *Four stages of life.* San Francisco: Jossey-Bass.

MacArthur Foundation. (n.d.). The John D. and Catherine T. MacArthur Foundation Research Network on Successful Midlife Development. Retrieved from http://midmac.med.harvard.edu

Marks, N. F. (1996). Caregiving across the lifespan: National prevalence and predictors. *Family Relations, 45,* 27–36.

McGuire, F. (2000). What do we know? Not much. The state of leisure and aging research. *Journal of Leisurability, 26,* 97–100.

McNally, S., Ben-Shlomo, Y., & Newman S. (1999). The effects of respite care on informal carers' well being: A systematic review. *Disability and Rehabilitation, 21,* 1–14.

MetLife Mature Market Institute. (1999). *The MetLife juggling act study: Balancing caregiving with work and the costs involved.* Retrieved from http://www.caregiving.org/data/jugglingstudy.pdf.

Moen, P., & Wethington, E. (1999). Midlife development in a life course context. In S. L. Willis & J. D. Reid (Eds.), *Life in the middle* (pp. 3–23). San Diego: Academic Press.

National Alliance for Caregiving & AARP. (1997). *Family Caregiving in the U.S.: Findings from a National Survey.* Bethesda: Authors.

National Alliance for Caregiving & AARP. (2004). *Caregiving in the U.S.* Retrieved from http://assets.aarp.org/rgcenter/il/us_caregiving.pdf.

Neal, M. B., Ingersoll-Dayton, B., & Starrels, M. E. (1997). Gender and relationship differences in caregiving patterns and consequences among employed caregivers. *Geronologist, 37,* 806–816.

Neugarten, B. L. (1977). Personality and aging. In J. E. Birren & W. K. Schaie (Eds.), *Handbook of the psychology of aging* (pp. 626–649). NY: Van Nostrand Reinhold.

Neugarten, B. L., & Datan, N. (1996). The middle years. In D. A. Neugarten (Ed.), *The meanings of age: Selected papers of Bernice L. Neugarten* (pp. 135–159). Chicago: University of Chicago Press.

Neugarten, B. L., & Weinstein, K. K. (1964). The changing American grandparent. *Journal of Marriage and the Family, 26,* 199–204.

Olson, L. K. (Ed.). (2001). *Aging through ethnic lenses: Caring for the elderly in a multicultural society.* NY: Rowman & Littlefield.

Papalia, D. E., Sterns, H. L., Feldman, R. D., & Camp, C. J. (2002). *Adult development and aging* (2nd edition). Boston: McGraw-Hill.

Paproski, D. L. (2001). The role of spirituality in the transition through midlife: A narrative study. *Dissertation Abstracts International, Section A: Humanities and Social Sciences, 62*(1-A), 90.

Pearlin, L. I., Mullan, J. T., Semple, S. & Skaff, M. M. (1990). Caregiving and the stress process: An overview of concepts and their measures. *Gerontologist, 30*(5), 583–594.

Purcell, P. J. (2005). Older worker: Employment and retirement trends. *Journal of Pension Planning and Compliance, 30*(4), 49–70.

Putney, N. M., & Bengtson, V. L. (2001). Families, intergenerational relationships, and kinkeeping in midlife. In M. E. Lachman (Ed.), *Handbook of midlife development* (pp. 528–570). NY: Wiley.

Rabins, P. V. (1998). The caregiver's role in Alzheimer's Disease. *Dementia and Geriatric Cognitive Disorders, 9,* 25–28.

Roberts, J., Browne, G., Gafni, A., Varieur, M., Loney, P., & de Ruijter, M. (2000). Specialized continuing care models for persons with dementia: A systematic review of the research literature. *Canadian Journal on Aging, 19,* 106–126.

Sanders, G. F., & Trygstad, D. W. (1993). Strengths in the grandparent-grandchild relationship. *Activities, Adaptation, and Aging, 17,* 43–50.

Sands, R. G., & Goldberg-Glen, R. S. (2000). Factors associated with stress among grandparents raising their grandchildren. *Family Relations: Interdisciplinary Journal of Applied Family Studies, 49,* 97–105.

Santrock, J. (2002). *Life span development.* NY: McGraw-Hill.

Schaie, K. W. (2000). The impact of longitudinal studies on understanding development from young adulthood to old age. *International Journal of Behavioral Development, 24,* 257–266.

Schlossberg, N. K., Waters, E. B., & Goodman, J. (1995). *Counseling adults in transition.* NY: Springer.

Schulz, R., & Salthouse, T. (1999). *Adult development and aging: Myths and emerging realities.* Upper Saddle River: Prentice-Hall.

Schwiebert, V. L., & Myers, J. E. (1994). Midlife care givers: Effectiveness of a psychoeducational intervention for midlife adults with parent-care responsibilities. *Journal of Counseling & Development, 72,* 627–637.

Staudinger, U. M., & Bluck, S. (2001). A view on midlife development from lifespan theory. In M. E. Lachman (Ed.), *Handbook of midlife development* (pp. 3–39). NY: Wiley.

Stone, R., Cafferata, G. L., & Sangl, J. (1987). Caregivers of the frail elderly: A national profile. *Gerontologist, 27,* 616–626.

Szinovacz, M. E., DeViney, S., & Davey, A. (2001). Influences of family obligations and relationships on retirement: Variations by gender, race, and marital status. *Journal of Gerontology: Social Sciences, 56,* 20–27.

Toledo, J. R., Hayslip, B., Emick, M. A., Toledo, C., & Henderson, C. E. (2000). Cross-cultural differences in custodial grandparenting. In B. Hayslip & R. Goldberg-Glen (Eds.), *Grandparents raising grandchildren: Theoretical, empirical, and clinical perspectives* (pp. 107–124). NY: Springer.

Vaillant, G. E. (1989). The evolution of defense mechanisms in the middle years. In J. M. Oldham & R. S. Liebert (Eds.), *The middle years* (pp. 58–72). New Haven: Yale University.

Vitaliano, P. P., Schulz, R., Kiecolt-Glaser, J., & Grant, I. (1997). Research on physiological and physical concomitants of caregiving: Where do we go from here? *Annals of Behavioral Medicine, 19,* 117–123.

Wethington, E. (2000). Expecting stress: Americans and the “midlife crisis.” *Motivation and Emotion, 24*(2), 85–103.

Wykle, M., & Segall, M. (1991). A comparison of Black and White family caregivers' experience with dementia. *Journal of the National Black Nurses' Association, 5,* 29–41.

Yee, J. L., & Schulz, R. (2000). Gender differences in psychiatric morbidity among family caregivers: A review and analysis. *Gerontologist, 40,* 147–164.

Zarit, S. H., Johansson, L., & Jarrott, S. E. (1998). Family caregiving: Stresses, social programs, and clinical interventions. In I. H. Nordhus, G. R. VandenBos, S. Berg, & P. Fromholt (Eds.), *Clinical geropsychology* (pp. 345–360). Washington, DC: American Psychological Association.

Part III
Local, State, and National Issues Effecting Caregivers and Mental Health Caregiving

Loss, Grief, and Bereavement: Implications for Family Caregivers and Health Care Professionals of the Mentally Ill

Sherry R. Schachter and Jimmie C. Holland

In the present health climate of managed care, patients remain at home and a major burden is placed on the family as their primary caregivers. As caregivers, family members are expected to manage visits to clinic or hospital, change wound dressings and participate in other hands-on medical procedures that clinicians have prescribed needing to be done at home, while also maintaining their home environment and perhaps maintaining a full- or part-time job outside the home. It is a tall order that is frequently compounded by the graying of Americans with more who are older, and who will have chronic illnesses requiring lengthy care at home. After the death, the surviving family member is faced with the grief associated with loss, often without attention to his/her needs for counseling. Health care policy must increasingly address this burden in our society which will only grow in the next few decades. This chapter outlines some of the issues for the family caregiver and the medical caregiver team—both of whom face significant stresses in this new environment. When there is a dual diagnosis of mental illness as well as medical illness, the burden for patient and caregiver is much greater.

Anticipatory Grief

Individuals diagnosed with a life-threatening illness face many losses before their actual death. Alopecia, loss of energy, loss of limb, and changes in body image are just some of the losses that patients, families, and clinicians identify (Holland and Lewis 2000). Other losses are related to financial security (e.g., when the individual is

S. R. Schachter (✉)
Bereavement Services, Calvary Hospital/Hospice,
1740 Eastchester Road, Bronx, NY 10461, USA
e-mail: sschachter@calvaryhospital.org

J. C. Holl
Department of Psychiatry and Behavioral Sciences, Memorial Sloan-Kettering Cancer Center,
641 Lexington Avenue, 7th Floor, New York, NY 10022, USA
e-mail: hollandj@mskcc.org

R. C. Talley et al. (eds.), *The Challenges of Mental Health Caregiving*,
Caregiving: Research • Practice • Policy, DOI 10.1007/978-1-4614-8791-3_8,

no longer able to work; burdens related to health insurance; the hiring of housekeepers, baby-sitters, or health aides to assist at home; etc.) and isolation from friends or family members (Schachter 2009; Schachter and Holland 1995; Holland and Lewis 2000; Doka 1993). These losses, and the expression of sadness, occurring before the actual death, are also examples of anticipatory grief (Doka 1993; Rando 1986, 2000).

The concept of anticipatory grief (or anticipatory mourning), was first introduced by Lindemann (1944). It refers to the grief experience by loved ones as they anticipate an impending death, often grieving well before the death occurs. For family members who are able to recognize and talk about their feelings, this *can* be very supportive and healing offering opportunities for them to deal with "unfinished business," face the potential death and hopefully use the time with the patient for meaningful activities. However, not all individuals who are forewarned about a death can accept the reality (Schachter 2009; Rando 1986). Some families even after a lengthy downhill trajectory have reported saying: "I can't believe he's gone. I never thought he was going to die." Often, health care providers become frustrated when relatives, and even the patient, appear not to have "heard" the physician's discussion related to poor prognosis and maintain a denial of what is actually happening. Therefore, it is crucial for physicians (and other health care professionals) to acknowledge that knowing in advance about an impending death does not equate with patients or families actually preparing or discussing issues related to dying (Schachter 2008, 2009; Coyle et al. 2001). Just because a patient suspects (or has even been told) that they have a life-threatening illness or that their disease has progressed does not necessarily mean they (the patient or the family) give up hope and "accept" their impending death. There is often a disconnect between what people have (or have not) been told, what they believe, and how they incorporate that information into their consciousness (Schachter 2009).

Corr et al. (2003) stressed that anticipatory grief should not be viewed as a strategy for achieving completion or resolution of grieving prior to the death and that: "... it may affect the quality of post-death bereavement, but it need not be any more (or less) significant" than all other aspects of coping with dying (p. 237). Even when death is expected (e.g., with a chronic or life-threatening illness) the death of a loved one is an immense stressor impacting on physical, psychological, financial, emotional, and existential suffering (Corr et al. 2003; Coyle et al. 2001; Doka 1993). Of all diseases associated with the aging process, Alzheimer's is recognized as the one most stressful for families (Li and Lemke, 1998). These stressors exist for families whether caring for family members at home or in an institution as many are faced with having to quit their jobs or drastically alter their schedules to care for their loved ones. The course of the illness trajectory will affect caregivers' day-to-day living and the quality of life for both the patient and family member.

For 3 years prior to her husband's death, Wanda was able to care for him at home. At the age of 58, this high-powered Wall Street broker had been diagnosed with early Alzheimer's. Initially, Wanda was able to manage her own job as an office manager, her home, and her husband. However, as Jason's condition progressed he became physically abusive and the changes in his mental status no longer allowed him to remain safely at home despite the hiring of a home health aide. When Jason was placed in a nursing home, Wanda would visit him daily juggling her responsibilities as wife and caregiver. Wanda was compelled to spend 4–5 h a day with him and every day after work she would travel to the nursing home to have dinner and spend the evening together even though he could not converse with her. The stress of this situation contributed to Wanda's own physical and emotional decline.

Other chronic and debilitating diseases (e.g., amyotrophic lateral sclerosis (ALS), multiple sclerosis, myasthenia gravis, etc.) impact the family's day-to-day activities. Although frequently frustrating, challenging, and exhausting for family caregivers, there are potential benefits of being a caregiver.

As a society, we do not deal well with death. Whether one thinks we are a "death denying" society or a "death defying" society (Aries 1975), the subject of death is frightening and can provoke increased anxiety. Unlike years ago, when individuals died at home with family members present actively participating in their care, family caregivers today often have limited exposure witnessing and experiencing a death or going through the dying process with someone they love. Patients are apt to have their family of origin unavailable, perhaps residing scattered across the country or throughout the world. Increasingly common and problematic today is caring for the patient who is either geographically or emotionally distant from family or social supports. These challenges impact the context in which dying occurs and the grieving process (Corr et al. 2003).

Current Focus on Loss and Bereavement

The shift from an aggressive approach aimed at curing disease to a palliative focus aimed at aggressively treating physical, psychological, and existential symptoms and improving quality of life remains a continual and challenging problem causing distress for physicians, nurses, social workers, other health care professionals as well as the patient and family (Carver and Foley 2001). There is a general unease that exists among clinicians which often occurs when having to discuss poor prognoses, end-of-life issues, dying, or just introducing the option of hospice (Schachter 2009; Schachter 2008; Clayton et al. 2005; Murillo and Holland 2004; Buckman 1984, 1999; Girgis and Sanson-Fisher 1998). Yet the ability to effectively communicate, particularly at the end of life, is essential not only for good medical care but also for maintaining a positive relationship between the patient, family, and health care providers (Kirk et al. 2004). Clear, concise, open, and effective communications are potent tools in initiating and maintaining effective interventions (Schachter 2009; Schachter and Coyle 1998; Schachter and Holland 1995). They affect bereavement outcome for the survivors. The paucity of training programs for health professionals in communication skills and the lack of role models in medical, nursing, and social work schools have further contributed to this problem. Earlier studies by Ferrell et al. (1999) in a survey of nursing curriculum and nursing textbooks found that few schools addressed this important aspect of end-of-life care. In 50 nursing textbooks, an average 2 % of their total pages (total pages of 3,108) related to end-of-life care.

A similar study was conducted by Rabow et al. (2000) examining medical textbooks from multiple specialties. Texts having the highest percentage of end-of-life care content were located in family medicine, geriatrics, and psychiatry. Texts with the least information were found in surgery, AIDS, oncology, and hematology textbooks (Rabow et al. 2000).

Similarly, a survey by the American Medical Association (AMA) in 1997–1998 indicated that only 4 of 126 medical schools in the USA required a separate course in the care of the dying patient (EPEC Project 1999). This initiated the Education on Palliative and End-of-Life Care (EPEC) Project aimed at educating health care clinicians by providing advanced medical teaching skills (via conferences, workshops) and access to web-based curriculum on end-of-life issues, palliative care skills, and care of the dying. The EPEC curriculum combines didactic sessions, videotape scenarios, interactive discussions, practical exercises, and role modeling.

While nurses spend more time with patients and families than any other health professional, supporting the physical, psychological, emotional, and existential needs of patients and families, research has previously demonstrated that major deficiencies exist in clinical nursing education about end-of-life-care (http://www.okabcd.org/ELNEC.htm). The End-of-Life Nursing Education Consortium (ELNEC) Project and curriculum was developed and funded by The Robert Wood Johnson Foundation to improve nursing skills at the end of life. National ELNEC training seminars were initiated to train nurses who were expected to return to their own institutions to train their colleagues.

Frequently family caregivers prioritize the patient's needs as being more important than their own. Discussing with them that there is no "one right way" and no "one right place" to die is important (Schachter and Coyle 1998) irrespective of where the care is delivered (e.g., home, hospital, hospice, nursing home, or other facility). However, achieving clear communication between health care professionals, families, and patients does not readily happen. Communication skills must be and can be effectively taught and role modeled. Billings and Block (1997), in their study of deficiencics in medical education, reported that 41 % of medical students had never observed an attending talking about death with either the patient or family members, and 35 % had never discussed the care of a dying patient with a teaching attending. In a survey of oncologists, almost 50 % felt that their communication skills regarding breaking bad news to patients was poor to fair (Baile et al. 1999) and nearly one quarter of patients studied indicated that the information they received about their cancer diagnosis was unclear and not communicated to them in a caring way (Chan and Woodruff 1997). The medical models—EPEC Project (1999) and nursing ELNEC Project (2000)—are educational programs that were developed to address these deficiencies. Many institutions have benefited from these training programs.

An additional stressor for some physicians may be their unrealistic expectations about curing the disease. Health care providers may be left feeling helpless and powerless when they do not cure their patient (Holland 2002). To diminish these feelings, some clinicians distance themselves. They avoid the dying patient and family so much that families angrily say they felt abandoned by their doctors even prior to their loved one's death. After the patient dies, some physicians blame themselves

Table 1 Risk factors for severe grief in bereavement. (Parkes 2002)

Mode of loss
Sudden or unexpected losses (survivors are unprepared)
Death associated with an overly lengthy illness
Multiple losses
Violent or horrific losses
Death of a child (at any age)
Deaths perceived as preventable
Deaths for which the survivor feels responsible
Disenfranchised losses
Personal vulnerability
Dependence on deceased person (or vice versa)
Ambivalence to deceased person
Persons with poor self-esteem
Persons with a prior history of psychological vulnerability
Persons who are medically frail
Perceived lack of social support
Family absent or viewed as unsupportive
Social isolation
Concurrent stresses

and feel guilty. Dismayed at their inability to "save" their patient, they avoid calling or writing the family. Contact after the death is a crucial role for all health care clinicians and should routinely be incorporated as part of end-of-life care. Families often indicate how meaningful it was to them when the doctor showed "he cared" by sending them a condolence card or making a telephone call (Holland 2002).

Despite the bond between patient and the physician and primary team, it is not unusual that after the patient dies, physicians do not remain in contact with the surviving family (Holland 2002). Yet repeatedly in our clinical work with bereaved family members, we hear their anguish and disappointment when physicians and other health care professionals are no longer "present." Holland (2002) suggests that caring for the patient does not end when the patient dies and that clinicians have a responsibility to assess the family in order to determine how they are coping, and if they are at risk for complicated bereavement. However, in order to feel competent, one must have the basic skills and knowledge in how loss is experienced (Chochinov et al. 1998). Identifying resources, including referrals to a bereavement therapist or other appropriate mental health professional, if needed, should be a routine part of care. Table 1 indicates several risk factors for more severe grief reactions and Table 2 lists some of the manifestations of normal grief. Most individuals manage their grief well; in fact, studies show that about 80 % will go through a normal grieving process. However, about 20 % will experience more severe grief which may become an onset of depression.

Since caring for dying patients causes confrontation with mortality and death by the physicians and nurses, unacknowledged anxiety and fear related to personal death is an added stressor (Schachter 2009). Having some philosophy about life and death or some spiritual or religious beliefs appears helpful in coping with palliative and end-of-life care (Schachter 1999). Another factor is helping clinicians understand

Table 2 Manifestations of grief. (Schachter 1999)

Grieving the death of a loved one is very painful and at times can be overwhelming. Individuals often worry if they are grieving "the right way" and question if they are "normal." Grief is not just sadness or depression; it is a whole host of feelings and emotions. Besides affecting your emotions, grief reaches into every part of your life: your work, your relationships with others, and your image of yourself. Not everyone will have the same experiences

1. Profound feeling of sadness, emptiness, and loss of meaning
2. A feeling of tightness in your chest, your throat, or your abdomen
3. An empty feeling in the stomach
4. The need to sigh
5. Muscle weakness
6. Stomachaches, headaches
7. Weight loss or gain
8. An extreme weariness and lack of energy
9. The need to go through a detailed review of all the events that led to the death
10. An intense preoccupation with the life and memories of the deceased; and the need to re-examine past actions and behaviors toward your loved one
11. Occasional feelings of regrets over things that happened or did not happen in your relationship with the deceased
12. The urge to try and solve the puzzle which led to the death; attempting to make some sense out of the course of illness
13. The inability to concentrate; you may be absent-minded (get lost while driving, misplace money, miss appointments)
14. Profound loneliness
15. You may be sensitive to noise
16. May have difficulty sleeping
17. You may dream frequently about the deceased (or wish you did)
18. Occasional untypical anger (at the doctor, God, or the deceased for leaving you)
19. A feeling of numbness
20. A sense that nothing seems real to you
21. You may start or increase your smoking or drinking habits
22. You may have uncontrolled tears
23. You can become restless and engage in aimless activity
24. At times you try to avoid any reminder of the deceased, or you may become fascinated with objects, activities, or places associated with your loved one
25. You may withdraw or avoid seeing friends or families
26. You may hear or see your loved one—sensing their presence, like expecting the person to arrive home at the usual time, hearing their voice, or seeing their face
27. A fear you will forget what the person looked like or you will forget the "good" memories
28. You may take comfort in wearing the deceased's clothes or hold on to articles from the deceased
29. You may feel that your own "cancer diagnosis" is inevitable or worry that other loved ones will also be diagnosed with cancer and die
30. Ruminating over the last few hours, days, or months before the death

why they may find a death particularly painful. Knowing one's "loss history" is often beneficial because it frequently clarifies our previous relationships and experiences with death of loved ones. Personal experiences and past issues can influence one's clinical decisions as we identify with a particular patient. One physician noted: "I really liked her. She was so young—young enough to be my wife or my sister. I never wanted to discuss hospice or palliation with her. I didn't want her to give up hope even though down deep I knew the end was close" (Schachter 1999).

The opposite—an intense *dislike*, can also occur, without obvious cause but relates to prior attachments. These unconscious bonds (transference and countertransference) influence how we discuss bad news and initiate end-of-life discussions. Several years ago, an Israeli physician trained in our teaching hospital (MSKCC). He and his family (wife and two children) spent a year in the USA before returning home. One of his patients was a young doctor from Israel who had pancreatic cancer. The fellow could not understand why this patient caused him so much distress. He would often think about him on the weekends when he was not on call. He was frustrated when he could not control the patient's pain. His identification with the young doctor frequently complicated and impacted on his medical decisions and clinical care.

Another important concept is recognizing disenfranchised grief. Doka (1989) first described disenfranchised grief as "the grief that persons experience when they incur a loss that is not or cannot be openly acknowledged, publicly mourned, or socially supported" (Doka 1989, p. 4, 2002). Typical situations can be observed with situations including miscarriage, abortion, adoption, and perinatal deaths. Other situations leading to disenfranchised grief can be observed when the loss is experienced by an elderly or mentally impaired person; in socially awkward situations in which the grief or "the other woman" in an extramarital affair cannot be fully recognized. These bereaved individuals can easily become overwhelmed and frequently lack the emotional support so gravely needed.

Nearly all of the 2.5 million Americans who died in 2004 were admitted to a hospital within the past 12 months of their life and half of all deaths occurred in inpatient facilities (Imhof and Kaskie 2005; National Center for Health Statistics 2003). With the rise of the modern day hospice movement, and more recently the focus on end-of-life issues and quality-of-life, researchers have identified barriers contributing to what has come to be defined as a "good death" (Buckman 1984, 1999; Smith 2000; Steinhauser et al. 2000). These barriers can impact on the family's bereavement as the circumstances surrounding the death can leave vivid memories; grief is much easier when the components of a "good death" can be remembered. A "good death" can be defined as one in which the patient is kept comfortable and symptoms are controlled as well as possible, particularly pain (Howarth and Leaman, 2001). A "good death" is one that is "free from avoidable distress and suffering for patients, families and caregivers; in general accord with the patients' and families' wishes; and reasonably consistent with clinical, cultural, and ethical standards." A bad death "... is characterized by needless suffering, dishonoring of patient and family wishes or values..." (IoM 1998, p. 24). Table 3 indicates several components that have been identified as contributing toward a good death. Unfortunately, many individuals still die in pain causing distress that could have been prevented or relieved (Desbiens and Wu 2000; Huskamp et al. 2001; IoM 1998; Teno et al. 2004). The study to Understand Prognoses and Preferences for Outcomes and Risks of Treatments (SUPPORT 1995) found that 40–70 % of patients had substantial pain in the last days of their life. Additionally, nearly 40 % of patients spent the last 10 days of their life receiving care in an intensive care unit.

With the exception of the hospice concept of care, which includes the family, the focus for most medical teams has been on the patient; this is especially so in

Table 3 Components of a good death. (Adapted from *Principles of a Good Death* (Smith 2000))

Effective pain management
Effective symptom management
Relief of needless suffering
Clear decision-making
An understanding of what to expect
Preparation for death
Knowing when death was coming
Having a choice of where death occurs
Able to maintain control of what happens
Access to spiritual and emotional support
Control over whom is present
Having time to say goodbye

There are similar *Principles of a Good Death*; 12 principles that should be incorporated into the plans of individuals, professional codes, and the aims of institutions and health services

tertiary hospitals. However, in hospice, care is aimed at *both* the patient and the family ensuring attention to their needs. Hospice and palliative care continues to be a growing field in the USA as well as worldwide. In 2003, Robert Wood Johnson Foundation awarded a $ 4.5 million grant to The Center to Advance Palliative Care (CAPC) to establish palliative care programs. Since 1998, hospital-based palliative care programs have increased from 300 to 800 in 2001 (CAPC 2003a, b; Imhof and Kaskie 2005) to over 950 programs in 2002 (Health Forum 2004). However, most tertiary hospitals, even those providing pain and palliative care services, often do not offer bereavement services to families. In an audience of over 200 health care clinicians from throughout New York City (2005, Calvary Hospital), only about ten clinicians indicated that their institutions provided bereavement services; and less than half said that they continuously assessed whether their institutions were meeting the needs of the families they served.

In 1998, Memorial Sloan-Kettering Cancer Center in New York initiated a hospital-wide bereavement program that addressed these concerns and provided ongoing care for families after a patient died. Within two weeks of a patient's death, the family received a handwritten condolence card on behalf of the hospital. This was followed 3 months later by a letter providing them with information about bereavement resources, and 9 months later, another handwritten card was sent to the family acknowledging the 1-year anniversary of their loved one's death. Responses resulting from this program had been overwhelmingly positive and many families called or wrote notes thanking the hospital for their continued commitment and emotional support. In addition, many took advantage of the free weekly bereavement support groups which they described as being helpful. This program has since been terminated and a new decentralized program which utilizes Psychosocial Care Teams associated with each medical disease management team is being developed. They will follow up with relatives who have died on their service.

Founded in 1899, Calvary Hospital is the only fully accredited acute care specialty hospital in the USA devoted exclusively to providing palliative care to adult advanced cancer patients. This one-of-a-kind hospital has 225 beds. Embedded in the hospital's mission is the philosophy of nonabandonment evidenced by the numerous bereavement services the hospital provides without charge to family members and the community at large. A major focus of the bereavement services includes adult bereavement support groups that are closed, time-limited sessions meeting weekly for 1.5 h. All groups are free, and they are open to the community. In addition, there are weekly bereavement support groups for children (ages 6–11) and teens and Calvary's Camp Compass® a weeklong bereavement summer camp for children and teens (Schachter and Georgopoulos 2008; Schachter 2007).

Family Caregivers

Our experience in conducting numerous bereavement groups have identified recurring themes : acute symptoms of loss; loneliness; anger about terminal care and feelings of being abandoned during late stages of illness; recurrent images of the last days of illness; regrets or guilt over what the family perceived that they, or the health care team, did or did not do. Bereaved families frequently ruminate over the events of their loved one's death and recall the sensitivity (or lack of it) of the clinicians caring for their loved one (Schachter 2009; Murillo and Holland 2004).

For families, being a caregiver can be all consuming and it is not unusual for family members to neglect their own health while caring for their dying loved one. The psychological strain of caregiving and bereavement has been shown to put spousal caregivers and bereaved survivors themselves at heightened risk of death (Schaefer et al. 1995; Schulz and Beach 1999; Kaprio et al. 1987). It was only after Betty died of breast cancer that her husband Keith attended to the abdominal pains in his stomach. Although Keith had symptoms of nausea, vomiting, and pain for some time he attributed his symptoms to that of being a caregiver and did not seek help until several weeks after the funeral. He was diagnosed with an unresectable tumor and started experimental chemotherapy.

Studies, especially with older spouses (Zisook 2000), describe many adverse psychiatric (e.g., depression, panic attacks, suicidal ideation) and physical health ailments (decreased energy, high blood pressure, including a tenfold increase in hypertension; Prigerson and Jacobs 2001). Increased alcohol and tobacco intake, and changes in sleeping and eating behaviors are also noted during bereavement (Schulz et al. 1995; Schulz and Beach 1999; Stroebe et al. 2001).

Complex symptoms of grief at sufficiently high and persistent levels represent a distinct form of psychopathology. Sometimes called traumatic, prolonged, or complicated grief, this form of grief is painful and interferes with function and can continue for long periods of time with an inability of the survivor to accept their loved one's death (Ringold et al. 2005). Symptoms include: separation distress (e.g., yearning, pining for the deceased; excessive loneliness), feeling stunned and dazed; a sense of disbelief; numbness; bitterness; and a sense of vulnerability with intrusive thoughts (Shear et al. 2005).

Paradoxically, despite the heightened morbidity associated with complicated grief, it also coincides with a significantly lower utilization of health services (Shear et al. 2005; Prigerson et al. 2001) indicating that many bereaved family caregivers do not seek out or receive the health care services they need. This further illustrates the need for clinicians to be diligent in monitoring bereaved family members for complicated grief including suicidal risk.

A study (Prigerson et al. 2001) found that the duration of caregiving was directly associated with a greater number and greater length of hospital stays for medical problems by these bereaved survivors. One explanation may be that since bereaved caregivers underutilize and fail to obtain the health care they need, ultimately results in an increased severity of their illnesses often requiring hospitalization.

Appropriate resources, such as bereavement support groups, are available, although not often readily publicized or made easily accessible. Expecting the bereaved individual to search out and locate resources is not realistic since families often lack the energy required to find telephone numbers and websites and making phone calls for appointments. Another factor is the huge disparity in our health care system, putting African-Americans or other minorities at risk because of access to fewer services, coupled with distrust of the medical system (Crawley et al. 2000). Tertiary hospitals must be in tune with the needs of the discrete populations they serve and address cultural sensitivity issues such as religious beliefs, customs, rituals, understanding the meaning of the illness, suffering, and death.

Available support groups are highly variable due to the style and competency of those individuals who facilitate the bereavement support groups (psychologists, social workers, clergy persons, bereavement counselors, nurses, volunteers) and treatment modalities (individual therapy, supportive, cognitive, behavioral therapies). While there have been great strides in the area of credentialing professionals, variations in standards differ from state to state making this an area of concern (LoCicero 2002–2003). Although there are numerous views as to whether or not credentialing professionals is a benefit, supporters feel it protects the public from unethical or incompetent practitioners by establishing standards of practice in the field. Currently there are a few programs throughout the USA (e.g., College of New Rochelle in New York, Brooklyn College in New York, Hood College in Maryland) that offer a master's program in thanatology where clinicians (e.g., nurses, counselors, social workers, hospice personnel, etc.) can obtain more advanced knowledge and training in areas related to grief, loss, and bereavement. The Association for Death Education and Counseling (ADEC) is an international, professional organization "dedicated to promoting excellence and recognizing diversity in death education, bereavement counseling, care of the dying, grief counseling, and research in thanatology. Based on quality research, theory and practice, the association provides information, support, and resources to its international, multicultural, multidisciplinary membership and to the public" (ADEC website). A study of 394 grief counselors who were ADEC members was conducted exploring the similarities and differences between noncertified and certified grief counselors, indicating that certified grief counselors have greater experience and background (LoCicero 2002–2003).

ADEC provides training and offers a certification process for those individuals working with the dying or the bereaved. *Certification in Thanatology (CT): Death, Dying and Bereavement* is the foundation certification. The individual indicates a mastery of the body of knowledge, which was developed by topic experts in the field and later evaluated through an ADEC survey. Individuals pass an examination based on this core body of knowledge. The CT credential is perceived as a foundation certification and although a counselor/therapist or educator is defined by his/her education and work experience, the CT notes the special educational training in the field. Eligibility requirements include a bachelor's degree and 2 years of verified related experience or a master's or doctorate and 1 year of verified related experience plus 60 contact hours in thanatology and related topics plus two letters of support from supervisors or colleagues.

ADEC also initiated a Fellow in Thanatology in an effort to recognize practitioners and educators in the discipline of dying, death, and bereavement who have met specific requirements to demonstrate advanced levels of competency in teaching, research, and/or clinical practice. Requirements include a master's/doctoral degree with 5 years experience in thanatology, letters of verification and support, and a minimum of 12 units in a professional portfolio.

Future Needs/Directions

We have several recommendations for future directions so that bereaved family caregivers may receive the emotional support they need during this difficult period.

Practice Recommendations

- Clinicians need to be alert to survivors who come in with an ostensible medical problem which is a manifestation of grief, particularly in older individuals.
- Given that 2.5 million people die yearly in the USA (National Center for Health Statistics 2003) many individuals are grieving the loss of loved one. Clinicians need to assess individuals after a significant loss as there are those who will adapt well, but a significant percentage (at least 20 %) may require additional support and help.
- Encourage clinicians to assess surviving family members for complicated or prolonged grief reactions after the patient has died.
- Increase the sensitivity of physicians to cultural factors, coping styles, and gender differences in bereavement care.
- Encourage the emotional and psychological support of individuals in underserved populations, improving availability and access to care.
- Encourage bereavement support groups in community centers, senior citizen centers by collaborating with local hospice, home care facilities, and long-term care facilities.

- Develop brochures offering help, support, and information in languages other than English (e.g., Spanish, Chinese, Italian, etc.).
- Elderly bereaved individuals need special programs due to concurrent losses of physical well-being, loss of friends, and decreased financial and social supports.

Education and Training Recommendations

- Encourage more systematic approaches to the management of chronic and terminal illness through palliative care and hospice programs by accreditation by regulatory bodies (Meier 2004). Bereavement assessment at the end of life should be part of the standard of end-of-life care.
- Educate physicians and other health care professionals to address and care for their own personal psychological needs; acknowledge their feelings about mortality dealing with losses.
- Training of health care professionals to improve communication skills and address end-of-life issues by utilizing faculty from the individual's own discipline in conjunction with an expert skilled in teaching communication (Murillo and Holland 2004). Utilizing multidisciplinary consultant services facilitates learning (Imhof and Kaskie 2005). Currently, there are over 900 physicians certified in palliative care and more than 840 trained in end-of-life care with 7,600 nurses who are similarly certified (Imhof and Kaskie 2005; Last Acts 2002). In addition, currently there are over 800 international professionals (psychologists, social workers, nurses, chaplains from many countries who have completed the *Certification in Thanatology: Death, Dying and Bereavement* (Dr. G. Thornton, personal communication, July 26, 2005).
- Implementation of courses on dying and death into the curriculum of medical and nursing schools. Workshops and training utilizing techniques such as role playing or use of videotapes (Delvaux et al. 2005; Hulsman et al. 1999; Jenkins and Fallowfield 2002; Murillo and Holland 2004; Razavi et al. 2003).
- Lectures and workshops should be more accessible to community organizations such as churches, synagogues, and other places of worship.

Research Recommendations

- Identify most effective teaching methods;
- Examine grief in women and men with implications for interventions;
- Study factors related to complicated or prolonged grief;
- Evaluate efficacy of psychological interventions;
- Study cross-cultural factors which impact on grieving, its nature, and severity;
- Impact health policy to obtain parity for counseling in end-of-life care and bereavement (Murillo and Holland 2004).

Summary

This chapter has outlined the major issues facing family caregivers and their medical counterparts—demonstrating how psychological issues can complicate medical decisions, from both the patient-family and physician's viewpoints. The recommendations given should be carefully considered from several perspectives: the education of professionals for health care in the new century with a focus on chronic disease in an aging population, and attention to the potential for prolonged or complicated grief reactions in survivors. Health care policy makers must set standards for care that assure adequately trained professionals are available and that they follow clinical practice guidelines based on evidence. Palliative care, in particular, will need to address the needs of diverse populations and recognize the need to include care of the bereaved following the death of a patient receiving palliative care.

References

Aries, P. (1975). *Western attitudes toward death from the middle ages to the present* (P. Ranum, Trans.). Baltimore: The Johns Hopkins University Press.

Association for Death Education and Counseling. *Mission statement*. http://www.adec.org/about/index.htm#mission.

Baile, W. F., Glober, G. A., Lenzi, R., Beale, E. A., & Kudelka, A. P. (1999). Discussing disease progression and end-of-life decisions. *Oncology, 13*, 1021–1038.

Billings, J. A., & Block, S. (1997). Palliative care in undergraduate medical education: Status report and future directions. *Journal of the American Medical Association, 278*, 733–738.

Buckman, R. (1984). Breaking bad news: Why is it still so difficult? *British Medical Journal, 288*, 1597–1599.

Buckman, R. (1999). Communication in palliative care: A practical guide. In D. Doyle, W. C. Hanks, & N. MacDonald (Eds.), *Oxford textbook of palliative medicine* (2nd ed., pp. 141–156). Oxford: Oxford University Press.

Carver, A. C., & Foley, K. M. (2001). *Neurologic clinics: Palliative care, 19*(4). Philadelphia: W. B. Saunders Company.

Center to Advance Palliative Care (CAPC). (2003a). *Making the case for hospital-based palliative care: Benefits to hospitals: Meeting JCAHO accreditation standards*. http://www.capc.org/building-a-hospital-based-palliative-care-program/case/hospitalbenefits/index_html#meeting. Accessed 28 Aug 2013.

Center to Advance Palliative Care (CAPC). (2003b). *Press release*. http://www.capc.org/news-and-events/releases/August-2003-release. Accessed 28 Aug 2013.

Chan, A., & Woodruff, R. K. (1997). Communicating with patients with advanced cancer. *Journal of Palliative Care, 13*(3), 29–33.

Chochinov, H., Holland, J. C., & Katz, I. (1998). Bereavement: A special issue in oncology. In J. C. Holland (Ed.), *Psycho-oncology* (pp. 1016–1032). New York: Oxford University Press.

Clayton, J. M., Butow, P. N., & Tattersall, M. H. N. (2005). The needs of terminally ill cancer patients versus those of caregivers for information regarding prognosis and end-of-life issues. *Cancer, 103*(9), 1957–1964.

Corr, C. A., Nabe, C. M., & Corr, D. M. (2003). *Death and dying, life and living* (4th ed.). Belmont: Wadsworth/Thomson Learning.

Coyle, N., Schachter, S., & Carver, A. C. (2001). Terminal care and bereavement. In A. C. Carver & K. M. Foley (Eds.), *Neurologic clinics: Palliative care, 19*(4), (pp. 1005–1027). Philadelphia: W. B. Saunders Company.

Crawley, L. V., Payne, R., Bolden, J., Payne, T., Washington, P., & Williams, S. (2000). Palliative and end-of-life care in the African American community. *Journal of the American Medical Association, 284*(19), 2518–2521.

Delvaux, N., Merckaert, I., Marchai, S., Libert, Y., Conradt, S., Boniver, J., et al (2005). Physicians' communication with a cancer patient and a relative. *Cancer, 103*(11), 2397–2411.

Desbiens, N. A., & Wu, A. W. (2000). Pain and suffering in seriously ill hospitalized patients. *Journal of the American Geriatric Society, 48*(5 suppl), 183–186.

Doka, K. J. (1989). *Disenfranchised grief: Recognizing hidden sorrow.* Lexington, MA: Lexington Books.

Doka, K. J. (1993). *Living with a life threatening illness.* Lexington, MA: Lexington Books.

Doka, K. J. (2002). *Disenfranchised grief: New directions, challenges and strategies for practice.* Chicago: Research Press.

End of Life Nursing Education Consortium (ELNEC). (2003). End-of-life nursing education care: Train-the-trainer workshops. http://www.okabcd.org/ELNEC.htm. Accessed 28 Aug 2013.

Ferrell, B., Virani, R., & Grant, M. (1999). Analysis of end-of-life content in nursing textbooks. *Oncology Nursing Forum, 26*(5), 869–876.

Girgis, A., & Sanson-Fisher, R. W. (1998). Breaking bad news I: Current best advice for clinicians. *Behavioral Medicine, 24,* 53–59.

Health Forum. (2004). *Hospital Statistics 2004.* Chicago: American Hospital Association.

Holland, J. C. (2002). The management of grief and loss: Medicine's obligation and challenge. *Journal of the American Medical Women's Association, 57*(2), 95–96.

Holland, J. C., & Lewis, S. (2000). *The human side of cancer: Living with hope, coping with uncertainty.* New York: Harper Collins.

Howarth, G. & Leaman, O. (Eds.). (2001). *Encyclopedia of death and dying.* London: Routledge.

Hulsman, R. L., Ros, W. J., Winnubst, J. A., & Bensing, J. M. (1999). Teaching clinically experienced physicians communication skills: A review of evaluation studies. *Medical Education, 33,* 655–668.

Huskamp, H. A., Buntin, M. A., Wang, V., & Newhouse, J. P. (2001). Providing care at the end of life: Do Medicare rules impede good care? *Health Affairs, 20*(3), 204–211.

Imhof, S., & Kaskie, B. (2005). What do we owe the dying? Strategies to strengthen end-of-life care. *Journal of Healthcare Management, 50*(3), 155–169.

IoM Study (1998). Approaching death: Improving care at the end of life—A report of the Institute of Medicine. *Health Services Research, 33,* 1–3.

Jenkins, V., & Fallowfield, L. (2002). Can communication skills training alter physicians' beliefs and behaviors in clinics? *Journal of Clinical Oncology, 20,* 765–769.

Kaprio, J., Koskenvuo, M., & Rita, H. (1987). Mortality after bereavement: A prospective study for 95,647 widowed persons. *American Journal of Public Health, 77,* 283–297.

Kirk, P., Kirk, I., & Kristjanson, L. J. (2004). What do patients receiving palliative care for cancer and their families want to be told? A Canadian and Australian qualitative study. *British Medical Journal, 328,* 1343. http://bmj.bmjjournals.com/cgi/content/full/328/7452/1343?maxtoshow=&HITS=10&hits=10&RESULTFORMAT=&author1=kirk&fulltext=palliative&andorexactfulltext=and&searchid=1141000177629_17377&FIRSTINDEX=0&sortspec=relevance&resourcetype=1. Accessed 28 Aug 2013.

Last Acts. (2002). *Means to a better end: Report on dying in America today.* Messages for hospice and palliative care organizations and providers. www.nhpco.org/sites/default/files/public/messages. Accessed 31 Aug 2013.

Li, Y. B., & Lemke, D. (1998). Caregiving for elders with Alzheimer's in China. *Illness, Crisis & Loss, 6*(4), 357–371.

Lindemann, E. (1944). Symptomatology and management of acute grief. *American Journal of Psychiatry, 101,* 141–148.

LoCicero, J. P. (2002–2003). A comparison on non-certified and certified grief counselors in regard to education, experience, credentials, and supervision. *Omega Journal of Death and Dying, 46*(1), 5–13.

Meier, D. (2004). Variability in end of life care. *British Medical Journal, 328,* E296–297. http://bmj.bmjjournals.com/cgi/content/full/328/7449/E296. Accessed 28 Aug 2013.

Murillo, M., & Holland, J. C. (2004). Clinical practice guidelines for the management of psychosocial distress at the end of life. *Palliative and Supportive Care, 2,* 65–77.

National Center for Health Statistics. (2003). *Deaths final Data from 2003.* http://www.cdc.gov/nchs/products/pubs/pubd/hestats/finaldeaths03/finaldeaths03.htm.

National Center for Health Statistics. (2005). *FASTATS.* http://www.cdc.gov/nchs/fastats/popup_us.htm. Accessed 28 Aug 2013.

Parkes, C. M. (2002). Grief: Lessons from the past, visions for the future. *Death Studies, 26*(5), 385.

Prigerson, H. G., & Jacobs, S. C. (2001). Caring for bereaved patients: "All the doctor just suddenly go." *Journal of the American Medical Association, 286,* 1369–1376.

Prigerson, H. G., Silverman, G. K., Jacobs, S. C., Maciejewski, P. K., Kasl, S. V., & Rosenheck, R. (2001). Disability, traumatic grief and the underutilization of health services. *Primary Psychiatry, 8,* 61–69.

Rabow, M. W., Hardie, G. E., Fair, J. M., & McPhee, S. J. (2000). End-of-life content in 50 textbooks from multiple specialties. *Journal of the American Medical Association, 283*(6), 771–778.

Rando, T. A. (1986). *Loss and anticipatory grief.* Lexington: Lexington Books.

Rando, T. A. (1993). *Treatment of complicated mourning.* Champaign: Research Press.

Rando, T. A. (Ed.). (2000). *Clinical dimensions of anticipatory mourning: Theory and practice in working with the dying, their loved ones, and their caregivers.* Champaign: Research Press.

Razavi, D., Merckaert, I., Marchal, S., Libert, Y., Conradt, S., & Boniver, J. (2003). How to optimize physicians' communication skills in cancer care: Results of a randomized study assessing the usefulness of post training consolidation workshops. *Journal of Clinical Oncology, 16,* 3141–3149.

Ringold, S., Lynm, C., & Glass, R. M. (2005). Grief. *Journal of the American Medical Association, 293*(21), 2686.

Schachter, S. R. (1999). *The experience of living with a life-threatening illness: A phenomenological study of dying cancer patients and their family caregivers.* Unpublished dissertation, Union Institute University, Cincinnati, Ohio.

Schachter, S. R. (2007). Bereavement summer camp for children and teens: A reflection of nine years. *Palliative and Supportive Care, 5*(3), 315–323.

Schachter, S. R. (2008). *Palliative care, end of life and bereavement. The wellness community innovative models of international psychosocial oncology training: A training manual* (pp. 39–71). Washington DC: The Wellness Community.

Schachter, S. R. (2009). Cancer patients facing death: Is the patient who focuses on living in denial of his/her death? In M. Bartalos (Ed.), *Speaking of death: American's new sense of mortality* (2008; pp. 42–77). NY: Praeger Publishers.

Schachter, S. R., & Coyle, N. (1998). Palliative home care—Impact on families. Psycho-Oncology (pp. 1004–1015). New York: Oxford University Press.

Schachter, S. R., & Georgopoulos, M. (2008). Camps for grieving children: Lessons from the field. In K. J. Doka & A. Tucci (Eds.), *Living with grief: Children and adolescents.* Hospice Foundation of America (pp. 233–255). NY: Brunner Routledge.

Schachter, S. R., & Holland, J. C. (1995). Psychological, social and ethical issues in the home care of terminally ill patients: The impact of technology. In J. C. Arras (Ed.), *Bringing the hospital home: Ethical and social implications of high-tech home care* (pp. 91–106). Baltimore: Johns Hopkins University Press.

Schaefer, C., Quesenberry, C. P. J., & Wi, S. (1995). Mortality following conjugal bereavement and the effects of a shared environment. *American Journal of Epidemiology, 141,* 1142–1152.

Schulz, R., & Beach, S. R. (1999). Caregiving as a risk factor for mortality—The caregiver health effects study. *Journal of the American Medical Association, 282,* 2215–2219.

Schulz, R., O'Brien, A. T., Bookwala, J., & Flissner, K. (1995). Psychiatric and physical morbidity effects of Alzheimer's disease caregiving: Prevalence, correlates and causes. *Gerontologist, 35,* 771–791.

Shear, K., Frank, E., Houck, P. R., & Reynolds, C. F. (2005). Treatment of complicated grief: A randomized controlled trial. *Journal American Medical Association, 293*(21), 2601–2608.

Smith, R. (2000). A good death: An important aim for health services and for us all. *British Medical Journal, 320*(7228), 129–130. http://bmj.bmjjournals.com/cgi/content/full/320/7228/129. Accessed 28 Aug 2013.
Steinhauser, K. E., Clippo, E., McNeilly, M., Christakis, N. A., McIntyre, L., & Tulsky, J. A. (2000). In search of a good death: Observations of patients, families and providers. *Annals of Internal Medicine, 132,* 825–832.
Stroebe, M. S., Hansson, R. O., Stroebe, W., & Schut, H. (2001). Introduction: Concepts and issues in contemporary research on bereavement. In M. S. Stroebe, R. O. Hansson, W. Stroebe, & H. Schut (Eds.), *Handbook of bereavement research: Consequences, coping and care*. Washington, DC: American Psychological Association.
Teno, J., Clarridge, B. R., Casey, V., Welch, L. C., Wetle, T., & Shield, R. (2004). Family perspectives on end-of-life care at the last place of care. *Journal of the American Medical Association, 291,* 88–93.
The SUPPORT Principal Investigators (1995). A controlled trial to improve care for seriously ill hospitalized patients: The study to understand prognoses and preferences for outcomes and risks of treatments (SUPPORT). *Journal of the American Medical Association, 264,* 1591–1598.
Zisook, S. (2000). Understanding and managing bereavement in palliative care. In H. M. Chochinov & W. Breitbart (Eds.), *Handbook of psychiatry in palliative medicine* (pp. 321–336). Oxford: Oxford University Press.

Caring for a Family Member with Mental Illness: Exploring Spirituality

Thomas R. Smith and Mary G. Milano

The authors wish to dedicate this chapter to the memory of David B. Larson, MD, MSPH, former President of the International Center for the Integration of Health and Spirituality.

Sir William Osler, the Canadian physician whose pioneering clinic at Johns Hopkins Hospital was so acclaimed that he has been called one of the most influential physicians of all time, expressed a profound insight about the role of spirituality in health. He said, "Nothing in life is more wonderful than faith—the one great moving force which can neither be weighed in the balance nor tested in the crucible... mysterious, indefinable, known only by its effects, faith pours out an unfailing stream of energy while abating neither jot nor tittle of its potency" (1910). Efforts to measure faith, religious commitment, or spirituality during the latter part of the twentieth century tended to support Osler's thesis that such a concept remains challenging for researchers. By now, enough research of varying degrees of quality, in numerous different settings, with a large variety of respondents has shown a moderate yet consistent association between various aspects of health and this other mysterious variable, regardless of how it is defined or measured. This fact has been especially found relevant in the area of mental health associated with coping skills. The direct application of these data to the mental health of caregivers and those who receive their care will hopefully become apparent.

One must be careful not to assume that profound spirituality or faithful adherences to religious practices will, in themselves, prevent anyone from enduring chronic or painful illness or being responsible to care for someone in that condition. Research has not yet identified convincingly any direct mechanism by which one's spiritual

T. R. Smith (✉)
Cheaha District, The United Methodist Church,
5230 Red Oak Drive, Oxford, AL 36203, USA
e-mail: TomSmith39@aol.com

M. G. Milano
International Center for the Integration of Health and Spirituality,
4660 Tall Maple Ct., Ellicott City, MD 21043, USA

R. C. Talley et al. (eds.), *The Challenges of Mental Health Caregiving*,
Caregiving: Research • Practice • Policy, DOI 10.1007/978-1-4614-8791-3_9,

practices or personal faith influences the ways in which one deals emotionally or mentally with the stresses of caregiving. Evidence is convincing, however, that the mental health of people under stress is often ameliorated if they can place their stress in a larger context with some redemptive or humanitarian purpose or with the hope associated with an improved future defined in some meaningful way. That is to say that spiritual strength seems to be associated with an improved ability to withstand the emotional burden of caring for someone and the personal sacrifices associated with it.

Although people may define spirituality in different ways, there tends to be general consensus across cultures that spirituality is the aspect of humanity that searches for transcendent meaning in life. For many, spirituality includes a search for Ultimate Reality including a relationship with a personal God. For others, Ultimate Reality is primarily a philosophical concept, but not personal. In any event, for purposes of this chapter, the spiritual dimension of human beings will be thought of as that which gives individuals a sense of connectedness between themselves and others, their environment, and ultimately the universe. It gives a depth of meaning to experiences in life that otherwise might seem disconnected or utterly impossible to understand.

While spirituality and religion are not synonymous, for most people, religious traditions and belief systems form the primary means on which personal spiritual expressions are based. In the last several decades, during a general decline among Americans in a commitment to organized religion, there has been a growing interest in spirituality. Nevertheless, the primary ways personal spirituality is fostered and the benefits enjoyed continue to reflect aspects of religious beliefs and practices. A Gallup poll (Gallup 1996) revealed that 95 % of Americans say they believe in God or a Universal Spirit and that 40 % attend religious services weekly or more and 60 % at least monthly. Thus, a majority of Americans are involved in an organized expression of faith that has the potential of producing spiritual resources within them. Only 5 % of Americans identify themselves as atheist or agnostic. Although many of them would not call themselves spiritual, any humanitarian concerns and interests that they may have and the meaning that they often attach to such caring for others may be considered spiritual according to this broad definition.

It is important to note that the connections between spirituality and religion are not nearly as discreet as might seem likely. Many who are devoutly religious and faithful in a particular religious community hold views of spirituality that are inconsistent with the official teachings of the faith group to which they belong. An extreme example would be a Baptist who believes in the eastern tenet of reincarnation. Similarly, avowed atheists may adhere to moral codes that promote humanitarian and social goals that are similar to those that arise from theological premises, and, without calling such priorities spiritual, nevertheless find such meaning in pursuing those humanitarian goals that it would appear to some that they are spiritual people. Some atheists stood alongside Dr. Martin Luther King, Jr. in the struggle for civil rights and support other social causes that have their origins within religious institutions. The extent to which such humanitarian activism expresses the pursuit of Ultimate Reality and/or provides meaning for those involved defines the extent to which those activities are spiritual.

Despite the complexity of these interrelationships, the terms spirituality and religion are often used interchangeably because of the scarcity of scientific research in this area. When the years of research neglect have been overcome, it can be anticipated that a greater degree of clarity among the concepts of religion, spirituality, faith, beliefs, and other similar terms will be achieved.

All of these terms, however, reflect the dimension of life that gives meaning to human experiences. Spirituality applies to all people, yet is unique to each individual. It is very often the means of hope to people in the midst of suffering and provides a source of meaning and purpose to their lives (Astrow et al. 2001). Not surprisingly, an individual's religious and spiritual beliefs are often brought to the forefront during times of crisis. Mental illness, indeed, all illness calls into question the way one has lived life; what life's meaning has been or might be; whether one's life has any genuine value; and whether the quality of one's relationships with the Transcendent or with other human beings are in right order. These are spiritual issues that, if left unresolved, can cause spiritual distress and suffering. Foglio and Brody (1988) explained the relationship in this way:

> For many people, religion forms a basis of meaning and purpose in life. The profoundly disturbing effects of illness can call into question a person's purpose in life and work, responsibilities to spouse, children, and parents, and motivations and fidelity priorities. Healing, the restoration of wholeness (as opposed to merely technical healing) requires answers to these questions. (p. 474)

Surveys have found that 94 % of patients consider their spiritual health to be as important as their physical health (King and Bushwick 1994; see Elmore, this book). Nearly 80 % of Americans believe in the power of God or prayer to improve the course of illness (Fitchett et al. 1997), while 96 % of family physicians stated that they believed spiritual well being was an important factor in health (Ellis et al. 1999). Additional findings from the 1996 Gallup poll demonstrated that 65 % of Americans claim that religion is central to their lives and that a majority feel that spiritual faith can help them recover from illness (Gallup 1996).

A growing body of research has begun to examine the links that exist between health and spirituality. In fact, more than 1,200 peer-reviewed, published studies have documented this relationship. Researchers have found a variety of links between health and spirituality including lower rates of depression, lower levels of early mortality, lower levels of hypertension, improved surgical outcomes, enhanced recovery from addictions, shorter hospital stays, and better compliance with clinical care (Koenig et al. 2001b).

Patients' Use of Religious and Spiritual Coping

Among these published studies, a large body of research focuses on the impact of religious and spiritual beliefs on coping with illness (Pargament 1997). Just what is it about religious or spiritual coping that seems to be so effective? Koenig et al. (2001a) posited that the religious tradition of emphasizing relationships—relationship to God, others, and self—can provide significant support when facing illness or crisis. As they explain:

> Religious beliefs and practices may reduce the sense of loss of control and helplessness that accompanies physical illness. Religious beliefs provide a cognitive framework that can reduce suffering and increase one's purpose and meaning in the face of other previously relied upon sources of self-esteem. Private religious activities such as prayer reduce the sense of isolation and increase the patient's sense of control over the illness. Praying to God may not only relieve the patient's loneliness, but belief in an all powerful, loving, and responsive God can give patients the sense that they can influence their own condition by possibly influencing God to act on their behalf. (p. 355)

Koenig et al. (1988) examined the ways in which religious coping assists the elderly in dealing with the stresses of aging and disability. The researchers asked a sample of 100 older adults about how they had coped with some of the most difficult circumstances in their lives, including physical and mental illness. Nearly two-thirds of the women and one-third of the men replied that they used religious coping mechanisms (i.e., prayer, trust and faith in God, reading religious scriptures, depending on religious institutions or religious leaders).

Koenig et al. (1998b) followed this prior work by examining 850 male veterans at the Durham Veterans Affairs Medical Center who were admitted to the acute medical and neurological services unit and 330 men and women who were admitted to the medical, neurology, and cardiology units at Duke University Medical Center. The researchers sought to examine how religious coping was used to deal with acute medical illness in these two populations. Using the Religious Coping Index (RCI), the researchers found that 20 % of veterans and 42 % of the other patients reported that their spiritual and religious beliefs were the most important factors that they used in coping with their illness. When asked further questions, seven out of ten veterans and nine out of ten of the other patients reported that they used religion at least to a moderate extent in coping with their illness. In addition, 55 % of the veterans and 75 % of the other patients indicated that they used religious coping to a large or very large extent.

Interestingly, among the 850 hospitalized veterans, the use of religious coping was significantly and inversely correlated with depressive symptoms and predicted lower levels of depression up to six months later. In fact, religious coping was the most powerful of all 14 covariates measured at baseline in predicting low depression scores on follow-up (accounting for 45 % of the explained variance). Other studies have found that spiritual coping, such as seeing God as benevolent, collaborating with God, seeking a connection with God, or receiving support from clergy or church members not only resulted in less depression, but also improved quality of life and compliance with medical care (Koenig 1998). These characteristics of spiritual coping were also found to be related to enhanced stress-related growth, which resulted in greater psychological growth as a result of the illness.

In the Fitchett et al. (1997) study of patients' spiritual coping, 68 % of the psychiatric patients indicated that religion was, to "a great deal," a source of comfort and support. This compared to 76 % of the medical-surgical patients who responded that strongly to the question. This area of research is in its infancy, requiring much more data on the role of spiritual coping among psychiatric patients. The issue is complicated by the fact that the symptoms of some diseases may include hallucinations or delusions that include religious themes.

Holland et al. (1999) and Baider et al. (1999) both examined the impact of religious or spiritual beliefs on coping styles among patients suffering from melanoma. Both researchers found that those patients who relied more on religious or spiritual beliefs in coping with their illness used a more active coping style that allowed them to accept their illness and deal with it in a positive, meaningful way. The researchers noted that these findings reverse past views of religious coping as a passive or even avoidant psychological phenomenon.

Roberts et al. (1997) examined the role that religious and spiritual coping might play among women suffering from gynecologic cancer. Among this patient population, 91 % stated that religion helped them to sustain their hopes, 76 % said that religion had a serious place in their lives, and 41 % said that religion sustained their sense of self-worth. Interestingly, nearly half of these female patients stated that they had personally become more religious since their diagnosis, while no patients stated that they had become less religious since learning they had cancer.

Similarly, high levels of religious and spiritual coping were found among women battling breast cancer (Johnson and Spilka 1991). Among these women, 88 % considered religion to be important or very important, 85 % felt religion helped them to cope with their diagnosis, and 95 % reported being very satisfied with clergy home and hospital visits.

Among patients undergoing hemodialysis, more than half of the patients saw their religious beliefs as an important factor in adjusting to their illness. In addition, nearly half of the patients re-surveyed three years later felt that their religious beliefs had become even more important to them in coping with their illness (O'Brien 1982).

While numerous studies have found significant correlations between religion or spirituality and improved coping skills, other studies have found that not all spiritual or religious beliefs predict better outcomes. For example, a study of 90 HIV positive patients found that patients' perceptions of God can influence their coping style (Kaldjian et al. 1998). The researchers found that patients who felt guilty about having HIV or who viewed their infection as punishment from God had greater fear of death.

In contrast, those HIV-positive patients who read the Bible frequently, attended church regularly and saw God as having a central role in their lives, had less fear of death. Interestingly, the researchers also found that those who believed in God's forgiveness were also more likely to have discussions about resuscitation status, possibly indicating more of an acceptance of their condition and less overall fear. The researchers commented, "Belief in a God who forgives and comforts may signify an ability to accept HIV or premature death."

Pargament et al. (1998) also supported the idea that God images play a role in shaping an individual's coping style and efficacy. They found that negative coping strategies (i.e., seeing the crisis as God's punishment or questioning God's love or power) were linked to more depression and lowered quality of life as well as a greater callousness towards others. Other studies have noted that individuals who employ coping behaviors that focus primarily on themselves rather than God are at a greater risk of suffering from depression, lower quality of life, and experience significantly lower stress related growth (Koenig 1998; Koenig et al. 1998a).

Research has demonstrated that spiritual resources can be useful to patients as they cope with the rigors of chronic and serious physical and mental illness as well as other physical and mental disabilities. Similar spiritual resources are available to caregivers as well. It is useful to examine some of the research results regarding the ways professional and non-professional caregivers rally the resources of their own spirituality to help them cope with the physical and emotional demands of taking care of others.

The Role of Spiritual Coping in Caregiving

The history of medicine has long emphasized the importance of caring for the whole person—body, mind, and spirit. In fact, the foundation of medicine is deeply based in religious traditions from the Egyptian culture (Imhotep in the twenty-seventh century B.C.), Greek antiquity (Aesculapeus, known in mythology as the god of healing), native American "medicine men," African "healers and root doctors," and Buddhist concepts of physical health as deriving from spiritual health, as well as Judeo-Christian traditions uniting physical and spiritual aspects of health.

The history of modern nursing also places its roots firmly in the solid soil of theological commitments. Florence Nightingale, to whom much credit is given for founding the modern profession of nursing, believed that she was called by God to respond to the pain and suffering around her. While she promoted improved sanitation and cleanliness, and incidentally kept records to show the improved outcomes from following these rigors, she always contended that the nursing profession was a sacred one (McDonald 1999).

However, as technology has advanced over the last 50 years, the emphasis in medical practice has changed. The curriculum has become understandably packed with volumes of scientific data on disease diagnosis and treatment. This development has left little time to emphasize the compassionate part of caregiving. Traditional medical training has emphasized the study of many of the hard sciences, often leaving out spiritual issues and focusing on treating the disease rather than the patient. Americans have felt the impact of this training and have reported their dissatisfaction with our current health care system. Clinicians need to be encouraged to listen more carefully when patients wish to talk about what gives their lives meaning.

Today, many clinicians are recognizing the need to return to the roots of their profession—to reclaim the tradition of caring, not only for patients' bodies, but also for their minds and spirits. Clinicians are recognizing the importance of "person–alizing" medicine—something educators now term patient-centered care. Integral to a more personalized educational and clinical approach is enhancing practitioners' recognition of the importance of spirituality in the lives of both patients and caregivers. Training health care providers to pay attention to their patients' beliefs and values is necessary to ensure that patients have their spiritual as well as physical needs met. At the core of training health care providers is teaching them to respect the whole patient and cultivating an effective way of communicating with the people they serve.

Bergin and Jensen (1990) stated quite directly the issue:

> For the more than 70 % of the population for whom religious commitment is a central life factor, treatment approaches devoid of spiritual sensitivity may provide an alien values framework. . . a majority of the population probably prefers an orientation. . . that is sympathetic, or at least sensitive to, a spiritual perspective. We need to better perceive and respond to this public need. (p. 6)

To underscore this, the Association of American Medical Colleges (AAMC) Medical School Objectives Project stated that physicians must seek to understand the meaning of patients' stories in the context of their beliefs, family, and cultural values (AAMC 1998). Other professional associations have also counseled their members to attend to the psychosocial, existential, or spiritual suffering of their patients confronting serious medical illness (Lo et al. 1999). The U.S. Joint Commission on the Accreditation of Healthcare Organizations requires the assessment of patients' spiritual needs (Miller 1998), while the American Psychiatric Association recommends that patients be asked about their religious or spiritual beliefs so that "they may properly be attended to in treatment" (Committee on Religion and Psychiatry 1990).

Attending to patient's religious or spiritual issues in clinical care can often have unexpected rewards, not only for patients, but for the caregivers as well. Researchers at the University of Pennsylvania found that asking patients if they have religious or spiritual beliefs that would affect their medical decisions if they became gravely ill increased the patient's level of trust in their doctor (Ehman et al. 1999). Sixty-six percent of study respondents indicated that if their physician inquired about their religious or spiritual beliefs, their level of trust in the clinician would be deepened. In addition, of those patients who indicated that their religious or spiritual beliefs would affect their medical decision-making, 94 % believed that their physician should ask about these beliefs. Unfortunately, only 15 % of these patients indicated that their doctors had asked them about the relevance of their beliefs in the medical setting—a large discrepancy between patient desire and physician practice.

Indeed, while most patients place significant importance on their religious faith, physicians often misunderstand or even ignore this dimension of patient care. Koenig et al. (1991) found that while 44 % of hospitalized patients rate their faith as being very important in coping with their illness, only 9 % of physicians placed this same level of importance on their patients' religious beliefs.

These findings confirm earlier studies that found a similar gap between patient desire and doctor provision. A study published in *The Journal of Family Practice* surveying more than 200 inpatients found that 77 % of those surveyed believed physicians should consider patient's spiritual needs (King and Bushwick 1994). In addition, more than one-third of these patients wanted their physician to discuss religious beliefs with them more frequently, and nearly one-half wanted their physician to pray with them. A similar survey conducted by *USA Weekend* in 1997 found that nearly two-thirds of patients wanted to talk with their physicians about their spiritual or religious beliefs, but only 10 % of their doctors had initiated any type of conversation on the subject (McNichol 1997).

While spirituality and religion can, and often do, play an important role in the coping patterns of those facing a variety of illnesses, physicians often seem hesitant to inquire about their patients' belief systems. The fact that so few physicians address the spiritual concerns of their patients is understandable since spirituality, until recently, had long been overlooked in research, medical school curricula, and in the standards of medical care. How can clinicians better respond to this area of patient interest? What guidelines should physicians follow in addressing their patient's spiritual and religious issues?

A variety of published studies have suggested ways in which clinicians can deal sensitively and ethically with their patients' belief systems. One of the primary ways that physicians can learn how best to address their patients' religious or spiritual beliefs is by taking a spiritual history. Like a social history, a spiritual history can gauge a patient's level of religious or spiritual commitment as well as highlight how these beliefs might best be used to support the patient during their illness. The spiritual history can also uncover possible spiritual or religious struggles or problems—areas that may be best handled by a referral to a chaplain or other clergy person. For example, Pargament et al. (2001) noted that certain beliefs of patients reflecting their spiritual struggles could be correlated with early death among seriously ill patients. In this two-year study of patients 55 years of age and older who suffered from serious illness, they learned that those who believed that God had abandoned them, questioned God's love for them, or believed that the devil caused their illness, were statistically more likely to have died by the end of the study than those who did not have those beliefs.

Indeed, the consequences of failing to raise spiritual issues as a part of an overall assessment and treatment plan may be more significant than previously thought. Limiting questions about patients' spirituality to asking them their religious preference may not delve deeply enough into the beliefs of the patients to be useful. One must keep in mind that the particular beliefs of those being cared for may or may not represent the official beliefs of the faith community he or she professes. In fact, patients may not connect their distress or their comfort with their belief system if no one providing care to the patient raises the question.

Larson et al. (2000) detailed some aspects of taking a spiritual history in *Primary Care Reports:*

> Taking a spiritual history can occur in a time efficient manner and can save time in the long run by discovering potential treatment resources like religious social support on the one hand, or potential road blocks, such as a patient's reluctance to take a certain medication or a concern about procedures like blood transfusion. . . A spiritual history may be taken at an initial visit as part of the social history, at each annual exam, and at follow up visits, as appropriate. Some patients, particularly those with chronic or serious illnesses, might want to bring up their spiritual beliefs more frequently. The physician should also remain aware that religion can be associated with guilt and conflict indicating an appropriate referral to a counselor or chaplain. It is important to keep the discussion centered on the patient and work within the patient's frame of reference or spiritual belief system. It is crucial that physicians not impose their own beliefs or lack of them on their patients. (p. 168)

A spiritual history can consist of a variety of questions and formats. Various researchers and clinicians have suggested the following questions to facilitate clinical discussions about patient spirituality (Kass et al. 1991; Maugans 1996; McBride et al. 1998):

1. What does your spirituality /religion mean to you?
2. What aspects of your religion/spirituality would you like me to keep in mind as I care for you?
3. Would you like to discuss the religious or spiritual implications of your healthcare?
4. As we plan for your care near the end of life, how does your faith impact your decisions?
5. How close do you feel to God or a higher power?
6. How strongly religious/spiritual do you consider yourself to be?
7. How has your religious or spiritual history been helpful in coping with your illness?
8. How has your belief system been affected by your illness?

The answers to these questions can help to guide physicians' interactions with patients and aid in medical decision-making. However, certain guidelines in handling patient spirituality should be observed, according to Post et al. (2000):

> Patients should be permitted to express their spirituality, should they wish to, in a respectful and supportive clinical environment. It would, however, be disrespectful and not beneficial or supportive of autonomy to encourage patients to "get" religious or spiritual beliefs if they do not have them. Referrals to chaplains can be critical to good healthcare for many patients and can be as appropriate as referrals to other specialists. Because many clinicians do not routinely inquire about patient spirituality and do not appreciate its frequent patient relevance, such referrals are often not made. The lack of appropriate clinical spiritual referrals can constitute a form of negligence. (p. 580)

Inquiring non-judgmentally and thoroughly about patients' beliefs and securing appropriate assistance from properly trained individuals who can help the patient address any identified struggles has growing acceptance as the appropriate standard of professional care. Such a standard, however, requires that an interdisciplinary partnership be forged between physicians and nurses who provide overall direct care, and clinically and theologically trained chaplains, spiritual directors, or other clergy persons in each healthcare environment.

Spirituality as Coping Mechanism for Professional Care Providers

Without a doubt, providing care for patients who suffer chronic and serious illnesses and disabilities produces enormous amounts of stress for those who provide the care. The demands upon the caregivers often accrue to such an extent that they must fall back on their own belief system in order to maintain their emotional equilibrium.

Though little research has been done in the area of physicians' spirituality, one study by Waldfogel (1997) suggested that physicians' religious faith can provide tools for coping with the rigors of medical training and practice. Spiritual beliefs can also help medical professionals apply meaning not only to their own problems, but to the difficulties and suffering their patients may experience. Brallier (1999) commented that integrating a provider's spirituality into the caregiving experience can transform medical care—for the physicians as well as for the patient:

> Integration of our spiritual consciousness allows even a nanosecond of caregiving to be felt as a spiritual connection. Consider how many choices of consciousness we can generate and project as we take someone's blood pressure. A patient can experience feeling painfully squeezed or lovingly hugged by the cuff, largely dependent upon the spiritual and psychological states of the caregiver. Patients treasure caregivers who practice their science and art soulfully in spite of time and profit pressures. Testimony to this is the relief and gratitude seen in the misty eyes of patients who fondly refer to a caregiver as their angel, a trustworthy presence who has created a meaningful connection with them. The genuine caring in this quality of connection is likely to also enhance the spiritual strength of the recipient. Meanwhile the "angels" are also energized by their own expressions of altruism and caring. (p. 1)

Even as they provide critically important and often demanding services to their patients, it is simply a matter of time until each healthcare provider will become a patient as well. The spiritual resources that professional providers can accrue in the midst of their provision of clinical services can eventually prove to be invaluable when they are confronted with their own human issues and seek meaning from their personal life experiences.

Spiritual Coping for Family Caregivers

While professional caregivers often face issues of burnout and stress in their professional lives, it often falls to patients' family members to endure the most intense, persistent, and continuous demands for providing care to chronically ill and disabled patients. It has been estimated that family caregivers provide 80–90 % of all long-term care in the United States (National Family Caregivers Association 1998). The stress placed upon such family caregivers is often intense, resulting in adverse physical and emotional health outcomes for these individuals. Family caregivers have to endure the constant demand to provide critical care to someone they have loved for a long period of time. Unresolved issues from experiences in their relationship can require emotional support that is especially difficult to produce if there is residual anger, resentment, or a sense of injustice arising from that history. In these instances, it often falls to the caregiver to find adequate spiritual strength to administer care faithfully while seeking to forgive the very individual who requires their care.

Recognizing the unique physical and emotional stresses placed on family caregivers, Rabins et al. (1990) sought to identify coping mechanisms that facilitated long-term adaptation among those family members caring for chronically ill loved ones. Religion was found to be one of the most important and helpful resources for these caregivers. In fact, the strength of the caregivers' religious faith was related to a better emotional state two years later. Pargament (1997), in his seminal text on religion and coping, probed a bit further with this study, asking,

> What is it about religious faith that is helpful? Does it reassure them that their relative will recover? Does it help them view the illness in a more positive light? Does it provide them with direction and guidance in their struggles? Does it enable them to find meaning in what may seem to be a senseless disease? It is not enough to find that general measures of religious faith or practice relate to general measures of adjustment of well-being. The central question remains: How does religion come to life in the immediate situation? (p. 166)

Segall and Wykle (1988) asked caregivers of patients suffering from dementia to identify one special way that they used to deal with their caregiving responsibilities. By far, the vast majority of family caregivers stated that they relied on prayer and faith in God to deal with the stresses and strains of their caregiving. Wright et al. (1985) noted that caregivers who found support in their religious beliefs tended to have a more positive outlook about their caregiving responsibilities and were more able to find the "silver lining" in their demanding role. Kaye and Robinson (1994) found that wife caregivers of dementia patients were more likely than non-caregiving wives of healthy husbands to have a spiritual orientation or perspective on their lives and roles. Caregiving wives reported engaging in private prayer and seeking spiritual guidance with everyday decisions more than non-caregiving wives. Caregiving wives were also more likely to read spiritual materials, discuss spiritual issues with friends weekly, and believe that spirituality is an important part of life. While the study did not assess the caregiving wives' level of spiritual or religious involvement prior to their husband's illness, one can venture to guess, given prior research in the area of coping with illness, that religion and spirituality became more important to these women as they confronted the stress of caring for an ailing spouse.

Folkman (1997) studied coping strategies of caregivers and partners of persons dying of AIDS over a two-year period. He concluded that "spiritual beliefs and experiences may be especially helpful in supporting adaptive coping during the days and weeks surrounding the partner's death" (p. 1214).

Nearly three-fourths of caregivers in Baines' (1984) study of caregivers of Alzheimer's disease patients said that prayer was their primary coping strategy.

A study of 30 married elderly couples by Salts et al. (1991) sought to determine the interaction of religiousness and their ability to cope with the status of caregiver. Researchers concluded that "... the role of religion appeared to vary systematically in relation to the various health-related patterns observed" (p. 51). All the couples involved with short-term care used religious faith to cope, as did the couple with live-in caregiving responsibility.

Spiritual Resources for Caregivers

Completing the section on religious coping among caregivers, Koenig et al. (2001b) state, "In summary, religious or spiritual beliefs and behaviors are commonly used to cope with the stress of caring for a sick family member or loved one. These behaviors are generally associated with greater meaning and purpose, more positive appraisals, greater well-being, and faster adaptation to the caregiving role" (p. 90). Individuals cannot be expected to sustain the benefits of these spiritual resources alone. Competent community agencies and institutions are essential to provide a supporting role in nurturing these beliefs as experiences of stress and sacrifice challenge them.

Communities of faith and houses of worship, particularly African American Churches, have a strong tradition of working to meet their community's needs—both spiritual and physical (Tuggle 2000). Churches have established parish nursing programs, community health clinics, soup kitchens, housing shelters, and clothing programs to help meet the needs of disadvantaged community members.

However, some have suggested that faith communities are not maximizing their ability to meet the needs of family caregivers. In response to this perceived lack of support, the National Family Caregivers Association (1998) conducted a poll of congregations in the Washington, DC, area to determine the nature of programs and services offered by these congregations to family caregivers. Less than one-third of responding congregations stated that they currently offered programs targeted at the disabled, chronically ill, elderly, and/or their family caregivers. Only 7 % of those congregations currently running programs planned on expanding them, and less than 25 % of those who did not have programs for caregiving families planned on starting one.

The poll also found that congregations tended to provide traditional services such as pastoral counseling, transportation to services, bereavement support and counseling, accessible accommodations for worship, and regular phone calls. Congregations were least likely to provide caregiver respite, end-of-life education and counseling, and support groups for caregivers and/or care recipients. Unfortunately, studies have shown that it is these very services that mean the most to family caregivers. Future efforts should perhaps be directed at assisting communities of faith to design and staff programs that more fully meet the expressed caregiving needs of their members and the communities that they serve.

Communities of faith often find that their most effective use of resources lies in collaborating with other such communities across denominational lines or within the denomination, to expand their ability to provide the necessary services. In fact, most recently some of these services have qualified for additional funding from government agencies to produce an even more advanced level of service resulting from government and faith-based partnerships.

Spiritual resources, however, are not limited to those from organized religious bodies. As critical as religious institutions often are and as effective as they can be, many people nourish and express their spirituality in private. Prayers prescribed by various denominations can be quite helpful to individuals when they read them and find them to fit their life situation. However, personally and privately created prayers are even more meaningful for many individuals than those written by others, regardless of how eloquent the language or theologically sound the concepts in them.

Others find meditation, Yoga, Tai Chi, or other disciplines from eastern cultures to be efficacious in producing renewed inner strength and purpose for their lives. Still others gain comfort for their souls by listening to music, reading, or listening to poetry or other literature, experiencing the vastness of the universe under the evening stars, or enjoying a leisurely walk in a beautiful natural setting.

Furthermore, many agencies that are not necessarily identified as representations of religious or spiritually oriented institutions exist as support systems for caregivers, especially family caregivers. A number of these programs include sensitivity to spiritual and religious issues associated with caregiving and can provide multi-faceted support to those who seek it.

Among these groups with varying explicit interests in spirituality are:

- Caregiver.com
- Christian Caregivers
- Directions in Caregiving
- Family Caregivers Alliance
- National Family Caregivers Association
- National Organization for Empowering Caregivers
- Rosalynn Carter Institute for Caregiving
- Today's Caregiver Magazine

No single effort to discover a means to find inner strength, peace, and meaning fits every individual, and no single approach is likely to be effective with any individual every single time it is employed. Varieties of experiences that produce a renewal of one's spirit are often helpful. Patients and caregivers alike may benefit from the help of a spiritual director or their own trial and error in finding the appropriate processes to assist them in developing spiritual resources to deal with their own suffering or the demands of caring for someone who is suffering.

Policy/Advocacy Issues

Given that medical care at the end of life consumes 10–12 % of the total health care budget and 27 % of the Medicare budget (Emmanuel 1996), and that the value of the services family caregivers provide is estimated to be US$ 257 billion a year (Arno 2002), it is critical that a comprehensive national policy of support for these family caregivers be established. A national policy supporting the spiritual needs of family caregivers would not only be good for the families burdened with the emotional and physical responsibilities of caring for a loved one, it would be cost-effective and consistent with our national "soul."

For example, the stress of family caregiving for persons with dementia has been shown to impact a person's immune system for up to three years after their caregiving ends, thus increasing their chances of developing a chronic illness themselves (Glaser and Glaser 2003). Providing resources that would replenish the immune capacity of caregivers, as spiritual renewal is shown to do, could reduce the overall cost of healthcare associated with chronic illness and disability. Current initiatives that have awarded limited resources to faith-based agencies that provide social services to individuals have been inadequate, at best, to address this growing concern as medical science enables chronically ill patients to live longer.

A comprehensive national policy that would be a beginning must include, but not be limited to:

- Recognizing the importance of the role of non-professional family caregivers
- Providing tax incentives to families that care for chronically ill or disabled family members
- Funding time off for family caregivers to renew their spiritual resources
- Funding "circuit riding" chaplains to make home visits to chronically ill or disabled patients who are being cared for at home

Since the national interest is enhanced by the contributions of non-professional family caregivers, a policy of giving overt recognition to the debt the nation owes to these people would be a starting point. Organizations of family caregivers have begun this practice. Importantly, they augment support given by the federal government, which provides the bulk of dollars supporting family caregivers. However, the amount allocated by Congress to this effort is lacking.

Caring for a chronically ill or disabled family member is an expensive proposition. The services of Medicare and Medicaid are indeed useful and essential. On the other hand, tax breaks to families providing around-the-clock care to loved ones would not only demonstrate the nation's resolve in recognizing their contribution to society, but in some cases, help these families avoid financial disaster. Family caregivers need a break. Their supply of spiritual stamina cannot endure for long periods of time without some attention being given to spiritual nourishment. A national policy that pays for a substitute caregiver to relieve the family caregiver at least once a month would enable the family caregiver to spend some time in reflection, meditation, or other spiritual practice that could restore his or her ability to maintain a self identity while focusing primarily on the one for whom most attention is given.

Many, but not all, families with a chronically ill or disabled patient have a connection to a community of faith with resources that can be useful. However, most of the spiritual leaders of these faith communities are not trained to deal with the spiritual issues that arise in clinical situations. Furthermore, a large number of these families have no connections at all with communities of faith. Having access to clinically trained chaplains who can work cohesively with the team of medical and social caregivers would be a most valuable contribution to the health of the patient and the caregiver. Clinically trained chaplains are able to provide spiritual care to people regardless of their faith background or religious orientation. They are trained not to proselytize those with whom they interact. The focus of the services of these chaplains is the patient and the patient's family.

These aspects of a national policy could go far to strengthen the ability of non-professional caregivers to continue to provide the invaluable services they contribute to the national good while taking care of a family member.

Conclusion

It is evident that more research on the role of spirituality in caregiving is essential. There is enough research, especially in the area of coping, to justify continued investigation of the potential links between spirituality and coping with the stresses of illness or of caregiving. However, more sophisticated research designs will be required if we are to better understand how spirituality enhances emotional stability and reduces physical symptoms even for those under considerable stress by virtue of illness, disability, or caring for such individuals.

Educational opportunities are also urgently required to apprise those who received their professional training before these new research findings revealed the importance of including spirituality as an integral aspect of healthcare. Continuing education workshops, seminars, and distance learning modules could all produce enormously beneficial results for those providing professional care.

In addition, family caregivers could benefit from educational experiences that enable them to learn what to expect in the course of caring for their loved one. Those who expect far more from themselves than is reasonable could gain the benefit of setting reasonable goals for their own performance. Those whose coping resources have been depleted could learn methods for securing renewed spiritual strength in the midst of their dilemmas.

Ongoing support groups conveniently located so that additional stress is not caused by efforts to become engaged in them are needed. No one can provide assistance to others better than those who either have been or continue to be in a similar situation. It is amazing that a group of individuals, all of whom are overtaxed and burdened, can produce in each other a reservoir of inner strength. Such small groups are not only invaluable for providing a sense of identification and connectedness but in providing insights from their own experience that can assist caregivers in very practical ways.

Experience has shown that most people have strength they are not aware of until they are put to the test. This inner reserve of emotional and mental capacity required for such situations can be seen as a manifestation of the human spirit. It is the capacity for an otherwise seemingly self-absorbed soldier to willingly sacrifice his or her life for the sake of a fellow soldier. It is the additional burst of energy that allows a marathoner to overcome pain and fatigue to finish the race. It is no less the selfless commitment to faithfully tend to the needs of others that sustains one despite the personal sacrifices and postponed gratification required.

Caregiving is inherently spiritual. Admittedly, researchers have difficulty identifying spirituality as precisely as other variables may be defined. However, as Sir William Osler noted, it may be measured by its effects. Some of these effects parallel those described in the Christian *New Testament. Galatians 5:22–23a* (New Revised Standard Version) reads, "The fruit of the Spirit is love, joy, peace, patience, kindness, generosity, faithfulness, gentleness, and self-control." We increase our capacity to give care when we nourish that part of ourselves that we call our spirits. When our spirits are cared for, we achieve our greatest potential for finding meaning in the care we provide. May that process of self-care synergistically and reciprocally strengthen those who care for others? May our cultural expectations for those who are dedicated to caring for others include resources to nourish the spirits of the caregiver as well as those requiring care.

References

Arno, P. S. (2002). *Economic value of informal caregiving*. Presented at the annual meeting of the American Association of Geriatric Psychiatry, Portland, OR.

Association of American Medical Colleges. (1998). *Report 1: Learning objectives for medical student education: Guidelines for medical schools*. Washington: Association of American Medical Colleges (http://www.aamc.org/meded/msop/msop1.pdf).

Astrow, A. B., Puchalski, C., & Sulmasy, D. P. (2001). Religion, spirituality, and health care: Social, ethical, and practical considerations. *American Journal of Medicine, 110,* 283–287.

Baider, L., Russak, S. M., Perry, S., Kash, K. M., Gronert, M. K., Fox, B., et al. (1999). The role of religious and spiritual beliefs in coping with malignant melanoma: An Israeli sample. *Psycho-Oncology, 8,* 27–35.

Baines, E. (1984). Caregiver stress in the older adult. *Journal of Community Health Nursing, 1,* 257–263.

Bergin, A. E., & Jensen, J. P. (1990). Religiosity and psychotherapists: A national survey. *Psychotherapy, 27,* 3–7.

Brallier, L. (1999). The spiritual care of the caregiver. *Spirituality and Medicine Connection, 3*(2), 1–2.

Committee on Religion and Psychiatry. (1990). Guidelines regarding possible conflict between psychiatrists' religious commitments and religious practice. *American Journal of Psychiatry, 147,* 542.

Ehman, J. W., Ott, B. B., & Short, T. H. (1999). Do patients want physicians to inquire about their spiritual or religious beliefs if they become gravely ill? *Archives of Internal Medicine, 159*(15), 1803–1806.

Ellis, M. R., Vinson, D. C., & Ewigman, B. (1999). Addressing spiritual concerns of patients: Family physicians' attitudes and practices. *Journal of Family Practice, 39,* 564–568.

Emmanuel, E. J. (1996). Cost savings at the end of life: What do the data show? *Journal of the American Medical Association, 275,* 1807–1914.

Fitchett, G., Burton, L. A., & Sivan, A. B. (1997). The religious needs and resources of psychiatric in-patients. *Journal of Nervous and Mental Disease, 185*(5), 320–326.

Foglio, J. P., & Brody, H. (1988). Religion, faith and family medicine. *The Journal of Family Practice, 27*(5), 473–474.

Folkman, S. (1997). Positive psychological states and coping with severe stress. *Social Science and Medicine, 45,* 1207–1221.

Gallup, G. (1996). *Religion in America: 1996*. Princeton: Princeton Religious Research Center.

Gallup, G. (1997). *Spiritual beliefs and the dying process*. National survey for the Nathan Cummings Foundation and The Fetzer Institute.

Glaser, J., & Glaser, R. (2003). *Proceedings of the National Academy of Sciences: Chronic stress and age-related increases in proinflammatory cytokine IL-6*. Chicago: National Academy of Sciences.

Holland, J. C., Passik, S., Kash, K. M., Russak, S. M., Gronert, M. K., Sison, A., et al. (1999). The role of religious and spiritual beliefs in coping with malignant melanoma. *Psycho-Oncology, 8,* 14–26.

Johnson, S. C., & Spilka, B. (1991). Coping with breast cancer: The roles of clergy and faith. *Journal of Religion and Health, 30,* 21–33.

Kaldjian, L. C., Jekel, J. F., & Friedland, G. (1998). End-of-life decisions in HIV-positive patients: The role of spiritual beliefs. *AIDS, 12*(1), 103–107.

Kass, J. D., Friedman, R., Leserman, J., Zuttermeister, P. C., & Benson, H. (1991). Health outcomes and a new index of spiritual experience. *Journal for the Scientific Study of Religion, 30,* 203–211.

Kaye, J., & Robinson, K. M. (1994). Spirituality among caregivers. *Journal of Nursing Scholarship, 26*(3), 218–221.

King, D. E., & Bushwick, B. (1994). Beliefs and attitudes of hospital patients about faith healing and prayer. *Journal of Family Practice, 39,* 349–352.

Koenig, H. G. (1998). Religious beliefs and practices of hospitalized medically ill older adults. *International Journal of Geriatric Psychiatry, 13,* 213–224.

Koenig, H. G., George, L. K., & Siegler, I. (1988). The use of religion and other emotion regulating coping strategies among older adults. *Gerontologist, 28,* 303–310.

Koenig, H. G., Hover, M., Bearon, L. B., & Travis, J. L. (1991). Religious perspectives of doctors, nurses, patients, and families: Some interesting differences. *Journal of Pastoral Care, 45,* 254–267.

Koenig, H. G., Cohen, H. J., Blazer, D. G., Pieper, C., Meador, K. G., Shelp, F., et al. (1998a). Religious coping and depression in elderly hospitalized medically ill older adults. *International Journal of Geriatric Psychiatry, 13,* 213–224.

Koenig, H. G., Pargament, K. I., & Nielsen, J. (1998b). Religious coping and health outcomes in medically ill hospitalized older adults. *Journal of Nervous and Mental Disease, 186,* 513–521.

Koenig, H. G., Larson, D. B., & Larson, S. S. (2001a). Religion and coping with serious medical illness. *Annals of Pharmacotherapy, 35,* 352–359.

Koenig, H. G., McCullough, M. E., & Larson, D. B. (2001b). *Handbook of religion and health.* New York: Oxford University Press.

Larson, D. B., Larson, S. S., Puchalski, C. M., & Koenig, H. G. (2000). Patient spirituality in clinical care: Clinical assessment and research findings part one. *Primary Care Reports,* 6(21), 165–172.

Lo, B., Quill, T., & Tulsky, J. (1999). Discussing palliative care with patients. ACP-ASIM End-of-Life Care Consensus Panel, American College of Physicians, American Society of Internal Medicine. *Annals of Internal Medicine, 130,* 744–749.

Maugans, T. A. (1996). The SPIRITual history. *Archives of Family Medicine, 5,* 11–16.

McBride, J. L., Arthur, G., Brooks, R., & Pilkington, L. (1998). The relationship between a patient's spirituality and health experiences. *Family Medicine, 30*(2), 122–126.

McDonald, L. (1999, October). The faith of Florence Nightingale. *Niagara Anglican,* 15 (newspaper of the Anglican Church's Diocese of Niagara).

McNichol, T. (1997, April 5–7). The new faith in medicine. *USA Weekend,* 4–5.

Miller, W. R. (1998). Researching the spiritual dimensions of alcohol and other drug addictions. *Addiction, 93,* 979–990.

National Family Caregivers Association. (1998, November). Survey of Washington, DC, congregations. Presentation to St. Johns Church, Washington, DC.

O'Brien, M. E. (1982). Religious faith and adjustment to long term hemodialysis. *Journal of Religion and Health, 21*(1), 68–80.

Osler, W. (1910). The faith that heals. *British Medical Journal, 1,* 1470–1472.

Pargament, K. I. (1997). *The psychology of religion and coping*. New York: Guilford.

Pargament, K. I., Smith, B. W., & Koenig, H. G. (1998). Patterns of positive and negative religious coping with major life stressors. *Journal for the Scientific Study of Religion, 18,* 412–419.

Pargament, K. I., Koenig, H. G., Taraeshwar, N., & Hahn, J. (2001). Religious struggle as a predictor of mortality among medically ill elderly patients. *Archives of Internal Medicine, 161,* 1881–1885.

Post, S. G., Puchalski, C. M., & Larson, D. B. (2000). Physicians and patient spirituality: Professional boundaries, competency, and ethics. *Annals of Internal Medicine, 132*(7), 578–583.

Rabins, P. V., Fitting, M. D., Eastham, J., & Zabora, J. (1990). Emotional adaptation over time in caregivers for chronically ill elderly people. *Age and Ageing, 19,* 185–190.

Roberts, J. A., Brown, D., Elkins, T., & Larson, D. B. (1997). Factors influencing views of patients with gynecologic cancer about end of life decisions. *American Journal of Obstetrics and Gynecology, 176,* 166–172.

Salts, C. J., Denham, T. E., & Smith, T.A. (1991). Relationship patterns and role of religion in elderly couples with chronic illness. *Journal of Religious Gerontology,* 7, 41–54.

Segall, M., & Wykle, M. (1988). The black family's experience with dementia. *Journal of Applied Social Sciences, 13,* 170–191.

Tuggle, M. (2000). *It is well with my soul.* Washington: American Public Health Association.

Waldfogel, S. (1997) Spirituality in medicine. *Primary Care, 24*(4), 963–976.

Wright, S., Pratt, C., & Schmall, V. (1985). Spiritual support for caregivers of dementia patients. *Journal of Religion and Health, 24,* 31–38.

Part IV
Issues in Policy and Research

Caregiving and Mental Health: Policy Implications

Michael J. English, David de Voursney and Kana Enomoto

Evidence that family caregiving is both effective and burdensome is presented throughout this volume. Lack of public support for family caregiving is also a consistent theme. In this chapter, we will examine the public policy context of family caregiving and suggest an innovative approach for achieving increased public support. The policy discussion is important because much of the national health care infrastructure is built on the assumption that family caregiving will fill needs that the professional health care delivery system cannot meet. As a result, efforts to improve health care that do not address family caregiving will be limited in their ability to produce comprehensive care. This chapter reviews some of the dynamics that are important to family caregiving policy for families facing mental illness and makes a range of recommendations. Chief among these is the proposal to build locally based systems of support for family caregiving.

Unsustainable growth in health care spending has brought health reform to the forefront of our national agenda. The past half decade has also seen a series of important developments in health policy which will have a substantial impact on caregivers of people with mental and substance use disorders. These policy changes will lead to expanded health insurance coverage, expanded benefit packages that cover mental health and substance use treatment and services, growth in the use of health information technology like electronic medical records, increased support for community-based long-term care, and a wide variety of other important shifts in health care systems.

These changes come in a time of fiscal constraints and efforts to reduce spending which may present an opening for advocates for family caregiving. Family caregivers

D. de Voursney (✉)
Office of the Assistant Secretary for Planning and Evaluation,
U.S. Department of Health and Human Services, Rockville, MD, USA
e-mail: david.devoursney@samhsa.hhs.gov

M. J. English · K. Enomoto
Substance Abuse and Mental Health Services Administration,
U.S. Department of Health and Human Services, Rockville, MD, USA

R. C. Talley et al. (eds.), *The Challenges of Mental Health Caregiving*,
Caregiving: Research • Practice • Policy, DOI 10.1007/978-1-4614-8791-3_10,

reduce costs by providing needed services at a cheaper rate than professionals or institutional placements, meeting the call for increased coverage while helping to contain costs.

In order to take advantage of this opportunity, advocates of family caregiving should demonstrate that family caregivers are effective in providing care and that they can provide care in a cost-effective manner. Policies that support caregiving can be crafted in a way that avoids crowd out, a situation where family caregivers bill for work that they would have done in the absence of policy change. If crowd out is likely, policymakers will be unlikely to support policy changes. Instead of direct support, proposed policies may be more viable if they focus on support of the caregiving role through training and educating family caregivers, providing respite care, and building community supports to enable family caregiving. In fact, successful advocates may be able to make the case that supports for family caregiving will reduce reliance on publicly supported services, allaying policymakers' concerns about cost while improving the scope of supports for family caregivers and those they care for.

The complex interaction between public sector commitments to treat illnesses and traditional family and community values that expect families to "take care of their own" complicates the formulation of public policies that support family caregiving. Why should society pay someone to take care of his or her own parent, spouse, or child? U.S. democratic traditions envision government as having a limited role in regulating relationships among individuals and groups, who are otherwise free to fend for themselves. Values of rugged individualism and free enterprise are prized. At the same time, a tradition of helping those who are less fortunate, and ensuring that people have access to necessary care provides a basis for the social programs at the core of the nation's domestic agenda. The rational for public support of family caregiving lies at the intersection of these ideological premises. Viewing these principles in cooperation rather than opposition is the best way to explain the need for an expanded caregiver support policy. We can help families help themselves.

In addition to ideological issues, there are also concrete reasons for the lack of a clear consensus about public support of family caregiving. On the one hand, concerns about costs make any expansion of services difficult in the current fiscal climate. Additionally, the notion of family caregiving contradicts the traditional medical model, where medical experts provide and are reimbursed for the treatment of clearly defined problems in offices or hospitals. On the other hand, there are very practical reasons to support caregiving. Care provided by family caregivers is less expensive than care provided by specialty medical personnel and is often provided in settings that are more comfortable and convenient for the care recipient and their family. Family caregiving provides the opportunity for a more integrated and comprehensive approach that may be more successful at managing chronic disease. Support of family caregiving can also improve the ability of caregivers to adapt to the caregiving role, increasing their ability to provide care and reducing demand on the public system and corresponding costs. As with the ideological issues mentioned above, a compromise that addresses concerns about family caregiving while harnessing its strengths is most likely to be successful. Taking an integrated approach that involves family caregivers in the treatment team and maintains a focus on effective practice would augment the current model of care, better address the needs of health care consumers and their families, and also manage costs.

Support for family caregiving has significant implications for the field of mental health. Because mental disorders are relatively common, often strike early in life, and can be highly disabling without being terminal, they create a particularly heavy burden for caregivers. Although recovery is an increasingly realistic prospect for many, severe mental illnesses tend to be long-term in nature (Kessler et al. 2005).

Individuals with disabling mental illness often rely on family resources to remain in their communities, to perform activities of daily living, and to participate in school or gainful employment. Also, people with mental illness are more likely to go without professional treatment than are those with physical illness (HHS 1999). Left untreated, mental illness can cause disabling symptoms that worsen over time. Without the benefits of specialized treatment or family caregiving, children with serious emotional disturbances are more likely to end up in foster care or juvenile detention, and adults are more likely to become homeless or incarcerated (National Council on Disability 2002). Under these circumstances, even small changes in the availability of family caregiving can have dramatic effects on the demand for specialty mental health services and public institutions.

Improvements in care associated with family caregiving may also reduce costs and improve outcomes related to other chronic health conditions, especially if they improve care for mental disorders. The cost of treating common diseases is higher when a patient has untreated behavioral health problems (Melek et al. 2008). Successful interventions for depression can lead to improved self-care of diabetes and heart medication compliance (Gehi et al. 2005; Gonzalez et al. 2007). Noncompliance with medical treatment is three times greater for depressed patients compared with nondepressed patients (DiMatteo et al. 2000). Beyond fiscal costs, there is also human toll that comes with behavioral health problems. People with mental disorders face higher rates of smoking, obesity, physical inactivity, diabetes, cardiovascular disease, and asthma than the general population (National Association of State Mental Health Program Directors 2008). People with mental and substance use disorders are also nearly twice as likely as the general population to die prematurely, often of preventable or treatable causes (Harris and Barraclough 1998).

Involving caregivers could enable treatment teams to address broader health outcomes of people with mental illness, allowing for interventions that promote general wellness in addition to addressing mental illness. In addition to addressing the considerable monetary and human costs associated with mental disorders, it seems likely that support of family caregiving could have other positive health effects as well.

While caregiving is important to the mental health outcomes of care recipients, it is important to remember the increased risk of mental health problems faced by caregivers. Although the value and risk of caregiving are interrelated issues, this chapter will not address the direct societal costs of mental illness among caregivers. This discussion focuses on policies and other factors that affect the caregiver's ability and willingness to provide un- or undercompensated monetary, social, and emotional support we know as family caregiving.

This approach is sensible for a chapter on public policy because care recipients are already a primary focus of policy in the United States. Large entitlement programs provide health care and disability benefits for people with mental disorders. Changes in caregiving policy are likely to have implications for these programs. Of course, promoting and preserving the mental health of caregivers should be a crucial objective of the public health system. The onset of mental disorders among caregivers not only adds to the burden on the health care system, it also affects the extent to which caregiving is available to the original recipient. As a result, public support for family caregiving will result in value not only to the care recipient, but also to the family caregiver and the professional health care community. After a brief summary of what we know about family caregiving and a review of the critical factors affecting caregiver support, this chapter discusses policy and describes possible approaches to increasing public support for family caregiving.

What We Know About Family Caregiving

We define *family caregiving* as caring for an individual with a mental disorder for reasons other than compensation by persons without professional training or whose professional training is not a formal prerequisite for providing care. Of course, the term "family caregivers" refers to family members providing care, but it can also refer to a variety of individuals volunteering to be of service. The terms *formal* or *professional care* are used to distinguish the many caregivers who are paid to provide care and who do so on the basis of certain required qualifications.

Regardless of whether family caregiving is provided by family members or others who volunteer to help, the services rendered are not only valuable and generally effective, but also burdensome. Every day millions of uncompensated family caregivers struggle to maintain a home with a child or adult disabled by a mental disorder. A tailored approach to caregiving support that addresses discrimination against people with mental disorders can help these caregivers as they contribute to care recipients' recovery.

Family Caregiving Is Valuable The health caregiving literature estimates the value of family caregiving for adults with conditions that limit their daily activities at US$ 450 billion per year (Feinberg et al. 2011). These estimates are limited to the value of services to the recipient; they do not include the caregiver's lost earning potential and directly related costs. Seven percent of caregivers report mental illness as the main problem or illness driving the need for caregiving (National Alliance for Caregiving and AARP 2004), so a significant proportion of this cost is directly attributable to mental illness. Furthermore, mental illness is often comorbid with other chronic conditions that require family caregiving, so mental illness is likely responsible for increased demand on caregivers beyond the 7 % in which mental illness is their primary concern.

Family Caregiving Is Effective for the Recipient Other chapters in this volume describe a wide variety of effective caregiving and caregiver support practices across a number of fields. This material demonstrates the value of these practices, both in generating positive client outcomes and in reducing caregiver burden. In mainstream public mental health programs, family psychoeducation is an evidence-based practice that is becoming increasingly common. As part of its evidence-based practice initiative, the Substance Abuse and Mental Health Services Administration (SAMHSA) has developed a Family Psychoeducation Implementation Resource Kit for use by communities in expanding their use of this intervention (SAMHSA 2009). In addition to family psychoeducation, a number of other family support and education interventions have been shown to be effective in improving mental health consumer outcomes (Dixon et al. 2004; Lefley 1997; Luckstead et al. 2012; Mueser 2001; Rummel-Kluge and Kissling 2008).

Family Caregiving Is Burdensome Burden includes physical, emotional, financial, social, and symptom-specific burdens associated with difficult behaviors. Many studies establish both the magnitude and extent of the burden associated with caregiving for persons with serious mental disorders (Baronet 1999; Schultz and Rossler 2005). Both objective and subjective burden has been documented (Cuijpers and Stam 2000). The stress and burden associated with caregiving for persons with serious mental illness can cause declines in the physical and emotional well-being of caregivers and can exacerbate the recipient's mental illness (Heyde 1997). Caregiver burden also has been associated with poorer self-reported physical health, increased risk of activity limitations, and increased health care utilization by the caregiver (Perlick et al. 2008; Gallagher and Mechanic 1996). For parents of children with serious emotional disturbances, perceived caregiving burden is a better predictor than the child's psychiatric status of how parents view the parent–child relationship (Pickett et al. 1997).

Negative Attitudes, Discrimination, and Blame Add to the Burden of Caregiving The belief that poor parenting and dysfunctional families cause mental disorders remains strong even among professional clinicians, despite the fact that little evidence supports this theory (Mohr et al. 2000). Negative attitudes toward consumers and their families are related to increased difficulty for caregivers and families of people with serious mental disorders (Struening et al. 2001). Increased stigma is also related to increased stress and reported emotional and social burden among caregivers (Mak and Cheung 2008).

The Rise of the Consumer and Recovery Movements, with Their Emphasis on Self-Direction and Wellness, Could Have a Significant Effect on Caregiver Burden The recovery and consumer movements have brought a focus on the real possibility of healing and independence. Currently, mental health services are moving toward self-direction, and consumers are becoming more autonomous. As a result, dependence on family caregivers may decrease, reducing burden and stress for caregivers (Lefley 1997; New Freedom Commission 2003). Federal encouragement of the consumer and recovery movements, exploration of self-directed care models, and increased supported education, competitive employment, and independent housing programs for people with disabling mental disorders could be important elements of an overall caregiver support initiative (HHS 2005).

The federal government has recognized the importance of recovery and has made it a central focus of its behavioral health policies. SAMHSA recently released a definition of recovery, "A process of change through which individuals improve their health and wellness, live a self-directed life, and strive to reach their full potential." This definition (SAMHSA 2012) was accompanied by a recognition that recovery from mental and substance use disorders is inseparable from four dimensions of life:

- "Health: overcoming or managing one's disease(s) or symptoms—for example, abstaining from use of alcohol, illicit drugs, and nonprescribed medications if one has an addiction problem—and for everyone in recovery, making informed, healthy choices that support physical and emotional wellbeing.
- Home: a stable and safe place to live;
- Purpose: meaningful daily activities, such as a job, school, volunteerism, family caretaking, or creative endeavors, and the independence, income and resources to participate in society; and
- Community: relationships and social networks that provide support, friendship, love, and hope."

The recovery definition is also supported by a list of guiding principles, among which is the principle that recovery is supported through relationship and social supports, noting that family members are a vital part of support networks for people in recovery. Efforts to increase supports for family caregiving should engage the recovery movement to ensure that family caregivers respect the right to self-determination and support individuals as they pursue their own recovery.

Critical Factors in Developing Caregiver Capacity

Money There is little public investment in family caregiving for people with mental disorders. In a study conducted by the Schizophrenia Patient Outcomes Research Team (S-PORT), the reimbursement records of persons with schizophrenia revealed little evidence that medical or mental health systems provide services to families. Of 15,425 consumers included in the study, only 0.7 % had any claim for family therapy under Medicare and 7.1 % under Medicaid. Of those consumers with reported family contact, 30 % reported that their families received information about their illness and 8 % reported that their families had attended an educational or support program (Dixon et al. 1999).

Health insurance policy is oriented to reimbursement for diagnosed individuals rather than supporting family-based interventions. Unfortunately, this neglects evidence that caregiver burden appears to be at least as important in predicting formal service utilization patterns as clinical symptoms. Greater strain/burden on the family is associated with greater demand on the formal treatment system (Brannan 2001).

As mentioned earlier, a grave consequence of psychological distress among caregivers is their elevated risk for mental illness. This risk results in increased demand for formal psychiatric treatment. These costs should be included in the cost–benefit equation for family caregiving support along with the other cost savings and benefits achievable through increased public support of family caregiving.

There has been some federal support for caregivers through the National Family Caregiving Support Program which was established in 2000 through the Administration on Aging (AoA). In 2011, the program provided approximately US$ 150 million to support family caregiving (AoA 2012). This program serves family caregivers who support elderly care recipients and elderly people acting as caregivers of children or adults with disabilities. While some caregivers of people with mental disorders can receive support through the National Family Caregiver Support Program, its primary focus is on the elderly, and many families facing issues related to mental illness are ineligible. In 2009, the AoA also established Aging and Disability Resource Centers (ADRCs) which are authorized through the Affordable Care Act. These centers are designed to integrate and coordinate the full range of long-term supports and services from across public and private systems and payers for individuals with physical disabilities, serious mental illness, and/or developmental/intellectual disabilities. The program provides information and assistance to people in need of public or private help and to professionals providing or planning long-term care. ADRC programs are also a single point of entry to long-term supports funded through a variety of sources (AoA 2012).

In another development that will be important for caregivers, the Obama administration combined the AoA, the Administration on Developmental Disabilities, and the Office on Disability into the Administration on Community Living in 2012. This new agency will work with the Centers for Medicare and Medicaid Services (CMS) and other government agencies to meet the needs of seniors and people with disabilities, by:

- Better coordinating programs and improving policies across federal programs that support community living
- Enhancing access to quality health care and long-term services
- Acting as a central resource for information
- Complementing community infrastructure (Health and Human Services 2012)

CMS has also instituted changes to support caregiving. In 2008, CMS launched the "Ask Medicare" website to provide information to caregivers. In addition, CMS approved billing codes for Medicare which providers can use in a number of settings to pay for some caregiver education in conjunction with medically necessary face-to-face visits (CMS 2012). Additional Medicaid policy changes, which may help caregivers, were enacted as a part of the Affordable Care Act in 2010. An existing waiver for states called the Money Follows the Person (MFP) program will be extended through 2016 and allow the investment of an additional US$ 2.25 billion to states to help institutionalized individuals return to their homes or other community settings. The Affordable Care Act also expanded the scope of services and the eligibility requirements under the 1915(i) program, allowing states that receive a waiver to offer a comprehensive package of home and community-based services to Medicaid beneficiaries. The Balancing Incentive Program created under the Affordable Care Act will provide up to US$ 3 billion in extra Medicaid matching funds to states before 2015 so that they can make structural reforms that increase access to noninstitutional services and supports and avoid nursing home placements. The Community First Choice program is another new optional state plan benefit created by the Affordable Care Act that enables federal Medicaid support to states that choose to provide home and community-based attendant services to Medicaid recipients facing institutional placement.

The Affordable Care Act also included significant health insurance coverage expansions that will affect people with mental and substance use disorders and their caregivers. Under the law, starting in 2014, individuals living under 138 % of the poverty line in many states will be newly eligible for Medicaid and others who are not eligible for Medicaid will receive subsidies for health insurance coverage based on their income level. This, paired with regulations that stop insurers from excluding individuals with preexisting conditions, will greatly reduce the number of people who do not have health insurance. The law also lists coverage of treatment for mental health and substance use disorders as "essential benefits" that must be covered, though the details of what this will mean across states are not available at the time this chapter is being written. This means that caregivers and the people they care for should have increased access to and reduced financial costs related to treatment for mental and substance use disorders.

Recognizing these developments, there has been a historical shortage of supports for caregivers of people with mental disorders. When polled about support services for families of adults with serious mental illness, 80 % of state mental health authorities reported that their state had no policy about funding any form of family support intervention. Many states reported that support was provided, mostly by funding NAMI's (National Alliance on Mental Illness) Journey of Hope program, but that their average statewide investment was generally less than US$ 100,000 per year (Dixon et al. 1999).

While there have been some advances related to caregiving in recent years, evidence about the effectiveness of family caregiving for mental health suggests that there could be a greater public role in the support of family caregiving for people with mental disorders. Much of the attention paid to caregiving is currently focused on the elderly as a result of the aging of the baby boomer generation. Policy makers should be mindful of the role that caregiving can play for people with disabilities, and of craft programs that can respond to the needs of these caregivers in addition to those providing care to the elderly.

Training and Education With a few exceptions, public programs in the United States are not designed to educate and train caregivers who are caring for people with disabling mental disorders. Rather, education and training is embedded in some therapeutic interventions, like family psychoeducation, where treatment objectives for the consumer predominate. This lack of training is unfortunate because caregiving for people with mental disorders can be extremely complex and demanding, and is more effective with evidence-based training and education (Dixon et al. 2001).

Whatever their prior educational or professional experiences, few people are prepared with the knowledge and skills relevant to the job of caregiving. A frequent refrain begins, "If I had only known this a few years ago...." The dearth of educational programs for caregivers about the nature, course, and outcomes of mental disorders contributes both to ineffective caregiving and to increased stress from stigma, discrimination, and uncertainty. Managing the aggressive, violent, or oppositional behaviors of a child with serious emotional disturbance is extremely difficult and stressful for any parent, and those without specialized training are at a distinct disadvantage. Unfortunately, promising approaches such as problem-solving skills training and parent management training are not readily available in most communities (Farmer et al. 2002).

Clarity of Roles The traditional medical model emphasizes the role of the professional clinician and his or her relationship with an individual patient even though most care is actually provided by family caregivers. The role of the caregiver is given little attention within the therapeutic process. One result is that neither clinicians nor caregivers have a clear understanding of how to relate to one another and how to take best advantage of the strengths each brings to the treatment process. Despite the wealth of knowledge and skills clinicians offer their patients, families often express dissatisfaction with professional services because they feel left out or blamed. Caregivers report feeling marginalized by providers who do not seek their opinion and do not inform them about the illness experienced by the person they are caring for (Shankar and Muthuswamy 2007). At the same time, clinicians may feel that family members are uncooperative or resistant to their recommendations and are therefore unable to partner with them in caring for the recipient. As a result, roles remain unclear, the unique strengths and capabilities of both parties go underutilized, and the opportunity to provide the most effective care possible is lost.

As family members become more active participants in the therapeutic process, family–provider relationships can experience strain. Family members feel more engaged and committed when they feel they are respected by professional providers and seen as an important source of information (Doornbos 2002). More active participation in policy formulation and collaborative relationships between caregivers and professionals also appear to reduce caregiving stress (Winefield 2000). It is critical that professional providers include family caregivers in treatment planning so that stress and burden can be minimized, allowing the caregiver to contribute more effectively to the person's care (Vaddadi et al. 1997; Greene 1995). Improved practice standards in support of including family caregivers are effective in supporting increased participation by caregivers (Lakeman 2008). Policies and programs that emphasize the value of family caregiving and the importance of collaboration between professionals and family caregivers are a critical avenue for caregiver support.

The literature indicates that the role of family caregiver can lead to both burden and reward (Heru 2000). Some aspects of caregiving act as incentives for family caregivers including altruism, self-actualization, and bringing meaning to life (Rhoades 1999). The satisfaction of fulfilling parental duties and personal growth are also critical incentives for parents providing caregiving to their mentally disabled children (Chen and Greenberg 2004; Schwartz and Gidron 2002).

Spirituality and Faith-Based Initiatives Religious factors are recognized as important coping mechanisms that family caregivers rely on while caring for family members with disabling mental illness (Chang et al. 1998). Spirituality incorporates many of the values most closely associated with family caregiving: love, charity, self-sacrifice, the importance of family, etc. Therefore, it is sensible to acknowledge and incorporate spirituality into caregiver support programs. Caregivers report that religion can be an important source of support (Murray-Swank et al. 2006). While the constitutional principle of separation of church and state complicates the picture, opportunities exist to deliver support through community-level faith-based organizations that can yield high "supportive" returns at relatively low costs and without significant government involvement. Faith-based organizations have the advantage of being community-based, and they may be effective partners reaching and providing support to caregivers within their faith communities.

Multiculturalism and Caregiver Support As discussed in *Mental Health: Culture, Race, and Ethnicity*, the U.S. Surgeon General recognizes that individuals and families from different cultural groups perceive mental disorders and their symptoms differently (HHS 2001). Not only do they differ in their conceptions of the cause and source of illness, they vary in levels of perceived burden and in their access to supportive services for easing the burden and improving the quality of their caregiving (Guarnaccia 1998).

Culture, socioeconomic status, geography, education, race, disability, sexual orientation, and other demographic characteristics can be significant strengths and challenges in caregiving. For example, there is some evidence that African-American families perceive caregiving as less burdensome and derive more positive benefits from it when compared with European-American families. This suggests that ethnicity can be a factor affecting levels of family caregiving for persons with serious mental illness (Mak 2005; Horwitz et al. 1996). Lesbian, gay, bisexual, and transgender (LGBT) caregivers face unique hurtles when working with insurers, hospitals, employers, and others to provide care to their partners. Beyond discrimination, LGBT caregivers may encounter formal policy and legal barriers to visiting loved ones in inpatient settings or making decisions about their care (Coon 2003).

Caregiving burden has different meanings and implications across different cultural, racial, and ethnic groups. For example, in an immigrant Chinese-American family, the perceived shame of having a family member with mental illness and a reduced social support network in the United States, and unwillingness to seek help from individuals outside the family may combine to create increased caregiver burden. Culture influences the degree to which a community values self-sufficiency and independent living for all its members, regardless of disability. Cultural differences may contribute to intergenerational conflicts within families. Furthermore, divergent views of mental health, mental illness, and their etiologies may lead to disagreements or misunderstandings between the family caregiver and the professional provider cultures (Kung 2001). Culture and ethnicity may also play a role in responses to the caregiving role. Differences in ethnicity have been associated with variation in aspects of caregiver well-being such as growth, worry, and perceived benefits (Mak 2005).

Because factors related to demographics can both support and add to the burden of caregivers, prudent programs and policies must be sensitive to the roles of culture, race, ethnicity and other demographic factors for both professional providers and family caregivers. The objective of emphasizing cultural factors is not only to extend opportunities for effective caregiving to fast-growing, underserved populations, but also to learn more from all caregivers about how their cultures (and the cultures of others) enrich the caregiving experience.

Policy Discussion

Family caregiving is a critical element of successful health care, especially mental health care. Because family caregiving is valuable and effective, it should be considered an essential component of the public health system. Caregiving burden is also well documented, so it makes sense for government at all levels to foster policy environments supportive of caregivers and the services they provide. Support can be provided through funding, training, education, research to identify best practices, and formal acknowledgment of the important role that caregivers play in the health care delivery system. Caregivers should be appropriately trained and credentialed if they are providing specialized services, included as members of the treatment team, compensated for the care they provide, offered continuing education, and recognized for their expertise and important contributions to health care. Assistance to family caregivers can be provided in many different ways. Beyond financial aid, caregivers would benefit from other supports like respite care, and increased respect and involvement in care planning.

Confounding significant needs for resources to support caregivers, the United States is struggling with rapid increases in the cost of already expensive health care. The infrastructure is not in place to deliver the education, training, and other supports necessary for increasing the efficiency and effectiveness of family caregiving. Although evidence of the effectiveness of family caregiver services continues to develop, many gaps in that evidence base still exist. Furthermore, in the cases where effectiveness has been demonstrated, there is little careful documentation of exactly what is effective and why. The nation's mental health services research agenda should be explicit about learning more about family caregiving as an effective and sustainable part of our health care system. The yield from investments in caregiver effectiveness research could be substantial given the broad roles that caregivers play for persons with mental disorders and the likelihood that lessons learned from these families can be shared. Findings may also be generalizable to families coping with other forms of illness or disability.

There is no reason to wait for the results of more research before action is taken. Family caregiving is effective and moderates demand on the costly professional health care delivery system. Increased family caregiver support should be contingent on a number of factors:

- First, support should help improve caregiver capacity to care for persons with health problems. Policy should be grounded in what works.
- Second, policy should encourage caregivers to care for their loved ones. Policies and programs should address discrimination and negative attitudes related to mental illness. Unlike other health disorders, such as diabetes or heart disease, the negative attitudes and discrimination related to mental illness can be a profound barrier to effective family caregiving. Nationwide activities and policies against stigma and discrimination are critical supports for local efforts in this area.
- Finally, policies should support care options as close to the consumer as possible, empowering consumers to address their own problems. Taking advantage of existing strengths and relationships is central to this approach and caregiving can be a vital part of this approach. Individually tailored and locally based solutions accommodate unique conditions, preserve human scale, rely on relationships, and succeed on the basis of manageable partnerships among people who have personal investments in the outcomes. This perspective is captured in what can be called *the community-level problem-solving approach*. It has special appeal within public health because it embodies many characteristics of the public health approach: It is population-based, seeks involvement from the entire community, has a strong prevention element, and is wellness oriented rather than pathology-based.

Community-Level Problem Solving

Community-level problem solving seeks solutions implemented under local leadership that incorporate the unique characteristics of the locality in question. A community can be large or small, but it represents the public entity that people relate to most directly. A community-level problem-solving approach implements solutions in individual communities rather than at the federal level. The role of a state government in this approach depends on its organization, size, and complexity. Some states are closely linked to communities and their residents. Others are large, complex, decentralized, and reliant on county, municipal, or town governments as the basic governmental units serving communities. Both the states and the federal government can participate in, or offer support to, community-level problem-solving efforts. This approach has a fundamental policy implication: By adopting a community approach, the federal government takes on a supportive and promotional role, leaving direct responsibility to local leadership.

Several conditions make the community-level problem-solving approach especially attractive for increasing caregiver support:

- Family and uncompensated caregiving is a uniquely local phenomenon. Care is provided by individuals who share a community context. The benefits of caregiving are felt most strongly at home, but neighbors, friends, and other community members are also invested in outcomes, consciously or not. Relationships are built on a personal basis and involve close proximity between the caregivers and the recipient of care. With a community care perspective, family members are nurtured and protected, neighbors are involved, negative attitudes and discrimination are challenged, and community providers can be better coordinated.

- Most of the incentives to solve the problem exist locally. Many of the costs of formal services and service failure related to mental illness are borne by local communities. Personal funds, partially supported by state and local taxes, pay for the majority of mental health treatment. In many states, counties govern public mental health services. In others, local authorities manage community programs, supplemented by state oversight. A person who is unable to care for him or herself becomes a burden on local health and social agencies. In extreme cases, persons with mental disorders and no family caregiver network become homeless or involved in the local criminal justice system. Children without effective support are more likely to use public systems, and some cases families are forced to give up custody to the state to receive needed care (GAO 2003). Adults and children with serious mental illnesses or emotional disturbances can also be forcibly removed from their communities and placed in state hospitals or out-of-state residential treatment programs. Providing locally based support to caregivers may help avoid some of these negative outcomes.
- Increased caregiver support can take many forms besides direct payment. Many forms of support are uniquely local. Improved provider relationships, participation on the treatment team, meaning derived from caregiving, and improved social roles—all have community overtones.
- Problem solving is best accomplished where the resources for solving the problem are located and the burden for not solving it is most directly felt. Communities have different values and demographics. They have a variety of governance structures and different sets of organizations in their service networks. As a result, a locally tailored approach can best account for these variables.

Several key strengths are associated with the community-level problem-solving approach:

- The community-level problem-solving approach emphasizes family solutions. In most communities, families are the primary social unit and are expected to support their members. Furthermore, family involvement is central to a number of effective interventions,
- Communities are made up of natural collaborative relationships that mirror the collaborations demanded by improved family caregiving. Communities often rely on partnerships to address common problems, for example, hospitals, police stations, fire stations, and neighborhoods all play a role in local emergency response. A similar coordinated response that involves families can help improve care and supports for people with mental disorders.
- Community readiness, a key condition affecting successful change (Edwards et al. 2000; Thurman et al. 2003), can be assessed and accounted for. Broader approaches that do not take readiness into account may attempt to implement programs before communities are ready resulting in reduced effectiveness, or retrace ground already covered, wasting resources and frustrating stakeholders.

- Communities are integrated in a manner that better sustains a more comprehensive and tailored approach to problem solving. Communities are often served by a group of stakeholders with existing relationships and a nuanced understanding of local dynamics, improving the changes of program success if there is buy-in.
- Communities provide the best forum for consumer, caregiver, and family leadership. Connecting with state or federal government can be difficult for consumers, caregivers and family members. Access at these broader levels can be difficult because of transportation and time constraints. Also, policy at the state or national level may be so diffuse and removed from the personal situation of a consumer, caregiver, or family member, that there is little incentive for them to get involved. The community level provides better opportunities for involvement because access is less of a problem, and local policies and practices have direct effects on the lives of community members.
- Communities naturally gravitate to community-based rather than institutional solutions. Because of natural connections to their own communities, community members have a more intuitive understanding of solutions at a community level. This understanding can drive decision making and political will around solutions tailored at the community level.

Adopting a community-level problem-solving approach has important federal policy implications. In particular, the federal role changes from directive to supportive. Using this approach, federal dollars do not buy the result, but rather fuel the process. This approach is embedded in SAMHSA's Theory of Change. Under SAMHSA's Theory of Change, innovation coming from research and practice-based evidence is translated into interventions and policies ready for implementation. These interventions and policies are then disseminated and implemented on a broader scale, leading to wide-scale adoption. Federal investments are made throughout this process with the expectation that communities and other systems will respond by shifting available resources to more effective approaches.

In SAMHSA's Theory of Change, the federal role includes the following:

- *Sponsoring more synthesis and transactional research*. Scientific evidence about what works in caregiving and caregiving support is not useful until it has been synthesized into a body of knowledge, translated into information that is useful and usable for practitioners and consumers, and converted into strategies for changing community practices and policies.
- *Sponsoring cost-effectiveness and cost-offset studies* that provide communities with the financial information they need to make sound decisions about the investment of resources in family caregiver support. The lack of reliable cost and cost-offset data represents a critical gap in the knowledge base needed for problem solving in this area. Local communities are not in a position to develop extensive cost–benefit studies both because such research is very expensive and because cost data can be extremely difficult to access across systems. Indeed, sponsoring pilot demonstrations may be the only way to obtain useful cost-effectiveness and cost-offset data.

- *Sponsoring more effectiveness research* to determine the extent to which positive findings of efficacy in research settings can be replicated under real-world conditions. Such research is especially important for family support and education programs which must compete with direct clinical services for scarce community resources (Solomon 1996).
- *Sponsoring demonstrations*. One lesson learned from SAMHSA's work is that implementation of model interventions in a real-world settings is difficult and complex. It is one thing to implement an intervention or program, and another to do it with sufficient fidelity, implementation supports, and the appropriate level of adaptation to obtain consistent outcomes. Also, implementation itself is both an art and a science. The field is still learning about effective methods for introducing new programs with staying power. Pilot demonstrations can be crucial laboratories for communities to use to guide their own implementation efforts.
- *Identifying and supporting change agents*. In addition to sponsoring the customary meetings and conferences designed to introduce interested community leaders to new ideas that could benefit their community, federal agencies can offer discretionary grant funds to individuals and groups who are willing to champion changes like improving community support for family caregivers. This function is especially important because it allows caregivers themselves and their care recipients to become engaged in the change process. Support can include activities such as training in exemplary practices, or education about the art of change agency itself. It can also include funds for convening key stakeholders, a critical resource for persons who wish to champion change. For example, SAMHSA's Statewide Consumer and Family Network grants are designed to encourage and empower change agents to step forward and initiate change in their states and communities. Many communities include coalitions of active citizens focused on a variety of issues from substance abuse prevention to health promotion. These existing bodies can be engaged as allies in advancing change.
- *Providing tools*. A number of tools are needed to build consensus for change in communities. These tools can include carefully documented standards and guidelines that accurately describe the practice to be adopted; data on the costs and benefits of the proposed change; training and education curricula that provide key stakeholders with the information they need to participate meaningfully in the process; information on maintaining fidelity to evidence-based practices while accommodating local needs and interests; support for local data collection, use, and evaluation; information-sharing and telecommunication technologies that aid coalition building; and information about the alternatives available for building the political and programmatic support necessary to achieve success.

Process facilitation is a key ingredient to consensus building and decision making in a democratic setting. Effective facilitation strategies can be employed to encourage active participation, retain interest, encourage compromise, cement shared commitments, and make concrete goals, objectives, and commitments. Information about financing options and accountability mechanisms is critical in providing the comfort decision makers need to have before committing limited resources. All of these tools can be organized and supplied by state and federal agencies for use by local change agents:

- *Supporting implementation.* Technical assistance, training, and performance measurement are classic governmental support devices. They are key elements of any successful implementation strategy and should be a core element of a program for supporting increased family caregiver support. In addition, state and federal support could be provided to assist communities to develop financing strategies that take advantage of multiple funding streams to supply dollars to caregiver support initiatives. Although categorical funding streams are a political reality at the federal and state levels, there are many reasons to assist communities to coordinate and aggregate funding streams so that comprehensive programs can be implemented locally. For example, increased caregiver support for families with children who suffer from serious emotional disturbances could include respite care funded by the federal Community Mental Health Services Block Grant, caregiver training funded by discretionary grants, self-/family-directed care models funded through Medicaid, screening and assessment funded under the Early and Periodic Screening, Diagnostic, and Treatment (EPSDT) provisions of Medicaid, wraparound service supports designed to meet caregiver needs funded through the Children's Mental Health Initiative, and antistigma and discrimination campaign resources available from state and federal public education initiatives.
- *Including caregiver support in federal financing programs,* such as Medicaid, TANF, and Family Preservation. In the best of all worlds, federal health-care-financing policy changes to increase funds available for caregiver support would provide flexibility to communities to choose financing strategies that include federal payments as part of the funding package for caregiver support services. Consideration should be given to allow reimbursement for effective family interventions rather than limiting reimbursement to medical treatment provided only to the individual with the diagnosis.
- *Paying for what works.* More than any other strategy, limiting federal reimbursement to demonstrably effective interventions will go far toward increasing family caregiver support and, ensuring the best possible return on investment in such services. This approach allows dollars to be diverted from ineffective interventions to ones with demonstrated effectiveness. An increased focused on outcome-based financing instead of fee-for-service model could also change incentives to support caregiving. Under the fee-for-service system, health care providers are rewarded for providing services regardless of quality. An outcome-based reimbursement system would remove this incentive, and provide health providers with incentives to engage caregivers with effective supports in order to drive better outcomes.
- *Insisting on accountability.* In any case where federal funds are used to pay for improved family caregiver support, funding agencies can insist that the funds be accompanied by appropriate quality assurance and other accountability mechanisms, especially outcome-oriented performance measurement. Insistence on accountability means monitoring the extent to which evidence-based practices are implemented with fidelity, data is collected routinely on relevant outcomes (e.g., outpatient and emergency service utilization rates, hospitalization,

perceptions of caregiving burden, consumer satisfaction, housing stability, etc.), and family caregiving is integrated into the overall treatment plan for the recipient who is suffering from a mental disorder.

Avoiding Unfunded Mandates

The downside to policies that promote community-level problem solving is that they may be interpreted as unfunded mandates for communities to solve problems that state or federal governments cannot. Recognizing this, communities need to feel ownership over programs and therefore should share some portion of the costs for these programs. Increasing caregiver support will require more funding. Most of the potential avenues for caregiver support—compensation, education and training, respite services, therapy—require a significant financial commitment. At the same time, most communities already feel that their budgets and their systems are stretched to the limit. Current budgetary conditions at the state and federal levels also make funding increases from these sources unlikely. At any level, demonstrating the effectiveness of caregiving in managing costs and the existence of near-term cost savings associated with caregiving will be central to obtaining increased funding.

Although funding for caregiver support will be difficult to obtain, policymakers cannot risk the public health consequences of failing to support family caregiving programs. Creative solutions must be found. Here we group the possibilities in two categories: nonfinancial incentives and resource sharing through community partnerships.

Nonfinancial Incentives A key nonfinancial incentive for family caregivers of persons with mental disorders is the elimination of the negative public attitudes about having a family member with a mental disorder. Local sponsorship of campaigns against stigma and discrimination can include messages that convey to communities that mental illness is not a moral weakness, mental illness is not the fault of the individual or family, recovery is possible, and treatment works. These messages may reduce societal stigma and negative attitudes, thereby easing family guilt and making caregiving a more purposeful and rewarding experience.

Improving relationships between family caregivers and professional treatment providers appears to be especially important. Improved relationships set the stage for better communication which permits more education and training, gives family caregivers reassurance because they understand better what is going on, and sets the stage for mutual respect. Most important, improved relationships yield supports that reduce feelings of isolation and give caregivers—both professional and family—a sense that they are supported and part of a team.

Community Partnerships Lack of family caregiving support can result in more severe illness and publicly supported institutional care, and increased homelessness, foster care, and/or criminal justice involvement for people with mental disorders. Untreated mental disorders have ramifications in almost all domains of life and can create high costs across community-level service systems, both public and private. Lack of family caregiver support also can result in increased physical and mental illness treatment costs for both the caregiver and the care recipient. However, the costs and the savings are often realized in agencies and organizations that are fiscally independent of one another. For example, if a community were to reduce the demand for nursing care through increased caregiver support, an incentive to continue the program would exist only if the savings are redirected to provide increased supports for caregivers. Thus, a need for partnerships is created at the local level. Public policies that support partnerships that pool power, resources, and commitments would enable communities to leverage their existing assets and direct them toward the goal of increasing family caregiver support. Experience tells us that communities can and do pool categorical resources to achieve common goals more effectively than most federal agencies or large state governments.

Measures should also be taken to support caregiver participation in employment and other settings. The Family and Medical Leave Act ensures that caregivers can take leave to care for sick relatives (Lohrer et al. 2007). Using regulations like the Family and Medical Leave Act and working in partnership with employers around issues like flexible work schedules can play a role in supporting family caregivers. Such measures not only reduce the opportunity cost of caregiving, they can also allow caregivers to participate more fully in other aspects of life.

Faith-based support for family caregiving is a vital and feasible area for improvement. Religion provides a culturally sensitive avenue for caregiver support. Religiosity among caregivers is associated with better mental health and adjustment to the caregiver role (Murray-Swank et al. 2006). Communities are in a unique position to engage their religious institutions in building partnerships for the support of family caregiving. Given encouragement and some tools, religious organizations can improve their effectiveness in providing education and training, operating support groups, linking caregivers to each other, and in publicly recognizing the great contributions of family caregivers. All of this can be done within the framework of religious practice that cherishes good works, encourages social responsibility, and is grounded in the love of self and neighbor. Community partnerships with faith-based organizations for the purpose of improving caregiver support may be a cost-effective approach to working toward this goal.

Cultural traditions also provide opportunities to leverage community strengths and to support family caregiving. Many ethnic groups in the United States have traditions of extended family involvement and family self-help, so the potential for improving the mental health of care recipients through increased support to the family is great. In communities that strongly emphasize filial piety and family cohesiveness, caregiving can be celebrated as an expression of personal and family values. Community leaders can encourage their neighbors to learn about being caregivers and to support others serving in this important role. But communities, especially those with limited English proficiency or literacy, need information that is accessible, in languages that they can understand. Caregiving education and training need to be readily available to all, whether they speak Spanish, Swahili, or American Sign Language.

Reducing Discrimination and Negative Attitudes as an Overarching Policy Goal

Although communities can and should actively seek to reduce the stigma and discrimination associated with mental illness, federal and state commitments to reducing discrimination and negative attitudes are critical as well. It is unconscionable that the American people have not been given the information they need to understand the physiological basis of mental illness and the effectiveness of mental health services. Continuing to assign fault to families and individuals with mental disorders seriously limits the ability to counteract the seriously disabling effects of these illnesses. Nationwide antistigma and antidiscrimination activities will help to ensure that local efforts are successful.

Summary

Substantial evidence exists to show that caregiver support can yield significant societal benefits. Specific supportive interventions have been shown to reduce caregiver burden, reduce use of expensive health care services, increase positive outcomes for care recipients, and improve the health and mental health of caregivers. This evidence, coupled with data on the value of care provided by families to persons with chronic illnesses (including mental disorders), suggests that it is good policy to increase caregiver support. But it is impractical to suggest that the policy "solution" is simply to invest great sums of public dollars in the support services that seem to help caregivers most. Rather, more realistic policies are exploring the extent to which the federal government and the states can provide support to communities that are interested in keeping families intact, reducing the burden on public institutions, and optimizing the fundamental values of family and community.

By using the community-level problem-solving approach, federal and state governments can play a supportive role to communities that seize the opportunities family caregiving offers to improve health care and control costs. Community solutions involve an increased investment in the backbone of the community—families. But they also strengthen caregiving by:

- Increasing personal fulfillment by recognizing and respecting the contribution family caregivers make
- Treating caregiving as an undertaking that requires expertise gained by training and education, not just experience
- Helping caregivers learn strategies to improve effectiveness and increase self-esteem as persons who help others
- Reducing negative attitudes and guilt unfairly associated with having a family member with a mental disorder
- Reducing burden and stress by providing respite and coping skills development opportunities

- Connecting caregivers with their peers so that they can learn from one another, share successes, and feel supported

The policy implications of this approach are dramatic. They make effective support the prerequisite for federal involvement. They involve making a place at the policy table for many different community interests, including providers, consumers, activists, agency officials, religious leaders, payers, and families.

The key to success will be achieving the best balance between burden and opportunity. Public systems are strained financially, and caregiving is not an issue that can be solved by money alone. Families and others caring for loved ones acknowledge their responsibility for providing care. They do so for many reasons. Absent support, they cannot give the best and most lasting care possible. When family caregiving breaks down, the community and its institutions bear the costs. Increased family caregiving support represents an investment opportunity that could yield dividends in caregiving capacity, lower health care costs, and better partnerships among families and professional providers. These results are worth changes in policy that support family caregiving.

References

Administration on Aging (AoA). (2012). National Family Caregiver Support Program. http://www.aoa.gov/AoA_programs/HCLTC/Caregiver/index.aspx#funding. Accessed 31 July 2012.

Baronet, A. M. (1999). Factors associated with caregiver burden in mental illness: A critical review of the research literature. *Clinical Psychology Review*, 19(7), 819–841. doi:10.1016/S0272-7358(98)00076-2.

Brannan, A. M. (2001). The role of caregiver strain in determining children's mental health service utilization patterns. *Dissertation Abstracts International, 61,* 5794.

Chang, B. H., Noonan, A. E., & Tennstedt, S. L. (1998). The role of religion/spirituality in coping with caregiving for disabled elders. *Gerontologist, 38,* 463–470. doi:10.1093/geront/38.4.463.

Chen, F. P., & Greenberg, J. S. (2004). A positive aspect of caregiving: The influence of social support on caregiving gains for family members of relatives with schizophrenia. *Community Mental Health Journal, 40,* 423–435. doi:10.1023/B:COMH.0000040656.89143.82.

Coon, D. (2003). *Lesbian, gay, bisexual, and transgender (LGBT) issues and family caregiving*. San Francisco: Family Caregiver Alliance. http://www.caregiver.org/jsp/content_node.jsp?nodeid=981. Accessed 31 July 2012.

Centers for Medicare and Medicaid Services (CMS). (2012). CMS archive site MS Document # 11390. http://wayback.archive-it.org/2744/20110930214257/https://www.cms.gov/Partnerships/downloads/ProviderBillingforCaregiverEducation.pdf. Accessed 31 July 2012.

Cuijpers, P., & Stam, H. (2000). Burnout among relatives of psychiatric patients attending psychoeducational support groups. *Psychiatric Services, 5,* 375–379.

DiMatteo, M. R., Lepper, H. S., & Croghan, T. W. (2000). Depression is a risk factor for noncompliance with medical treatment: Meta-analysis of the effects of anxiety and depression on patient adherence. *Archives of Internal Medicine, 160*(14), 2101–2107. doi:10-1001/pubs.Arch Intern Med.-ISSN-0003-9926-160-14-ioi90679.

Dixon, L., Goldman, H., & Hirad, A. (1999). State policy and funding of services to families of adults with serious and persistent mental illness. *Psychiatric Services, 50,* 551–553.

Dixon, L., Lyles, A., Scott, J., Lehman, A., Postrado, L., Goldman, H., et al. (1999). Services to families of adults with schizophrenia: From treatment recommendations to dissemination. *Psychiatric Services, 50,* 233–238. doi:10.1176/appi.ps.52.7.903.

Dixon, L., McFarlane, W. R., Lefley, H., Lucksted, A., Cohen, M., Falloon, I., et al. (2001). Evidence-based practices for services to families of people with psychiatric disabilities. *Psychiatric Services, 52,* 903–911. doi:10.1176/appi.ps.52.7.903..

Dixon, L., Lucksted, A., Stewart, B., Burland, J., Brown, C. H., Postrado, L., et al. (2004). Outcomes of the peer-taught 12-week family-to-family education program for severe mental illness. *Acta Psychiatrica Scandinavica, 109,* 207–215. doi:10.1046/j.0001-690X.2003.00242.x.

Doornbos, M. M. (2002). Family caregivers and the mental health care system: Reality and dreams. *Archives of Psychiatric Nursing, 16*(1), 39–46. doi:10.1053/apnu.2002.30541.

Edwards, R. W., Jumper-Thurman, P., Plested, B. A., Oetting, E. R., & Swanson, L. (2000). Community readiness: Research to practice. *Journal of Community Psychology, 28,* 291–307.

Farmer, E. M., Compton, S. N., Bums, B. J., & Robertson, E. (2002). Review of the evidence base for treatment of childhood psychopathology: Externalizing disorders. *Journal of Consulting Clinical Psychology, 70,* 1267–1302. doi:10.1037/0022-006X.70.6.1267.

Feinberg, L., Reinhard, S. C., Houser, A., & Choula, R. (2011). *Valuing the invaluable: 2011 update. The growing contributions and costs of family caregiving.* Washington: AARP. http://assets.aarp.org/rgcenter/ppi/ltc/i51-caregiving.pdf. Accessed 31 July 2012

Gallagher, S. K., & Mechanic, D. (1996). Living with the mentally ill: Effects on the health and functioning of other household members. *Social Science and Medicine, 42,* 1691–1701.

Gehi, A., Haas, D., Pipkin, S., & Whooley, M. A. (2005). Depression and medication adherence in outpatients with coronary heart disease: Findings from the Heart and Soul Study. *Archives of Internal Medicine, 165,* 2508–2513. doi:10.1001/archinte.165.21.2508.

Gonzalez, J. S., Safren, S. A., Cagliero, E., Wexle, D. J., Delahanty, L., Wittenberg, E., et al. (2007). Depression, self-care and medication adherence in Type 2 diabetes: Relationships across the full range of symptom severity. *Diabetes Care, 30,* 2222–2227. doi:10.2337/dc07-0158.

Government Accountability Office (GAO). (2003). *Child Welfare and Juvenile Justice: Federal Agencies Should Play a Stronger Role in Helping States Reduce the Number of Children Placed Solely to Obtain Mental Health Services* (GAO-03-397). Washington: General Accounting Office. http://www.gao.gov/new.items/d03397.pdf. Accessed 15 Aug 2012.

Government Accountability Office. (2012). *Medicaid: States' plans to pursue new and revised options for home- and community-based services* (GAO-12-649). Washington: http://www.gao.gov/assets/600/591560.pdf. Accessed 15 Aug 2012.

Greene, R. R. (1995). Family involvement in mental health care for older adults: From caregiving to advocacy and empowerment. In M. Gatz (Ed.), *Emerging issues in mental health and aging* (pp. 210–230). Washington: American Psychological Association.

Guarnaccia, P. J. (1998). Multicultural experiences of family caregiving: A study of African American, European American, and Hispanic American families. In H. P. Lefley (Ed.), *Families coping with mental illness: The cultural context* (pp. 45–61). San Francisco: Jossey-Bass.

Harris, E. C., & Barraclough, B. (1998). Excess mortality of mental disorder. *The British Journal of Psychiatry, 173,* 11–53. doi:10.1192/bjp.173.1.11.

Heru, A. M. (2000). Family functioning, burden, and reward in the caregiving for chronic mental illness. *Families, Systems, and Health, 18*(1), 91–103. doi:10.1037/h0091855.

Heyde, A. P. (1997). Coping with the threatening, intimidating, violent behaviors of people with psychiatric disabilities living at home: Guidelines for family caregivers. *Psychiatric Rehabilitation Journal, 21,* 144–149.

Horwitz, A. V., Reinhard, S. C., & Howell-White, S. (1996). Caregiving as reciprocal exchange in families with seriously mentally ill members. *Journal of Health and Social Behavior, 37*(2), 149–162.

Kessler, R. C., Birnbaum, H., Demler, O., Falloon, I. R. H., Gagnon, E., Guyer, M., et al. (2005). The prevalence and correlates of non-affective psychosis in the National Comorbidity Survey Replication (NCS-R). *Biological Psychiatry, 58*(8), 668–676. doi:10.1016/j.biopsych.2005.04.034.

Kung, W. W. (2001). Consideration of cultural factors in working with Chinese American families with a mentally ill patient. *Families in Society, 82*(1), 97–107.

Lakeman, R. (2008). Practice standard to improve the quality of family and carer participation in adult mental health care: An overview and evaluation. *International Journal of Mental Health Nursing, 17,* 44–56. doi:10.1111/j.1447-0349.2007.00510.x.

Lefley, H. P. (1997). The consumer recovery vision: Will it alleviate family burden? *American Journal of Orthopsychiatry, 67,* 210–219. doi:10.1037/h0080224.

Lohrer, S. P., Lukens, E. P., & Thorning, H. (2007). Economic expenditures associated with instrumental caregiving roles of adult siblings of persons with severe mental illness. *Community Mental Health Journal, 43*(2), 129–1512. doi:10.1007/s10597-005-9026-3.

Luckstead, A., McFarlane, W., Downing, D., Dixon, L., & Adams, C. (2012). Recent developments in family psychoeducation as an evidence-based practice. *Journal of Marital & Family Therapy, 38*(1), 101–121. doi:10.1111/j.1752-0606.2011.00256.x.

Mak, W. W. (2005). Integrative model of caregiving: How macro and micro factors affect caregivers of adults with severe and persistent mental illness. *American Journal of Orthopsychiatry, 75,* 40–53. doi:10.1037/0002-9432.75.1.40.

Mak, W. W. S., & Cheung, R. Y. M. (2008). Affiliate stigma among caregivers of people with intellectual disability or mental illness. *Journal of Applied Research in Intellectual Disabilities, 21*(6), 532–545.

Melek, S., & Norris, D. (2008). *Chronic conditions and comorbid psychological disorders.* Seattle: Milliman. http://publications.milliman.com/research/health-rr/pdfs/chronic-conditions-and-comorbid-RR07-01-08.pdf. Accessed 31 July 2012.

Mohr, W. K., Lafuze, J. E., & Mohr, B. D. (2000). Opening caregiver minds: National Alliance for the Mentally Ill's (NAMI) provider education program. *Archives of Psychiatric Nursing, 14,* 235–243. doi:10.1053/apnu.2000.9814.

Mueser, K. T. (2001). *Family services for severe mental illness.* Chicago: Behavioral Health Recovery Management. http://www.bhrm.org/guidelines/Family%20Services.pdf. Accessed 31 July 2012.

Murray-Swank, A. B., Lucksted, A., Medoff, D. R., Yang, Y., Wohlheiter, K., & Dixon, L. (2006). Religiosity, psychosocial adjustment, and subjective burden of persons who care for those with mental illness. *Psychiatric Services, 57,* 361–365. doi:10.1176/appi.ps.57.3.361..

National Alliance for Caregiving and AARP. (2004). *Caregiving in the U.S.* Bethesda: National Alliance for Caregiving. http://www.caregiving.org/data/04finalreport.pdf. Accessed 31 July 2012.

National Council on Disability. (2002). *The well-being of our nation: An inter-generational vision of effective mental health services and supports.* Washington: National Council on Disability. http://akmhcweb.org/Docs/ncd9–16-2002mentalhealth.htm. Accessed 31 July 2012.

New Freedom Commission on Mental Health. (2003). *Achieving the promise: Transforming mental health care in America* (Final report; HHS Publication No. SMA-03-3832). Rockville: Department of Health and Human Services.

Perlick, D. A., Rosenheck, R. A., Miklowitz, D. J., Kaczynski, R., Link, B., Ketter, T., et al. (2008). Caregiver burden and health in bipolar disorder: A cluster analytic approach. *Journal of Nervous and Mental Disease, 196*(6), 484–491. doi:10.1097/NMD.0b013e3181773927.

Pickett, S. A., Cook, J. A., & Laris, A. (1997). *The journey of hope: Final evaluation report. Presentation at the* University of Illinois at Chicago, National Research and Training.

Rhoades, D. R. (1999). Caregiver meaning and self-actualization: A homeshare provider study. *Dissertation Abstracts International, 59*(7-A), 2366.

Rummel-Kluge, C., & Kissling, W. (2008). Psychoeducation in schizophrenia: New developments and approaches in the field. *Current Opinion in Psychiatry, 21,* 168–172.

Schultz, B., & Rossler, W. (2005). Caregiver burden in mental illness: Review of measurement, findings, and interventions in 2004–2005. *Current Opinion in Psychiatry, 18*(6), 684–691.

Schwartz, C., & Gidron, R. (2002). Parents of mentally ill adult children living at home rewards of caregiving. *Health & social work, 27*(2), 145–154.

Shankar, J., & Muthuswamy, S. S. (2007). Support needs of family caregivers of people who experience mental illness and the role of mental health services. *Families in Society, 88*(2), 302–310.

Solomon, P. (1996). Moving from psychoeducation to family education for families of adults with serious mental illness. *Psychiatric Services, 47,* 1364–1370.

Struening, D. L., Perlick, D. A., Link, B. G., Hellman, F., Herman, D., & Sirey, J. A. (2001). Stigma as a barrier to recovery: The extent to which caregivers believe most people devalue consumers and their families. *Psychiatric Services, 52,* 1633–1638.

Substance Abuse and Mental Health Services Administration. (2009). *Family Psychoeducation: How to use the Evidence-Based Practices KITs.* (HHS Pub. No. SMA-09-4422). Rockville: Center for Mental Health Services, Substance Abuse and Mental Health Services Administration, U.S. Department of Health and Human Services. http://store.samhsa.gov/product/Family-Psychoeducation-Evidence-Based-Practices-EBP-KIT/SMA09–4423. Accessed 15 Aug 2012.

Substance Abuse and Mental Health Services Administration (2012). *SAMHSA's Working Definition of Recovery Updated.* Rockville: Substance Abuse and Mental Health Services Administration. http://blog.samhsa.gov/2012/03/23/defintion-of-recovery-updated/. Accessed 31 July 2012.

Thurman, P. J., Plested, B. A., Edwards, R. W., Foley, R., & Burnside, M. (2003). Community readiness: The journey to community healing. *Journal of Psychoactive Drugs, 35*(1), 27–31.

U.S. Department of Health and Human Services (HHS). (1999). *Mental health: A report of the Surgeon General.* Rockville: U.S. Department of Health and Human Services.

U.S. Department of Health and Human Services (HHS). (2001). *Mental health: Culture, race, and ethnicity—A supplement to Mental health: A report of the Surgeon General.* Rockville: U.S. Department of Health and Human Services.

U.S. Department of Health and Human Services (HHS). (2005). *Transforming mental health care in America. Federal Action Agenda: First steps* (HHS Publication No. SMA-05-4060). Rockville: U.S. Department of Health and Human Services.

U.S. Department of Health and Human Services (HHS). (2012). *About Us: Questions and Answers on the Establishment of the Administration for Community Living.* http://www.hhs.gov/acl/about.html. Accessed 31 July 2012.

Vaddadi, K. S., Soosai, E., Gilleard, C. J., & Adlard, S. (1997). Mental illness, physical abuse and burden of care on relatives: A study of acute psychiatric admission patients. *Acta Psychiatrica Scandinavica, 95*(4), 313–317.

Winefield, H. R. (2000). Stress reduction for family caregivers in chronic mental illness: Implications of a work stress management perspective. *International Journal of Stress Management, 7*(3), 193–207.

Research in Caregiving

Elizabeth A. Crocco and Carl Eisdorfer

Between 1950 and 2050, the proportion of those aged 65 years and older in the population will more than double (Himes 2001). As the population ages, the likelihood of frailty, dementia, and disabling illness increases. This unprecedented growth in the elderly population in need of support presents multiple challenges for society and in particular, for families who are frequently called upon to act as caregivers for impaired spouses, parents, and siblings. A tremendous degree of burden and psychological distress are associated with the caregiving role (Schulz et al. 1995). For this reason, research is essential to identify those caregivers who are most susceptible to adverse outcomes and to identify and alleviate the burden associated with different aspects of the caregiving experience. Furthermore, innovative caregiving research can lead to the development of constructive interventions that will aid families, older adults, and society at large.

This chapter will present an overview of research in mental health and caregiving. It will cover the prevalence and demographics of caregiving, consequences of caregiving on mental health, areas of study related to risk factors for caregiver's depression and "distress," interventions to prevent or ameliorate the negative consequences associated with caregiving, and research priorities in this important field. Variables related to both caregivers and care recipients will be addressed and we will conclude with our observations on future challenges in this area.

E. A. Crocco (✉) · C. Eisdorfer
Division of Geriatric Psychiatry, Department of Psychiatry and Behavioral Sciences, Miller School of Medicine/University of Miami,
1695 NW 9th Avenue, Suite 3204A, Miami, FL 33136, USA
e-mail: ecrocco@med.miami.edu

C. Eisdorfer
e-mail: carlandsusan@gmail.com

R. C. Talley et al. (eds.), *The Challenges of Mental Health Caregiving*,
Caregiving: Research • Practice • Policy, DOI 10.1007/978-1-4614-8791-3_11,

Prevalence and Demographics of Caregiving

The majority of dependent older adults live in private households, dispelling the myth that most are placed in long-term care facilities (Hobbs and Damon 1996). The need for caregiving from family members, such as spouses and children, is increasing. Data collected in a comprehensive survey of caregivers to the elderly by the National Alliance for Caregiving (NAC) and the AARP in 2004 provides the following findings. There are an estimated 44.4 million US households, or nearly one in four, providing care for disabled or seriously ill relatives. From all the primary caregivers, 61 % are female. About one-quarter of the caregivers are caring for dementia patients, most commonly, those with Alzheimer's disease (AD). Approximately four million people in the USA have AD, and this number will increase to 14 million by 2050 unless a cure or prevention is found (Volicer 2001).

More than half of all caregivers are employed full- or part-time (NAC and AARP 2004). Many experience significant loss of income due to the changes they must make in their work environment to accommodate caring for a loved one. In addition, the burden of reduced employment is more likely to be incurred by women and families of ethnic minorities (Covinsky et al. 2001) than by white men. In a study by Arno et al. (1999), it was estimated that the national economic value of informal caregiving was US$ 196 billion in 1997, a figure that dwarfs the national spending for formal home health and nursing home care. For AD specifically, a similar trend in caregiving cost was described (Harrow et al. 2004). In terms of lost productivity among employees providing hands-on care, a conservative estimate is that US$ 11.4 billion are lost annually to US businesses (Langa et al. 2001).

Clearly, the epidemiological data demonstrate that caregivers of those elderly who suffer from disabling illnesses such as AD are challenged by significantly large and growing problems. Both government agencies and researchers alike have demonstrated concern for maintaining caregivers' health and ability to perform their duties. Through public policy and advocacy, caregiving research has become an increasingly significant priority for funding through the National Institute on Aging and the National Institute of Mental Health. In addition, research to prevent caregiver depression has been supported through the National Institute of Nursing. Caregiver research has also been coupled with elder abuse as a vital area in need of further research and funding. Only through conclusive data can one advocate for real changes in public policy.

Caregiver Burden and Its Mental Health Consequences

Caring for a family member with AD has been shown to result in significant psychological distress and a subjective or perceived burden (Schulz et al. 1995; Schulz and Williamson 1991). Psychological distress includes emotions such as anger, anxiety, low levels of life satisfaction, and depression. It is important to note that the negative consequences of caregiving, such as isolation, anger, resentment, loss of control, and work pressures are not identical to objective burden, which refers to the care recipients' needs and deficits that affect the caregivers' practices (Zarit et al. 1986). Examples of objective burdens include disruption of lifestyle, increased caregiver vigilance due to patient wandering (in instances of dementia), physical burden for those who care for the bed-ridden, and alterations in sleep due to disruption by the care recipient. Other objective variables associated with the caring transaction may include time spent on caregiving, economic burden (e.g., management of parental or familial finances), and interpersonal challenges (e.g., hiding the car keys).

Objective burden needs consideration independent of subjective burden, since the caregivers' mental state can alter their perception of personal burden and the patients' abilities to care for themselves, independent of their actual burden. As an example, caregivers, at times, may feel responsible and want to help, or they may feel burdened and angry about their situation, or even both at the same time. The caregivers' mental state may then, in turn, alter their subjective impression of actual care burden, i.e., actual hours spent on their loved one, independent of the actual number of hours spent providing care. Surprisingly, the severity of actual burden is not always reflective of poorer caregiver outcome. Caregiving may at times actually have positive influences such as family cohesiveness, improved self-worth, and enhanced personal growth (Czaja et al. 2000). These differences may explain why there is a considerate amount of variability in what caregivers typically appraise as stressful. In both clinical practice and research, this can be most challenging as not all caregiving burdens are universally stressful or distressful.

To complicate matters, caregivers often differ in their subjective response to similar stressful events due to individual differences, such as coping ability, social support, and additional life stressors (Zarit et al. 1998). In addition, subjective burden may differ based on the nature of the relationship with the care recipient and vary as a function of personal qualities of both the caregiver and care recipient. The age, gender, culture, and ethnicity of the caregiver also play a role in this dichotomy between perception and measured events (Czaja et al. 2000). Clearly, research into caregiver outcomes must include a multiple array of variables that may add to or diminish burden.

Due to the amount of stress and burden suffered by caregivers, it is not surprising that they suffer from greater risks to their health than non-caregivers. Prevalence rates of self-reported depression among individuals caring for a person with dementia within the community have ranged from 30 % (Kiecolt-Glaser et al. 1991a) to as high as 83 % (Drinka et al. 1987). These rates are significantly higher than those reported in demographically similar controls. In addition, caregivers use prescription drugs for depression, anxiety, and insomnia 2–3 times as often as compared the rest of the population (Schulz et al. 1995), implying they have an increased number of psychiatric disturbances.

In general, spousal caregivers tend to report more symptoms of depression and overt distress relative to adult child caregivers (Baumgarten et al. 1992; Grafstrom et al. 1992; Meshefedjan et al. 1998). Wives appear to have particularly high levels of depression and psychological distress (Bookwala and Schulz 2000; Pruchno and Potashnik 1989; Pruchno and Resch 1989; Rose-Rego et al. 1998), and women, in general, may be more prone to negative emotional outcomes associated with the caregiving experience (Yee and Schulz 2000). Differences in adverse psychological outcomes among different types of family caregivers may be affected by such factors as attentiveness to one's own emotions, coping styles, and specific caregiver roles (Rose-Rego et al. 1998).

The consequences of caregiving not only effect the emotions but also the physical health of the caregiver (Haley 1997). A prospective study of elderly spousal caregivers showed that the subjects that reported a high level of emotional strain had a 63 % higher mortality risk than non-caregivers (Schulz and Beach 1999). Adverse changes in the autonomic and immune systems in caregivers have also been empirically documented (Kielcolt-Glaser et al. 1991; Wu et al. 1999), and these alterations in the immune system may lead to increased susceptibility to illness (Kiecolt-Glaser et al. 1991b). In addition, chronic stress and bereavement have also been associated with increased medical risks (Bodnar and Kiecolt-Glaser 1994). Well-established models have suggested that repeated increases in stress hormones, such as cortisol and catecholamines from the hypothalamic-pituitary-adrenal (HPA) axis and sympathetic nervous system respectively, due to chronic stress may lead to allostatic load and physiological dysregulation, making an individual more prone to diseases (McEwen 1998). Other theoretical models imply that stress triggers poor lifestyle choices, such as poor diet, substance abuse, and sedentary behavior, which, in turn, are risk factors for cardiovascular and metabolic dysfunction (Vitaliano et al. 2003).

Several studies demonstrate that caregivers suffer more chronic illnesses than non-caregivers. In a recent meta-analysis, Vitaliano et al. (2003) compared the physical health of caregivers with similar non-caregivers in 23 studies over a 38-year period. Caregivers were found to have a 23 % higher level of stress hormones and 15 % lower level of antibody responses than the demographically matched control group. When examined across 11 health categories, such as global health, health service utilization, and medication use, caregivers demonstrated only a slightly greater risk than non-caregivers. Though these findings do not add credence to the proposal that caregiving causes illness, they suggest that there are, indeed, potential risks to one's health.

A recently proposed theoretical model that integrates caregiver stress, poor health habits, and physiological mediators with subsequent illness outcomes was constructed by Vitaliano et al. (2003). In the caregiver experience, individual differences, such as vulnerability (i.e., age, sex, disposition, race, family history) and resources (coping mechanisms, social supports) as well as caregiving exposure directly interacted with psychological distress (i.e., depression). Caregivers' health habits, in turn, directly affected their physiological response, which leads to illness expression. By adding two-way interactions between exposures, vulnerabilities, and/or resources, the authors predicted distress and health habits better than by using any one variable alone. Data support this theory (Vitaliano et al. 1991), and allow for the summative influence of individual characteristics of each specific caregiver on illness risk and expression. Individual variation and lack of integration of similar stress models may be one plausible explanation of why studies on caregivers and the risk of physical illness are conflicting. Future research design needs to integrate multifactorial stress models that incorporate these numerable variables.

Caregiver burden can also have consequences for the care recipient. It has been demonstrated that negative reactions due to poor-quality care were quite common among those receiving care and may lead to depression and low life satisfaction (Newsome and Schulz 1998). What is more alarming is that violence has emerged as a significant clinical challenge in families living with a relative diagnosed with AD. A study by Paveza et al. (1992) suggests that a person with AD is at 2.25 times greater risk for a physically abusive episode than an older person living in the community and that 17 % of Alzheimer's families experience familial violence. A study comparing the characteristics of older married men who committed homicide-suicide with an age-matched group of older married men who committed suicide demonstrated that half of the homicide-suicide perpetrators were caregivers as compared with 13 % of the suicides (Cohen et al. 1998). Given their dependent position, frail, medically ill elderly are potentially vulnerable to abuse and neglect from burdened caregivers. We may assume that select caregivers with a high degree of perceived burden and possible psychopathology may place their family members at risk, but specific risk factors among caregivers are unclear and warrant further investigation.

In practice, due to the high level of morbidity and even possible mortality associated with caregiving, health care providers need to be well-informed of the risks the caregiving role assumes and be able to treat caregivers appropriately. Caregivers often turn to physicians for help and support. In the case of dementia and AD, early diagnosis and education are paramount to prevent delays in receiving needed support and intervention strategies to put caregivers at less risk for depression and burden. Health care providers must be able to recognize and appropriately treat clinical depression and other mental health illnesses in caregivers who can respond to medications and/or psychotherapy. Screening for elder abuse and violence is also needed.

In terms of education and training, geriatrics is still woefully lacking for general physicians, nurses, and social workers (Spector and Tampi 2005). However, the greater recognition of family caregivers as an essential component in treating many chronically ill and cognitively impaired older adults has facilitated the integration of caregivers' needs into the study of geriatrics. For example, physicians training specifically in geriatric subspecialties, such as geriatric medicine and geriatric psychiatry, are expected to achieve competence in family caregiver assessment for risks associated with burden and to understand effective treatments and interventions as part of the larger picture in achieving positive outcomes for their elderly patients.

Risk Factors for Caregiver Depression

As previously described, the negative mental health effects of caring for family members are well documented. Caregivers experience such emotions as anger, anxiety, low levels of life satisfaction, and clinical depression as well as chronic stress (Schulz et al. 1995).

Table 1 lists variables that have been shown in various studies to affect caregiver mental health. These represent important areas known to have an influence on caregivers and each is worthy of investigation.

Table 1 Risk factors for caregiver depression

1	Gender
2	Relationship to patient
3	Ethnicity
4	Cultural adaptation
5	Patient's behavioral and emotional changes
6	Impairment in activities of daily living (ADLs)
7	Coping style of caregiver
8	Interfamily support
9	Community support
10	Religiosity or spirituality
11	Psychiatric history
12	Isolation
13	Alcohol abuse

Gender

Gender is among the most powerful predictors of caregiver depression. Female caregivers have a higher prevalence of depression than their male counterparts (Cohen 2000). Wives are at the highest risk, followed by husbands, daughters, and daughters-in-law, sons, and other relatives (Dura et al. 1991). The basis for these differences is not entirely clear, although the style of caregiving may play a role, with women tending to provide direct, comprehensive care, as in mothering behavior for children, while men tend to delegate care and orchestrate it, creating a greater degree of interpersonal separation and the perception of more control and mastery. Their expectations for positive outcomes may be defined as when children grow and require less care; successful care for frail and demented patients cannot be defined by the same type of outcome.

Recent data suggest that although women appear more vulnerable to depression than men, male caregivers may be at an increased risk of physiological dysregulation, such as decreases in immune function. Scanlan et al. (2001) demonstrated that male caregivers with depression had less lymphocyte proliferation than non-depressed men. The same was not replicated in depressed woman subjects. Male caregivers may be more vulnerable to physical illness through stress mediators due to chronic stress. This clearly has implications for clinical practice as male caregivers may require health care providers to pay closer attention to the physical risks they incur, and plan for intervention to alleviate both physical and psychological pathology.

Relationship to the Patient

Caregiving has a positive component both to caregiver and recipient (MacPhail 1993), which may, in part, be a result of the relationship the caregiver has with an impaired relative. There is only scant literature on motivation for family caregiving and the relationship between caregivers' motivation and behavior, or their consequences on the patient or caregiver. Cohen and Eisdorfer (1995) have proposed a theoretical model that includes such variables as love, morality, equity, ethics, envy, and greed, but there are minimal empirical data that examine the significance of such factors, despite what would seem to be their obvious importance.

Love, arguably our most powerful positive emotion, is poorly understood by scientists despite its crucial role in interpersonal relationships. Morality recognizes what is right or wrong, reflects our social code of conduct, and may be associated with social embarrassment if one does not provide care. Equity refers to a sense of social justice and an implicit accounting (e.g., look at all that my mother did for me, and I owe her). Ethics is an inner concern with what is the right thing to do even if one's relative has been historically selfish or abusive to the caregiver and felt to be undeserving. Envy may be a complex motivation related to a history of sibling or familial rivalry and may be expressed in competition to win the care recipient's respect and affection by being the principal helper. Greed speaks for itself as a motivation to provide care to a wealthy relative, but greed can also create caregiving conflicts since there is the possible issue of spending the care recipient's assets on them or preserving them, while these same assets also represent a possible inheritance for the caregiver. Although hard to objectify and quantify, these and other possible motivational issues should be investigated since they represent the unique relationship the caregiver has with the dependent relative and can play a role in the outcome of the caregiving process for all of those involved.

Ethnicity and Cultural Adaptation

Race as a variable plays a role. African-Americans had lower rates of caregiver depression then Caucasians or Hispanics, whereas Caucasian caregivers appraised behavioral problems as more stressful in comparison to African-Americans, Hispanic, or Asian caregivers (Connell and Gibson 1997; Gallagher-Thompson et al. 2000). African-Americans may be less prone to depression because they perceive caring as less burdensome and have a higher expectation that they should provide care. They are also more likely to have extended family and kinship networks within the community to provide care. Haley et al. (1996) found that mastery, or a sense of competence in the caregiving role, was higher among African-American than among Caucasians, which may reflect increased cultural acceptance and family support of that role. In addition, African-Americans may more likely use spirituality and religion to cope with the burdens of caregiving (see *Caring for a Family Member with Mental Illness: Exploring Spirituality*, this volume, this book).

The link between Hispanics and depression is not entirely clear due to conflicting results in the literature. Mexican-Americans appraise caregiving as less stressful than other ethnic groups (John and McMillian 1998), but in a study by Mintzer et al. (1992) it was demonstrated that among caregivers for Alzheimer's patients, Cuban-American female caregivers had more symptoms of depression than white, non-Hispanic matched counterparts. These differences may reflect the diversity among the various Hispanic groups. Mexican-American daughters have demonstrated higher self-efficacy, or belief about their abilities to organize and execute planning (Depp et al. 2005), and place their family role in caregiving as an honor and an expected function. For more on cultural/racial caregiving for the mentally ill, see *Cultural Considerations in Caring for Persons with mental Illness*, this volume, this book.

Care Recipient Characteristics

In terms of patient characteristics, the impaired elders' behavior problems and emotional changes are consistently linked to psychiatric morbidity in the caregiver (Zarit et al. 1998). In general, the patients' emotional state seems to be a good predictor of caregiver distress. Greater severity of patient cognition or physical deterioration clearly plays an important role, but this is more influential in the late stages of dementia. In caring for the AD patient, the amount of time spent caring for the patient, misidentifications of the caregiver by the patient, and nocturnal arousal by the care recipient have all been noted to accumulate to create an emotional "breaking point" for the caregiver that can lead to clinical depression and placement of a dependent relative in a long-term care facility. Overall, caregivers found patients' impairment in activities of daily living (ADLs; i.e., dressing or bathing) to be less stressful, possibly due to their greater predictability.

In practice, interventions which improve the cognitive, functional, and psychiatric/behavioral impairments can lessen the objective burden to caregivers and, in turn, potentially alleviate caregiver stress. Medications, such as cholinesterase inhibitors, as well as cognitive retraining may improve cognitive impairment. Psychotropic medications and behavioral interventions can be affective for psychiatric and behavioral disturbances that most likely appear to cause caregiver stress. Functional impairment in ADLs can be improved through behavioral intervention and appropriate supportive care (Beck et al. 1997). These interventions can lead to reductions in objective burden for the caregiver and possibly better the outcomes for both caregiver and patient.

Spirituality and Religiosity

The degree of religiosity may also be a significant variable which interacts with ethnicity/race. Caregivers, especially African-Americans, often rely on prayer and religion as a helpful coping mechanism, whereas Caucasians more commonly rely on professional assistance. Attendance at religious activities and membership in a church, mosque, or synagogue may give them a larger sense of community support, which further explains why African-Americans suffer less caregiver burden and psychological distress than other ethnic groups. See *Caring for a Family Member with Mental Illness: Exploring Spirituality*, this volume, this book, for additional details.

Coping Style

The specific relationship between family caregivers' coping styles or the way in which they process and handle stressors and the resultant degree of experienced psychological distress is also an important factor. Caregivers that demonstrate distressed or poor coping styles have poorer long-term mental health consequences. Aneshengel et al. (1995) found that mastery, which indicates more active coping, was generally related to better well-being of caregivers caring for an impaired relative at home. Pruchno and Resch (1989) report that different coping styles have effects on different emotions. The use of emotion-focused coping mediated the impact of stress on depression, and problem-focused coping styles were associated with a more positive effect. Female caregivers may use more "emotion-focused" coping rather than "problem-focused" coping, which might result in higher levels of reported depression and general distress. Goode et al. (1998) suggest that active approaches rather than avoidant coping styles are associated with better emotional and health outcomes for dementia caregivers. On the other hand, emotion-based coping, such as cognitive reappraisal, may be superior to problem-based coping when situations are unchangeable, such as caring for a loved one with a dementing illness. Clinically, understanding coping skills is important because they are behaviorally modifiable.

Interfamily Support

Research into the nature and structure of the family as a social network and the role of caregivers within the family is an important concern. Becoming a caregiver has detrimental effects on social relationships. Female spouses tend to have higher rates of social isolation from family and friends than other family caregivers. Caring for a family member with AD, in particular, can lead to more social isolation and family conflict and disruption (Pillemer and Suitor 1996).

Select qualities in a family relationship can have a positive outcome for caregivers. Qualities that are associated with decreasing caregiver burden include the integrity, closeness, and cohesiveness of family members. Positive feedback from family and friends can also be positive for caregivers.

Lack of nearby relatives, decreased frequency of interaction, and history of conflict and abuse (e.g., old sibling rivalries that resurface with the stress of increased family responsibility for caregiving) are detrimental to caregivers and can further add to both the objective and perceived burden on the part of the caregivers, which add to worsening health outcomes.

The nature of the caregiver's marriage (e.g., late life, 2nd or 3rd marriage), their longevity, and the relationship of children to the care recipient and caregiver doubtlessly play a role. In the instance of families with older members born abroad and younger members born and educated in the USA, acculturation will affect expectations and reactions.

Community and Group Support

Examples of community programs available to support caregivers include adult day care programs, which provide structured, supervised activities during the day for impaired elderly individuals, and respite programs, which give temporary care at home or in an institution by people other than the primary caregiver. The purpose of these programs is to provide personal time to caregivers to rest or tend to other responsibilities. Support groups are used to discuss experiences and ideas about caregiving for caregivers to provide emotional support to each other. Such support can be seen as a social factor to reduce isolation and appreciated for its value in practical support.

Although qualitatively, day care and respite can be practical, they provide mixed benefit to caregiver burden and well-being (Zarit et al. 1998). This may be due, in part, to the caregiver's low rates of use of community programs. Caregivers may feel guilty leaving the responsibility of a relative to a stranger, feeling that caregiving should be kept in the context of the family, or even have a lack of transportation for themselves or their loved one. Support groups intervention research has also had mixed results. This may also be explained by low rates of use, as caregivers need to find a safe place for their impaired relative to receive care.

Caregiver Isolation and Psychiatric History

Many caregivers have limited access to information and resources that exist in their communities, and they frequently report feelings of isolation and inadequate social support (Stoltz et al. 2004). Perceived isolation and lack of social and practical support also increase the likelihood of depression and related symptoms as well as physiologic events (Bodnar and Kiecolt-Glaser 1994). A history of psychiatric illness or alcohol abuse prior to assuming the caregiver role is another risk factor for caregiver depression. Those with a premorbid psychiatric history appear to be more likely to show distress or an exaggeration of symptoms (Schulz et al. 1990) and are more likely to have an exacerbation of clinical symptoms and functional impairment. In addition, experiencing acute stressful life events, such as bereavement, increases the risk over the chronic, day-to-day stressors of caring for an impaired loved one. Previous roles and role expectations within the family unit may also affect the individual's adaptation to the caregiving role. There is a paucity of research on whether cognitive flexibility, hardiness, and prior efficacy expectations impact the individual assuming the caregiving role.

Interventions to Assist Caregivers

There have been numerous studies aimed at developing useful interventions to alleviate caregiver burden and lessen the negative consequences of caring for the mentally ill. The data seem to indicate that there is no single, easily implemented, consistently effective method for eliminating the stresses of caregiving. Programs studied have included family support groups, respite care programs, community and home services, and psychoeducational programs, which can range from groups getting information on illnesses to specific instructions on techniques of care. These interventions have not always demonstrated consistently positive results, especially when measuring outcomes of clinical significance (Schultz et al. 2002), which translates to the practical value of the effects of an intervention. Another reason that these studies may not have shown consistent positive results is that they are too narrowly focused and that multicomponent interventions would be better to address all of a caregivers' needs.

Recent studies have attempted to incorporate a more comprehensive approach to intervention and evaluate outcomes that are more likely to translate to clinical significance. For example, subjective appraisals of caregiving stressors and the caregiver's depressive symptoms are better predictors of outcome than the frequency of objective stressors. The adaptation of stress process theory has been applied to research (Schulz et al. 2000) to help guide and evaluate caregiver interventions. Interventions can assist caregivers by incorporating multiple variables needed to improve caregiver burden. They may reduce real or objective stressors, such as behavioral problems, alter the caregiver's subjective appraisal of the problems, and strengthen psychosocial support, which may decrease isolation and teach improved coping mechanisms, and help the caregiver perceive problems as less threatening.

As a part of the New York University caregiver intervention study by Mittelman et al. (2004), a structured, comprehensive psychosocial intervention for caregivers was evaluated to see if caregivers' subjective appraisal of patients' behavioral problems due to AD became more benign over a 4-year period. The intervention initially consisted of individual and family counseling sessions, which were personalized to the individual characteristics and needs of the caregivers and their entire family. Next, caregivers joined support groups that provided emotional support and education. Lastly, counselors were available by phone, as needed, to help deal with patient crises and worsening symptoms. The results show substantially reduced caregivers' negative reactions to patients' behavioral problems despite the fact that the interventions did not reduce the frequency of behavioral problems. In addition, these results were consistent over time regardless of worsening of the patients' behavioral symptoms. In previously published results, this approach of comprehensive intervention has also demonstrated other clinically significant outcomes, such as delay in nursing home placement (Mittelman et al. 1996) and a decrease in the symptoms of caregiver depression (Mittelman et al. 1995).

As previously described, caregivers often underutilize community programs and support groups designed to alleviate burden. In this regard, computer- and communication-based technologies are an up-and-coming approach to provide services for caregivers and their families. The report of the REACH (Relief for Energy Assistance through Community Help) program, a 6-year project of the National Institute on Aging, indicated that the use of computer-assisted phone to allow for regularly scheduled group support by conference calls when combined with a structured family therapy intervention over a six-month period significantly reduced depression in an Anglo- and Cuban-American (CA) sample of caregivers (Eisdorfer et al. 2003). The use of this technology-based intervention was well received by the participants and has shown promise as a novel way for caregivers to receive help and support without leaving their homes. In addition, the inclusion of a structural family therapy intervention, which identifies and restructures specific interactions within the family and other systems that may be linked to caregiver burden, when combined with the phone technology, demonstrated a greater, clinically significant reduction in caregiver depression than the phone calls alone. Of interest, the most depressed group (CA wives), showed the least favorable responses to the intervention. More intensive interventions, including psychiatric treatment, may be warranted in more severe cases.

Environmental designs have also been of interest. Specifically, controlling the level of stimulation for older patients in the later stages of dementia, using color to enhance recognition and orientation, separating more confused patients from the larger groups for meals, and having the staff supply orienting information as part of interacting with patients in a facility, all seem to show promise. A study conducted by Gitlin et al. (2003) as part of the Philadelphia REACH Initiative demonstrated caregivers' of Alzheimer's patients improved in management ability, affect, and select stressors when receiving intervention from the environmental skill-building program, which combines strategies that provide education, instruction in problem-solving, and implementation of home environmental strategies, which are tailored to the needs of each caregiver. Again, a multidimensional approach was theorized and implemented, and the methods led to good outcomes for the caregivers.

Studies of intervention have targeted the care recipient with medication to enhance the patients' abilities to care for themselves or reducing the untoward clinical problems, such as agitation or depression of the patient. This should, of course, act to reduce caregiver burden and distress, but the specifics are critical to planning any intervention and measuring outcome. Again, intervention studies that target multiple variables, including both the caregiver and care recipient, are needed and would be most beneficial.

Caring is a time-based process: time per days and weeks, and time over years. Our ability to extend life also extends the length of the caregiver's burden. Does experience over time make it easier or does it wear down the caregiver? Support is generally valued, but the pattern of support needs to be considered. Is it constant and predictable or unreliable? If family members pitch in, do they convey emotional support to the primary caregiver or anger, guilt, and criticism?

Future Considerations

Because of the tremendous challenges that caregivers face now and in the future, innovative strategies are needed to alleviate the burdens that are likely to emerge from the needs of a rapidly growing elderly population. Research is needed to articulate the factors affecting caregiving; help policymakers, professional caregivers, and family caregivers improve the quality of caring; reduce the possibility of causing harm.

Recent research attention has been focused on the continuing problems experienced by caregivers after nursing home placement or death of the patient. What we have learned is that in most instances, caregivers may continue to be distressed even when the burden is lifted. Bereavement has clear consequences on the emotions as well as the autonomic nervous system and on immune parameters. Specific interventions are needed to help families adjust to nursing home placement and bereavement.

The age of the caregiver should be considered and age cohorts also may differ along various dimensions, including demands outside the home, the likelihood of employment, educational attainments, information about community resources, caregiver health, and other salient variables.

In reaction to caregiving, a greater understanding of gender differences is needed. Not only are women more likely to be caregivers but also in contemporary society, they often have careers outside the family. Does this conflict create pressures that push women over the threshold? Are there stylistic differences involved in the process of caregiving by women that cause more distress to the caregiver? In addition, men appear to have a stronger physiological response to caregiving than women. Does that put them at an increased risk of physical illness?

The nature of stressors relatable to the caregiving transaction also needs to be separated from the range of those circumstances which are independent of caregiving and the cumulative load assessed as a factor. In much of caregiving research, only the caregiving process is assessed. Perhaps there is insufficient attention to other crises in the caregiver's life.

In terms of practice and education, professional caregivers will need to better understand the caregiving role and the need for recognition, diagnosis, and specific interventions that may benefit both the caregiver and their dependent relative. They must also be better trained in geriatrics, and recognize caregiving as an important source of morbidity and even mortality.

In terms of public policy, as data continue to emerge, national funding sources that target research in caregiving will more than likely take on a more complex, multidirectional approach, which can answer these and other pending questions.

Conclusion

Caregiving for the mentally ill and their caregivers is a major and growing issue among families and the community at large. The data show that caring for older patients or spouses is a powerful risk factor for distress and increases the risk of mental and physical health problems. A wide array of variables influence the caregiver's transaction with the patient; these may either ameliorate or increase subjective burden associated with the caregiving experience. These factors may be associated with characteristics of the caregiver, such as age, gender, cultural background, coping style, religiosity, premorbid psychiatric morbidity, and susceptibility to distress as well as with the caregiver-care recipient relationship. Patient characteristics include level of cognitive and functional impairment, degree of agitation and behavioral disturbance, and psychiatric comorbidity. Other variables, such as objective and subjective burden, social support from others, and knowledge and availability of community resources are all important variables in any models investigating caregiver depression and perceived burden. There are also subtle, but important motivations that underlie the caregiving experiences. These transactions occur within the context of caring and extraneous stimuli, which complicates the lives of caregivers who may already be in distress. Clearly, future models will have to account for the interactive as well as the reciprocal relationships present between many of these variables.

Interventions are being explored ranging from pharmacologic treatment of those receiving care to psychosocial interventions relating to the stage of the patient's illness. Caregiver-focused interventions also run the gamut from family therapy and personal help ranging from coping styles to techniques of support and day care for the patient. It is likely that one therapy will not fit the needs of every caregiver, and it will be important to identify the profiles of caregivers that are most likely to benefit from specific types or combinations of interventions.

While we know that many caregivers are at risk for adverse outcomes, most models of caregiving distress are not sufficiently complex to allow for the potential interactions of patient- and caregiver-specific and environmental variables on caregiver outcomes, although recent studies are better adapted to these models. The advent of latent structural modeling and growth curve analysis offer methods of better accounting for all mediating and moderator variables that may affect outcomes. Highly operationalized multicenter interventions, such as REACH, will also serve to identify those interventions that have the most efficacy with different types of caregivers.

It is important to continue to recognize the price caregiver's pay for their invaluable help. The role they play for our larger society in terms of lost earnings and opportunities is barely recognized, while their role in setting ethical standards and models for care in our communities is obvious. It is imperative that we do everything possible to understand and ameliorate the challenging care situations we now face, including high levels of caregiver dysfunction and disease. Research that addresses appropriate prevention and intervention is the key.

References

Aneshengel, C. S., Pearlin, L. I., Mullan, J. T., Zarit, S. H., & Whitlatch, C. J. (1995). *Profiles in caregiving: The unexpected career*. San Diego: Academic Press.

Arno, P. S., Levine, C., & Memmott, M. M. (1999). The economic value of informal caregiving. *Health Affairs, 18*, 182–188.

Baumgarten, M., Battista, R. N., Infanti-Rivard, C., Hanley, J. A., Becker, R., & Gauthier, S. (1992). The psychological and physical health of family members caring for an elderly person with dementia. *Journal of Clinical Epidemiology, 41*, 61–70.

Beck, C., Heacock, P., Mercer, S. O., Walls, R. C., Rapp, C. G., & Vogelpohl, T. S. (1997). Improving dressing behavior in cognitively impaired nursing home residents. *Nursing Research, 46*, 126–132.

Bodnar, J. C., & Kiecolt-Glaser, J. K. (1994). Caregiver depression after bereavement: Chronic stress isn't over when it's over. *Psychology of Aging, 9*, 372–380.

Bookwala, J., & Schulz, R. (2000). A comparison of primary stressors, secondary stressors, and depressive symptoms between elderly caregiving husbands and wives: The caregiver health effects study. *Psychology and Aging, 15*, 607–616.

Cohen, D. (2000). Caregivers for persons with Alzheimer's disease. *Current Psychiatry Reports, 2*, 32–39.

Cohen, D., & Eisdorfer, C. (1995). *Caring for your aging parents: A planning and action guide*. New York: G. P. Putnam's Son.

Cohen, D., Llorente, M., & Eisdorfer, C. (1998). Homicide-suicide in older persons. *American Journal of Geriatric Psychiatry, 155*, 390–396.

Connell, C. M., & Gibson, G. D. (1997). Racial, ethnic and cultural differences in dementia caregiving: Review and analysis. *Gerontologist 37*, 355–364.

Covinsky, K. E., Eng, C., Lui, L., Sands, L. P., Sehgal, A. R., Walter, L. C., et al. (2001). Reduced employment in caregivers of frail elders: Impact of ethnicity, patient clinical characteristics, and caregiver characteristics. *Journal of Gerontology, 56A*, M707–M713.

Czaja, S. J., Eisdorfer, C., & Schulz, R. (2000). Future directions in caregiving: Implications for intervention research. In R. Schulz (Ed.), *Handbook on dementia caregiving: Evidence-based interventions for family caregivers* (pp. 283–312). New York: Springer.

Depp, C., Sorocco, K., Kasl-Godley, J., Thompson, L., Rabinowitz, Y., & Gallagher-Thompson, D. (2005). Caregiver self-efficacy, ethnicity, and kinship differences in dementia caregivers. *American Journal of Geriatric Psychiatry, 13*, 787–794.

Drinka, T. J., Smith, J. C., & Drinka, P. J. (1987). Correlates of depression and burden for informal caregivers of patients in a geriatric referral clinic. *Journal of the American Geriatrics Society, 35*, 522–525.

Dura, J., Stukenberg, K., & Kiecolt-Glaser, J. (1991). Anxiety and depressive disorders in adult children caring for demented parents. *Psychology and Aging, 6*, 467–473.

Eisdorfer, C., Czaja, S. J., Loewenstein, D. A., Rubert, M. P., Arguelles, S., Mitrani, V. B., et al. (2003). The effect of a family therapy and technology-based intervention on caregiver depression. *Gerontologist, 43*, 521–531.

Gallagher-Thompson, D., Arean, P., Coon, D., Menendez, A., Takagi, K., Haley, W., et al. (2000). Development and implementation of intervention strategies for culturally diverse caregiving populations. In R. Schulz (Ed.), *Handbook on dementia caregiving: Evidence-based interventions for family caregivers* (pp. 151–186). New York: Springer.

Gitlin, L. N., Winter, L., Corcoran, M., Dennis, M. P., Schinfeld, S., & Hauck, W. W. (2003). Effects of the home environmental skill-building program on the caregiver-care recipient dyad: 6-month outcomes from the Philadelphia REACH initiative. *Gerontologist, 43*, 532–546.

Goode, K. T., Haley, W. E., Roth, D. L., & Ford, G. R. (1998). Predicting longitudinal changes in caregiver physical and mental health: A stress process model. *Health Psychology, 17*, 190–198.

Grafstrom, M., Fratiglioni, L., Sandman, P. O., & Winblad, B. (1992). Health and social consequences for relatives of demented and non-demented elderly. *Journal of Clinical Epidemiology, 45*, 867–870.

Haley, W. E. (1997). The family caregiver's role in Alzheimer's disease. *Neurology, 48*(Suppl. 6), S25–S29.

Haley, W. E., Roth D. L., Coleton, M. I., Ford, G., West, C., Collins, R., et al. (1996). Appraisal, coping, and social support as mediators of well-being in black and white family caregivers of patients with Alzheimer's disease. *Journal of Consulting and Clinical Psychology, 64*, 121–129.

Harrow, B. S., Mahoney, D. F., Mendelsohn, A. B., Ory, M. G., Coon, D. W., Belle, S. H., et al. (2004). Variation in cost of informal caregiving and formal service use for people with Alzheimer's disease. *American Journal of Alzheimer's Disease and Other Dementias, 19*, 299–308.

Himes, C. L. (2001). *Elderly Americans*. Washington, DC: Population Reference Bureau.

Hobbs, B. F., & Damon, B. L. (1996). 65 + in the United States. In *United States Bureau of the Census: Current Population Reports, Special Studies*. Washington, DC: U.S. Government Printing House.

John, R., & McMillian, B. (1998). Exploring caregiver burden among Mexican Americans: Cultural prescriptions, family dilemmas. *Journal of Aging and Ethnicity, 1*, 93–111.

Kiecolt-Glaser, J., Dura, J., Speicher, C., Trask, O. J., & Glaser, R. (1991a). Spousal caregivers of dementia victims: Longitudinal changes in immunity and health. *Psychosomatic Medicine, 53*, 354.

Kiecolt-Glaser, J. K., Glaser, R., Shuttleworth, E. C., Dyer, C. S., Ogrocki, B. S., & Speicher, C. E. (1991b). Chronic stress and immunity in family caregivers of Alzheimer's disease victims. *Psychosomatic Medicine, 49*, 523–535.

Langa, K. M., Chernew, M. E., Kabeto, M. U., Herzog, A. R., Ofstedal, M. B., Willis, R. J., et al. (2001). National estimate of the quantity and cost of informal caregiving for the elderly with dementia. *Journal of General Internal Medicine, 16*, 770–778.

MacPhail, J. (1993). Intergenerational caring in professional and family life. *Geriatric Nurse, 14*, 104–107.

McEwen, B. S. (1998). Protective and damaging effects of stress mediators. *New England Journal of Medicine, 3*, 171–179.

Meshifedyan, G., McCusker, J., Bellavance, F., & Baumgarten, M. (1998). Factors associated with symptoms of depression among informal caregivers of demented elders in the community. *Gerontologist, 38*, 247–253.

Mittelman, M. S., Ferris, S. H., Shulman, E., Steinberg, G., Ambinder, A., Mackell, J. A., et al. (1995). A comprehensive support program: Effect on depression in spouse-caregivers of AD patients. *Gerontologist*, 35, 792–802.

Mittelman, M. S., Ferris, S. H., Shulma, E., Steinberg, G., & Levin, B. (1996). A family intervention to delay nursing home placement of patients with Alzheimer's disease: A randomized control trial. *Journal of the American Medical Association, 276*, 1725–1731.

Mittelman, M. S., Roth, D. L., Haley, W. E., & Zarit, S. H. (2004). Effects of a caregiver intervention on negative caregiver appraisals of behavior problems in patients with Alzheimer's disease: Results of a randomized trial. *Journal of Gerontology Series B: Psychological Sciences and Social Sciences, 59*, P27–P34.

Mintzer, J. E., Rupert, M. P., Loewenstein, D., Gamez, E., Millor, A., Quinteros, R., et al. (1992). Daughters caregiving for Hispanic and non-Hispanic Alzheimer's patients: Does ethnicity make a difference? *Community Mental Health Journal, 28*, 293–303.

National Alliance for Caregiving & AARP. (2004). *Caregiving in the U.S.: Findings from a national survey*. Washington, DC: Authors.

Newsome, J. T., & Schulz, R. (1998). Caregiving from the recipient's perspective: Negative reactions to being helped. *Health Psychology, 17*, 172–181.

Paveza, G. J., Cohen, D., Eisdorfer, C., Freels, S., Semla, T., Ashford, J., et al. (1992). Severe family violence and Alzheimer's disease: Prevalence and risk factors. *Gerontologist, 32*, 493–497.

Pillemer, K., & Suitor, J. (1996). Family stress and social support among caregivers to persons with Alzheimer's disease. In G. R. Pierce, B. R. Sarason & I. G. Sarason (Eds.), *Handbook of social support and the family* (pp. 467–494). New York: Plenum Press.

Pruchno, R. A., & Potashnik, S. L. (1989). Caregiving spouses: Physical and mental health in prospective. *Journal of the American Geriatric Society*, 37, 697–705.

Pruchno, R. A., & Resch, N. L. (1989). Husbands and wives as caregivers: Antecedents of depression and burden. *Gerontologist, 29*, 159–165.

Rose-Rego, S. K., Strauss, M. E., & Smyth, K. A. (1998). Differences in the perceived well-being of wives and husbands caring for persons with Alzheimer's disease. *Gerontologist, 38*, 224–230.

Scanlan, J. M., Vitaliano, P. P., Zhang, J., Savage, M., & Ochs, H. D. (2001). Lymphocyte proliferation is associated with gender, caregiving, and psychosocial variable in older adults. *Journal of Behavioral Medicine, 24*, 537–559.

Schulz, R., & Williamson, G. M. (1991). A 2-year longitudinal study of depression among Alzheimer's caregivers. *Psychology and Aging, 6*, 569–578.

Schulz, R., & Beach, S. R. (1999). Caregiving as a risk factor for mortality: The caregiver health effects study. *Journal of the American Medical Association, 282*, 2215–2260.

Schulz, R., Visintainer, P., & Williamson, G. M. (1990). Psychiatric and physical morbidity effects of caregiving. *Journals of Gerontology: Series B: Psychological Sciences and Social Sciences, 45*, P181–P191.

Schulz, R., O'Brien, A. T., Bookwala, J., & Fleisser, K. (1995). Psychiatric and physical morbidity effects of dementia caregiving: Prevalence, correlates, and causes. *Gerontologist, 35*, 771–791.

Schulz, R., O'Brien, A. T., Czaja, S., Ory, M., Norris, R., Martitire, L. M., et al. (2002). Dementia caregiver intervention research: In search of clinical significance. *Gerontologist, 42*, 589–602.

Spector, J., & Tampi, R. (2005). Caregiver depression. *Annals of Long-Term Care, 13*, 34–40.

Stoltz, P., Uden, G., & Willman, A. (2004). Support for family carers who care for an elderly person at home—a systematic literature review. *Scandinavian Journal of Caring Services, 18*, 111–119.

Vitaliano, P. P., Russo, J., Young, H. M., Teri, L., & Maiuro, R. D. (1991). Predictors of burden in spouse caregivers of individuals with Alzheimer's disease. *Psychology and Aging, 6*, 392–401.

Vitaliano, P. P., Zhang, J., & Scanlan, J. M. (2003). Is caregiving hazardous to one's physical health? A meta-analysis. *Psychology Bulletin, 6*, 946–972.

Volicer, L. (2001). Management of severe Alzheimer's disease and end-of-life issues. *Clinics in Geriatric Medicine, 17*, 377–391.

Wu, H., Wang, J., Cacioppo, J. T., Glaser, R., Kiecolt-Glaser, J. K., & Malarkey, W. B. (1999). Chronic stress associated with spousal caregiving of patients with Alzheimer's dementia is associated with down regulation of B-lymphocyte GH mRNA. *Journal of Gerontology: Series A: Biological Science and Medical Science, 54*, M212–M215.

Yee, J. L., & Schultz, R. (2000). Gender differences in psychiatric morbidity among family caregivers: A review and analysis. *Gerontologist, 40*, 147–164.

Zarit, S. H., Todd, P. A., & Zarit, J. M. (1986). Subjective burden of husbands and wives as caregivers: A longitudinal study. *Gerontologist, 26*, 260–266.

Zarit, S. H., Johansson, L., & Jarrott, S. E. (1998). Family caregiving: Stresses, social programs, and clinical interventions. In I. H. Nordhus, G. R. VanderBos, S. Berg & P. Fromholt (Eds.), *Clinical geropsychology* (pp. 345–360). Washington, DC: American Psychological Association.

Part V
Conclusions

Mental Health Caregiving: A Call to Professional Providers, Family Caregivers, and Individuals with Mental Health Challenges

Donald Lollar and Ronda C. Talley

The chapters in this volume have provided a wealth of information addressing the mental health of both family and professional caregivers. The perspectives have ranged from individual and family approaches to cultural perspectives to public health prevention models. The first section began with broad themes addressing the impact of caregiving, the cultural and contextual environments of caregiving, and the relationship between physical and mental health. The second section focused on age-related caregiving, beginning with systems for children followed by emphasis on mid-life caregiving, and ending with mental illness prevention issues and opportunities. Sections three and four address spirituality and bereavement and implications for caregiving, along with policy and research challenges and directions. If you are reading this chapter culmination to this volume, hopefully this reading will consolidate some ideas that pervade the chapters. If, on the other hand, you are reading this chapter as an attempt to forego reading the full text so as to glean the crux of the material in less time and with less energy, I think you will be disappointed. While you will find an attempt to organize some of the major themes, you will, however, miss the enormous wealth of material, both broad and deep, that will help you to understand the varied dimensions of mental health and caregiving. I encourage you to start from the beginning. Themes are presented next.

First, let us discuss the array of issues addressed in this volume, beginning with the *caregiving* part of the caregiving / mental health dyad. Two types of caregiving are outlined—family and professional. Several of the chapters outline issues and strategies to help family caregivers, while others focus on professional caregivers—

D. Lollar (✉)
Oregon Institute on Disability & Development, Oregon Health & Science University, 707 SW Gaines Street, Portland, OR 97239, USA
e-mail: lollar@ohsu.edu

R. C. Talley
Department of Psychology, Western Kentucky University, 1906 College Heights Blvd., 3023 Gary Ransdell Hall, Bowling Green, KY 42101, USA
e-mail: Ronda.Talley@wku.edu

R. C. Talley et al. (eds.), *The Challenges of Mental Health Caregiving*, Caregiving: Research • Practice • Policy, DOI 10.1007/978-1-4614-8791-3_12,

that is, nurses, doctors, therapists, and other professionals who work with care recipients and their families. Implicit in this distinction is a primary theme—that is, family caregiving is part of a broader system. There is an attempt to define that "system" in several chapters, but it is also clear that a second theme addresses the fragmentation of the system for caregiving in this country. Support of those who provide care to others is less than optimal. While the chapters outline programs and policies that have been shown to be support caregiving and caregivers, there is no coherent national perspective on this important societal activity.

The issue around systems to assist caregivers turns on the notion in our country that caregiving is an individual and family tragedy. It is clear that these authors wish that those needing care and those giving care be seen as part of the community—that is, caregiving is not a family but rather a community responsibility. This basic tenet of American society—individualism—has been the driving force for our success as a nation. Caregiving is a part of life where that tenet needs to be complemented with a sense of group responsibility so that families feel support in their tasks. As this volume suggests, our society recognizes the contribution of caregiving, but the mechanisms to support this enormous activity have not been implemented, though we know much about what could help.

Caregiving is also described across age groups and diagnostic conditions, acknowledging the breadth of caregiving in our country. And across ages and conditions, the clearest theme is that caregiving is a risk factor for physical and mental health issues for the caregiver—more so for family than professional caregivers. Throughout the book there is an acknowledgment of the emotional stress and physical strain, some would use the term "burden," of caregiving. It is clear that caregiving is often associated with substantial negative impact. On the other hand, the positive emotional impact of caregiving is discussed rather often, providing a balance to the assumption that all caregiving is arduous, difficult, and a drain on the physical and emotional well-being of the caregiver. Myers describes the positive benefits of caregiving as self-esteem and confidence. Gibson, likewise, reinforces the rewards of caregiving. Elmore reports that if caregiving is not overly strenuous it is associated with higher optimism and lower stress. Conversely, more stress is associated with greater physical effects.

Both positive and negative perspectives of caregiving are influenced by environmental factors, especially cultural context. A crucial notion espoused by the Gibson and Jumper-Thurman article is that culture influences perceptions of illness and caregiving, and therefore, mental health. In addition, they suggest that the United States is but one cultural context, and that within the USA, there are numerous cultural differences. The notion of caregiving as a burden, then, is a social construct.

Mental health is the second part of the dyad. Mental health, as used in this volume, indicates the spectrum of perceptions, emotions, beliefs, and behaviors and from health to illness. That is, varied components of mental health and mental illness are addressed, with programs for family and professional caregivers' emotion, attitudes, and behaviors being included. Mental health is also influenced by environmental barriers and facilitators, from family to community to national policy environments. The most cogent observation by Taylor-Brown is that there is a mental health component in every caregiving experience. This most elemental, and yet overlooked, dynamic needs to be acknowledged and affirmed as caregiving is addressed from the individual through the family and to the public health population level. To forget this connection for a moment makes of caregiving a sterile set of physical actions without the attendance emotional dimension.

Questions regarding caregiving and mental health were answered across the volume. The next section will synthesize the answers to some of the most pervasive questions. How many are there and what do they do? What are the mental health effects on family caregivers? What affects the impact of caregiving on family or professional caregivers? What and where are the supports for caregivers? What services and programs are needed? What policies will support caregivers more fully?

Taylor-Brown reports that there are 27 million Americans providing long-term care to family members. Most authors in this text report that women are more likely to be caregivers. Myers indicates that women who are caregivers report high rates of clinical depression, between 46 and 79 %. The more caregiving is provided, the greater stress is reported, with the average duration by women caregivers being 4.3 years, and 17 % giving care for more than 10 years. Schachter indicates that a spouse caregiver has a greater probability of dying early due to emotional and physical stress.

It is clear that the environment, using that term broadly, impacts caregivers' emotional health. Cultural issues, most specifically the ways in which illness and caregiving are interpreted by a group will affect the mental health of those who become limited, ill, and need and receive care as well as those giving the care. Environment was often discussed but the chapter by Gibson and Jumper-Thurman best clarified the substantial importance of cultural perceptions for mental health and caregiving. Given the multicultural nature and growth in the USA, this thread cannot be underestimated for future research, practice, and policy. In addition, the spiritual dimension of life, seen as a backdrop, is the second environmental factor interacting with caregiving to influence caregiving. The perception of caregiving as burden or blessing, at different times both, is intimately related to the spiritual interpretation and beliefs of the caregiver and family. Smith and Milano focus their chapter on the family member with a mental illness, but spirituality is a theme often reported as a protective factor in research throughout the volume.

Broader environmental factors flow from this cultural issue. That is, if the general culture looks askance at those with emotional problems, and sees caregiving as a family issue, the community support will be reduced and the physical and emotional stress for caregivers will be increased. In addition, cultural changes will be needed to reduce or eliminate disparities.

National policies are also part of the environment affecting caregiving and mental health. Taylor-Brown and McDaniel are clear that the USA has no coherent long-term care policy, much less a broader approach and policy toward caregiving. Several specific policies are ubiquitous. Throughout the volume, authors emphasize the need for parity between physical health and mental health benefits under private or public insurance payments. Reforms in this area have been discussed and implemented in focused areas. There are not, however, the kind of systemic changes needed so that mental health coverage is on par with physical health benefits. This policy affects both those who need assistance by virtue of living with a primary mental illness as well as those who are giving care of others with physical or emotional conditions. Mental health is often a carve-out, separated from and given less strength than physical health benefits.

It is amazing that informal caregivers, primarily family members, are projected to provide US$ 306 billion of care (Becker 2006). Crocco indicates that, in addition, US$ 11.4 billion is lost to US business from employees giving hands-on care. Policies, such as social security credits for caregivers, have not been implemented. Financial incentives such as cash and counseling, as discussed by Elmore, and policies relative to direct respite services are crucial to an integrated set of policies that support caregiving and thereby the mental health of the caregivers. English and Enomoto want policies that allow families to address their caregiving and mental health concerns as close to their homes and neighborhoods as possible. They impress on the reader the importance of local solutions. Of course, this approach must be connected with the previous emphasis on community acceptance and positive attitudes toward caregiving and mental health. Societal attitudes are a foundational aspect of the community environment.

Another set of themes from the volume address services and programs that support caregivers' mental health. Myers has indicated the inverse relationship between caregiving and support—that is, the more caregiving, the less support. Implicit again is the notion that more caregiving is often associated with greater isolation for the caregiver, raising the risk for emotional difficulties. Community support seems to fall away. At the same time, Elmore has indicated that family function is central to the physical and mental health of caregivers. If families are not cohesive, therefore, or become less so under the strain of caregiving, outcomes are undermined. This paradox is apparent; that is, the importance of family and community support is crucial to the physical and emotional health of caregivers; but, it is also clear that services and programs described are not sufficiently integrated or ubiquitous to provide a coherent net of support for caregivers.

The volume, however, is replete with services and programs designed to assist caregivers at various levels—individual, family, community. It would be most helpful to individuals and families if the services and programs proceed from policies that show respect for and awareness of the array of needs to be addressed. Myers discusses the importance of respite services for families—acknowledgment that caregiving, even when affirmed by the community, can take a toll on the individual caregiver. Counseling and family intervention are integral to shoring emotional resources of caregivers. Schachter discusses the importance of group counseling to reduce the emotional stress for caregivers. A specific approach to counseling is the educational and guidance services that can be provided over the Internet. Using technology can be one component of support services, but must have an interpersonal element if it is to provide the human dimension needed by caregivers.

It is important for community leaders to be cultivated so that they can develop an awareness of the important role communities have to play in supporting caregiving, specifically as it affects the emotional health of many of its citizen caregivers. As awareness of the importance of the role emerges, the second, and often, parallel step is an assessment of community resources, including specific programs and services, available for caregivers.

This synthesis began with emphasis on the public health data suggesting a national issue related to caregiving and mental health. The themes presented have become progressively more focused—from environmental and cultural issues, through policy, practices, and systems. The final focus is on those themes addressing practice at the individual and family level. An important emphasis at this level is that provided by Taylor-Brown and McDaniel, as well as Elmore. Elmore suggested that primary care providers, especially with aging patients, are in a strong position to identify caregivers experiencing stress and strain. Myers refers to the caregiver as the "hidden patient." Taylor-Brown and McDaniel recommended including families in primary care visits and information gathering and intervention discussions so that critical identification of difficulties and support of individuals and families can be initiated. To the extent that caregivers often have several professionals assisting them, inclusion in interdisciplinary teams is also essential for the caregiver to feel a part of the treatment process. The authors suggest even further inclusion—that is, setting primary care visits for the family. Gibson discussed critical consciousness for professionals working with caregivers and those receiving assistance. Schachter recommends that caregivers be assessed for complicated grief, a process that undermines both physical and emotional health. Elmore also discussed the need to manage behavior problems that might present to professionals. Of course, families are integral to any interventions to influence difficult behavior. This attention to mental health of the families and caregivers of individuals experiencing a need for care is presented by the authors throughout the volume as a basic and relatively straightforward approach using existing personnel and services.

Across all chapters, the issue of preparation of professionals emerged. While much of the volume has focused on mental health and family caregiving, parts of numerous chapters addressed the mental health of providers—professional caregivers. Motes indicated that fewer than 5 % of pediatricians are trained in the mental health needs of youth. The usual health care professionals were often included, specifically nurses, pediatricians, and family physicians. Emphasis included training on screening for mental health problems among anyone doing caregiving. This is not usual education for health professionals, but should be an integral part of sensitivity regardless of the area of medical or health specialty. In addition, however, authors such as Motes and Smith discussed the need to train teachers, chaplains, community workers. Motes noted that two-thirds of teachers feel overwhelmed with students' mental health needs.

In summary, the health infrastructure depends on "free" family caregiving, according to English. Of course, this process is, by no means, free. Its costs are measured in the mental and physical health of those family members who take the responsibility for helping their mothers, fathers, sisters, brothers, uncles, aunts, cousins, and other family members. The corporate responsibility needs to be accepted at all levels of society—certainly beginning with families—but including communities, states, institutions, and the nation. The supports and resources are not beyond our reach. What is required is the will to assess and intervene coherently and so that each family feels support to assist their family member—helping the helpers.

Index

A
Activities of daily living (ADLs), 17, 135, 183, 212
Administration on Aging (AoA), 187
Adolescents, 7, 103, 104, 108–110, 115–117
African American, 34, 41, 44, 154, 211, 212
African American caregivers, 38, 39, 46, 47, 134, 212
Agency, 67, 107, 195, 198
Aging, 5, 15, 71, 125, 126, 129, 133, 146, 157, 188, 229
  premature, 18, 68
  stresses of, 164
Aging and Disability Resource Centers (ADRCs), 187
Agitation, 216
  degree of, 217
Alaska Native, 25
Alzheimer's disease, 5, 25, 65, 146, 171, 206, 209, 211, 213, 215
American Indian, 25
Anger, 17, 64, 136, 153, 170, 206, 209, 216
Anxiety, 16, 18, 23, 43, 60, 68, 70, 125, 134, 135, 147, 149, 206, 207, 209
Anxiety disorder, 36
Arthritis, 125
Asthma, 183

B
Behavioral disorders, 83, 104, 106, 107, 113, 116
Behavioral Risk Factor Surveillance System (BRFSS), 2
Bereavement, 9, 91, 147, 149, 151–156, 208, 214, 217, 225
Biopsychosocial model, 6, 16, 67
Bipolar disorder, 36, 49
Bitterness, 153
Breast cancer, 153, 165

C
Cancer, 3, 5, 87, 165
Cardiovascular disease, 3, 94, 183, 192
Care recipient, 1, 4, 9, 21, 22, 24, 29, 39, 40, 68, 135, 172, 182–184, 187, 198, 199, 207, 226
Caregiver burden, 8, 64, 132, 136, 185, 186, 190, 199, 208, 212–216
  impact of, 9
  levels of, 22
Caregiver depression, 9, 73, 206, 210, 211, 214–216, 218
Caregiver education, 24, 187
Caregiver experiences, 68, 208
Caregiver research, 206
Caregiver–care recipient dyad, 2, 41, 205, 217
Caregivers, 1, 2, 4, 5, 10, 21, 60, 61, 69, 74, 108, 189–191, 208, 209, 212–214
Caregiving, 1, 2, 4, 6–10, 15–21, 24, 70, 74, 123, 124, 130, 138, 207, 226
  burdens of, 19, 21, 27, 185, 190, 191, 207
  challenges of, 71
  definition of, 4
  dynamics of, 124
  effects of, 9, 17, 19, 39
  impact of, 20
  issues of, 8
  perceptions of, 197
  risks of, 21
Caregiving demands, 16, 60, 68
Caregiving education and training, 198
Caregiving research, 17, 20, 46, 205, 206, 217
Caregiving stressors, 2, 20, 139, 162, 174, 215
Caregiving wives, 171
Caring, 4, 10, 15, 17, 39, 46, 55, 56, 68, 70–72, 84, 87, 149, 174, 206, 212, 213, 216

R. C. Talley et al. (eds.), *The Challenges of Mental Health Caregiving*, Caregiving: Research • Practice • Policy, DOI 10.1007/978-1-4614-8791-3,

Centers for Disease Control and Prevention (CDC), 2, 4
Cerebral palsy, 68
Child welfare, 103, 104
Children, 3, 25, 26, 58, 59, 67, 68, 74, 86, 88, 90, 91, 94, 99, 104, 108–110, 114–117, 128–130, 134, 163, 193, 206, 210
  depression in, 89
Chronic disease, 16, 21, 22, 26, 125, 130, 157, 182
Chronic illness, 1, 8, 56, 60, 61, 68, 145, 173, 199, 208
  impact of, 57
  prevalence of, 56
  treatment of, 55, 64
Chronic stress, 208–210
  role of, 18
Clinical depression, 209, 212, 227
Cognitive flexibility, 214
Cognitive impairment, 22, 212, 217
Cognitive problems, 17
Cognitive reappraisal, 213
Cognitive-behavioral interventions, 39
Collaborative Family Healthcare (CFH) model, 72
Colon cancer, 65
Cultural competency, 7, 103, 104, 107, 108
Cultural competency training, 45
Cultural considerations, 6, 46
Culture, 34, 35, 38, 67, 94, 116, 124, 131, 138, 190, 191, 207, 227
  analysis of, 35
  dynamics of, 33
  impact of, 134
  importances of, 6

D
Death, 3
Delayed wound healing, 18
Dementia, 22, 35, 36, 38–42, 44, 46, 47, 49, 69, 136, 171, 173, 205–207, 209, 213
  stages of, 136, 212, 216
Depression, 2, 16, 17, 60, 64, 73, 90–95, 115, 134, 206, 209, 216
  cure of, 89
  diagnosis of, 95
  impact of stress on, 213
  levels of, 112, 132, 164, 207
  occurrence of, 87
  onset of, 149
  prevention of, 85, 88, 89
  symptoms of, 69, 207, 214
  treatment for, 90, 115, 207
Depressive symptomatology, 41, 47, 88, 89, 135
Developmental disabilities, 103
Developmental issues, 7, 138
Diabetes, 3, 183, 192
Diagnostic services, 103
Direct care, 4, 63, 169
Disability, 2–5, 39, 56, 127, 164, 173, 175, 190, 191
  causes of, 4
  long-term, 1
  types of, 4
Distress, 3, 4, 17–19, 136, 147, 151, 153, 168, 205, 213, 216–218

E
Economics, 27, 33
Education, 6, 7, 9, 10, 15, 16, 20, 21, 23, 69, 73, 103, 104, 117, 186, 190, 191, 199, 216, 217
Emotional care, 4
Emotional disorders, 83, 104, 106, 107, 113, 116
Emotional problem, 17, 136, 227
Emotional stress, 69, 132, 170, 226–228
End of life issues, 148
End-of-life care, 147, 149, 156
Ethnicity, 34, 35, 38, 41, 96, 124, 127, 131, 134, 138, 190, 191, 207, 212

F
Family, 62–64, 68, 70, 73, 94, 107, 110, 139, 189
family, 55
Family caregiver, 6, 8, 9, 16, 20–25, 28, 29, 60, 63, 69, 71, 72, 85, 104, 139, 147, 153, 155, 170, 174, 181, 182, 185, 187, 189, 191, 195, 197, 198, 213
  burden of, 24, 27, 33, 39, 40
  definition of, 4, 184
  eduation and training, 24
  needs for, 15
  needs of, 24, 28, 172
  role of, 15, 18, 55
  significance of, 7, 103
  types of, 208
Family caregiving, 4, 9, 24, 27, 35, 56, 127, 181–187, 191–193, 197, 200, 210, 226, 229
  burdens of, 61
  effectiveness of, 188, 191
  efficiency of, 191
  faith-based support for, 198
  lack of, 197

levels of, 190
stress of, 61, 173
value of, 189
family caregiving, 184
Family dynamics, 59
Family life cycle, 133
Family physicians, 73, 163, 229
Fatigue, 175
Fear, 70, 125, 149, 165
Fear of death, 165
Federal policymakers, 8, 26
Financial care, 4
Frustration, 93–95, 136

G
Gender, 41, 42, 69, 124, 127, 131–133, 138, 155, 207, 210, 217
Gender identity, 129
Grief, 8, 9, 107, 145, 146, 149, 151, 153–157, 229

H
Health care providers, 21, 22, 29, 44, 45, 66, 73, 146–148, 196, 209, 210
Healthcare, 7, 175
Healthcare professionals, 7, 9
Hemodialysis, 59, 165
Hospice, 5, 9, 65, 147, 148, 150–152, 155
Hypertension, 57, 125, 153, 163
Hypothalamic-pituitary-adrenal (HPA) axis, 208

I
Immune dysregulation, 18
Individuals with disabilities, 16, 21, 27
Informal caregiver, 4, 61, 68, 228
Insomnia, 16–18, 59, 207
Interagency collaboration, 109, 110, 117
Intervention
caregiver-focused, 218
community-based, 7, 103, 108, 109, 116
evidence-based, 114, 116, 117
family-based, 7, 22, 23, 136, 186, 196
multi-center, 218
technology-based, 24, 137, 215

J
Juvenile justice, 103

L
Lesbian, gay, bisexual and transgender (LGBT) caregivers, 190
Life span, 5, 46, 84, 86
Longevity, 56, 127, 213
Loss, 8, 9, 66, 107, 126, 134, 145, 149, 151, 154–156, 164, 206
symptoms of, 153

M
Mediation care, 4
Mental disability, 4, 166
Mental disorders, 3, 67, 103, 183–191, 193, 197, 199
Mental health, 2, 3, 6, 9, 16, 17, 19, 20, 23, 24, 60, 83, 96, 103, 112, 135, 190, 205, 226, 228
definitions of, 3
Mental health caregiving, 2, 9
Mental health issues, 2, 3, 10, 61, 67, 115, 226
Mental health system, 107, 108, 186
Mental illness, 2, 3, 6, 10, 34–40, 42, 46, 48, 49, 91, 103, 133, 163, 164, 166, 181, 183–185, 190, 193, 227, 228
burden of, 3
dual diagnosis of, 145
prevention of, 7, 83
risk of, 187
signs of, 3
symptoms of, 4
treatment of, 2, 35
Mentally ill, 41, 42, 45, 49, 85, 88, 212, 214, 217
Midlife concerns, 123
Modern nursing, history of, 166

N
National Alliance for Caregiving (NAC), 4
National Ambulatory Medical Care Survey (NAMCS), 2
National Family Caregiver Support Program (NFCSP), 25, 70, 187
National Family Caregivers Association (NFCA), 4, 173
National Family Caregiving Support Program, 187
National Health and Nutrition Examination Survey (NHANES), 2
National Health Interview Survey (NHIS), 2
National Hospital Ambulatory Medical Care Survey (NHAMCS), 2
National Hospital Discharge Survey (NHDS), 2
National Nursing Home Survey (NNHS), 2
Native American Caregiver Support Program (NACSP), 25
Nervios, 36
symptoms of, 36

Non-caregiving wives, 171
Non-professional caregivers, 166, 174
Nurses, 5, 87, 114, 147–149, 154, 156, 169, 209, 226, 229

O
Obesity, 3, 183
Objective burden, 40, 60, 134, 206, 207, 212

P
Pain, 3, 151, 153, 166, 175
Pancreatic cancer, 151
Parent–child relationship, 185
Patient-centered care, 166
Pediatricians, 229
Physical disability, 4, 166
Physical health, 6, 9, 16, 17, 60
Physical illness, 3, 10, 60, 133, 164, 166, 183
Physical therapy, 55
Physicians, 5, 73, 146–149, 155, 156, 161, 167–170, 209
Policy, 5, 8–10, 28, 34, 38, 40, 45, 57, 61, 63, 71, 99, 106, 173, 174, 181, 182, 190, 194, 199, 200, 206, 217, 225, 227–229
Policy makers, 8, 29, 33, 37, 46, 62, 70, 85, 106, 139, 182, 188, 197, 216
Pregnancy Risk Assessment Monitoring System (PRAMS), 2
Primary care, 6, 21, 59, 63, 64, 66, 70
Professional caregivers, 3, 5, 9, 85, 94, 166, 170, 216, 217, 225, 226, 229
Psychiatric illness, 214
Psychoeducation, 21, 23, 24, 40, 42, 48, 69, 185, 188, 215
Psychological distress, 187, 205–208, 212, 213
Psychopathology, 153, 209

R
Race, 34, 38, 96, 124, 127, 190, 191, 211, 212
  effects of, 35
Religious Coping Index (RCI), 164

S
Schizophrenia, 36, 42, 46, 49, 186
Sexual orientation, 190
Siblings, 38, 69, 74, 94, 109, 205, 211
Socioeconomic status, 134, 190
Spiritual coping in caregiving, role of, 166
Spirituality, 5, 8, 126, 161–163, 165, 166, 168–175, 190, 211, 212, 227
Stigma, 2, 10, 106, 115, 185, 189, 192, 197, 199
  of HIV disease, 69
  of mental illness, 108
Stress caregiving, 2
Stress hormones
  levels of, 17, 18, 208
Support program, 186

T
Training caregivers, 24
Training health care providers, 166
Trauma, 153
Triangulation, 47

W
Western cultures, 62
World Health Organization (WHO), 3, 70

CPSIA information can be obtained at www.ICGtesting.com
Printed in the USA
LVOW01*1243130215

426929LV00001B/27/P

9 781461 487906